STAGING PHILOSOPHY

THEATER: THEORY/TEXT/PERFORMANCE

Series Editors: David Krasner and Rebecca Schneider
Founding Editor: Enoch Brater

Recent Titles:

Staging Philosophy

Intersections of Theater, Performance, and Philosophy

~

EDITED BY

David Krasner and David Z. Saltz

The University of Michigan Press
Ann Arbor

2009   2008   2007   2006   4   3   2   1

A CIP catalog record for this book is available from the British Library.

Library of Congress Cataloging-in-Publication Data

Krasner, David, 1952–
    Staging philosophy : intersections of theater, performance, and
philosophy / edited by David Krasner and David Z. Saltz.
        p.   cm.
    Includes index.
    ISBN-13: 978-0-472-09950-4 (cloth : alk. paper)
    ISBN-10: 0-472-09950-7 (cloth : alk. paper)
    ISBN-13: 978-0-472-06950-7 (pbk. : alk. paper)
    ISBN-10: 0-472-06950-0 (pbk. : alk. paper)
    1. Performing arts—Social aspects.   2. Performing arts—
Philosophy.   I. Saltz, David Z., 1962–   II. Title.
PN1590.S6K73 2006
791.01—dc22   2006006237

ACKNOWLEDGMENTS

We especially wish to thank LeAnn Fields for her commitment to this
project, Rebecca Rostov for her valuable assistance, and Marcia
LaBrenz for her superb copyediting. Our wives, Lynda Krasner and
Lizzie Zucker Saltz, have been steady supporters throughout. We wish
to thank Diane Quinn for permission to use her husband's essay, and
the Frederick Hilles Fund of Yale University for its support. The contributors deserve special credit; it is their intellectual insights that
enlighten this work.

Portions of Alice Rayner's "Presenting Objects, Presenting Things"
appears in *Ghosts: Death's Double and the Phenomena of Theatre* (Minneapolis: University of Minnesota Press, 2006).

~

This book is dedicated to
Michael Quinn and Bernard Williams.

Contents

Introduction

David Krasner and David Z. Saltz

Why This Book?

Though the past fifteen years have observed a veritable golden age of performance theory—a lively discourse that draws on anthropology, sociology, linguistics, psychoanalysis, political theory, cultural studies, feminism, and queer theory—performance theorists rarely draw on works emanating from American philosophy departments.[1] Similarly, very few professional philosophers have focused in depth on questions pertaining to the phenomena of theater or performance.[2] This situation is especially surprising given the attention recent philosophers have lavished on other art forms, such as painting, music, and film.

The guiding principle of this book is a sustained engagement with philosophy and performance theory. The goal is to raise issues of critical importance by providing case studies of various philosophical movements and schools of thought. The book is designed to be accessible to nonspecialists who might be unfamiliar with philosophy of theater and performance, yet stimulating to experts in the field. Each chapter addresses fundamental questions about theater and live performance from a philosophical perspective. The contributors are performance scholars and philosophers, with one contribution jointly authored by a representative from each discipline. The chapters encompass a wide range of philosophical approaches, from analytic philosophy to phenomenology, and from deconstruction to critical realism. The concepts put forth in this book are meant to provoke, stimulate, and engage the reader, and ultimately bring the concept of theater to the foreground of intellectual inquiry. No single ideology dominates this work; inclusivity, not dogma, guides our entries.

This collection will, we hope, invite further challenges, so that the ongoing dialogue, as Plato might imagine it, continues.

As the title suggests, the aim of this book is to examine key issues in theater and performance from a philosophical perspective. What exactly do we mean by a "philosophical" approach to theater and live performance? We can begin by broadly distinguishing a philosophical analysis from a critical study, on the one hand, and prescriptive manifesto, on the other. A critical study interprets particular dramatic texts, performances, individuals, groups, periods, or movements. A manifesto is a statement about how practitioners *should* go about creating texts and performances. A philosophical analysis might examine the assumptions made by critical studies and prescriptive manifestos. Most significantly, however, it advances new arguments about—and new approaches to—the nature of theater and performance in general.

There are many different approaches to philosophy. The question, "What is philosophy?" is itself a philosophical question—as, for that matter, is the question, "What is theater?" For the purposes of this book, we have established two pragmatic criteria for philosophical analysis: It is first an analysis of theater broadly construed, or more generally of live performance (a phenomenon encompassing theater); second, it is a theoretical inquiry that does not merely report philosophical claims, but advances new arguments and constitutes an original contribution to the philosophical discourse. We will examine both of these criteria in greater detail. But first we will consider an enduring connection between theater and philosophy that renders these two disciplines natural allies.

Theater and Philosophy: Kindred Disciplines

In *Connections to the World: The Basic Concepts of Philosophy,* Arthur Danto suggests that philosophy has risen "only twice in the history of civilization, once in Greece and once in India." Both times, Danto posits, it emerged because "some distinction between appearance and reality seemed urgent."[3] Significantly, both of these civilizations, at much the same time and, arguably, for much the same reason, also gave rise to theater. Like philosophy, theater often sheds light on a reality obfuscated by appearances. Moreover, theater, like philosophy, exposes that reality by representing and analyzing human action and demonstrating causal relationships.[4] In theater, writes philosopher Bruce Wilshire, "we can see 'writ large' the theatre-like conditions of the coherence and being of actual selves—large enough to see conditions which would otherwise be easily missed."[5] Theater and philosophy shed light on thought, behavior, action, and existence while simultaneously enhancing our comprehension of the world and ourselves.

The critical link that holds theater and philosophy together is the act of seeing. Observing events, actions, responses, gestures, and behaviors, along with hearing sounds, voices, tones, and rhythms, brings us closer to understanding the realities that underlie surface appearances. In his essay "Philosophy and Theatre," Aldo Tassi draws similar observations about theater and philosophy, noting that they are inexorably joined by an "unconcealment process." Philosophy, he says,

> is an activity that seeks to transport us to the place where boundaries are established so that we may "see" how things come to be. Like the theatrical stage, the theatre of the mind is a place for seeing, and it is philosophy's task to bring to light and allow us to see what usually remains obscure or hidden in our perceptual dealings with things. Both philosophy and theatre, then, originally arose as activities to take us beyond the empirical level to involve us in the pursuit of truth as an unconcealment process.[6]

Both theater and philosophy represent humans actively engaging with and in the world, and a basic technique both employ to that end is dialogue. Dialogue is one of the most important tools of Plato's famous Socratic method, and remains a common format for presenting philosophical arguments through the Enlightenment. Less obviously, dialogue remains integral, in a subtler way, to the method of most contemporary philosophers. Philosophical positions typically develop through a process of dialogue between philosophers: one philosopher advances a proposition, another picks that proposition apart and revises and refines it, or proposes a radically different proposition in its stead. A third philosopher might then join in to argue that the entire debate rests on faulty premises and propose an entirely new approach to the topic. Philosophers tend to welcome trenchant criticisms of their positions. The most valuable works of philosophy are those that challenge other philosophers to respond. A philosophical statement plays a vital role in the discourse, not necessarily by contributing knowledge that most other philosophers accept as "truths" (as in the sciences), but by stimulating further dialogue and keeping the philosophical ball rolling.

Works of philosophy tend to assume a dramatic form internally. Philosophers often begin an argument by formulating an initial hypothesis and then responding with counterarguments to their own provisional thesis. The best philosophy does not rush to conclusions—a restraint that can be very frustrating for nonphilosophers who are not acclimated to an incremental development of ideas. Furthermore, after all of the twists and turns that result from the arguments, the conclusion emerging can often appear obvious. The significance of a philosophical proposition only becomes clear when one situates that proposition in context. Claims, for example, that people have free will, or that there is no such thing as sense data, are meaningful and interesting only in the face of compelling contradictory arguments. Philosophical arguments often reveal propositions with intuitive appeal to be ultimately flawed or incoherent, or to have unexpected and unwelcome implications. In other words, to appreciate the significance of a philosophical statement, one must recognize the force of the statement as an *action* performed within a dramatic exchange of arguments and assertions. The hope of provoking an active exchange of ideas about theater and philosophy provides the fundamental impetus for this work.

Continental and Analytic Philosophy

For much of the twentieth century, it was commonplace to distinguish between two broad traditions of philosophy, dubbed "continental" and "analytical." Since nearly all of the contributors to this volume owe their ideas to these movements, a brief summary of the key differences will provide a useful background. In *Twentieth-Century Analytic Philosophy* Avrum Stroll describes analytic philosophy as "directed toward articulating the meaning of certain concepts, such as 'knowledge,' belief,' 'truth,' and 'justification.'" One of the guiding principles of the analytic tradition, Stroll adds, is that "one cannot make a judicious assessment of any proposed thesis until one understands it and its constituent concepts."[7] Along similar lines, Bernard Williams describes the analytic tradition as distinctively "workmanlike," sustained by the conviction that "no philosophy which is to be worthwhile should lose the sense that there is something to be got right, that it is answerable to argument and that it is in the business of telling the truth."[8] Analytic philosophy emerged during the period from 1879 to World War I, and was led by Gottlob Frege, G. E. Moore, and Bertrand Russell (who often referred to their work as the logical analysis of language).[9] The speech-act theories of J. L. Austin and John Searle fall within the tradition of analytic philosophy. Among the most prominent philosophers to develop theories of art in the analytic tradition—often with explicit implications for theater and performance—are Richard Wollheim, Nelson Goodman, Kendall Walton, Arthur Danto, and Noël Carroll (whose work appears in this volume).

The continental approach holds sway among professional philosophers in Germany and France. Continental philosophy continues the tradition of G. W. F. Hegel, and owes much to Nietzsche, the phenomenological traditions emanating from Husserl and Heidegger, the hermeneutics of Gadamer and Ricoeur, the existentialism of Sartre, Simone de Beauvoir, and Maurice Merleau-Ponty, and the Frankfurt School social theories of Max Horkheimer, Theodor Adorno, and Walter Benjamin. Frankfurt School social theories have had a profound and pervasive impact on theater and performance scholarship. The most prominent theater theorists to embrace phenomenology are Bert O. States, Stanton Garner, and Alice Rayner, the latter of whom is a contributor to this volume. Phenomenology's emphasis on the body has proven especially useful to performance theorists such as Peggy Phelan and Amelia Jones, who investigate the way performance art manipulates the perception and construction of gender and sexuality. For the most part, performance theorists have been drawn to the skeptical style of thought typified by poststructuralist theory.

During the second half of the twentieth century, theories derived from Nietzsche and Heidegger, Saussure's structural linguistics, Marxism, existentialism, and Frankfurt School social theory have opened up new vistas of philosophy primarily known as poststructuralism. Poststructuralism can be described as generally skeptical of epistemology (knowledge), grounded truth claims, and assertions of certainty, often the bedrock of the analytic tradition. It views reason skeptically, as a rhetorical strategy masking power relations and the status quo. Instead of a fundamental vocabulary anchored in the analytic tradition of science, knowledge, and most importantly language, poststructuralist theory uproots claims of truth, morality, self, value, and the certainty of language. John Passmore somewhat caustically remarks that poststructuralists "are often willfully obscure, or wholly silent, precisely at the epistemological and ontological points where the Anglo-American philosopher seeks illumination."[10] Passmore's sarcasm notwithstanding, this willful obscurity is owing to the fact that poststructuralists view language as something too frequently taken for granted. Rather than assuming language's certainty, poststructuralists attempt to avoid the solidification of ideas through linguistic terms. Instead, they open up ideas and language to doubt and skepticism by subverting, deconstructing, and challenging the very meaning of language that attempts clarification. As a result, the continental-poststructural tradition sets out to undermine the structures that define our world. In his two-volume *History of Structuralism*, François Dosse accurately describes the development of continental-poststructural philosophy as a school that rejected the "binary" descriptions of linguistic and anthropological "structuralism," shifting the emphasis to a playful indeterminacy of meaning and form:

> The various binary couples—signifier/signified, nature/culture, voice/writing, perceptible/intelligible—that compose the very instrument of structural analysis were each put into question, pluralized, disseminated in an infinite game that peeled, disjoined, and dissected the meaning of words, tracking down every master word, every transcendence. A whole Derridean language destabilized traditional oppositions by bringing undecidables into play as veritable units of simulacrum, organizers of a new, carnivalesque order of reason.[11]

Instead of certainty, poststructuralist theories search for what might be termed breaks, or fissures in events, revealing inconsistencies, contradictions, interstices, and ruptures in the fabric of universal truths, organized reason, and the division between objectivity and subjectivity. Whereas the analytic tradition seeks refinement by probing minutia, detail, and the fine points of logic, linguistics, and aesthetics, the poststructuralists look to overturn the establishment and anything associated with truth, closure, and definitive clarity. The paradigmatic examples of poststructuralist theory include the psychoanalysis of Jacques Lacan, the deconstructionism of Jacques Derrida, the antiepistemology of Michel Foucault, the postmodernism of Jean-François Lyotard, the gender performativity of Judith Butler, and the psychoanalytic feminism of Julia Kristeva. The typical analytic philosopher is logical, systematic, scientific, abstract, and sometimes reductive. The typical continental philosopher is speculative, poetic, nonlinear, paradoxical, and sometimes obscure. While these stereotypes have some basis in fact, there are important exceptions to virtually any generalization one might make about either analytic or continental philosophers; the variations among individual philosophers *within* each of the two traditions is at least as great as the difference between the two traditions themselves. Some prominent continental philosophers, such as Roman Ingarden and Mikel Dufrenne, set forth highly rigorous and systematic arguments similar to those associated with analytic philosophy, while some prominent analytic philosophers, such as Wittgenstein and Stanley Cavell, write in nonlinear, poetic, and sometimes enigmatic style. Both traditions encompass philosophers who view truth as absolute and ahistorical as well as those who construe it as culturally and historically relative; those who believe that human identity is innate and immutable as well as those who view it as a social construct; and those who erect sweeping philosophical systems as well as those who actively resist system-building. In both traditions, the general trend over the past thirty years has been toward denying the purity of abstract philosophical reasoning and advancing philosophical arguments that try to account for the messy contingencies of the empirical world.[12] Indeed, the late Bernard Williams, a distinguished philosopher in the analytic tradition, suggests that the dichotomy between analytic and continental philosophy is largely meaningless:

> It is absurd to mark philosophical differences with these two labels. Apart from involving a strange cross-classification—rather as though one divided cars into front-wheel drive and Japanese—the labels are seriously misleading, in helping one to forget that the origins of analytical philosophy itself lay in continental Europe (notably so, when its founding father is taken to be Frege and its greatest representative Wittgenstein), and that the interests of "continental" philosophy are not confined to the European continent.[13]

Doing versus Using Philosophy

Many theorists who have addressed the phenomenon of theater and performance have applied theories developed by other disciplines, for example literary theory and cultural studies. A performance theorist might apply the theories of feminists Judith Butler or Luce Irigaray to an analysis of a performance by the performance group Split Britches; or a cultural studies theorist might apply theories from French poststructuralist Jean

Baudrillard or sociologist Pierre Bourdieu to analyze the reconstructed Globe Theater in London. Such applications of preexisting theories have yielded, and will continue to yield, insightful and valuable contributions to our understanding of theater and performance. Still, the validity of performance theories ultimately rises or falls on arguments proffered by the theorists upon which the theory draws, rather than on the theorists' own argument. The shape of this type of analysis is conditional: *if* we accept the arguments of Butler, Irigaray, Baudrillard or Bourdieu, *then* certain ideas about theater or performance follow accordingly. One result of this approach to theory is that the sequence of theoretical discourse about theater and performance flows almost exclusively from *elsewhere* and *into* performance theory, and only occasionally does it flow out again to influence other disciplines. Jill Dolan has noted this trend, lamenting that "theatre studies' historical borrowings from other fields to theorize itself" creates the impression that there is "something second-class about theatre."[14] One of the goals of this book is to reverse that trend.

This book collects fifteen essays that advance original and thoughtful philosophical arguments about issues in theater and performance. The essayists here, of course, draw deeply on the work of previous theorists. Ultimately, however, their arguments stand—or fall—on their own. Much of this work challenges received wisdom. Indeed, in the venerable spirit of philosophical debate, some of the contributors to this book advance positions that are at odds with those defended by others.

Introduction to the Essays

We have sorted the diverse collection of chapters that comprise this book into three parts: (1) history and method, (2) presence, and (3) reception. These parts highlight important connections between the chapters, with chapters in each section sometimes building off one another as they address an overarching theme, and sometimes contradicting each other as they present alternative solutions to similar problems. These sectional divisions, however, represent only one possible path through the book. Each chapter is self-contained, with interesting links between chapters throughout. Instructors using this anthology can assign the chapters in any order to highlight different thematic links and serve different pedagogical objectives.

PART I: HISTORY AND METHOD

The book begins with three essays investigating the intersection of the history of theater and performance studies with the history of philosophy. Julia A. Walker's chapter, "The Text/Performance Split across the Analytic/Continental Divide," analyzes the historical origins of the schism between those who regard theater as literature and those who regard it as performance, suggesting that this schism arose at the same time, and within the same intellectual climate, as the one between analytic and continental philosophy. Walker carefully examines the relationship between these two debates, finding similar nodal points of interest.

Martin Puchner's essay, "Kenneth Burke: Theater, Philosophy, and the Limits of Performance," explores philosophers' increasingly frequent appeal to theatrical performance as a metaphor describing a wide range of phenomena. He dubs this philosophical trend the "theatrical turn," linking the movement to the rise of performance studies. Both philosophers and performance studies advocates, Puchner contends, need to devote more effort to ascertaining the limits of the theater metaphor. He points to Kenneth Burke as a rare instance of a thinker who embodies the theatrical turn while directly confronting its limits.

Part I concludes with Tobin Nellhaus's "Critical Realism and Performance Strategies." His ambitious goal is to provide a new theoretical foundation for the study of theater history, using as his point of departure the methods and insights of critical realism and cognitive science. With that larger project in mind, Nellhaus critiques the traditional notion of "genre" and proposes to replace it with a new concept, which he calls a "performance strategy." He illustrates this concept and demonstrates its effectiveness by applying it to two historical examples: medieval theater and the Broadway stage of the mid-1950s.

PART II: PRESENCE

The six contributors to part II address the meaning and significance of "presence" in the context of live performance. Over the past decade, Philip Auslander has written a series of highly provocative essays and books challenging a sacrosanct belief: that liveness matters. He maintains that mediatized performances on film, video, and digital media exhibit virtually all of the qualities people describe as unique to live performance and vice versa. In his contribution to this volume, "Humanoid Boogie: Reflections on Robotic Performance," Auslander extends his challenge to the privileged status of the live human performer by arguing that robots can "perform" in precisely the same sense that people do. In other words, human presence, according to Auslander, is not a necessary condition for an event to qualify as a performance.

Noël Carroll provides a rebuttal to Auslander's ontological skepticism. Carroll grants Auslander the aesthetic and ideological points regarding the significance of liveness. He agrees with Auslander that theorists such as Peggy Phelan, who maintain that the mere fact of theatrical presence has political ramifications, overstate their case. However, Carroll refutes Auslander's negation of ontological signification, insisting instead that there exists a definitive ontological difference between live performance and mass media. He bases his account of the difference between live and mediatized performance on the role interpretation plays in performance, in contrast to the purely mechanical process of media presentation. Carroll, one of the most respected and prolific philosophers of art in the analytic tradition, carefully engages Auslander's arguments, exemplifying the sort of dialogue that typifies the discipline of philosophy but is all-too-rare in theater and performance studies. Carroll wrote this essay in response to work that Auslander has previously published, and so it is quite remarkable to find that he has anticipated the analysis of robotics in Auslander's original contribution to this volume. Yet Auslander's position is a worthy adversary, especially in the emphasis on the audience reception of robots as emotionally and aesthetically equivalent to human performance.

Suzanne M. Jaeger's chapter, "Embodiment and Presence: The Ontology of Presence Reconsidered," also defends the distinctive ontology of live performance against Auslander's challenge and those of poststructuralist theory in general. Like Carroll, Jaeger proposes a positive account of theatrical presence. Her account differs from Carroll's, however, being grounded in Merleau-Ponty's theory of embodied interaction and human interconnectedness: presence, she proposes, is the capacity to adjust to unanticipated events in the here and now.

Jon Erickson, who is also a performance theorist with an uncharacteristically analytic bent, contributes significantly to the debate about presence. Unlike Carroll and Jaeger, who focus on the ontological issue, Erickson's main concern is the ethical significance of human presence. Erickson analyzes in considerable detail the notion of human agency and the empathic connections between beings. His position clearly comes down on the side of human presence as the main source of these human connections. While acknowledging the potential for presence to be used malevolently, Erickson nonetheless strongly defends its importance in what he astutely terms "psychic investment."

Robert P. Crease and John Lutterbie challenge the idealized conception of performance that opposes presence and spontaneity to technique and repetition. They develop a general phenomenological account of "technique," drawing close parallels between its functions in contexts such as scientific research and in performance. Technique, according to Crease and Lutterbie, is the mechanism through which people adopt socially defined habits of behavior. They argue that those who view technique as a threat to creativity and freedom radically underestimate the pervasiveness of technique. Technique, they argue, is unavoidable; there is no such thing as purely "natural" behavior, unencumbered by social convention.

Similar to the other essays in this part, Alice Rayner's "Presenting Objects, Presenting Things" probes the concept of presence. In contrast to the other writers, however, her focus avoids human presence, even the quasi-human presence of "performing" robots; instead, she investigates the presence of inanimate objects—that is, props—in the context of live performance. Rayner, likewise Jaeger, employs a phenomenological perspective, which draws primarily on the work of Heidegger. Using Heidegger's theories of *Dasein* (being there, or presence in the moment), Rayner suggests that objects can "dwell poetically," shading their meaning and value as they move from one context to another, and in particular as they move in and out of the theatrical frame. She provides an insightful analysis of the phenomenological impact of an object's history and (perceived) authenticity, both in theatrical and nontheatrical contexts. Rayner's essay exemplifies the distinctive power of phenomenological analysis to startle us with the conceptual richness of seemingly prosaic objects, such as the backstage prop table, that we ordinarily take for granted or dismiss as insignificant.

PART III: RECEPTION

The six chapters in part III examine, with varying emphasis, the relationship between the spectator and the performance event. Specifically, they investigate how audiences perceive and comprehend theatrical performances. The first chapter in this part, David Z. Saltz's "Infiction and Outfiction: The Role of Fiction in Theatrical Performance," provides a transition between the discussions of presence in the previous part and the

analyses of reception here. For Saltz, these issues are inextricably intertwined. His primary concern is with the ontological dimension of performance: the fact that spectators in the theater encounter real people and
objects. Theater functions not merely as a medium for representing
fictions; theatrical reception is, according to Saltz, more than a matter of
decoding signs to extract meaning. The fictional context of a play provides a framework that governs performers' real actions, allowing spectators to understand the significance of these actions. In developing his
account of fiction in performance, Saltz picks up on a line of reasoning
that Wittgenstein initiated with his reflections on "seeing aspects," and
that Kendall Walton has developed further in his theory of representation
in the arts.

Along similar lines, James R. Hamilton—one of the few philosophers in
the analytic tradition who has devoted extended attention over many years
to the phenomenon of theater—adopts a nonsemiotic approach to the
problem of theatrical reception. In "Understanding Plays," he argues that
an audience understands a theatrical performance by engaging with it as it
unfolds in the present, from moment to moment, rather than by gradually
constructing an image of the play as a whole and retrospectively analyzing
the significance of individual elements in the context of that whole. Hamilton relates his theory of theatrical reception to Levinson's "concatenationist" theory of musical reception. Following Levinson's thinking, he posits
that pleasure in listening to music derives from an appreciation of the way
each musical moment builds on the one that immediately precedes it,
rather than on an understanding of the structure of the work as a whole.
Interestingly, Hamilton's account of theatrical reception lends implicit
support to Plato's complaint that theater is unable to supply the whole.
But while Plato condemns theater's tendency to direct the audience's
attention toward the particular (which Plato regards as an illusion) and
transitory and away from the ideal and universal, Hamilton regards that
very quality of theater as key to its ability to offer delight.

Like Hamilton, Bence Nanay is concerned with how the audience
makes sense of the events on stage from a moment-to-moment basis. Similar to Rayner, Nanay's main focus is on the perception of objects onstage,
though Nanay and Rayner ask different questions and adopt different
methodologies. Nanay's chapter, "Perception, Action, and Identification
in the Theater," argues that the spectator's perception of the performance
event is action-oriented rather than detached. In other words, spectators
regard objects onstage as something teleological, which one might use to

achieve a goal. When observing a performance, spectators perceive objects onstage not in terms of their own potential actions, but the characters' actions. Hence, for him, a process of character identification accompanies the most basic act of perceiving an object on stage.

While the process of identification plays a supporting, albeit crucial, role in Nanay's analysis of audience reception, that process takes center stage in David Krasner's contribution. In "Empathy and Theater," Krasner depicts empathy as an act of cognitive as well as emotive identification. Tracing the philosophical development of the term *empathy,* he carefully formulates the concept within a Husserlian template. He uses his understanding of the concept of empathy to refute the arguments, both explicit and implicit, that empathy is an inherently reactionary force in the theater, inhibiting the spectator's ability to respond to a performance in a critical, politically engaged manner.

Rather than using philosophy to elucidate performance, Mike Sell's chapter, "The Voice of Blackness: The Black Arts Movement and Logocentrism," turns the tables to suggest that performance can be read as a kind of philosophical critique. Specifically, he examines the Black Arts Movement of the 1960s, seeing it not only as a radical turn to self-determination and cultural pride, but a centralized vocalization that critiques Derrida's concept of logocentrism.

The part on reception concludes with a previously unpublished essay by the late Michael L. Quinn, whose promising career as a theorist was cut tragically short upon his death in 1994. Quinn, like the other contributors to this part, sets out to determine the conditions that make understanding possible in the theater, building his account around the concept of theatrical convention. In the course of his analysis, he draws on the work of analytic philosophers David Lewis and Donald Davidson. Quinn's arguments, and in particular his appeal to Davidson's "principle of charity," constitute a savvy, sophisticated challenge to poststructuralist skepticism of truth.

Conclusion

Each chapter in this volume is designed to engage in, and dialogue with, a philosophy of theater. Along these lines, we have assembled chapters that we hope inspire new areas of thinking about theater, both as a practice as well as an intellectual discipline. The contributors have asserted themselves in the hopes of breaking new ground, initiating new discussions, and stimulating new ideas. Throughout this work, the commitment has been to introduce new approaches to theater and performance. It is our hope that this work will stimulate a fresh and dynamic debate among theorists of arts and culture from all disciplines.

NOTES

1. For firsthand accounts of the period in the 1980s when theory first became a prominent part of theater scholarship, see Sue-Ellen Case, "Theory/History/Revolution," in *Critical Theory and Performance*, ed. Janelle G. Reinelt and Joseph R. Roach (Ann Arbor: University of Michigan Press, 1992), 418–29; Philip Auslander, *From Acting to Performance* (London: Routledge, 1997), 1–6; and David Savran, "Choices Made and Unmade," *Theater* 31, no. 2 (2001): 89–95.

2. Among the exceptions are James Hamilton and Robert Crease, both of whom have written new essays for this collection. One of the only book-length philosophies of the performing arts by an analytic philosopher is Paul Thom, *For an Audience: A Philosophy of the Performing Arts* (Philadelphia: Temple University Press, 1992). See Timothy Murray, ed., *Mimesis, Masochism, and Mime: The Politics of Theatricality in Contemporary French Thought* (Ann Arbor: University of Michigan Press, 1997) for essays on theater by prominent contemporary French thinkers, including philosophers Gilles Deleuze, Jacques Derrida, Philippe Lacoue-Labarthe, and Jean-François Lyotard. A number of philosophers of art—such as Susanne Langer, Richard Wollheim, Nelson Goodman, Nicholas Wolterstorff, and Kendall Walton in the Anglo-American tradition, and Roman Ingarden and Mikel Dufrenne in the phenomenological tradition—have briefly examined theater in the context of aesthetic theories developed through detailed analyses of the visual arts, literature, or music.

3. Arthur Danto, *Connections to the World: The Basic Concepts of Philosophy* (Berkeley and Los Angeles: University of California Press, 1997), 14.

4. The term *appearance* can be vague, and has been used in a variety of ways. Primarily it refers to what contrasts with reality, something that is not readily available to experience and observation. For some, objects are what they appear to us, being entities unrelated to the mind of the perceiver. However, the history of appearances has been fraught with opinions. For philosophers like Hume and Berkeley, perceptions are the objects; from the appearances of objects to us, Hume asserts, appearances are the objects themselves. For Kant, appearances cannot directly tell us what the things in themselves are; we can only use intuition and a priori reason to tease out the meaning of appearances. For an interesting history of the subject, see John W. Yolton, *Realism and Appearances: An Essay on Ontology* (Cambridge: Cambridge University Press, 2000).

5. Bruce Wilshire, *Role Playing and Identity: The Limits of Theatre as Metaphor* (Bloomington: Indiana University Press, 1991), 4.

6. Aldo Tassi, "Philosophy and Theatre: An Essay on Catharsis and Contemplation," *International Philosophical Quarterly* 35, no. 4 (1995): 472. See also Tassi, "Philosophy and Theatre," *International Philosophical Quarterly* 38, no. 1 (1998): 43–54.

7. Avrum Stroll, *Twentieth-Century Analytic Philosophy* (New York: Columbia University Press, 2000), 7.

8. Bernard Williams, "Contemporary Philosophy: A Second Look," in *Blackwell Companion to Philosophy*, ed. Nicholas Bunnin and E. P. Tsui-James (Oxford: Blackwell, 1996), 26.

9. It subsequently underwent modifications by Wittgenstein (his later work), and its tradition was carried on by such luminaries as Tarski, Quine, Kripke, G. E. Moore, A. J. Ayers, C. D. Broad, Gilbert Ryle, P. F. Strawson, Hilary Putnam, Donald Davidson, Winfred Sellars, and Rudolph Carnap, as well as the logical positivism of the Vienna Circle.

10. John Passmore, *Recent Philosophers* (Chicago: Open Court, 1985), 12. See Samuel C. Wheeler, *Deconstruction as Analytic Philosophy* (Stanford: Standard University Press, 2000), for an interesting discussion on how these two strands of thinking can converge.

11. François Dosse, *History of Structuralism*, trans. Deborah Glassman, vol. 2 (Minneapolis: University of Minnesota Press, 1997), 22.

12. See W. V. O. Quine, "Two Dogmas of Empiricism," in *From a Logical Point of View: Nine Logico-Philosophical Essays* (Cambridge: Harvard University Press, 1953), 20–46.

13. Bernard Williams, "Contemporary Philosophy," 25. Owing to the pervasive influence of the Vienna Circle, Wittgenstein, and other Austrians on analytic philosophy, Michael Dummett suggests that "Anglo-American philosophy" should more accurately be called "Anglo-Austrian." See *Origins of Analytical Philosophy* (Cambridge: Harvard University Press, 1993), 2.

14. Jill Dolan, "Geographies of Learning: Theatre Studies, Performance, and the 'Performative,'" *Theatre Journal* 45, no. 4 (1993): 417.

PART ONE

History and Method

ONE

The Text/Performance Split across the Analytic/Continental Divide

Julia A. Walker

No topic has dominated contemporary scholarship in theater and performance studies more than the text/performance split. From Susan Harris Smith's critical assessment in 1989 of the "anti-dramatic bias" in both canonical and revisionist models of American literature, to W. B. Worthen's critique in 1995 of the textual presuppositions inherent in performance studies in the pages of *TDR,* to a number of attempts to understand the relationship between textual and performative modes of signification,[1] scholars have begun seriously to explore the seeming incommensurability yet persistent interdependence of performances and texts. Although it is often traced back to the antitheatrical prejudice evident in the writings of Plato, the text/performance split—as we know it—is a specifically modern formation. This modern formation developed at the turn of the twentieth century out of an academic debate that isolated textual study from the practice of performance. In the following I show that poetic theorists such as George Santayana and T. S. Eliot located meaning in the text alone in reaction to the popular teachings of speech educator S. S. Curry, who held that meaning was a function of voice and gesture as well. Ultimately resolving in the formation of separate disciplines, this debate posed the question of where exactly meaning lay: did it reside in words alone, or in the bodies that gave them voice?

Such questions were not simply the province of literature and theater and speech departments. Insofar as they raised fundamental concerns about the very nature of human experience, they were taken up by departments of philosophy as well. In the second half of this chapter, I briefly examine the analytic and phenomenological traditions of the early twentieth century, showing that the opposition upon which they are founded is essentially the same as that of the text/performance split. As I argue, the homology between them lies in an inside/outside relationship between the knowing subject and the object of its investigation. Where, in the text/performance split, the reader is either "inside" the text he or she performs or "outside" explicating its meanings, in the analytic/continental divide, the knowing subject is either "inside" the object of its investigation by means of a transcendental consciousness or "outside" the formal language in which that object's truth value is recorded. Having identified this inside/outside opposition as a common presupposition of each, I conclude by proposing a dialectical method of analysis that combines the advantages yet avoids the limitations of each. As applied to the study of theatrical performance, this proposal offers a possible remedy for repairing the text/performance split that has beset theater studies for the past century.

The Modern Formation of the Text/Performance Split

In *American Drama: The Bastard Art* Susan Harris Smith follows up on her *American Quarterly* article of 1989 by tracing the historical roots of the "anti-dramatic bias" that she observes in American literary study. What she discovers is that these roots, while extending back to a Puritan distrust of theatrical representation, are nourished by several precipitating conditions in the nineteenth century, including the lack of adequate copyright protection for dramatic works, a producing emphasis upon spectacle (as opposed to narrative), and the marketability of plays with an emotional (as opposed to intellectual) appeal. By the turn of the twentieth century, however, these conditions had begun to change as the art and little theater movements began to cultivate both homegrown talents and audience tastes for a more serious "literary" drama. Unfortunately, the often experimental plays written and mounted by these groups frequently relied upon contextual references, making them ill-suited for the model of textual autonomy soon to be institutionalized in departments of English by the New Critics. Thus an "anti-dramatic bias" shaped the study of American literature.

Martin Puchner has more recently demonstrated that modern drama itself bears just such a bias, arguing that it generally (not just in the United States) reveals a "theatre at odds with the value of theatricality."[2] Analyzing the work of writers such as Stéphane Mallarmé, James Joyce, and

Gertrude Stein, Puchner identifies a modernist proclivity for "closet drama"—drama that not only is meant to be read but whose full realization can only be achieved within the reader's imagination. He also examines the work of playwrights such as W. B. Yeats, Bertolt Brecht, and Samuel Beckett, suggesting that theirs is a "diegetic drama"—a drama in which theatricality is tightly controlled (if not denied, as in closet drama) by the playwright. Both strains, Puchner argues, reveal the extent to which modern drama seeks to resist theatricality.

While Smith and Puchner are correct to note an antidramatic bias both in the literary-critical establishment and in the drama itself, neither identifies the cultural origin of this bias or explains its rationale. As I have shown,[3] that origin lies in the cultural history of the expressive culture movement, a broad-based popular movement advocating the performing arts as an antidote to modernity, and, more specifically, in the influential strain of literary high modernism that developed in reaction to it. The two figures associated with this cultural movement and its reaction were respectively S. S. Curry, whose theory of "expression" insisted upon the coordination of the body's three modes of signification (verbal, vocal, and pantomimic), and T. S. Eliot, whose early critical essays insist upon the autonomy of the poetic text. To understand the debate that swirled around the two positions represented by these figures, we must delve into the cultural history of the expressive culture movement.

Encompassing poetry and drama, music and dance, the expressive culture movement taught that, through these forms of artistic expression, one could overcome the dehumanizing influence of the modern industrial age. Expressive culture offered a program of exercise designed to release the body from bad habits of breathing, speaking, gesturing, and moving, which, if left unchecked, inhibited authentic self-expression. These bad habits, its proponents held, were the direct result of having allowed the alienating conditions of modernization to alter the body's natural rhythms. Proposing to restore those natural rhythms and thus allow for freer self-expression, the expressive culture movement promised to reestablish the individual's relationship to the spiritual forces of the universe.

Offered through summer Chautauqua programs as well as independent schools of expression, the teachings of the expressive culture movement originally derived from the work of Boston University professor of oratory S. S. Curry, whose theory of "expression" transformed the practice of elocution by shifting its emphasis away from the vocalization of sounds toward the full bodily expression of ideas. This shift was necessitated in large part by changes within the American university system at the turn of the twentieth century, when various traditional fields of study were reconfigured into "scientific" disciplines, in keeping with the model of the German research institution. Thus, in order to redefine oratory as a "science," Curry, along with his mentor Lewis B. Monroe, outlined for it a new theory and practice. That theory was American transcendentalism; its practice was the reproduction of the various modes of communication that had been observed and recorded by French vocal instructor François Delsarte.

Although now largely forgotten, the Delsarte method revolutionized theatrical and vocal performance in the late nineteenth century by offering performers a more realistic model of human action that they could reproduce on stage. Its "realism" came from Delsarte's own observations of people in the streets, parks, and cafés of Paris. Recording the expressions, stances, and gestures he witnessed, Delsarte compiled them into a comprehensive system in which a specific meaning was ascribed to each. Introduced to the United States in 1870 by his student Steele MacKaye, the Delsarte method was like the neoclassical system of rhetorical gesture in its codification of bodily movement. Unlike neoclassical decorum, however, it held that its significations were discovered in nature rather than produced by convention, having been based upon Delsarte's own empirical observations. In this way, it offered Curry a "scientific" basis for his theory of expression.

Beginning with the subjective impressions the text evoked within the reader's mind, Curry's student was asked to conceptualize the meaning of the work as a whole. Then, after concentrating upon the various figures and images that produced that conception, the student was instructed to use the expressive means of his or her entire body to communicate that meaning to the audience. Those expressive means included the three primary "languages" of the body: verbal (the conventionalized symbols of language), vocal (e.g., tone color and inflection that register emotion), and pantomimic (gesture and bodily comportment). Although modern culture had disarticulated these three languages, often alienating speakers from their own bodily means of making meaning, students of expressive culture could learn to bring them back into alignment and thus give effective expression to their thoughts. Indeed, it was only through the effective and unified use of these three languages that an orator could arouse the sympathetic identification of his or her auditors so as to make the conceptualization that had manifested itself to the orator manifest itself to them.

The problem with Curry's method—as Harvard philosopher George Santayana pointed out—was that it located the text's meaning within the spiritual universe, suggesting that the student simply become attuned to its emanations in order to convey the true meaning of the text. In his essay "The Elements and Function of Poetry," Santayana implicitly challenges the assumptions underlying Curry's method. While he acknowledges that emotions are the stuff out of which poetry is made, he goes on to insist that poetry does not present us with an unmediated experience of them as they occur in the natural world; rather, it presents us with emotions that have been transformed first within the poet's imagination. The key to the poet's success, Santayana avers, lies in an ability to find the "correlative object" by which that emotion may be expressed. "Expression," Santayana contends, "is a misleading term which suggests that something previously known is rendered or imitated; whereas the expression is itself an original fact, the values of which are then [mistakenly] referred to the thing expressed, much as the honours of a Chinese mandarin are attributed retroactively to his parents. So the charm which a poet, by his art of combining images and shades of emotion, casts over a scene or an action, is attached to the principal actor in it, who gets the benefit of the setting furnished him by a well-stocked mind."[4] In other words, expression—as theorized by Curry—not only misattributes to the poem the poet's skill, but effectively denies poetic agency by suggesting that the poet is simply a conduit of some larger universal truth that the poet merely inscribes upon the page.

As a student at Harvard in the first decade of the twentieth century, Eliot probably would have known about expression and the expressive culture movement. Additionally, as a student of Santayana, he most certainly would have been aware of his critique. After all, it is from Santayana that he derives his notion of the "objective correlative," and it is around this critical phrase that he constellates his concerns over language and its ability to fully express the author's meaning. That phrase first appears, of course, in his essay "Hamlet and His Problems" (1919). Here, Eliot engages Nietzsche's critique of Shakespeare's famous play, in which he argues that the play's "problem" lies in its overemphasis upon language. For Nietzsche, the play was simply one of many examples of post-Euripidean drama in which the dialogue of Apollonian reason dominated or, indeed, supplanted the music of Dionysian feeling that was once an integral part of the dramatic ritual. Without it, Nietzsche maintained, drama tended to appeal only to the *principium individuationis,* failing to transport audience members out of their individual consciousnesses and into an experience of *communitas*. Eliot, however, diagnosed the play's problem differently. For him, it failed because Shakespeare was unable to express in language the emotion motivating Hamlet's dialogue. Note that it is not a problem of the actor's interpretation of the character, but the playwright's construction of his character in words. Introducing his famous critical term, Eliot explains that "[t]he only way of expressing emotion in the form of art is by finding an 'objective correlative'; in other words, a set of objects, a situation, a chain of events which shall be the formula of that particular emotion; such that when the external facts, which must terminate in sensory experience, are given, the emotion is immediately evoked."[5] Where Nietzsche believed that the drama's meaning could not be reduced to language, Eliot maintained that it must be.

Like Santayana, Eliot implicitly challenges Curry's theory of expression with its emphasis upon the integration of the three languages of the body. Like his mentor, he suggests that it does not adequately account for the importance of the significatory work performed by the poet on the verbal level. Although Curry did allow that "verbal expression . . . is the most complete and adequate means of revealing ideas,"[6] he maintained that it is not adequate unto itself; vocal and pantomimic languages complete the expression by introducing nuances that can augment or even reverse the presumed meaning of a verbal utterance.[7] "The writer arranges his ideas and endeavors to embody thought in words," Curry explains, "while the speaker not only endeavors to embody his ideas in words, but to reveal all the phases of experience arising from these ideas or associated with them through a co-ordination of all the living languages of his personality. Not only must he have 'words that burn,' but tones and inflections, motions and actions, which breathe and live with the deepest life of his soul."[8]

In many of his critical essays throughout the 1920s, Eliot elaborated his critique of Curry's theory of expression, refuting Curry's claim that performative modes of signification were necessary to convey the meaning of a text. In "The Possibility of a Poetic Drama" (1920), for example, Eliot's antiperformative bias is evident in his claim that performance is the greatest obstacle to the creation of a poetic drama. "[W]e must take into account the instability of any art—the drama, music, dancing—which depends upon representation by performers," Eliot remarks. "The intervention of performers introduces a complication of economic conditions which is in itself likely to be injurious. A struggle, more or less unconscious, between the creator and the interpreter is almost inevitable. The interest of a performer is almost certain to be centred in himself: a very slight acquaintance with actors and musicians will testify. The performer is interested not in form but in opportunities for virtuosity or in the communication of his 'personality.'"[9]

Although, later in his career, Eliot appears to assume a more ambivalent stance toward performance, writing several full-length dramas himself, his early critical writings helped to establish an antiperformative bias within literary high modernism. The fact that his later plays were critically acclaimed for their literary qualities speaks as much to the way that the category of the literary came to be defined by his early critical writings as to their ability to conform to that definition. Canonized within the Anglo-American university through the work of New Critics Cleanth Brooks and Robert Heilman, as well as I. A. Richards and F. R. Leavis, this influential model of literary high modernism thus bore within it a bias against explicitly performative genres that, as Smith cogently argues, made much of drama a "bastard art."[10] Effectively banished from English departments through the adoption of an antiperformative literary standard, the practice of expression set up its own dominion within the university structure with the formation of departments of theater and speech. As a result, the text/performance split institutionalized within the academy was exacerbated.

The Text/Performance Split in Twentieth-Century Western Philosophy

Although originally focused upon the problem of literary interpretation, the text/performance split pervades other areas of modern thought as well. Indeed, it can be seen to structure thought itself within the Western philosophical tradition of the past century. Consider the two major branches of philosophy within twentieth-century thought: the analytic tradition of Bertrand Russell and the phenomenological tradition of Edmund Husserl. Although typically characterized as a distinction between Anglo-American and continental (i.e., French and German) philosophy departments, the difference between the two traditions is less geographical than perspectival. For, as Jan Patocka points out, both derive from the work of Gottlob Frege, and both attempted to remake philosophy into a more rigorous science.[11] Where Russell's analysis was trained on the formal relations among propositions in statements made about the world, Husserl's phenomenology focused on the knowing subject who engaged in those relations with the world. Where Russell created a science of logical constructionism, Husserl created a science of experiential knowledge. The following will demonstrate the difference between the two is essentially that underlying the text/performance split.

When Husserl published his *Philosophy of Arithmetic* in 1891, he found himself having to rethink his assumption that the origin of all mathematical inquiry lies in the knowing subject after a critical review by Frege called his "psychologism" into question. Remarkably, Husserl actually gave Frege's critique thoughtful consideration and acknowledged the unquestioned assumptions in his work. Specifically, he came to reject the tautology that all acts of cognition are necessarily subjective, where, for example, the abstraction of a number from a particular set of objects would be understood as a psychological process rather than the recognition of an *a priori* category of knowledge. For Frege, such insistent subjectivism compromised the purity of formal logic by denying the possibility that universal categories of knowledge could exist apart from our understanding of them. Frege's critique startled Husserl into realizing that the relationship between a knowing subject and the objects of its knowledge was not yet properly understood.

Rejecting the mysticism of Kantian "noumena," Husserl set his focus on "phenomena," actual things in the world, but things whose essence eludes ordinary understanding. His method of phenomenology is meant to uncover that essence (in Kantian terms, the thing-in-itself) but without recourse to speculative theory; rather, Husserl explicitly formulates it as a *science*. As we have already seen, science at the turn of the twentieth century was the dominant paradigm of knowledge, claiming greater authority over the other "softer" disciplines. Philosophy was no less vulnerable to the hegemony of science in the German research academy than was oratory in the United States. Indeed, it was in response to Frege's stinging rebuke of his psychologism that Husserl set out to remake his epistemological method into a truly rigorous science in his *Logical Investigations* (1900–1901).

Husserl began by distinguishing between two basic types of knowledge: primary and psychical. Primary knowledge was that which was available through a sensory engagement with the empirical world. Colors, textures, shapes, smell—these were things that could be known through a direct encounter with the world. Psychical knowledge, on the other hand, was that which was *a priori*, intuitive, and categorical. It was knowledge that did not necessarily have to have a referent in the real world. But these two types of knowledge, Husserl held, were neither distinct nor mutually exclusive. That is, in order to get around the old problem that primary or sensuous knowledge came to us from an experience with the "outer" world while *a priori* or categorical knowledge was an "inner" experience, Husserl maintained that both types of knowledge pertained to both types of experiences. In other words, one could imagine a pink-and-green spotted elephant (where sensuous knowledge would appear in psychical form), and one could also experience, say, time through the process of feeling one's body age (where categorical knowledge would appear in sensuous form). As historian of philosophy Jonathan Rée observes, "Husserl's phenomenology could be described as uniting the two great tendencies in philosophy since Descartes: on the one hand, the loving attention to contingent and perhaps chaotic perceptual detail characteristic of Locke, Berkeley and Diderot, and on the other, the rigorous explication of orderly transcendental forms characteristic of Kant." But more than simply uniting these two tendencies, Rée argues, Husserl resolved the implicit contradiction between "inner" knowledge and "outer" data that had beset philosophers for centuries: "The prephenomenological philosophers had tried to persuade us that our experience is fundamentally subjective; but they were ignoring the irrepressible objective worldly reference of all our perceptions. The world is not an afterthought, a quality we tentatively infer from regular correlations amongst our sensory ideas. Nor is it a subjective three-dimensional geometrical form that we clamp on to certain ideas in order to differentiate them from the inner experiences that take place only in the single dimension of time." By refuting the centuries-old opposition between internal subjective experience and the external world in which we live, Husserl opened up a new way of thinking about knowledge as a subjective experience that was both in and of the world. "Husserl, as Sartre put it, liberated us from the stuffy old philosophy of the 'inner life.' We were finally out in the open air and philosophy could breathe again."[12]

The significance of Husserl's phenomenology was the fact that it recognized the world as both the object of knowledge and the context in which such knowledge was obtained. The world, for Husserl, was not merely a static place in which things had empirical existence; nor was it simply a place in which to locate our own subjective experiences; it was a fully textured, four-dimensional, dynamic environment—or "horizon" in Husserl's terms—that we actively engaged in knowing the things we know. It was thus to purify our knowledge of such things from the contamination of both our subjectivism and the fact of the object's empirical existence in the world that Husserl developed his phenomenological method as a science. The key to his method was the process of reduction whereby the subject learned to "bracket" things apart from the context of the world in order to understand their true essence, that which made them what they were and nothing else. Thus he prescribed the knowing subject to direct his or her consciousness toward the object of investigation in an act of intentionality not unlike that described by Curry in his "think-the-thought" method. Then, by focusing on the features of that object (often features that are presented to consciousness through the senses), the intending consciousness can deduce whether they are constitutive of the thing or merely incidental to it. For example, the redness of an apple may be constitutive of that particular apple, but it is not necessarily constitutive of apples as such. Thus, that feature would be deemed literally inessential to the nature of apples. As this example illustrates, the means by which an intending consciousness is able to deduce the essential nature of an object is by imagining all possible variations of all identifiable features in order to isolate only those that are invariant and thus constitutive of the object as such. Once having arrived at this understanding of the object under consideration, the intending consciousness is thus appraised of its essence or "eidos," the meaning that is immanent in it, the same meaning that is able to transcend any one intending consciousness and be presented to another. In this way, Husserl was able to avoid the charge of subjectivism (through the concept of transcendence) as well as the manacles of empiricism (in that meaning was immanent, not bound to the facticity of the thing itself, much like the abstract and *a priori* categories of mathematics).

Husserl went on to focus less on the immanence of meaning in things than on the transcendent consciousness that comes to know it, taking consciousness itself as the primary topic of his investigations. Meanwhile, in England, Russell was busy developing his own scientific approach to many of these same problems. The two thinkers had much in common: both inherited a Hegelian understanding of the world as an absolute totality; both followed Frege in allowing for the independent existence of *a priori* truths; both assumed a relationship between *a priori* categories of knowledge and our experience of the material world; and both sought to avoid the pitfalls of psychologism and empiricism in outlining a method for understanding that relationship. As we have observed, Husserl tried to address these problems by developing his method of reduction whereby consciousness directed itself toward the discovery of *a priori* truths in the world that were held to be both independent of our knowing them and transcendent of their material conditions.

Russell, however, took a slightly different tack. While he, too, held that *a priori* truths are independent both of our knowing them and of the particular conditions of their instantiation, he turned to the principles of pure mathematics to translate experiential knowledge into a symbolic form whose validity could be tested.[13] One of the reasons for the difference in these two philosophers' approaches had to do with their different attitudes toward the Hegelian legacy that they had both inherited. Where Husserl assumed with Hegel that everything in the world was part and parcel of the whole and thus developed his method of reduction as a heuristic tool for analyzing a single object in abstraction from the whole, Russell vehemently denied the Hegelian totality, dismissing it as mystical nonsense. In particular, he objected to its "doctrine of internal relations," which held that the relations between things informed the essence of each. So, for example, inherent to the idea of a bridge are its relations to the river, the two banks, the feet and vehicles that pass over it, and so on. Russell pointed out that, within the realm of pure mathematics, this would lead to an infinite number of relations inhering within any one number and thus refuted the doctrine of internal relations, asserting the existence of isolated or "atomic" facts that could be analyzed on their own.

Positing a "doctrine of external relations" instead, Russell held that relations have their own reality separate from that of the things related. For example, if a squirrel is on a park bench, the squirrel's relationship to the bench has a different ontological reality than does either the squirrel or the bench. The squirrel and the bench are particularities existing in real space and time; the relation of being "on," however, is not contingent upon those particular realities but exists as a formal dimension of their relationship to each other. Form was what most interested Russell. As he noted in his *Introduction to Mathematical Philosophy* (1919), "we do not . . . deal with particular things or particular properties: we deal formally with what can be said about *any* thing or *any* property."[14] Where matter is always particular, form is generalizable from any specific instantiation of it. So, too, are *a priori* truths generalizable from the material world in which we come to know them (e.g., the number of apples in the set "red" as a proportion of the number of apples in the set "bowl"). Thus, by isolating form and analyzing the formal relations between atomic facts, Russell sought to arrive at *a priori* truths about the world.

Russell's method of formal analysis takes its name from Kant's distinction between synthetic statements (which are informative) and analytic statements (which serve merely to instantiate facts). Taking the latter as the object of his study, Russell focuses on the formal relations among the terms within such statements in order to test their validity, believing that only valid forms are capable of conveying substantive truths about the world. This process assumes a correspondence between statements made about the world and the world itself, as well as a transparent relationship between language and the things it names. Known as the correspondence theory of truth and the referential theory of meaning respectively, these premises formed the backbone of Russell's early method. Yet, almost immediately, Russell was made aware of some of the inherent problems they posed, particularly with regard to language and its relation to the world. He followed Frege in distinguishing between "formalized" and "ordinary" language; the former referred to "conceptual content" alone, while the latter referred to the ways that that content could be shaped rhetorically "for the hearer to grasp."[15] In effect, it is a distinction not unlike that made by Curry between verbal signification and vocal and pantomimic languages; just as Eliot excluded all but verbal signification from his purview, so did Russell. Accordingly, Russell may be seen to have built his method upon an antiperformative foundation as well.

Having purified language of its rhetorical variability, Russell sought further to diminish any possibility of imprecision by translating it into a symbolic system of notation. As he explains in the introduction to the first volume of his and Alfred North Whitehead's *Principia Mathematica* (1910), "Any use of words would require unnatural limitations to their ordinary meanings, which would be in fact more difficult to remember consistently than are the definitions of entirely new symbols."[16] In other words, it is more expedient to use a symbol than a word that, by virtue of its being a word, has more than one strictly defined meaning; or, as Jacques Derrida might say, is subject to "citationality." What Russell does here is all but acknowledge the inherent problems in the referential theory of meaning upon which his method is based. Unwilling to forsake it completely, however, he devised a solution to the various problems that arose. The solution was known as *logical constructionism.*

Logical constructionism held that problematic statements were problematic because they were still in a compound linguistic form and needed to be broken down into their most fundamental units. So, for example, the ideas in sentences containing certain words such as "of" or "the" that seemed to have a specific referent but did not correspond to any particular fact could be restated in a more fundamental way. To make his case, Russell cited a sentence that clearly had no real-world referent in order to demonstrate that the problem was one of logic and not of fact. His famous example was "The present king of France is bald." As there is currently no king, let alone a bald king, in France, the "the" is without an obvious referent. Nonetheless, the sentence is not without logical form; it is just difficult to see since it is, in fact, a compound sentence, being composed of the atomic facts "there *is* a present king of France," "there is *only* one king of France," and "he is bald." Russell temporarily solved the problem inherent to the referential theory of meaning by locating it not within the structural conditions of language but within the logician whose language is not precise enough. (Like Eliot's Shakespeare, Russell's logician has not sufficiently mastered his craft.) What was needed was an "ideal" language, one that expressed ideas in their most elemental form, and was the basis for all manner of paraphrase. The test of this ideal language would be what Russell called "the principle of acquaintance," the rule that all ideas must refer to things we have experienced in the world. In this way, Russell effectively collapsed the referential theory of meaning into the correspondence theory of truth, insisting that ideas match experience when words and meanings became too difficult to regulate.

The referential theory of meaning (the primary flaw in Russell's method) presumes that language exists apart from yet mirrors the world by referring to its meanings. Since Russell's whole method is premised on this theory, it, too, presupposes a distinction between language and the world it names. But, as J. L. Austin later discovered, language sometimes has no referent outside itself but effects the very thing it names (what Austin referred to as a "performative" in *How to Do Things with Words* [1962]). As Russell's own student Ludwig Wittgenstein pointed out in his *Philosophical Investigations* (1953), language is *of* the world, and *in* the world, being a set of conventions by which we communicate. This observation situates the knowing subject back in the world, reintroducing the problem of psychologism that Husserl tried to solve with his method of reduction. Russell's solution to that same problem had been to imagine a realm of *a priori* truths that existed apart from the world of the knowing subject but that was accessible to that subject through means of linguistic representation. Part of its appeal was its presumed scientific objectivity. By imagining the knowing subject as existing apart from the realm of the language by which *a priori* truths may be represented, it posited the investigator outside the object of investigation.

Husserl's method, by contrast, situated the knowing subject fully inside the world that was the object of his or her investigations. But it was no less scientific for acknowledging the subject's implication within the world of the investigation. Indeed, its scientific appeal came from the heuristic tool of bracketing that allowed for a sort of tactical objectivity. Nonetheless, as Derrida argues in *Speech and Phenomena* (1967), Husserl succumbs to a "metaphysics of presence," imagining himself able to access the essence that inheres within the object of his investigation.[17] Husserl's mistake, for Derrida, is in believing that his intuition is self-present and unmediated when, in fact, to render an experience into thought is to (re)present it to one's consciousness as an idea. Representation, as Derrida points out, necessarily involves a process of self-alienation—a structural condition that Derrida later neatly refers to by the term "dehiscence."[18] Because of this structural condition, we have epistemological access only to the signifier of a thing, never the thing itself. Husserl tries to get around this problem by distinguishing between "expression" *(Ausdruck)* and "indication" *(Anzeichen),* understanding the former to bear an inherent "meaning" subject to intuition while the latter operates through a system of signs to communicate "sense." But Derrida deconstructs this structural opposition, demonstrating that Husserl's notion of expression as a sort of internal monologue or "solitary discourse" nonetheless depends upon a system of representation to mean.

The inside/outside opposition that marks the distinction between these two traditions is the same one that underlies the text/performance split. For just as Husserl posited his knowing subject inside the object of its investigation, so, too, did Curry believe that his oral interpreter could experience the literary object from within. Where Husserl's method of reduction allowed the subject to bracket out the world of variant features and intuit the essence of the object of investigation, Curry's think-the-thought method invited the subject to open up his or her sympathetic imagination to the forces of the spiritual universe in order to arrive at an unmediated understanding of the work's meaning. As a result, in both Husserl's phenomenological and Curry's performance-oriented methods, the knowing subject is understood to have direct, unmediated access to the object of study by occupying a position inside the field of investigation. And, in both Russell's analytic and Eliot's text-based methods, the knowing subject is understood to be outside the object of study, assuming a perspective of scientific objectivity. For, just as Russell posited his knowing subject outside the realm of *a priori* truths and the symbolic language by which they could be represented, so, too, did Eliot insist that his reader stand outside the literary text whose sympathetic effects were the result of the poet's conscious design. Where Russell imagined language as a transparent medium, Eliot imagined it as opaque, but both had the same goal; both focused on language as a means of representing something true about the world, whether *a priori* or poetic knowledge. Thus we can see a homology between the text/performance split and the analytic/continental divide.

Husserl's phenomenological and Russell's analytic methods have had their critics. But, while Derrida and Wittgenstein have usefully identified the limitations in each, we should not assume that these methods are totally without merit, particularly as brought to bear upon the study of theater and performance today. Critics such as Bert O. States and Stanton Garner have demonstrated the usefulness of phenomenological methods to study theatrical performance, especially those methods developed by post-Husserlian thinkers such as Maurice Merleau-Ponty. As Garner forcefully argues, poststructuralist rejections of phenomenology tend to fix the whole "tradition in its opening, most preliminary articulations, robbing it of its developments and internal revisions—in short, of its historical contingency."[19] Noting a persistent "scriptocentrism" underlying much contemporary poststructuralist theory, Garner correctly identifies a textual bias that informs many of the approaches that have been brought to bear upon theater studies.[20] Derridean deconstruction itself may be seen as one such "scriptocentric" approach, given its emphasis upon writing as a means of general communication (which, as such, is no different than speech). It, like Russell's analytic method, persists in understanding the thing represented by attending to the form of its representation. Even so, Derridean explorations of "différance" have been productively applied to theatrical signification by Peggy Phelan, Herbert Blau, and Philip Auslander, while Derrida's notions of "iteration" and "citationality" have been provocatively considered in relation to performance by Judith Butler and William Worthen.

While poststructuralist methods of interpretation such as deconstruction maintain an analytic focus on the form of representation as a means of understanding the thing represented, they are not necessarily subject to the same sort of critique that Wittgenstein made of the analytic tradition. Where they differ is in the relation they construct between the investigator and the object of investigation. Unlike Russell, poststructuralist approaches imagine their investigator *inside* the field of investigation, even as they set up a tactical "outside" perspective within it. Thus, for example, Derrida posits Husserl's *Logical Investigations* as the object of his study, analyzing its dependence upon a structural opposition between indication and expression for its coherence, even as he slyly acknowledges his own implication within that same system of structural oppositions (i.e., language) with his witty puns. In this way, Derrida sets up what anthropologists might refer to as a participant-observer relation to the object of his study.

For all of their tactical manipulation of the inside/outside opposition, however, participant-observers are not "inside" the object of their study in the way that Husserl and Curry intended, for what Husserl and Curry sought was an intuitive knowledge that transcended the form of its representation—what Derrida disparages as a "metaphysics of presence." Derrida's complaint is that, because of the structural conditions of representation, we can never know the referent except as it is presented to our consciousness through signification. And signification, by definition, automatically entails the process of "dehiscence" or self-alienation. That is, the signified is never fully present to itself. What this presumes is that knowledge is always an epistemological process, one that appeals solely to the cognitive faculty of reason.[21] But what if there are other aspects of knowledge that don't appeal to reason? What if those other ways of knowing appeal to other faculties such as emotion or spatiotemporal experience? This, in effect, is exactly what Curry suggested in describing his three "languages." Distinguishing between verbal, vocal, and pantomimic modes of signification, Curry insisted that all three were necessary to the act of communicating meaning; where verbal signification appeals to reason, vocality appeals to emotion and gesture appeals to our sense of existing in space and time.

The problem, as Derrida would undoubtedly point out, is that, insofar as vocality and gesture are languages, they are subject to the same structural conditions that inhere within any other system of signification that is based upon difference. But what if they are not languages? What if they are not dependent upon a system of difference to mean? What if those "meanings" are communicated in some other way? Consider a plaintive wail, sounded from the depths of a grieving mother's being. Consider the dilated pupils of a lover gazing into the eyes of his beloved. Although we could consider that both of these examples are subject to the same structural conditions that Derrida describes as pertaining to all modes of communication—the wail could *signify* "grief" or "pain," the gaze could *signify* "love" or "infatuation"—they nonetheless affect us without our having to translate them into such terms. What is suggested here is that vocality and gesture are not always subject to a process of dehiscence; they simply are what they are. Or, rather, they both are and are not subject to dehiscence, depending upon how one views them. If, for example, we ascribe a certain meaning to a certain inflection or gesture (as did Delsarte), then, of course, vocality and gesture may be subject to dehiscence. But if we consider them as pure sound or movement, they are not subject to dehiscence in that they do not function as arbitrary signs within a system of difference. This is why any attempt to analogize vocality or gesture to language is ultimately limited. "Meaning," in other words, *is* self-present. But, by "meaning," I do not mean a significance that is registered within the conceptual bandwidth of the brain. Rather, I mean a "significance" that is registered within the body's viscera, as emotional or experiential "knowledge." The fact that I have to keep using quotation marks to make myself understood points to the fact that, to *be* understood—conceptually speaking—I have to recur to the metaphors of "meaning," "significance," and "knowledge" in order to approximate in verbal form the types of knowledge these modes of communication relay.

In theater studies, the extraverbal meaning of vocality and gesture was first described by Richard Wagner in *The Artwork of the Future* (1849). Rediscovered by Antonin Artaud in *The Theatre and Its Double* (1931–36), this insight has since been discredited by Derrida in his essay "The Theatre of Cruelty and the Closure of Representation" (1967). Predictably, Derrida accuses Artaud of a "metaphysics of presence," criticizing him for believing that his "theater of cruelty," with its all-out sensory assault upon spectators, would be purer and less mediated than writing.[22] Indeed, insofar as the "animated hieroglyphs" that Artaud proposed are a form of representation, Derrida is right. Theatrical forms of signification are no less subject to the process of dehiscence than is language. Yet, insofar as what Artaud was proposing was an encounter with pure sound and movement—albeit placed within a theatrical frame—Derrida's critique falls short. For, in the theater, vocality and gesture are always both immediate and dehiscent; they always have the ability to appeal to both our affective and our experiential registers directly yet to function as signs within a system of theatrical signification.

In his responses to Husserl and Artaud, Derrida argues that knowledge is never as pure and unmediated as either would have it. But it is suggested here that Derrida's critique—though valid on its own terms—unnecessarily insists upon a strict definition of knowledge, one that speaks only to a classic epistemological sense, foreclosing the possibility that there are other ways in which we "know" things in our world. The question for us now is, why should we continue to abide by this restricted definition of knowledge, especially since it has been historically used to validate certain types of academic inquiry at the expense of others, with theater studies often getting short shrift? Even with the implementation of performance studies programs in our own moment, we should be wary of adhering to this restricted definition of knowledge in an attempt to gain academic legitimacy, especially since it seems inadequate to a consideration of the many ways in which a performance can mean.

Theater, perhaps more than any other art form, has the power to appeal to all of these ways of knowing in its very form. Combining visual, auditory, and often olfactory (if not gustatory) and tactile effects, theater simply cannot be understood from an "outside" perspective that flattens its multiple sensory appeals into a text to be read. Insofar as we see, hear, smell, or feel ourselves in relation to the event that takes place on stage (and often in the aisles and all around us), we are participating in an experience of understanding, not just registering the knowledge of something that stands in objective relation to our own subjectivity. By the same token, that experience cannot be fully understood until it *is* apprehended in objective relation to our own subjectivity. Just as rational cognition is inadequate by itself, so is sensuous participation. Theater has the unique ability to shift us between these two perspectives by situating us both inside an imaginative fiction and outside the proscenium frame.[23]

To illustrate, I cite one of my favorite theatrical anecdotes—Boston socialite Anna Cabot Lowell Quincy's reflections on Fanny Kemble's 1833 performance of Bianca in Henry Milman's play *Fazio*. Referring to the jail scene in which Bianca visits her husband. who has been charged with a murder he did not commit but nonetheless profited from, Quincy confessed to her journal:

> The moment which I think produced most effect on the house was at the moment when Fazio is to be led off to execution in the prison. She has just been imploring the jailer to delay a few moments in the most passionate manner, when the bell tolls, the sound of which seemed to turn her into marble. She stood riveted to the spot—her eyes fixed, her cheek pale and ashen. Fazio embraces her, but she is entirely insensible of it, and he is led off the stage leaving her the solitary figure. She stood,

I should think, five moments, a perfect statue, and the deathlike still-ness that reigned over the crowded audience, every person seeming to hold their breath, was very striking. "She stood the bloodless image of despair" until the bell tolled again.[24]

As the shifting referent of "she" reveals, Quincy simultaneously marvels at Kemble's technical skill and vicariously experiences the pathos of the situation her character is in. She is both "inside" the imaginative fiction of the play and "outside" it, observing Kemble's technique. Applying Husser-lian terms to her analysis, it is as if she is concentrating on Kemble's per-formance in such a way as to abstract its essence, perhaps isolating the character of Bianca from variant features such as costume, hair color, accent, etc. But, at the same time, Quincy is fully aware of the fact of Kem-ble's performance, commenting on the formal properties of Kemble's technique. Applying Russell's terms to her analysis, we may say that it is as if she maps the formal relationships among the atomic elements of the performance in order to arrive at its essential truth. Perhaps responding to the play's fundamental conflict between Christianity and capitalism that is represented as a tension between the "value" of life and death, Quincy notes the "deathlike stillness" that came over the audience as Kemble affected Bianca's shock by rendering her body immobile like a "statue." Here the elements of the representational language of performance stand in relation to each other as do the "truths" they represent. The lifeless aspect of Kemble's character, affected in response to the imminent death of her beloved, is recapitulated by the audience, even as its response is implicitly differentiated from Kemble's by Quincy's language. Kemble assumes the pose of a "statue," a work of art, while the audience can only approach what Kemble represents on stage, an approximation indicated by Quincy's use of the adjective "deathlike." Thus we see how Quincy's words reveal a double consciousness of the theatrical event; she is both imaginatively inside it, feeling what the character feels, while practically outside of it, appreciating Kemble's technique as a discerning connoisseur.

This anecdote undoubtedly dates to a period when performance con-ventions more easily allowed audiences to shift back and forth between an imaginative "inside" and practical "outside." But, while in our own moment the (still dominant) conventions of realism and the medium of film have shaped audience habits of consumption, this oscillating dynamic nonetheless persists. I memorably experienced it a few years ago while attending Julie Taymor's marvelous production of Disney's *The Lion King*.

During the scene where Simba wanders alone on the savannah, vulnerable to all sorts of unexpected dangers, a rhinoceros appears on a distant hill, quickly descending into the valley. Two more appear in its path, followed by several others until, just as the first rhinoceros mounts a hill in the foreground, we realize that this is a stampede. Within the fictional narrative of the play (however thin its rendering of the traditional African folktale), we are made to feel the terror of this rampage as it presses down on Simba, our hero and point of identification. Still, because Taymor exposes the technical apparatus behind her puppetry, we are simultaneously aware of the device that creates the illusion we find so terrifying. In this case, it is a series of rotating drums, graduated in size to render a sense of relative distance, on which are mounted papier-mâché rhinoceroses, also of graduated size to create the total effect of a rampage coming toward the audience. Part of my appreciation of this scene was that sense of shifting between being inside the narrative, imaginatively occupying Simba's place in the veldt, and outside the proscenium, sitting in my seat marveling at Taymor's artistry. But, like Quincy's response to Kemble, my response was not simply one of creating a tactical "inside" from which to observe the performance (as the participant-observer model would allow). It was an "inside" perspective that was predicated on an affective and experiential relationship to what I saw, heard, and felt. It was an affective and experiential relationship that made my rational comprehension of the play's moral about the importance of community all the more complete.

What is suggested here is that, to understand something fully, we must inhabit both "inside" and "outside" perspectives while interpolating the difference between them in a *reductio ad absurdum*. What I describe, of course, is the Hegelian dialectic. But, while I do not mean to suggest that we can achieve "absolute knowledge," I do mean to insist upon the necessity of keeping both perspectives in mind, acknowledging the utility and limitations of each. We are both inside and outside the field of investigation that is our world. We, in theater and performance studies, could benefit from remembering this fact more often. Rather than battle with each other over the superiority of our disciplinary methodologies, we should reshape those methodologies by learning to tack back and forth between an "inside" experiential knowledge and an "outside" analytical knowledge, for both offer insights into the other's blindness. The irony of all this is that theater—the object of our respective investigations—is an art form devoted to just this kind of oscillation, offering us a glimpse of the world as it can be imagined from an objective analytical viewpoint and an experience of the world as registered within our body's viscera in the form of an affective engagement that is very much in the moment and real. It is my hope that, by understanding the origins of the text/performance split and by understanding it in relation to the analytic/continental divide, we can not only heal the disciplinary divide that has wounded the cause of theater and performance studies over the course of the past century, but join together in developing a methodology that can adequately address the many facets of theater—the object of our knowledge and the subject of our passions.

NOTES

This essay is dedicated to Professor Jan Smucker, in whose classes I first experienced the pleasures of philosophical thought.

1. See Susan Harris Smith, "Generic Hegemony: American Drama and the Canon," *American Quarterly* 41 (1989): 112–22; William Worthen, "Disciplines of the Text/Sites of Performance," *TDR* 39, no. 1 (T-145) (1995), 13–28. Examples of attempts to map the relationship between textual and performative modes of signification are almost too numerous to cite, but see, for instance, Darko Suvin, "Weiss's Marat/Sade and its Three Main Performance Versions," *Modern Drama* 31, no. 3 (1988): 395–419, and David Z. Saltz, "When is the Play the Thing?—Analytic Aesthetics and Dramatic Theory," *Theatre Research International* 20, no. 3 (1995): 266–76. Suvin discusses productions of Weiss's text in terms of "variants," "adaptations," and "rewrites," while Saltz critiques such a "two-text model," proposing instead a Peircean distinction between type and token.

2. Martin Puchner, *Stage Fright: Modernism, Anti-theatricality, and the Drama* (Baltimore: Johns Hopkins University Press, 2002), 7.

3. See, for example, my essay "Bodies, Voices, Words: Modern Drama and the Problem of the Literary," in *Modernisms, Inc.,* ed. Jani Scandura and Michael Thurston (New York: New York University Press, 2000), 68–80, which discusses the text/performance split in relation to modern American drama. See also my article "Why Performance? Why Now? Textuality and the Rearticulation of Human Presence," *Yale Journal of Criticism* 16, no. 1 (2003): 149–75, which discusses the text/performance split in relation to the concept of performance in twentieth-century thought. Both articles—as well as this essay—draw from my research into the relationship between the expressive culture movement and literary high modernism, detailed in my book *Expressionism and Modernism in the American Theatre: Bodies, Voices, Words* (Cambridge: Cambridge University Press, 2005).

4. See George Santayana, "The Elements and Function of Poetry," in *Interpretations of Poetry and Religion* (Cambridge: MIT Press, 1989).

5. T. S. Eliot, "Hamlet and His Problems," in *Selected Essays: 1917–1932* (New York: Harcourt, Brace, 1932), 268.

6. S. S. Curry, *The Province of Expression* (Boston: School of Expression, 1891), 52.

7. Curry, *The Province of Expression,* 54.

8. Curry, *The Province of Expression*, 39.

9. T. S. Eliot, "The Possibility of a Poetic Drama," in *The Sacred Wood* (London: Methuen, 1920), 69.

10. Susan Harris Smith, *American Drama: The Bastard Art* (New York: Cambridge University Press, 1997). This book is an elaboration of the historical background to the argument first put forward in her 1989 *American Quarterly* article.

11. The following discussion of Husserl's phenomenology is thoroughly indebted to Patocka's brilliant explication. See Jan Patocka, *An Introduction to Husserl's Phenomenology*, trans. Erazim Kohák, ed. James Dodd (Chicago: Open Court Press, 1996).

12. Quoted in Jonathan Rée, *I See a Voice: Deafness, Language and the Senses—a Philosophical History* (New York: Metropolitan Books, Henry Holt, 1999), 343.

13. My synopsis of Russell's early writings is indebted to Paul Edwards, William P. Alston, and A. N. Prior's entry on Russell in volume 7 of the *Encyclopedia of Philosophy*, ed. Paul Edwards (New York: Macmillan and Free Press, 1967), 235–58.

14. Bertrand Russell, "Introduction to Mathematical Philosophy," in *The Basic Writings of Bertrand Russell*, ed. Robert Egner and Lester Denonn (1961; rpt. New York: Routledge, 2001), 176.

15. See *Translations from the Philosophical Writings of Gottlob Frege*, ed. P. Geach and M. Black (New York: Philosophical Library, 1952), 2–3.

16. Bertrand Russell and Alfred North Whitehead, "Introduction to *Principia Mathematica*," vol. 1 in *Basic Writings of Russell*, 162.

17. Jacques Derrida, *Speech and Phenomena and Other Essays on Husserl's Theory of Signs*, trans. David B. Allison (Evanston, Ill.: Northwestern University Press, 1973), 51.

18. Jacques Derrida, "Signature, Event, Context," *Glyph* 1 (1977). Reprinted in *Margins of Philosophy* (Chicago: University of Chicago Press, 1982), 307–33. In *Speech and Phenomena*, Derrida refers to this same idea when he speaks of the impossibility of being "in absolute proximity to oneself" (58).

19. Stanton Garner, *Bodied Spaces: Phenomenology and Performance in Contemporary Drama* (Ithaca: Cornell University Press, 1994), 22.

20. Garner, *Bodied Spaces*, 25.

21. Derrida's critique of Husserl is correct, but only insofar as it is an analysis of Husserl's *rhetoric*. Understood as such, it remains at the level of metacriticism; it does not disprove Husserl's central premise that experience provides us with a sort of intuitive "knowledge" (where my quotation marks are meant to signal the metaphorical value of this term). There is no reason to believe that experience is necessarily subject to the same structural conditions of representation that Derrida has so usefully identified with regard to language.

22. Jacques Derrida, "The Theatre of Cruelty and the Closure of Representation," in *Writing and Difference*, trans. Alan Bass (Chicago: University of Chicago Press, 1978).

23. Of course, the same could be said for reading a work of literature where one's immersion in the imaginative realm is disrupted by the "proscenium frame" of the language itself, but I would argue that such a claim operates by virtue of the metaphor of performance, thus essentially proving my point.

24. Quoted in Fanny Kemble Wister, ed., *Fanny, the American Kemble: Her Journals and Unpublished Letters* (Tallahassee, Fla.: South Pass Press, 1972), 116.

TWO

Kenneth Burke

Theater, Philosophy, and the Limits of Performance

Martin Puchner

Philosophy, a discipline concerned with truth, being, and the foundations of knowledge, was predestined to abhor the theater, which is premised on lying, appearance, and the construction of false worlds. Philosophical attacks on the theater, as they accompany the history of philosophy from Plato onward, are thus not only frequent but also unsurprising. At the same time, self-declared defenders of the theater, including many playwrights, have fought back by creating mock philosophers who are exposed as fools and charlatans on the stage, a tradition that begins with Aristophanes' unflattering portrayal of Socrates in *The Clouds*. Indeed, Plato and Aristophanes can be seen as representatives of the mutual distrust between theater and philosophy, a distrust that has been reified by the standard histories of both disciplines.

The inherited opposition between philosophy and theater must be challenged, and this challenge can begin at its origin, by pointing out that the opposition between Plato and Aristophanes is in fact situated *within* the field of theater, between two types of drama: Plato's philosophical dialogue and Aristophanes' old comedy. Both are populated by invented characters that talk and interact in a variety of circumstances, and in both the difference between abstract argument and scenic action is keenly felt and cunningly deployed. The common, if not similar, dramatic form chosen by these two authors can be taken as a point of departure for excavating the significance of drama and theater for the history of philosophy— and, conversely, the significance of philosophy for the history of the theater—which has been obscured by the seeming dichotomy between the two fields. Theatrical philosophies and philosophical dramas tend to be regarded as marginal phenomena, when they are recognized at all. Still, they assert themselves, against all odds, in the histories of both disciplines with some frequency.

The philosopher who not only invented a theatrical philosophy but who also managed to produce a host of followers, a full-fledged tradition of theatrical philosophy—a rarity within the history of philosophy—is Friedrich Nietzsche. Nietzsche's import for theatrical philosophy does not reside so much in his fascination with theater from Greek tragedy to Richard Wagner, even though this fascination might be taken as a first indication of the significance of the theater for Nietzsche's thought. Closer to the theatrical core of Nietzsche's works is his reliance on fictional characters and masks such as Dionysus and Zarathustra, but also his elusive theory of forces, which is based on a totalized concept of theatricality. When Nietzsche talks about masks, theatrical performances, and enactments, he always insists that we not understand this theatricality as a secondary modeling, as if there were stable agents that had suddenly acquired masks to hide their true faces. There is no stable agent behind the theatrical act, no unmasked actor behind the character; theatricality has become a primary condition of reality. Theatricalization here is in the service of an antiessentialist and antifoundational program: the essence, the firm ground—be it nonmetaphoric language, knowledge, or morals—is swept from under the feet of foundational philosophy and replaced by the boards of a stage. And true to the totalization of theatricality, it is stages all the way down.

Antifoundationalism or antiessentialism is the heritage with which Nietzsche endows his various heirs, including Gilles Deleuze's *Repetition and Difference* (1968),[1] but also Peter Sloterdijk, who casts Nietzsche as a "thinker on stage" in his volume of that title.[2] However, not all theatrical philosophy in the twentieth century derives directly from Nietzsche. Walter Benjamin, for example, turned his study of German tragic drama into a philosophical exercise, and a number of theorists, among them Philippe Lacoue-Labarthe and Jean-François Lyotard, have used theatrical concepts in their theories as well.[3] Once one pays attention to the role of theatricality in nineteenth- and twentieth-century philosophy, one begins to notice that even much pre-Nietzschean philosophy, from Hegel through Kierkegaard to Marx, relies on theatrical metaphors and concepts. After centuries, even millennia, of apparent rivalry, expressed in the so-called antitheatrical prejudice, theater and theory seem to have converged back to their common Greek root of *theōrein* and *theatron*.[4]

The convergence of theater and theory in the twentieth century made itself felt in a number of different disciplines. Studies in political science and sociology, such as Richard Sennett's *The Fall of Public Man* (1974), treat the theater as a privileged model for the formation of the public sphere, while Erving Goffman in his *Frame Analysis* (1974) uses what he calls "theatrical frame" as a means of theorizing the organization of experience. Moreover, Victor Turner brings theatrical models to the discipline of anthropology or, depending on how you look at it, anthropology to theater studies.

The field of study, however, that best exemplifies the resurgence of a theatricalized theory, and that in fact has drawn on these other theatricalized disciplines, is performance studies. Even though performance studies has frequently distanced itself from the concept of the theater (more about this shortly), the notion of performance can be seen as one more version of the expansion of theatricality to other disciplines. For this reason, I will use it as an occasion to raise the question of the limits of the theater in theory, and the limits of the concept of theatricality (or performance) as it organizes the expansion of this young discipline to an increasing number of fields and areas. The writer who invites such an inquiry, whose interests span the entire gamut of performance studies from ritual theater and anthropology to language philosophy and sociology, and who has often been taken as one of the precursors of performance studies, is Kenneth Burke. It is, therefore, through a reading of Burke that I propose to scrutinize the effects of the theater within theory as it applies to the question of the limits of performance studies.[5]

Kenneth Burke's Dramatism

An emerging discipline obsessed with foundational narratives and myths, performance studies has always remembered the work of Kenneth Burke, without being able to specify his place in the formation of the field. Marvin Carlson's *Performance: A Critical Introduction* (1996), for example, discusses Burke's contributions to the three areas most central to the origin of performance studies: anthropology, sociology, and the performance of language. And the founders of performance studies at New York University, Victor Turner and Richard Schechner, refer to Burke with frequency.[6]

I would like to suggest that Burke's centrality for performance studies resides in the fact that he more than anyone developed a form of theatrical philosophy and gave it a name: dramatism. I propose to read Burke with the hope of better understanding the disciplinary and philosophical conditions that gave rise to performance studies, for it is only by coming to terms with the emergence of theatrical theory and philosophy that we can hope to understand the philosophical assumptions of this discipline.

Burke's dramatism describes a gradual expansion of theatricality that begins with an interest in Greek tragedy, continues with a theatrical theory of language and sociology of human interaction, and culminates in the use of theatricality as the measure by which to judge the history of philosophy itself. The first book-length study to be devoted to what Burke would later call dramatism is *The Philosophy of Literary Form* (1941). Here, in the midst of a reading of poetry, Burke interrupts himself to observe that "the general perspective that is interwoven with our methodology of analysis might be summarily characterized as a *theory of drama*."[7] This theory of drama is not geared toward the analysis of different dramatic forms or the plays of various periods, but a theory of the origin of drama. Burke continues the passage above: "We propose to take *ritual drama* as the Ur-form, the 'hub,' with all other aspects of *human* action treated as spokes radiating from this hub." True to this interest in origins, references to the emergence of Greek drama from the goat song are extended to other forms of ritual, an interest driven in part by James Frazer's influential *The Golden Bough* (Schechner would later take up this thread and supply his own response to Frazer and to ritual theater).[8] Burke even "defends" ritual fertility and rain dances as being embedded in a structure of agricultural efficacy: "even the most superstition-ridden tribe must have had many very accurate ways of sizing up real obstacles and opportunities in the world, for otherwise it could not have maintained itself" (108). Burke here writes as an anthropologist interested in the functional aspect of ritual and ritual theater.

However, it becomes increasingly clear that Burke is less interested in the rituals of particular tribes than in the schemata derived from the study of early anthropologists, such as Frazer, that model general patterns of human behavior; ritual, after all, is supposed to allow Burke to analyze "all other aspects of human action." One of his favorite patterns is the scapegoat, which connects his interest in Greek tragedy to history (the beheading of kings) and all the way to sociology of different punitive systems. We are not surprised to hear that Burke ultimately did not care about possible objections raised against the historical accuracy of his theory of ritual and ritual theater, for what he was really after was "a calculus—a vocabulary, or a set of coordinates, that serves best for the integration of all phenomena studied by the social sciences" (105). Thus, step by step, Burke abstracts from his immediate objects of analysis, the ritual origin of Greek tragedy, and moves to a general theory that ends up encompassing not only all of human interaction but the study of nature as well. Burke writes: "The broad outlines of our position might be codified thus: 1) We have the drama and the scene of the drama. The drama is enacted against a background. 2) The description of the scene is the rôle of the physical sciences; the description of the drama is the rôle of the social sciences" (114). It is in the course of this radical expansion of the dramatic "hub" that Burke first mentions, in a footnote, what he later called the "dramatist pentad," a theatrical scheme of universal applicability.[9]

Even for a thinker as schematic as Burke, the move from the origin of Greek tragedy to all of human action and then to the natural sciences demands a number of mediating steps. Such mediation is achieved by the category of symbolic action that both anticipates and goes well beyond Austin's much more limited theory of speech acts, which entered the vocabulary of performance studies in the eighties.[10] The theory of language as symbolic action is best understood in contrast to what Burke calls the "semantic" ideal. The semantic ideal is a version of Austin's "constative" speech act, the attempt to use language as a regulative instrument of truth.[11] Burke sees this semantic ideal presented most clearly by the Vienna Circle philosopher Rudolf Carnap, who hoped to reduce language to a set of axiomatic, primary sentences from which truthful propositions could then be deduced purely by means of logic.[12] Burke discusses this ideal in order to expose its normative violence. Anticipating Adorno and Horkheimer's critique of instrumental reason as well as Foucault's attack on enlightenment rationality, Burke points out that the semantic ideal may be used to control human beings in a way that is similar to "an automobile license, with a record kept in some central bureau, like the Bertillon measurements of known criminals" (140).[13] Indeed, Burke refers to Bentham's panopticon as an example of the types of discipline and punishment exercised by a positivist and classificatory understanding of language.[14]

In order to counter the semantic ideal, which instrumentalizes language to function as a police record, Burke proposes a theory of symbolic action that takes its point of departure from the actions of the human body, even when it comes to analyzing poems. In what is probably his most well known phrase, Burke writes that "the symbolic act is the *dancing of an atti-*

tude. . . . In this attitudinizing of the poem, the whole body may finally become involved" (9). Burke's emphasis on enunciation, his desire to connect the act of speech to the whole body, is a corrective to the semantic ideal that had tried to detach language from the scene of its enunciation, its situatedness. Both Wittgenstein and Austin would later bring about a similar grounding, insisting that language be considered in its moment of enactment, which Austin labeled its performativity. However, while Austin stops at the classification of different situations, Burke takes the theory of language to the sphere of poetry and generally of art. His interest is to better understand the poesis that is at work in every act of speech but which is brought to the fore in those particular acts of speech called poetry. What does it mean to consider a poem in terms of the "dancing of an attitude"?

Burke here draws on a tradition that is interested precisely in the conjunction of body and language, namely the theory of gesture. Gesture is the category that connects corporeality to linguistic articulation and therefore promises to fill the gap left by theories of language based on the semantic ideal. Burke refers, for example, to the literary critic R. P. Blackmur, who also used the term *gesture* for readings in poetry.[15] Afraid that gesture would remain a merely metaphorical term, Burke finally turns to Richard Paget's theory of linguistic gestures, which presents a much more literal understanding of gestural language as based on the selection of clusters of phonemes. Both Blackmur and Paget participate in a long tradition of theorizing a gestural origin of language (Condillac, Vico, Herder, Warburton, Rousseau), which was frequently used by modernist writers to articulate their critique of abstract and therefore nongestural language (Beckett, Joyce, Hofmannsthal, Mallarmé). Most important, however, is the fact that the category of gesture connects language and literature to the sphere of the theater, where it was used extensively by theorists and practitioners of the theater, from Wagner and Meyerhold to Brecht and Artaud.[16] Burke thus pushes the analysis of speech acts precisely in the direction that Austin had tried to avoid because he deemed it parasitical and aberrant, namely theater and theatricality.[17]

But how can the theory of gestural, symbolic action be used to understand all forms of human interaction? Burke operates with something akin to Richard Schechner's definition of performance as "twice-behaved behavior." In order for any movement to become a gesture it must be "representative," and this means that it must be repeated. "One puts his arms on the table. This is a unique, real act. . . . Yet I have heard a portrait-painter exclaim at such a moment, when a man placed his arm on the table: 'There—just like that—that's your characteristic posture'" (19). A unique act becomes a gesture, a characteristic attitude, only if it is seen as being part of a series of repetitions. Gesture, or attitude, thus establishes a connection between various forms of symbolic action, from repetitive gestures in everyday life to the patterns of images and repeated associations in poems.

The last decisive step in the expansion of theatricality into a philosophical category occurred a few years later, in *A Grammar of Motives* (1945), where Burke develops a method of reading the entire history of philosophy in theatrical terms.[18] We can take this text as the culmination of the theatrical turn because here the entire history of philosophy itself is seen retrospectively through a theatrical lens. Unabashedly, Burke presents what he had referred to in a footnote previously, namely his dramatist pentad, which consists of five terms or categories derived from Aristotle: agent, agency, act, purpose, and scene. Four of these terms—agent, agency, act, and purpose—offer different perspectives on action, the primary dramatic category, while the fifth term—scene—describes the setting or field within which action occurs. Even though this dramatistic scheme seems to be geared toward the analysis of drama—we can use it, as Aristotle did, to say that action is more important than the agent (or character)—it is actually not meant to analyze drama, from which Burke nevertheless continues to quote at great length, but rather what could be called a theatrical history of philosophy. Slyly borrowing from sport, Burke writes: "In this chapter it is not my purpose at this late date merely to summarize and report on past philosophies. Rather, I am trying to show how certain key terms might be used to 'call the plays' in any and all philosophies" (201). There is perhaps no better definition of the theatrical turn than the assumption that the different philosophies are themselves based on different understandings of theatricality, that beneath each philosophical system we will inevitably find a play.

Once theatricality is firmly installed at the center of philosophy, Burke classifies and analyzes each and every philosopher worth mentioning—Plato, Aristotle, Hobbes, Spinoza, Berkeley, Hume, Leibniz, Kant, Hegel, Marx, James, Santayana, the list goes on—according to which of the five dramatistic terms is privileged. Those philosophers who foreground the scene are materialists; those focused on the agent are idealists; those putting emphasis on agency are pragmatists; those invested in the purpose are mystics; and those interested in the act are realists. This way the theatrical substrate, the play, of any philosophical notion is excavated and translated into the pentad. The notion of the "subject" in idealism, for example, becomes the theatrical "agent," while the material conditions in Marxism become the "scene." This exercise in translation can also serve to highlight the contradictions within a given philosophical system. In a reading of the *Communist Manifesto,* for example, Burke demonstrates that there is a tension between the privileging of the material conditions, that is, the scene, and the hope for the revolutionary act that will transform this scene. The five dramatistic terms thus not only constitute the frame within which the history of philosophy unfolds, but they also function as the analytic categories that highlight the contradictions and blind spots in each philosophy.

Theater and Dialectics

Since Burke's dramatism functions as a kind of metaphilosophy, a system for analyzing the history of philosophical systems, we must ask from where this philosophy itself is derived. Burke presents a direct answer: "The relation between 'drama' and the 'dialectic' is obvious. Plato's dialectic was appropriately written in the mode of ritual drama" (107). However, the actual source of Burke's metahistory[19] of philosophy is not the dialogism of Plato, but the dialectics of Hegel. What Burke inherits from Hegel is the understanding of history as a dramatistic process. Hegel's *Philosophy of History* begins by asserting that world history happens as if "in the theater" and ends by reflecting back on the history of the spirit in its various "theatrical presentations" *(Schauspiele).*[20] World history is thus aligned with the theater, and the different "stages" of world history are so many changes of theatrical scenes and characters. In a similar vein, Burke writes: "In equating 'dramatic' with 'dialectical,' we automatically have also our perspective for the analysis of history, which is a 'dramatic' process, involving dialectical opposition" (109). We are approaching here one of the central connections between philosophy and theater, namely the kinship between dialectics and drama. Both insist on a multiplicity of voices, and both trust that this multiplicity will generate transformation and change: the drama of history is the transformation that ensues from the encounter of irreducible positions. With the help of Burke, we can recognize that Hegel's view of a philosophy overcoming and inheriting Greek tragedy means that his own dialectical philosophy is nothing but a general or universalized abstraction from the dialogic theater. By reading the history of philosophy dramatically or, to use his own term, dramatistically, Burke thus restores dialectical philosophy to the theater from which it was originally derived.

Even though Burke thus reconnects theater and philosophy, his work nevertheless exhibits a characteristic oscillation between an interest in the theater and a tendency to extract from the theater a philosophical concept. Even and especially for this most theatrical of philosophers, it seems, there is no easy fusion of theater and theory. One way or another, all theorists of the theatrical turn derive their key metaphors and figures from the actual theater: Hegel from Greek tragedy; Nietzsche from Richard Wagner; Benjamin from Baroque tragedy; and Deleuze from Artaud. Sooner or later, however, they all turn away from the theater as their primary object of inquiry. Nietzsche's early work on the origin of Greek tragedy is not a text in the field of theater history, but a philosophical text that happens to take the form of a projected and highly speculative history of tragedy.[21] This view is confirmed by the fact that Nietzsche later turned against Wagner and even against the theater as such, denouncing Wagner by means of an antitheatrical vocabulary.[22] Likewise, Benjamin's study of Baroque theater has its ultimate purpose in the long philosophical introduction to that work, which extracts from this study the vocabulary of theatrical modernism.[23] Furthermore, Deleuze was not so much interested in the actual theater as in the speculative notion of theater he found in Artaud's theoretical writings and manifestos, themselves at odds with practically all existing theatrical practice.

Burke shows even more interest in the actual theater than these theatrical philosophers, and he quotes with obsessive frequency from the history of dramatic literature, including Greek drama, Shakespeare and Ibsen. However, despite this deep knowledge of and interest in the drama and the theater, Burke's texts never present themselves as studies in dramatic or theatrical criticism. Burke recognizes this dynamic, which ties the philosophy to the theater and which at the same time separates the two: "every philosophy is in some respect or other *a step away* from drama. Still, to understand its structure, we must remember always that it is, by the same token, a step away from *drama*" (230). We can push this double movement of attraction and repulsion even further. The closer philosophy moves to the theater, the more philosophy must distance itself from the theater so as to keep it from becoming nothing but a different form of theater.

It is at this point that we can recognize that Nietzsche's use of theater does not describe a simple conversion of philosophy from a prejudice against the theater to a newfound love for it. Plato's so-called antitheatrical prejudice and Nietzsche's turn toward the theater are different responses to the contentious affinity between theater and theory that has been part of philosophy since the beginning with the philosophical plays of Plato. Nietzsche's work describes not so much a turning of philosophy toward the theater as an object of study—which it had been since Aristotle's *Poetics*—but as a mode and method of doing philosophy. Indeed, one can find moments of an attraction to the theater in philosophical antitheatricalism just as one can find moments of a critique of the theater in Nietzsche's theatrical turn. There is no philosopher whose thinking was more permeated by references to plays and by abstract theatrical axioms than Burke, and therefore none who noticed more clearly the double gesture of attraction and repulsion between philosophy and the theater.

This tension between the theater as an object of study and as a theoretical paradigm, the critique of the theater that seems to accompany the history of theatrical philosophy, explains the similarly contentious relation between performance studies and theater studies. Although particular analyses undertaken in the name of performance studies continue to be interested in many forms of theater—most often nontraditional, ritual theater—performance studies as a field often distances itself from the theater as its central or constitutive object of analysis. One could even say that the term *performance* was coined to define the new discipline as something both related to and removed from the theater. This simultaneous approximation and distancing has an important consequence, namely that performance studies cannot and does not want to define itself through its object of study. Instead, what defines performance studies is a vocabulary and method of analysis based on the concept of twice-behaved behavior, which is ultimately derived from acting even though it is not limited to that concept. Descriptions of performance studies tend toward an additive model, for performance studies shares its objects of analysis with all of those disciplines to which it is said to be related: sociology, anthropology, linguistics, literary studies, philosophy, and even economy and technology. What provides the identity of performance studies in this contested field of objects of analysis is precisely what Burke called dramatism: a sense of the potential, even fundamental, theatricality of everything. How can we begin to consider such a limit that does not rely on delimiting objects of study but on the presumption of performance itself?

In search for such a limiting function, we can return once more to the work of Burke, because it is within his theory of dramatism that Burke recognizes the limits of what he calls dramatism, but what can also be extended to include performance as well. Since the basic unit of his analysis is action, and since "the basic unit of action is the human body in purposive motion" (*Grammar* 61), dramatism is a scheme that relies on the human agent, human agency, the human act, and human purpose. This is indeed what we should expect from a philosophical methodology derived from the theater, which is an art form that depends on live human performers. The result of this form of theatrical philosophy is a repeated deployment of characters or figures within philosophy, a tendency toward personification. We can understand this personifying tendency literally, for indeed many dialectical or dramatistic philosophers rely heavily on fictional or historical figures or characters in the presentation of their thought, including Plato's Socrates, Hegel's Napoleon, and Nietzsche's Zarathustra. When philosophy relies on personalization, the danger that always lurks in the background is allegory and prosopopeia (surrogate speaker), the personification of abstract entities. Should we understand Socrates as a portrait of Plato's teacher or as the personification of philosophy? And is Nietzsche's Zarathustra a figure for, or distinct from, the superman (another, though less tangible, Nietzschean character)?

The reliance on personification, I argue, constitutes a limit of theatrical philosophy. One way of gauging this limit is by looking at the history of theater itself. In the late nineteenth and early twentieth centuries, the reliance of the theater on human actors and on personification came under increasing scrutiny. A large number of avant-garde and proto-avant-garde theorists and practitioners, from Edward Gordon Craig and Vsevolod Meyerhold to Oskar Schlemmer and Tadeusz Kantor, tried to depersonalize the theater, to rid it of its reliance on the human figure. Actors were instructed to imitate puppets, objects, or machines when they were not replaced with inanimate objects altogether. This history of depersonalization in the history of the theater has not left theatrical philosophy untouched. Nietzsche, Benjamin, Deleuze, and Lacan present versions of the theatrical turn that are suspicious of the human, the personal, and the personified. At the same time, all these attempts in modernist theater to expel the personal from the stage encountered significant difficulties. Even when human actors are banished from the stage and replaced by objects, these objects are almost always repersonalized by being perceived as substitutions for the human, to which they therefore remain tied. In addition, just as rebelling against personification in the theater is a project ridden with complications, so is the attempt to exorcise the same personalizing tendency from dramatistic philosophy.

Burke's own dramatism was deeply entrenched in this problem of personalization and depersonalization. More importantly, Burke recognized that the problem of personification was intimately tied to his theatrical, or dramatistical, method itself. While four of its terms, namely act, action, agency, and purpose, are tied to the human and therefore to the personalizing tendency of dramatism, the fifth term, scene, exceeds personification. It can be seen as a kind of internal limit to the personification that is seemingly so inextricably part of the theater and theatrical philosophy. The problem with this internal limit, however, is that it does not represent the impersonal except as the limit of the personal; it cannot name the nonpersonal other than in terms of the ground or scene on which the personal drama of human acts, actions, agencies, and purposes unfolds. Hence, Burke makes the following, astonishing, discovery:

> Thus we have two kinds of scene: one designating a function within the pentad, another designating a function outside the pentad; for a term as highly generalized as the "dramatistic" calls for the "nondramatist" as its sole contextual counterpart. The fact that one of these usages "transcends" the other may be concealed by the fact that we can refer to either of them by the same word, scene. (440)

This reflection on the limits of the personifying pentad thus leads Burke to a term that is defined by its falling outside dramatism altogether, namely the "nondramatist." The interesting and disturbing thing about this limiting concept of the nondramatist, however, is that it is not only at the outer limit of dramatism, but also at its very core, namely hidden in the category of the scene. The scene is a double term, one that marks the outer limit (the "nondramatist") but that is at the same time part of dramatism. The result of this double limit, and Burke recognizes this very clearly, is nothing less than the collapse of dramatism:

> In the case of our pentad, for instance, after having stressed the need for the functioning of all five terms in rounded vocabularies of motives, we summed up our position as "dramatistical"—whereupon of a sudden we discovered that our terms had *collapsed* into a new title that had, as its only logical ground, the "non-dramatistic." (440; emphasis added)

Dramatism cannot remain a neat, self-enclosed system because the nondramatic has entered through the Trojan horse of the double "scene."

The scene outside the pentad may appear to be nothing but a second scene, but this homology is misleading, for the scene outside is nothing like the scene inside; instead it is the necessary "context" or "counterpart" that makes it possible for the scene inside to appear as scene. This dependence of the scene on something that can no longer be called simply scene interrupts the neat workings of dramatism because it carries the limits of dramatism into dramatism's very heart.

Burke draws a radical conclusion from the collapse he is forced to recognize in his dramatistical pentad: "The 'dramatistic' itself must have as its context a grounding in the 'non-dramatist.' . . . So there is a point at which the dramatist perspective, defined in terms of its contextual opposite, *must 'abolish itself' in the very act of its enunciation*" (441; emphasis added).

At the end of his dramatism, Burke thus announces a kind of self-erasure of dramatism, what he also calls the "dissolution of drama." This dissolution does not mean that his dramatistic pentad is wrong. It only means that by operating with it, he cannot ignore that this pentad is in the process of breaking down, that at the moment of its enunciation it must "abolish itself."

This self-critique can be understood as a plea that dramatism be always aware of its own limits, in particular of its tendency to personalize the nonpersonal, what Burke at a different moment called the "'agentification' of scene" (128). For the nonpersonal is also radically dissociated from the dichotomy between actor and scene; it lies entirely outside the theater and outside the pentad. Indeed, the pentad even depends on this nonpersonal that is beyond its horizon. The nonscenic scene is the limit of dramatism, and Burke calls upon us to never forget this limit, even if this means that we must be always in the process of abolishing dramatism. According to this line of thought, dramatism is not limited in a spatial sense, as if there were one sphere to which it can be comfortably applied and a second sphere from which it should be kept away. Rather, the limit of dramatism is a systemic and functional one; as a consequence, dramatism can never be applied comfortably to anything, not even to the theater. A faithful practice of dramatism thus requires a constant act of self-interruption and self-limitation.

We can draw some conclusions from Burke's powerful self-critique. Burke here not only anticipates the many features of performance studies and constitutes the link between theatrical philosophy and performance studies. He also indicates for us the necessity of thinking the limits of dramatism, which we can take as a point of departure for thinking the limits of performance. A number of scholars have began to work in this direction: Janelle Reinelt and Joseph Roach in their *Critical Theory and Performance* (1992); Judith Butler in *Bodies That Matter: On the Discursive Limits of "Sex"* (1993); Peggy Phelan's *Unmarked: The Politics of Performance* (1993); Philip Auslander in *Liveness: Performance in a Mediatized World* (1999); and Jon McKenzie in *Perform or Else: From Discipline to Performance* (2001). In various ways, these texts stand for a new spirit of methodological controversy, taking to task classical texts in the field and demanding new theoretical frames.

It is in this spirit that I raise here the question of the limits of performance. If we take Burke's lead, thinking the limits of performance would not necessarily imply delimiting the objects of analysis to which performance studies should apply itself. Rather, it would imply a critique in the Kantian sense, a meditation on the limits of the concept of performance (or theatricality) itself. For this project, we would need to develop a term counter to performance, something that plays the role of the second, radically external, notion of "scene" in Burke's reflection. What is the "scene" of performance, and what is the "scene of this scene," that which enables the interaction of scene and performance without being *of* it? Still, what would a performance studies look like that would "abolish itself" at the moment of its enunciation, that would inscribe the radically nonperformative at the center of performance?

NOTES

1. Michel Foucault recognized this theatrical bent in Deleuze early on, in his review essay "Theaturm Philosophicum," in *Language, Counter-Memory, Practice,* ed. Donald F. Bouchard (Ithaca: Cornell University Press, 1977), 165–97.

2. Peter Sloterdijk, *Thinker on Stage: Nietzsche's Materialism,* trans. Jamie Owen Daniel (Minneapolis: University of Minnesota Press, 1998).

3. Walter Benjamin, *Der Ursprung des Deutschen Trauerspiels* (Frankfurt am Main: Suhrkamp, 1955); Jean-François Lyotard, "The Unconscious as Mise-en-Scène," in *Mimesis, Masochism, and Mime: The Politics of Theatricality in Contemporary Thought,* ed. Richard Murray (Ann Arbor: University of Michigan Press, 1997), 163–74; Philippe Lacoue-Labarthe, "Theatrum Analyticum," in Murray, *Mimesis, Masochism, and Mime,* 175–96.

4. The verb form of *theoria* is *theoreo* (θεωρέω), seeing or viewing, including the particular meaning of viewing games. *Theoreo ta Olympia* (θεωρέω τα' Ολυμπια), for example, became an idiom for traveling to the Olympic games (Wilhelm Gemoll, *Griechisch-Deutsches Schul- und Handwörterbuch,* 9th ed. [Munich: Hölder-Pichler-Tempsky, 1997], 374). The form *theaomai* (θεαομαι), which is related to the word *theater* or *theatron* (θέατρον), likewise means seeing or viewing, but also, in conjunction

with the word *aletes,* seeing what is really the case or seeing reality in the sense that for Heidegger became the definition of philosophy (θεαομαι το ἀληθής). Indeed, Heidegger, in his essay *Wissenschaft und Besinnung* (Stuttgart: Verlag Günther Neske, 1959) explicitly relates theory to the root *thea* (θεα), which means seeing in all of these forms, including the seeing that takes place in the theater (48).

5. Martin Puchner, "The Theater in Modernist Thought," in *New Literary History* 33 (Summer 2002): 524.

6. Marvin Carlson, *Performance: A Critical Introduction* (London: Routledge, 1996) discusses Burke on pages 17, 36–38, and 57. Victor Turner's *From Ritual to Theatre: The Human Seriousness of Play* (New York: PAJ Publications, 1982) mentions Burke on pages 68 and 106.

7. Kenneth Burke, *Philosophy of Literary Form: Studies in Symbolic Action* (reprint Berkeley and Los Angeles: University of California Press, 1973), 103.

8. Richard Schechner opens his *Performance Theory* (London: Routledge, 1988) with a discussion of the Cambridge anthropologists, and in particular with Frazer.

9. In note 25, Burke writes: "Instead of the situation-strategy pair, I now use five terms: act, scene, agent, agency, purpose" (*Philosophy of Literary Form,* 106).

10. It was in fact only through the work of Judith Butler in the late eighties and early nineties that performance studies took an interest in speech act theory. For a detailed discussion of the tensions caused by the conjunction of Butler's Austinian theory of performativity and performance studies see Jon McKenzie, *Perform or Else: From Discipline to Performance* (London: Routledge, 2001).

11. J. L. Austin, *How to Do Things with Words* (Cambridge: Harvard University Press, 1962). For a discussion of the exclusion of the theater from speech act theory see Jacques Derrida, *Limited Inc.,* trans. Samuel Weber (Baltimore: Johns Hopkins University Press, 1988).

12. In accordance to this constructivist ideal, Carnap's main oeuvre is called *Der Logische Aufbau der Sprache* (The logical construction of the world).

13. Max Horkheimer and Theodor W. Adorno, *Dialektik der Aufklärung: Philosophische Fragmente* (Frankfurt am Main: Fischer, 1969).

14. Burke discusses Bentham in his essay "The Virtues and Limitation of Debunking," in *Philosophy of Literary Form,* 168ff.

15. R. P. Blackmur, *Language as Gesture: Essays in Poetry* (New York: Harcourt, Brace, 1952).

16. For a longer discussion of gesture, see my *Stage Fright: Modernism, Anti-Theatricality, and Drama* (Baltimore: Johns Hopkins University Press, 2002).

17. A number of efforts were necessary to make Austin's theory of speech acts useful for the study of literature and the theater. Important stepping stones were Derrida's *Limited Inc.,* Judith Butler's *Gender Trouble: Feminism and the Subversion of Identity* (London: Routledge, 1990), and most recently J. Hillis Miller's *Speech Acts in Literature* (Stanford: Stanford University Press, 2001).

18. Kenneth Burke, *A Grammar of Motives* (Berkeley and Los Angeles: University of California Press, 1969), 200ff.

19. Hayden White's influential *Metahistory: The Historical Imagination in Nineteenth-Century Europe* (Baltimore: Johns Hopkins University Press, 1973) takes its four master tropes from Burke.

20. Hegel writes: "Daß die Weltgeschichte dieser Entwicklungsgang und das wirk-

liche Werden des Geistes ist, under dem wechselnden Schauspiele ihrer Geschichten—dies ist die wahrhafte *Theodizee,* die Rechtfertigung Gottes in der Geschichte." G. W. F. Hegel, *Vorlesungen über die Philosophie der Geschichte* (Frankfurt am Main: Suhrkamp, 1970), 540. The second quote reads: "Der Geist ist aber auf dem Theater, auf dem wir ihn betrachten, in der Weltgeschichte, in seiner konkretesten Wirklichkeit" (29).

21. This theatrical reading of Nietzsche has become standard, thanks to Deleuze's subsequent book on Nietzsche and a number of other commentators, from Gianni Vattimo to Peter Sloterdijk, who casts Nietzsche as a "thinker on stage." Peter Sloterdijk, *Der Denker auf der Bühne: Nietzsche's Materialismus* (Frankfurt am Main: Suhrkamp, 1986). Gianni Vattimo, *I Sogetto e la Maschera: Nietzsche e il problema della liberatzione* (Milan: Bompiani, 1974).

22. Nietzsche's antitheatrical critique of Wagner breaks through in his "Der Fall Wagner," in *Richard Wagner in Bayreuth, Der Fall Wagner, Nietzsche contra Wagner* (Stuttgart: Reclam, 1966).

23. Reiner Naegele's *Theater, Theory, Speculation: Walter Benjamin and the Scenes of Modernity* (Baltimore: Johns Hopkins University Press, 1991), which includes a study of Benjamin's *Der Ursprung des deutschen Trauerspiels,* is an exemplary study of the relation between theater and theory.

THREE

Critical Realism and Performance Strategies

Tobin Nellhaus

One of the muddier topics in theater and drama studies is the concept of genre. Are comedy and tragedy each genres, or do they cover numerous genres? Is naturalism a genre, or a style (or is there even a difference between the two)? If it *is* a genre, is it the same genre when funny as when serious? Or should the term be reserved for narrower categories like gothic melodramas, mystery plays, modernist verse dramas, Jacobean revenge tragedies, and absurdism? Do Shakespeare parodies constitute a genre?

When a term can be used in such disparate ways, chances are good that it encompasses both too much and too little, and perhaps lacks a clear philosophical basis. However, there are other ways to sort through the similarities and differences among plays and performance styles. I will discuss one alternative, which distinguishes types of theater and drama in terms of *performance strategies*. That concept is grounded in the ideas of critical realism, a general philosophical framework that is emerging as a significant alternative to both positivism and poststructuralism. Since critical realism is not yet widely familiar to humanities scholars, particularly in the United States, the first part of this chapter will present its core ideas as fully as possible. The second part will then develop the concept of performance strategies, and how that concept is useful in analyzing the history of theater and drama (particularly the etiology of performance styles), and for grasping how audiences during some period may have understood the shows they went to see.

A Brief Introduction to Critical Realism

Critical realism is a relatively new philosophy with old roots. It began taking shape in the 1960s (most notably in the work of Rom Harré) primarily as a philosophy of science, and it reached a watershed in 1975, when Rom Harré and E. H. Madden's *Causal Powers,* Russell Keat and John Urry's *Social Theory as Science,* and Roy Bhaskar's *A Realist Theory of Science* all appeared. Due to the rigor of his analyses and his ceaseless pursuit of their implications, Bhaskar soon became the leading philosopher of critical realism, publishing some nine books on the subject by 2000.[1] But as Bhaskar himself points out, many of critical realism's fundamental ideas derive from (or are assumed by) the works of earlier writers. Some aspects have roots in Kant, Hegel, and even classical Greek philosophers, but the most prominent precursor is Marx. Not surprisingly, then, critical realism has advanced mainly in the fields of sociology, economics, political science, and law. Explorations of culture are still uncommon, but more are appearing as critical realism gains a wider following. The growth of interest that philosophy became evident first in the creation of a discussion listserv in 1995; critical realist research now also has the support of an international association, a series published by Routledge, and a peer-reviewed journal.[2]

The first premise of critical realism is simply that the vast majority of reality exists independently of our thoughts about it. In the face of some of the more extreme poststructuralist theories, this tenet may need more defending than I can provide here, but several arguments can be adduced to support it. Bhaskar develops his by investigating the conditions of possibility for knowledge and the intelligibility of science as a social practice.[3] The point can also be made by considering the conditions of possibility for error. Not knowing that fire is hot doesn't stop it from burning one's fingers; believing that we don't need oxygen doesn't free the body from breathing; doubting the existence of capitalism doesn't protect one from market forces. Such examples demonstrate the independence of both physical and social reality from our thoughts about it. One might object that the social world very clearly depends on thoughts, and wouldn't even exist without them; and this point is in fact true. However, it is true primarily *over time.* At any specific moment, however, social relationships are what they are, regardless of what you or I or even a large group of people think. The independence of reality from thought even holds for thoughts: once a thought has passed through the mind, it joins the unchangeable past. However, the assertion of reality's mind-independence does not entail a collapse into positivism. To the contrary, critical realism sharply opposes positivism, and arguably makes a better case against it than poststructuralism does.

One of positivism's weaknesses is its criterion for designating something as real. That criterion is perception: a thing exists only if it can be perceived to exist—or as Berkeley put it, "*esse* is *percipi.*"[4] Thus the condition for asserting the existence of something is our knowledge of it; we must understand being in terms of our knowledge. We can know our experiences, but not things themselves. In more philosophical language, ontology is dependent upon, collapsed into, or even disavowed in favor of epistemology.[5] It is worth noting that allegiance to perception (or another cognitive phenomenon, such as language) and skepticism toward ontology also characterize nearly all forms of poststructuralism.

In contrast, critical realism maintains that things are real if they have causal powers—one might say, "to be is just to be able to do."[6] Causality is the power to create a change, whether in some other thing or in the causal entity itself. If everything stayed exactly the same, if nothing were affected by anything anywhere, then no causal powers would be acting and nothing could be known to exist. But if changes happen—for example, if something moves or acquires a new shape or reflects light that we can see—then causal forces are at work. The concept of causality cannot be restricted to the mechanical interaction of discrete bodies or to the application of some external force upon an entity. A causal power can act at a distance (as in gravity), and it can arise from things that aren't physical objects (such as an intention to do something). Moreover, the causal power does not have to act at all times, nor always act with the same result: the power may be latent or inactive, and its action may be blocked, diminished, or displaced because action is always *interaction* with other entities in its environment. Consequently, causality concerns tendencies, and not behavioral regularities; it cannot be reduced to the logical formula "If cause C, then effect E." Whatever causes change, however, is a real entity, even if not necessarily a physical entity, and not necessarily one that is understood or even known to exist. It may be possible to demonstrate that this entity exists (through perceptions of its effects) even if it is not possible to perceive the entity itself.[7]

If reality consists of causal entities, then it must be stratified. In fact, it is stratified in two senses. One is familiar to most people: the way the world has "layers" of entities, in which entities at one layer are composed of entities at a lower layer. For example, molecules are formed from atoms, atoms combine subatomic particles such as protons and electrons, and subatomic particles consist of even lower level constituents, quarks. Even quarks may not be the most basic level of physical reality. Looking "upward," molecules may create lifeforms, which have their own strata.

On a high stratum we find humans as biological, social, and conscious beings.

The world is layered in this manner because of emergence. According to Bhaskar, "In emergence, generally, new beings (entities, structures, totalities, concepts) are generated out of pre-existing material from which they could have been neither induced nor deduced."[8] More precisely, emergence is "A relationship between two terms such that one term diachronically or perhaps synchronically arises out of the other, but is capable of reacting back on the first and is in any event causally and taxonomically irreducible to it."[9] Life emerged from chemical and physical reality, human society emerged from the biological realm, and capitalism emerged within the social realm. The entities that occupy an emergent stratum possess distinctive and relatively autonomous causal powers or properties that cannot be reduced to the stratum from which these powers emerged, and which affect the action of entities at that lower stratum (whether that means compulsion or constraint). Human intentionality, for example, is an emergent power that enables people to act upon biological, chemical, and physical entities, as well as upon each other. Such powers emerge from and are conditioned by lower strata; the lower strata determine an emergent capability's limits and may explain how it came into existence (e.g., what features of the brain make thought possible, or impossible if the thinker dies), but they explain little about what the emergent power actually is and does (in this example, what thought consists of and what a person thinks). Bhaskar calls this "emergent powers materialism."[10]

We might describe this first type of stratification as ontic: a layering of things that compose the world. The second type is more properly ontological, since it concerns objects' mode of existence. For Bhaskar, reality is stratified into three ontological domains. The fundamental domain is the *real*. As I have described, all real entities possess various causal powers and susceptibilities (in the form of structures and/or "generative mechanisms") that affect and are affected by other entities; and if something has causal power, it is real. Powers create potentialities or tendencies that may or may not be manifested, depending on the circumstances. But in this mode, they exist as a realm of possibilities awaiting their exercise. When (as a result of their causal powers) entities interact, they produce events, which occupy Bhaskar's second domain, the *actual*. The actual may be understood both as a higher stratum and as a subset of the real, since events and actualized possibilities possess causal powers (for instance, they may condition subsequent events). Finally, some of those events are or result in experiences or concepts. These constitute the third domain, which (depending on the account) is the *empirical,* the *subjective,* or the *semiosic.* The reasons for the variance need not detain us; in all three versions, consciousness and its contents are but the tip of the ontological iceberg, the contingent products of myriad underlying dynamics and conditions.[11]

Critical realism's stratification of ontology into three domains is radically at odds with positivism's view that reality must be understood strictly in terms of one domain, an epistemological one of experience or perception, and with poststructuralism's analogous interpretation of all things in terms of language. Critical realism maintains a consistent hold on issues of ontological alterity, such as the difference between reality and ideas about reality, between surface and depth, between praxis and its object, and between powers as capabilities or tendencies and the actual exercise of those powers. At the same time, because it conceptualizes causality as the exercise of powers, and not as a behavioral regularity that casts cause and effect as separate states marked only by difference, critical realism is able to sustain a concept of change, including ideas of process and work.[12]

Alterity and causality are related through negativity, in particular by the existence of specifiable absences (gaps, voids, lacks, limits, exclusions, differences, determinations, constraints, removals, ills, and so forth). Absence is centrally involved in causation, from physical dynamics (for example, entropy's leveling out of energy differences), to biological functions (e.g., finding food to reduce hunger, and eliminating wastes), to human praxis (purposeful activities such as seeking companionship to ease loneliness, or conducting research to fill gaps in knowledge). Ultimately, argues Bhaskar, causation is the process of absenting.[13]

Where there are absences (of one sort or another) there are also possibilities of connection and relationship. For instance, two planetary masses may be separated by a large distance but connected by their gravitational fields, so that one rotates around the other, forming an orbital system such as the earth and moon. Likewise, two people may be connected by their friendship, despite and because of their differences; and of course languages involve systems of differences and relationships. One can generalize the point by stating that things are existentially constituted by their relations with others. They belong to totalities, that is, systems of internal relations; and systems are emergent entities with causal powers underivable from their constituents. However, totalities do not have to be hermetic, with all their relations being internal and necessary: they may also have external or contingent relations (including with external or internal totalities), forming "partial totalities." But because within a totality there are two or more elements, the researcher can always switch perspectives from one to another; and changes to one element affect the system of relationships and the dynamics of the elements' interaction. In this sense, each element bears a trace or reflection of all the others; if we switch perspectives on totality itself, in its inward form totality is reflexivity.[14]

Reflexivity is an explicit element of human agency. For Bhaskar, agency must be understood as intentional, embodied, and causally efficacious. Reflexivity plays a role in this because it is fundamental to intentionality, that is, to a person's reasons for acting. Reasons are a form of reflexivity, in which people not only monitor what they are doing, but monitor that monitoring by means of a sign system (such as language) that allows them to assess their mental states and experiences, and thereby develop an understanding of what they are doing, have done, or are considering doing. Such understandings characteristically explain why an agent had taken or would take an action, that is, their reasons for acting. Reasons are themselves causes, when they are acted upon. Thus agency's intentionality and causal efficacy are intimately connected—not, of course, that all of an agent's actions or causal effects are intentional (far from it), but that agents are to a significant extent able to envision and *choose* among those possible actions and effects over which they do have control. Like any other causal power, agency is a process of absenting; further, it is a process of absenting absences, that is, an effort to remedy or eliminate ills, constraints, needs, and so forth.[15]

Agents are one part of what constitutes society. Society is more than simply the aggregate of individuals, or the sum of their individual interrelations. It is a complex emergent partial totality, possessing sui generis characteristics because its dynamics and very existence depend on the activities and inactivities of people (most of whom are now long dead). Society's ontology consists of three levels.[16] The middle level consists of agents, of both the individual and the collectively organized sort, each occupying various social positions (such as teacher, parent, employer, political contributor) and engage in various practices. Underlying their activities is the level of *social structures*—systemic relationships among people, and between people and material resources. These structures condition, constrain, but also enable agents' activities; they establish the possibilities of action, or more precisely, the system of social positions and the practices they make possible. Overlying the structural possibilities of action and the actions that agents actually conduct, there is society's uppermost ontological level: the systems of meanings and representations through which agents understand and shape their actions and the surrounding circumstances. These meanings are organized and articulated in various *discourses,* not just verbally but through signs of any sort. It should be noted that society's ontological framework of structures, agents, and discourses arises within the further circumstances of the natural environment, including geography.

Some currently popular sociologies (such as Anthony Giddens's structuration theory) treat structure and agency as inextricably interlinked and at every moment mutually constitutive; structures are "virtual" until instantiated by agents—a theory that is modeled on Saussure's concepts of *langue* and *parole.* In contrast, critical realism views society's stratified components as interrelated and interactive, but still ontologically distinctive, analytically distinguishable, and real (never virtual). Rather than being simultaneously mutually constitutive, they are mutually transformative *over time,* in a rhythmic or cyclic sense. People are born into and make their lives within a social structure not of their personal making (much less choosing), but one given to them from the past, the result of the activities of the long dead. Having been thrown into this social structure, they receive various enablements and constraints from their position within it, and as they work their way through the possibilities, choices, and necessities presented to them, they reproduce and transform that social structure, ultimately leaving it for the succeeding generation and a new cycle of social conditioning and social transformation. Even though billions of these cycles proceed concurrently across the globe, what any particular agent finds is not a mutual constitution of structure and agency, but rather a set of given conditions that the agent subsequently acts within and upon.[17]

I have said nothing yet about critical realism's epistemology. Against positivism but with poststructuralism, critical realism maintains that knowledge is socially produced. The process of producing knowledge is in fact much like the process of social change: on the basis of knowledge developed in the past, people develop new knowledge (which involves work). Being socially produced, perception and knowledge are necessarily theory-mediated. But the fact that observation is never theory-free, that our access to reality is always through signs and representations, does *not* mean that we are hermetically sealed within a world of signs and have no genuine contact with (and therefore no valid knowledge of) the world outside. We may have only indirect, mediated access to entities outside our minds, but since real entities have causal powers, they have direct access to us. Consequently they place limits on the sort of perceptions and interpretations we may have of them, and so the range of viable theories cannot be infinite. That said, there remains a range of theories, which can only be narrowed by undertaking practices (experimentation, field research, historical analysis, close reading, etc.) to turn up further evidence; we may obtain extremely high levels of certainty about some theory, but absolute certainty is unattainable. Critical realism is therefore *fallibilistic:* we can produce theories that fit the evidence available today, but as more (or other sorts of) evidence arise, the theories may need to be refined or replaced. Our experiences with reality force us to be modest about what we know. As Bhaskar strikingly argues, "To be a fallibilist about knowledge, it is necessary to be a realist about things. Conversely, to be a sceptic about things is to be a dogmatist about knowledge." A corollary is that the merit of a theory lies not in its predictive power (a notion that for the social sciences is ludicrous), but in its explanatory power. All told, critical realism upholds *epistemic relativism:* we can only know things under particular descriptions, within a socially and historically based theory. At the same time, however, it maintains that there are (or can be) rational grounds for preferring one theory over another: a *judgmental rationality* that opposes a relativism claiming that all beliefs are equally valid.[18]

Two aspects of critical realism's theory of knowledge lead the way to the concept of performance strategies. First, the development of knowledge involves a dialectical interchange between theory and practice. Bhaskar describes this as a theory-practice helix, in which practice predisposes and sometimes motivates theoretical judgments, and theory logically entails practical judgments and may directly cause practical actions.[19] The relationship between theory and practice is, I believe, one of emergence: practices may be motivated or governed by theoretical entailments, but theory emerges from practice. The latter point is underscored by the ontological argument that actual events emerge from the possibilities and necessities posited by real entities, and experiences and perceptions emerge from among those events.

Second, the process of forming new knowledge by means of older knowledge does not just refer to the use of current techniques to accumulate data that one can use to confirm or challenge a theory: it also concerns the use of something already understood as an analogy for something not as well understood. For critical realism, models—iconic images—are an essential part of an explanatory theory. The model does not "correspond" to its subject, but rather is (to a greater or lesser degree) adequate to the subject's characteristics. And at some point researchers may find that an existing model isn't sufficiently adequate and another must take its place, resulting in "paradigm shifts" in science.[20]

Iconic images are a fundamental part of theater, so it is important to establish a connection between the emergence of theory from practice, and the operation of models within theory. This can be accomplished by supplementing critical realist philosophy with the results of a particular science, namely cognitive science, which has perhaps become best known through the writings of George Lakoff and Mark Johnson. Supplementing critical realism in this manner is all the easier because Lakoff and Johnson derive from this research a philosophy they call "embodied realism," which has many commonalities with critical realism. There are some differences, but for present purposes the research is the matter at hand, not the philosophy, and these differences are not crucial.

Cognitive science's key finding is that thought is deeply shaped by human embodiment. The evidence for this claim arose from research in linguistics, psychology, gestural semantics, and other fields beginning in the late 1960s. Embodiment shapes the mind through our interactions with the material world, which provide the experiences behind our basic concepts of the world's contents and structure. For example, our concepts of containment emerge through our sensorimotor experiences of being inside something, trying to get inside something, removing or pouring materials from inside something, and so forth. As we build upon our experiences of the world, we turn these experience-based images, called image schemas, into metaphors that help us conceptualize other sorts of things—things that do not have the same physical topology (a runner is "in" a race), and things that cannot be physically perceived at all, nonmaterial and abstract objects such as gravity (the moon is "inside" the earth's gravitational field) and social relations (person A is "in" a relationship with person B).

Cognitive science has revealed image schemas of various sorts: position, orientation, movement, temperature, solidity, and much else. Lakoff and Johnson focus mainly on the emergence of image schemas from individual bodily experience; as human bodies are basically similar, we have these schemas in common. However, they also discuss image schemas that arise through social experiences, whether those are the aggregate of many individuals' embodied experiences with objects or activities that are sociohistorical products, or relational experiences that depend on personal interactions or social institutions. Social experiences are the basis of metaphors such as "the mind is a machine" or "time is money." Virtually all of our thoughts, perceptions, and knowledge—from basic concepts such as interiority and pathway, to advanced reasoning structures such as syllogisms, Boolean logic, and causal analysis, to entire philosophical systems—build upon image schemas.[21] Thus theory emerges from practice fundamentally through sensorimotor or social experience, the interaction of agential embodiment and intentionality; and metaphoric imagery is at the heart of the process, the link that makes it possible.

Performance Strategies

The value of cognitive science's research is already being explored in various fields of literary and cultural analysis; in theater studies, Bruce McConachie has done most to investigate its utility.[22] I will consider one of his studies toward the end of this article. Like McConachie, I believe that cognitive science should be incorporated within a larger explanatory framework. In my view, critical realism gives the concept of image schemas the greatest context and structural depth, and has the robust philosophical and social insights needed to develop coherent theoretical and historical analyses of theatrical performance. The key for undertaking such analyses is the concept of performance strategies.

Performance strategies embrace the entire arena of materials and techniques that playwrights, actors, directors, managers, and the like use or assume in constructing plays. A rough list would include performance space, performance time, dramatic action, scenery, sound, characterization, language, acting, genre concepts, expected audience behavioral norms, stage-audience dynamics, geography, attitudes, and pre- and post-performance discourse. The list is substantial, and not all of the elements can be controlled by theater personnel. However, in practice the elements within a single production and often across many productions tend to cohere into a single, regular system (akin to the regularities of a discursive formation).

Performance strategies emerge from agents' interactions with multiple social structures and forces, each other, and their own bodies, in the context of performing before an audience. The social environment sets the broadest conditions (enablements and constraints) on agents' activities. As noted earlier, the social environment must be analyzed on three levels:

structures, agents, and discourses. Each of these has in fact material, sociological, and meaningful aspects. The material aspect of social structures consists of the objects that make it possible for people to make things—equipment, buildings, materials, bodies. At the agential level, materiality concerns people's skills, habits, and coordinated activity, including the institutional and organizational arrangements through which they can undertake action. For discourses, the material element is the physical text, sound, or image required for semiosis. The sociological aspect of each level pertains to people's personal and collective interrelationships. At the structural level this means social relations of production and the system of positioned practices; at the agential level, actual individual and organizational interactions, including any social category or group that an agent normally engages (such as the students that schools require); and at the discursive level, intentions and illocutionary forces. Finally, the meaningful aspect of structures includes image schema and basic-level categories; for agents, it comprises their images of self and other, and their general strategies for conducting dialogue; and in the discursive domain it covers the articulation of thoughts and ideas in the form of reasoning, theories, fiction, drama, dance, and other cultural creations.[23]

Theatrical performance occurs as a specific collective formation and activity within this overall dynamic. It functions as a social agent possessing its own unique stratified ontology, one that closely parallels society's. Its theatrical level consists of the conventions, relationships, and spatial arrangements governing the interactions between performers and audience members. This is comparable to a social structure. Its dramatic level (analogous to the agential level) is the story as represented or narrated by the performers, the embodied actions and interactions of the characters that they perform. And its scriptive level is the "performance score," a discursive creation that can be a written play or simply an idea elaborated improvisationally. The homology between theatrical performance and society makes theater a kind of image of social ontology—an organ of social reflexivity. Moreover, by carrying out social reflexivity, it operates as a model of social agency.[24]

In theatrical performance, actors (real agents) create characters (virtual agents), who therefore are simultaneously products or causal *effects* of actual agency, *causes* of action in the dramas, and *indexes* of what it is to be an agent. As agents, characters typically strive to solve some problem, satisfy some need, ward off some danger, or in some other way remove some ill or threat or fulfill some desire. To do so, they adopt certain strategies, or at least ad hoc tactics. Performers, directors, and other theater artists likewise seek to solve problems, though their problems are usually very different: how best to make sense of a script, how to make the transition from page to stage, how to communicate with their prospective audience, how to make optimal use of their financial, material, and organizational resources, and so forth. They too take various strategies to achieve their ends. Not all of the strategies directly pertain to the performance itself, but the ones that do usually focus on the performance's intelligibility and artistic success. Performance strategies, then, are approaches to enacting agency by means of theater, conjoining the performer's imagination, intentionality, and embodiment toward direct or indirect dialogue with an audience. The strategies select and organize underlying image schemas deriving from sensorimotor and social experiences. And since some schemas derive from social experiences with institutions that themselves operate or depend upon fundamental social relationships, a few image schemas may obtain a dominant role in conditioning and enabling performance strategies.

A couple of examples will illustrate how such strategies operate. I will only hint at the structural bases for their emergence, and must describe the strategies with quite broad strokes. The examples will concern the mode of a performance's intelligibility, not its artistic success: more performances achieve the former than the latter, and the latter generally (though not always) depends on the former. My first example, the plays of the Middle Ages, are probably seldom as intelligible or meaningful to modern audiences as they were to their original audiences, in part because ideas about truth and reality have altered. Consequently the major performance strategies of medieval theater may seem quaint, even puzzling, while their cognitive import may be missed altogether. Medieval performance built strategies primarily upon two image schemas: "truth is writing" (meaning handwriting, manuscript), and "truth is repetition." (Other image schemas were of course called upon, if less centrally.) There was a degree of tension between these two schemas, since one derived from dominant institutions of literacy and the other from the pervasive oral and ritual background, but for the most part they maintained a fruitful symbiosis. The main way they conjoined was through the construction of similitudes, in symbolism, allegory, typology, and other forms. Similitudes were incorporated throughout the literature, art, sermons, political thought, music theory, and public punishments of the Middle Ages; they can be found operating in treatises on logic and theology, and even in works by writers who criticized analogical thinking.[25]

Allegory is one of the most recognized techniques in medieval art and literature. Allegorical personifications completely dominate morality plays such as *The Castle of Perseverance,* and they occasionally appear in mystery plays. However, allegory was primarily a method for interpretation, not characterization. Meaning was bifurcated into a literal and a figurative sense. Or many figurative senses: fourfold interpretation of the Bible—literal, allegorical, moral, and anagogic—was practically doctrine, and frequently appeared in sermons. The technique could be applied to mystery plays; in a few cases characters explained the allegory themselves. But spatial aspects of performance could also possess allegorical meaning. For example, the York Corpus Christi Cycle began its procession early in the morning by the Holy Trinity Priory at the outskirts of town, and concluded late at night at the Pavement, the marketplace where goods were weighed and sold and where public punishments took place—a path that signified the movement from God and Creation to the Last Judgment.[26]

However, in allegorical expansions, normally the literal level remained and was no less important than the figurative senses. (In fact it was not unusual for peasantry to interpret Scriptures literally as instructions for physical conduct, in a "re-ritualization of religious behavior" that often characterized their expression of religious feeling.)[27] The literal truth of words was critical for demonstrating the power of prophecy, a prevalent motif in the York Cycle. Prophecy was one way for textual truth to reveal repetition in history; another was typology, in which people and events in the Old Testament writings prefigure and are fulfilled by people and events in the New Testament. In the York pageant, Abraham's near-sacrifice of Isaac corresponds to God's sacrifice of Jesus. The play suggests this through both stage imagery and language: Isaac is somewhat over thirty years old, he willingly submits to his father's command and carries the wood for the sacrifice on his back, he uses phrases that Jesus later echoes, and so forth. Historical similitudes could be also established through anachronism. By peopling the plays with "dukes," "bishops," and "citizens," the dramatists quickly made the characters' essential social positions and moral types clear to the audience. This technique implies a figural conception of character, in the same sense (though not the same manner) as the allegorical characters.[28] Past and present repeat because they are united by moral and scriptural similarity.

Writing also provided the basis or motivation behind many physical symbols. For example, the image of a fish represented Jesus because *ichthus,* the Greek word for fish, was taken as an acronym for "Jesus Christ, Son of God, Savior." The cycle plays were replete with physical symbols. In the York Cycle, physical symbols often connected craft guilds to the pageants they staged. The shipwrights produced "The Building of the Ark," the bakers performed "The Last Supper," the pinners (makers of small, usually sharp, metal objects) did "The Crucifixion," and so forth. Since the symbols are part of communal culture (unlike modern symbolism, in which symbols often belong only to one particular author or play), they are inherently repeated. All ships were signs of arks; more, the trees they are made from are signs of the cross, and the ark itself symbolized the Church, preserver of souls. And like anachronism, the guild imagery makes a figural leap through time.[29]

The dichotomy between the literal and figural is connected to the philosophical distinction between the particular and the universal. In medieval philosophy, universals were understood as common natures, essences shared by similar individual entities—similitudes, in fact. The Latin term for this common nature was *species.* Thus there are different individual dogs, distinguished by particular but nonessential characteristics or circumstances such as age, friendliness, and so forth; but they are of the same species, that is, they have the same essence or common nature. Species were similitudes, understood as existing independently of the observer.

Medieval theatrical space was organized on the same principle. Whether the staging used one location, several emblematic locations, or a procession of pageants, it regularly divided the playing area into a *locus* (or several *loci*) and a *platea.* The *locus* was a particular location in which individuals found themselves. The *platea,* in contrast, was a generic space where individuals faded into types (species). Further, the *platea* was the realm of play, presentation, ritual embodiment, and audience engagement, while the *locus* was the domain of mimetic representation needing no interaction with the audience.[30] In performance the division between these spaces was always crossable and often crossed, but that does not contradict its underlying dynamic: the *locus* and *platea* structure consists of a realm of the particular at the center, a general realm surrounding it, and finally the spectators' universe at the outer edge. In order to see the particular place and people in the *locus,* the audience has to look through the *platea,* the general acting area; everything that is particular must pass through the general on its way to the audience (the catholic level, one might say), ultimately including God. The poles of the *locus* and *platea* set up a tension in which everything must be read through a generalizing filter, revealing its species or essence, as emblems or moral types.

Thus, people on the stage represented, even through their individuality, typical relationships to God. Consequently, medieval theater seldom pursued character in the modern sense (bearing internal, psychological depth and coherence) because its structure emphasized not personal motivation but fundamental moral meaning.[31] Social agency in the Middle Ages was defined in terms of moral species, and the performance strategies of the time both modeled and fostered that definition. Medieval theater invoked similitudes with a remarkable thoroughness in all areas of performance: language, plot, characterization, props, costuming, staging—the works. It was part of a culture imbued with similitudes as the dominant discursive strategy, forming a (partial, open) totality that constituted agency in moral terms.

Of course, medieval artistic methods had centuries to coalesce into this degree of integration. Such aesthetic unity contrasts sharply with the trend toward divergence that began during the last quarter of the nineteenth century, in which various performance styles and conditions compete or cohabit: naturalism, symbolism, expressionism, epic theater, historical reconstructions, performance art, forum theater, proscenium stages, thrust stages, black boxes, and so on. An implicit and sometimes explicit political intent has attended many of these developments. Some of them extend the dominant cognitive strategies and image schemas into new directions, which despite radically changed appearances remain consistent with the original assumptions; others take the dominant image schemas and switch perspectives, forming a sort of loyal opposition that fights the dominant approach to the teeth, yet surreptitiously agrees with it on certain basics; still others rely on different cognitive strategies and image schemas altogether. Sometimes contrasting approaches appear even within individual plays or productions. In previous eras, and often today, such inconsistencies were experienced as artistic flaws; in modern performance they may derive from an artistic approach, such as in eclecticism and postmodern pastiche; and in either case, they may articulate historical transitions, crises, collisions, and explorations, requiring efforts to grapple with change and the emergence of new cultural conditions that the old approaches, the old schemas, do not adequately accommodate.

But the proliferation of performance strategies in a variety of avant-gardes shouldn't obscure the fact that certain approaches are dominant. In his article "Doing Things with Image Schemas," Bruce McConachie proposes a way to use image schemas to understand how audiences may have experienced performances historically. His example is from mid-1950s mainstream American theater: *A Hatful of Rain,* by Michael Gazzo, on Broadway during 1955–56. His exploration produces intriguing insights, and is broadly compatible with critical realism. An explicitly critical realist framework can build upon this approach to reveal more fully the stratified and dynamic nature of audience responses, and suggests how in this instance the audience's response may have involved conflicting or even contradictory impulses.

As McConachie observes, certain images schemas and metaphors dominate or maintain cultural hegemony during historical periods. (My example of the Middle Ages also demonstrates this point.) He holds that during the 1950s, the image of "containment" was key. He is probably right about this, although I suspect that it rode at the surface above several other schemas that were more fundamental culturally and for the dynamics of theatrical performance; but he himself acknowledges that he has provided only the beginnings of a full historical analysis.[32] Having proposed containment as the primary metaphor, McConachie uses it to investigate the production's theatrical spatiality, narrative, and acting. In the terms I sketched earlier, these belong to the theatrical, scriptive, and dramatic levels of theater (respectively).

A Hatful of Rain played in a typical proscenium theater. McConachie notes that along with the image of containment, the schemas of "center-periphery" and "near-far" organized this space as well. Drawing on the proscenium theater's historical origins in Renaissance buildings such as the Teatro Farnese, McConachie finds that this space fosters a Cartesian objectivist gaze. The darkened house contributes to this effect by providing the spectator with a more privatized experience. According to McConachie, the spatial relationship strongly encourages what Lakoff and Johnson call "advisory projection." Advisory projection is one way in which people put themselves in another's shoes, in this case epitomized by the phrase, "If I were you, I'd do X." The alternative is "empathic projection," in which one adopts the other's viewpoint or experience, as in "I see why you feel that way." McConachie does not rule out the possibility of empathy in proscenium theaters, however, and he turns to other aspects of the production to find further evidence.[33]

The plotline and its critical reception provide some of that evidence.

The play focuses on Johnny, a Korean War vet whose life has taken a downward turn through heroin addiction; though harassed by pushers, he attempts to kick the habit and restore his family ties, but in the end his wife must call the police to take him to the hospital. McConachie finds signs in the reviews that several aspects of the play aroused anxiety about gender roles, while related elements hinted at fears of "subversion from within"; the two dangers were frequently associated in Cold War discourse. "Subversion" invokes the containment image, in this case of an inner essence. By spurring these worries in the audience, McConachie argues, *A Hatful of Rain* encouraged an advisory projection toward Johnny, whose psychological essence and authenticity was threatened with subversion.[34]

The containment schema also shaped the performance given by Ben Gazzara, the actor who played Johnny. Gazzara's Johnny was a man who was still decent and good on the inside, but who had taken the outer shape of a "Monster Addict" (in McConachie's phrase) that threatened to overwhelm him. Further, Method acting such as Gazzara's was itself built around the image of an inner self struggling to break free and sometimes bursting explosively into the light. Critics (and presumably audiences) found the resulting performance intensely honest, and sympathized with Johnny and his efforts to regain health and family. Such characters "could be sympathetic victims, [and] fellow sufferers."[35]

In demonstrating the coherence of the space, narrative, and acting of *A Hatful of Rain*, a coherence built around the image schema of containment and prevailing far beyond that one play, McConachie approaches the concept of a performance strategy. But the critics' sympathy for Johnny raises some questions, since such expressions do not necessarily indicate advisory projection. Audiences conceivably could sympathize with Johnny's passionate eruptions because they imagined themselves in similar psychological circumstances, from within his experiences and outlook on the world, in an act of empathic projection. McConachie notes that in principle, audiences may combine the two sorts of projection, but he doesn't discuss how that happens or explore the possibility when considering how audiences experienced *A Hatful of Rain*.[36] Of course, there are limits to what one can cover in a single article, he aims only to outline a methodology, and a different example might have pointed toward empathic projection. McConachie even enumerates a variety of questions that remain— most fundamentally, that while image schemas can help the historian describe and interpret a dominant culture, they explain little about where that culture came from or why certain schemas dominate.[37] Investigating that issue would require an extensive discussion that would surpass the limits of the present chapter. I can, however, consider how and why forms of projection might be combined and how they may have combined in *A Hatful of Rain,* by introducing certain concepts from critical realism and from a critical realist understanding of theatrical performance.

The first step is to reassess the Broadway theater space. It is true that its basic arrangement originated with Renaissance stages such as the Teatro Farnese. That design continued in use for centuries, with only modest modifications. But during the middle to late 1800s several major changes coalesced to form the modern stage. Perspective scenery, using the wing and groove or the chariot and pole system, was supplanted by three-dimensional objects often enclosed in rooms without a fourth wall. The audience was plunged into darkness during performances. And the U-shaped auditorium, with its explicit social hierarchy of pit, boxes, and galleries, was replaced with lightly arching rows in a fan-shaped orchestra and balcony. Vestiges of the old architecture often remained, but it seems a different sort of theater space had emerged, which by the 1950s had long predominated—and with it, perhaps different stage-audience dynamics.

The Farnese-style theater promoted an objectivist gaze in part because the perspective scenery could only line up properly if viewed from one special position, which is where the ruler sat. Not only did the rest of the audience have distorted perspectives, but its U-shaped seating arrangement paid at least as much tribute to the ruler as it did to the stage. Keeping the house lit was part of that relationship. Thus the ruler, sitting literally at the Archimedean vantage point, alone had the true perspective. The objective position was the ruler's view; the ruler's subjects had, well, subjective views. On this much McConachie and I concur, and also that dimming the house lights discouraged experiencing theater collectively and promoted a privatized experience instead.[38]

But I am not convinced that the objectivist dynamics of the Farnese-style theater operated so solidly in the modern playhouse. There were several inducements to subjectivism, and they could potentially be stronger than the contrary tendency. The rearrangement of seating so that the entire audience had a more or less straight-on view of the stage, and the shift to three-dimensional sets that never suffered from distorted perspective or outright fragmentation into wings, meant that everyone's view was roughly as good as everyone else's, and no one possessed a privileged position. Further, the objective view granted the ruler in the Farnese-type theater was one acknowledged publicly, by an audience facing inward and in the light—not a possibility in modern theaters, where only the personal gaze remained.

A tendency toward subjective perception was also prominent outside the theater, and was manifested in both the drama and the acting. A trend toward individualism had started as early as 1600 in Western culture, one of the principal ideas (in fact, image schemas) generated by capitalism. By 1950 it was almost universally trumpeted throughout the United States. In the nineteenth century it gained an increasingly psychological character (connected to positivism, which hypostatized perception), and around 1900 it was conjoined with an extended containment schema to produce the notions of psychological depth, the unconscious buried in the nether reaches of the mind (a mind within a mind), and the deep (and deeply sexualized) self associated with Freud, which were widely popularized in 1950s America. In theater, these developments provided the basis for the rise of psychological realism in drama and acting. Thus, as McConachie observes, *A Hatful of Rain* strove to "plumb the depths of Johnny's psychology," and the real sources of Johnny's problems "are mired in the search for the mother he never had and the Oedipal rage he still feels toward his father."[39]

The individualism, psychologism, and subjectivization that social forces generated in theater and drama could assume many forms. The first significant manifestation came in the early eighteenth century with the rise of sentimental comedy, and then sentimental drama. The latter touched Romantic drama, but mainly fed into various types of melodrama, which also often invoked the primacy of individualism. The essential dynamic of sentimental response is in fact still very alive. The most important development, however, was the psychological realism of the late nineteenth century. Psychological motivation, processes, and experience—the subjective realm—took center stage. From there it was but a short step to psychologically symbolist drama, expressionist theater, surrealist performances, Pirandellian enigmas on sanity/insanity and illusion/reality, memory plays and the like performed alongside the ever-dominant objective or naturalist form of psychological realism. Nor was it a large matter to patch elements from several of these styles into a single play. Thus a small set of image schemas permitted a wide assortment of permutations (inversions, reversals, perspective switches, focus shifts) that nevertheless always converged on the concept of individual subjectivity. A single premise, the schema complex of the deep self, laid the foundation for numerous performance strategies—or if you prefer, that schema was the strategy; all the rest were tactics.

The social forces that generated subjectivization in theatrical performance also produced it in the audience. Theater operates as a model of
social agency. In the Middle Ages, the agent was understood as moral
species; in twentieth-century America agency was (for many, still is)
defined as the Subject, a being primarily constituted through (or as) psychological depth. Audience response formed on that basis—as an emergent entity, theatrical performance has powers that can affect its audience
members and in principle can even alter their concept of agency, but it
emerges on the condition of the agent-form that already exists. Furthermore, theater is a partial totality that involves reflexivity and emerges from
other reflexive partial totalities. The dynamic of spectatorial reflexivity
involving a notion of individual inwardness probably was first clearly
articulated in the theory of sentiment that oriented eighteenth-century
plays. It postulated a reflex of seeing behavior, judging character, and
responding with spontaneous feeling. The emotions of one person thereby
inspired sympathetic feelings in the observer. In this system of self-
reflection, the meaning of an outward appearance lay in the observer's
inner response. The reflex of sentiment became the reflection of the
observer's inward self.[40] A roughly similar dynamic of reflexivity and
dialectical perspective-switching operated in twentieth-century mainstream performance, but now the self had been configured with embedded
interiorities, most deeply a seething morass of passions battling with an
ethical veneer to escape, within a Subject seated in the dark with his or her
own locally true perspective.

What sort of projection did these aspects of the Broadway playhouse
promote? Subjectivism, after all, could mean applying one's own values
and experience to others' actions, which would be advisory projection.
However, the Subject seated in the dark is a passive one: the characters on
stage are active, and so the darkness most likely encouraged spectators to
imagine their agency through the characters, vicariously. That impulse is
strengthened by psychological realism, which requires the audience to
piece together information and inferences in order to understand a character's past and motivations for acting, and interpret dramatic action from
the character's point of view. Method acting recommended that actors
undertake similar activities in order to get "inside" the character. Emotion
memory used the actor's own experiences not in order to assess the character, but to experience the character's feelings by proxy. Elements of the
script fed these tendencies further. The most explicit symbol in the play
arises when Johnny's father recounts how he once found Johnny, then a

little boy, in the backyard digging a big hole in the rain. Johnny had taken literally his father's statement that "the only way you get money in your pockets is to work." When his father convinced him to stop, Johnny picked up his hat, and the water in it poured all over him. In his father's words, "he worked and worked and all he got was a hatful of rain."[41] The story propels the spectators into Johnny's past and to imagine the world as Johnny experienced it, allowing them to grasp the context for some of Johnny's behavior. On theatrical, dramatic, and scriptive levels, there were many inducements toward empathic projection.

I would argue, then, that in an effective 1950s mainstream theater production like *A Hatful of Rain,* responding with empathic projection would not be an exception in a production that was heavily weighted toward advisory projection. It seems more likely that the dynamic version of the containment schema that this play relied upon, involving a struggle between container and thing contained, would systematically encourage audiences to feel both advisory and empathic projection (albeit not necessarily in equal measure). This theater's reflexivity involved empathy and judgment toward self as well as other. The tension between the two sorts of projection, the combination or alternation between them, probably supplied a considerable part of the gripping quality of the production. And the sense of authenticity achieved by both the character and the enacting of Johnny consisted in the first place in audience members' recognition of Johnny as a person like them, not in having a similar life, but in the sense of having a similarly fractured interiority of self. The authenticity of both the performer and the performed—their quality of truth and reality—is a function of theater's operation as a model of agency. Significantly, as McConachie notes, Method actors were often considered self-involved.[42] Their narcissism may have been an exaggeration of what was transpiring elsewhere in society, or just the exaggeration of reputation, but some degree of self-involvement was virtually inevitable with the sort of agency dominant at that time. For the audience too, the performance afforded an opportunity for self-involvement to the degree that empathy—seeing from the Other's perspective—can serve as a reflection of and attempt to fill one's own hollowed-out self. Agency is a process of absenting absences, an effort to overcome problems, constraints, needs. In the present case, there was a gap within agency itself, stipulated by its multiple interiorities, the disjunction required by the containment schema. In postwar America, agency was its own problem. The performance strategies of the time modeled it because that is what theatrical performance does; aimed to solve it because that is what agency does; and tried to do so by reinforcing it, even glorifying it, because unavoidable social forces established that Subjectivity is what agency is.

Performance Strategies: An Assessment

Performance strategies are inherently relational and dynamic. That is key to their value in analyzing theater. They ultimately concern the constitution and exercise of agency; agents devise them to achieve certain goals, solve certain problems, and answer certain questions about what it is to be an agent. However, as in any other endeavor, agents adopt strategies under conditions not of their own making. Were it otherwise, there would be no need for strategies at all. Agents form strategies to cross the divide between intention and present conditions, to struggle with and change realities. Strategies are always a matter of struggle, of contention between power and counterpower (for all things that are real have causal power), and they are always faced with the possibility of defeat. Performance strategies involve an overarching goal, a plan for achieving it, and intermediate steps requiring particular measures. On a larger scale one can also think in terms of an umbrella strategy under which various substrategies are possible. Probably that is the most straightforward way to think about the connection between (say) naturalism, symbolism, and expressionism in drama: they employ different approaches to staging and characterization, yet assume essentially the same concept of agency. They represent differing performance strategies that share a common basis or goal; from this perspective, one might consider individual plays or productions as tactics (which of course may or may not be successful).

Such variety is possible because the conditions for action always *under*-determine the actions undertaken. Though social structures place often enormous pressures on people to act in certain ways, options and choices always remain: people are not mere "bearers" of social relations, or marionettes manipulated by social forces—they are real agents who make real decisions that have real consequences that differ from what would have come from another choice. Operating with the dominant understanding of agency isn't obligatory: there are other concepts of agency, entailing other performance strategies. Of course, by the same token, choosing an alternative path means swimming against the current.

Within the variety, however, the concept of performance strategies allows one to see the common threads among divergent approaches, and to locate coherence among different elements such as acting, staging, narrative, costuming, and so forth not simply on a thematic level, but on an underlying conceptual level that becomes embedded even with the actor's body.[43] Or noncoherence: the theatrical, dramatic, and scriptive levels need not always be grounded in the same image schemas. But generally they are, due to the social dominance of one set of schemas or another. Some of the variety-in-commonality exists because reversals and perspective switches enable a single set of conceptual components to establish differing (complementary) strategies, essentially cognitive flip-sides. Many image schemas allow such perspective switches, such as between the container and the thing contained. Reversals of this sort do not merely exist in the imagination: they arise from sensorimotor experiences with real objects, and belong to their real entailments. The metaphorical implications or applications of image schemas may likewise make sense of non-metaphorical realities.

An example of switching perspectives on image schemas can be found in the contrast between advisory and empathic projection. Lakoff and Johnson state that the difference between the two sorts of projection rests on whether one applies one's own values or the other person's.[44] That analysis presents one type of perspective switch, but there is a deeper level. The co-occurrence of advisory and empathic projection does not depend on the fraught, multiply interiorized self of the 1950s: sociocultural conditions made the relationship between them bristle with the tensions and contradictions of the individual Subject (the foundation for both objectivism and subjectivism), but their co-occurrence has a basis in embodied metaphors—the two can be quite compatible. Underlying projection (as the term suggests) is the image schema of movement along a path. Thus the two types of projection involve not just perspective switches on values (mine vs. yours), but also on the image schema of source-path-goal. The image shows how the two projections are or at least can be complementary. However, the source-path-goal schema suggests that underneath the axiological element, the distinction between advisory and empathic projection has an epistemic foundation (involving experiential and anticipatory frameworks). Critical realism supports this proposal when it argues that values are not theory-free: values are grounded in theories, and theories generally entail value as well as practical judgments.[45] The epistemological ground of projection connects the two types of projection with the dialectics of perspective shifts, and supplants judgmental relativism toward value systems with epistemic relativism regarding values' underlying ideas about an independently existing world that makes judgments necessary. In other words, the complementarity of empathic (retrospective) and advisory (prospective) projection correlates with the critical realist distinction between, and conjoining of, epistemic relativism (recognizing that all theories are sociohistorically produced) with judgmental rationality (asserting grounds for recommending one theory rather than another).

And, I would argue, there are rational grounds for considering the concept of performance strategies more capable of providing viable explanations and analyses than the concept of genre. Performance strategies are founded in sociohistorical relations, resources, dynamics, and processes that emphasize or provide the sensorimotor and social experiences that play a key role in organizing that society's ideas and art. The researcher can investigate which social structures had the largest part in making certain image schemas prominent, and how exactly they accomplished that. Further, performance strategies reflect the choices that people make within their social conditions. Thus the concept of performance strategies concerns connections between structures, agents, and discourses—the whole of social ontology.

Theatrical performance, then, is not solely a matter of signs, representations, styles, or discourses. It is not even reducible to people doing things. It is a complex partial totality consisting of various social relationships, processes, products, and agents, which has emerged from and within the larger totality of society. It has a stratified structure of its own, arising in the context and conditions of society's ontological stratification. Its structure includes various component partial totalities, such as its physical arrangements, scripts, actors, and audiences. As an emergent totality, theater possesses sui generis powers; but how (or even whether) those powers are exercised, what their ultimate effects might be, depends upon the actual interaction of these numerous elements.

Genre, in contrast, is basically a formal or stylistic notion. It functions on the discursive level alone, without any necessary connection to people's actions, much less social dynamics. Moreover, the conceptual boundaries of genre are notoriously vague: comedy is a genre embracing Aristophanes and Shaw; naturalism is a genre with both serious and comic instances. But that said, the concept of performance strategies doesn't necessarily serve every research question: it is "scalable," in the sense of allowing broader or finer levels of substrategies, but it may or may not be effective for understanding (say) the nature of comedy as such, across differing performance strategies. Only further efforts to analyze theater in terms of performance strategies will prove the extent of its utility. In the meantime, the notion of genre remains useful, at least for indicating a loose "family resemblance" among plays or approaches to performance, even though it may not be a real analytical tool.

Many other questions remain as well. There is much more to be said about how, exactly, social structures make certain image schemas central for a specific era, how and why the dominant schemas change, whether theatrical performance requires adjusting the dominant schemas in some way, and so forth. The nature and relationships of concurrent styles (e.g., naturalism and symbolism) needs more detailed discussion. Differing social structures, such as gender, race, and class, have effects on audience experience that must be taken into account. Critical realism provides a strong philosophical framework for studying these issues by upholding both the reality of the world outside the mind and the social character of our thoughts about it, and by overcoming the chasm between world and mind without collapsing them together.

NOTES

1. Bhaskar's key works are *A Realist Theory of Science* (Sussex: Harvester Press; Atlantic Highlands, N.J.: Humanities Press, 1978); *The Possibility of Naturalism: A Philosophical Critique of the Contemporary Human Sciences,* 2nd ed. (New York: Harvester Wheatsheaf, 1989); and *Dialectic: The Pulse of Freedom* (London: Verso, 1993). His collection of essays, *Reclaiming Reality: A Critical Introduction to Contemporary Philosophy* (London: Verso, 1989), serves nicely as an introduction to his work. So too does Andrew Collier, *Critical Realism: An Introduction to Roy Bhaskar's Philosophy* (London: Verso, 1994).

2. Critical realism has of course evolved over the years, as its changing nomenclature suggests: it began as "transcendental realism" (as a philosophy concerning the natural sciences), which was expanded to encompass the social sciences under the rubric "critical naturalism," and in the late 1980s other writers amalgamated the two phrases to form "critical realism" (see *Reclaiming Reality,* 190). Strictly speaking, I should now refer to it as "dialectical critical realism" to accommodate the developments introduced in *Dialectic* (1993), some of which play a role in the present article. However, I consider the new dialectical elements to be continuous with the earlier critical realism, and use the latter phrase for both.

3. Bhaskar, *Realist Theory of Science,* 12–17, 21–24, and passim.

4. George Berkeley, *A Treatise Concerning the Principles of Human Knowledge* (1710), in *The Empiricists* (Garden City, N.Y.: Anchor Books, 1974), §3, p. 152.

5. Bhaskar, *Realist Theory of Science,* 36–40.

6. Ibid., 182.

7. Ibid., 79–90, 175–84.

8. Bhaskar, *Dialectic,* 49.

9. Ibid., 397.

10. Ibid., 49–56, 172, 400; *The Possibility of Naturalism,* 97–99.

11. Bhaskar's original formulation (in *Realist Theory of Science*) defined the third domain as the empirical, consisting of experiences. This version still appears, but in more recent work (*Dialectic* on) he often redefines it as the subjective, which includes both experiences and concepts. While I think the later version is superior insofar as it is more encompassing, both accounts have problems, and elsewhere I have argued that the third domain would be better understood as the semiosic (and that the concept of emergence applies not just ontically, but ontologically as well). See *Realist Theory of Science,* 59; *Dialectic,* 11, 393; and Tobin Nellhaus, "Signs, Social Ontology, and Critical Realism," *Journal for the Theory of Social Behaviour* 28, no. 1 (1998): 1–24.

12. Bhaskar, *Dialectic,* 231–38.

13. Ibid., 238–40.

14. Ibid., 123–27, 272–76, 401, 405. One might note that aside from quarks (and perhaps even them), all entities are composed of other entities. Hence for practical purposes, the elements of a totality are always themselves totalities (and consist of further subtotalities), contributing to the larger totality's stratified, dynamic complexity.

15. Bhaskar, *The Possibility of Naturalism,* 35, 81–83, 90–97; *Dialectic,* 51–52, 173–77, 276–79.

16. On this point I depart from Bhaskar, who recognizes only two tiers. See Nellhaus, "Signs," 13–21.

17. Bhaskar, *The Possibility of Naturalism,* 31–44; *Dialectic,* 154–64; Margaret S. Archer, *Culture and Agency: The Place of Culture in Social Theory,* rev. ed. (Cambridge: Cambridge University Press, 1996), 149–61. This "transformational model of social activity" is neatly summarized in *The Eighteenth Brumaire of Louis Bonaparte:* "Men make their own history, but they do not make it just as they please; they do not make it under circumstances of their own choosing, but under circumstances directly found, given and transmitted from the past. The tradition of all the dead generations weighs like a nightmare on the brain of the living." Karl Marx, in *The Marx-Engels Reader,* ed. Robert C. Tucker, 2nd ed. (New York: Norton, 1978), 595.

18. Bhaskar, *Realist Theory of Science,* 16–17, 43 (quoted), 185–87, 195–99, 249–50; *The Possibility of Naturalism,* 21, 57–58.

19. Roy Bhaskar, *Scientific Realism and Human Emancipation* (London: Verso, 1986), 172–75.

20. Bhaskar, *Realist Theory of Science,* 145–46, 158–63, 166–68, 194.

21. George Lakoff and Mark Johnson, *Philosophy in the Flesh: The Embodied Mind and Its Challenge to Western Thought* (New York: Basic Books, 1999), esp. 16–59, 161–66, 247. Cognitive science's case for the fundamental role of imagery in thought meshes with the semiotics of Charles S. Peirce, which holds that icons are deeply involved in symbolic signs: symbols, he says, "come into being by development out of other signs, particularly from likenesses or from mixed signs partaking of the nature of likenesses and symbols. . . . Now every symbol must have organically attached to it, its Indices of Reactions and its Icons of Qualities." *The Essential Peirce: Selected Philosophical Writings,* vol. 2 (1893–1913), ed. Peirce Edition Project (Bloomington: Indiana

University Press, 1998), 10, 193–94. I have argued for the compatibility of Peirce's semiotics with critical realism in "Signs," 1–8.

22. See McConachie's "Metaphors We Act By: Kinesthetics, Cognitive Psychology, and Historical Structures," *Journal of Dramatic Theory and Criticism* 8, no. 2 (1993): 23–45; "Approaching Performance History Through Cognitive Psychology," *Assaph* 10 (1994): 113–22; and "Doing Things with Image Schemas: The Cognitive Turn in Theatre Studies and the Problem of Experience for Historians," *Theatre Journal* 53 (2001): 569–94. McConachie cites several scholars applying cognitive science to other fields in "Doing Things," 575.

23. See Nellhaus, "Signs," 15–21.

24. Tobin Nellhaus, "Social Ontology and (Meta)theatricality: Reflexions on Performance and Communication in History," *Journal of Dramatic Theory and Criticism* 14, no. 2 (2000): 12–20.

25. See Judson Boyce Allen, *The Ethical Poetic of the Later Middle Ages: A Decorum of Convenient Distinction* (Toronto: University of Toronto Press, 1982), 180.

26. For an extensive discussion of the procession route's meaning, see Martin Stevens, *Four Middle English Mystery Plays: Textual, Contextual, and Critical Interpretations* (Princeton, N.J.: Princeton University Press, 1987), 50–77.

27. Brian Stock, *Implications of Literacy: Written Language and Models of Interpretation in the Eleventh and Twelfth Centuries* (Princeton, N.J.: Princeton University Press, 1983), 104–6. This tendency continued into the sixteenth century, as Carlo Ginzburg's study of a peasant heretic shows: "In his mental and linguistic world, marked as it was by the most absolute literalism, even metaphors must be taken in a rigorously literal sense." See *The Cheese and the Worms: The Cosmos of a Sixteenth-Century Miller*, trans. John Tedeschi and Anne Tedeschi (Harmondsworth: Penguin, 1982), 62.

28. Meg Twycross, "'Apparell Comlye,'" in *Aspects of Early English Drama*, ed. Paula Neuss (Cambridge: D. S. Brewer, 1983), 30–34. As Twycross points out, although characters might be designated by anachronistic terms, they did not necessarily wear contemporary clothing.

29. See Richard L. Homan, "Ritual Aspects of the York Cycle," *Theatre Journal* 33 (1981): 303–15.

30. W. F. Munson, "Audience and Meaning in Two Medieval Dramatic Realisms," in *The Drama of the Middle Ages: Comparative and Critical Essays*, ed. Clifford Davidson, C. J. Gianakaris, and John H. Stroupe (New York: AMS Press, 1982), 197; Robert Weimann, *Shakespeare and the Popular Tradition: Studies in the Social Dimension of Dramatic Form and Function*, ed. Robert Schwartz (Baltimore: Johns Hopkins University Press, 1978), 73–85.

31. See David Mills, "Characterization in the English Mystery Cycles," *Medieval English Theatre* 5 (1983): 5–17; and Lawrence M. Clopper, "Tyrants and Villains: Characterization in the Passion Sequences of the English Cycle Plays," *Modern Language Quarterly* 41 (1980): 3–20.

32. McConachie, "Doing Things," 584–86, 593–94.

33. Ibid., 586–88; Lakoff and Johnson, *Philosophy in the Flesh*, 281.

34. McConachie, "Doing Things," 588–91.

35. Ibid., 591–93.

36. Ibid., 581.

37. Ibid., 593–94.

38. Ibid., 587.

39. Ibid., 589.

40. See the discussion in Michael G. Ketcham, *Transparent Designs: Reading, Performance, and Form in the "Spectator" Papers* (Athens: University of Georgia Press, 1985), 13, 32, 41–43, 49–50, 53, 63.

41. Michael Vincente Gazzo, *A Hatful of Rain* (New York: Random House, 1956), 131.

42. McConachie, "Doing Things," 593.

43. The analytical approach I am proposing bears comparison with Foucauldian "archaeology," which if applied to painting "would try to discover whether space, distance, depth, colour, light, proportions, volumes, and contours were not, at the period in question, considered, named, enunciated, and conceptualized in a discursive practice; and whether the knowledge that this discursive practice gives rise to was not embodied perhaps in theories and speculations, but also in processes, techniques, and even in the very gesture of the painter. . . . It would try to show that, at least in one of its dimensions, it is discursive practice that is embodied in techniques and effects." Michel Foucault, *The Archaeology of Knowledge and The Discourse on Language,* trans. A. M. Sheridan Smith (New York: Pantheon, 1972), 193–94.

44. Lakoff and Johnson, *Philosophy in the Flesh,* 281.

45. Bhaskar, *The Possibility of Naturalism,* 54–55; *Scientific Realism,* 173. This is part of a larger argument (against positivism) that one can move from facts to values, and (in certain senses) vice versa. See also Collier, *Critical Realism,* 169–81.

PART TWO

Presence

FOUR

Humanoid Boogie

Reflections on Robotic Performance

Philip Auslander

> Some people say it with flowers, some people say it with Lloyd's.
> But you don't find many trying to say it with humanoids
> —THE BONZO DOG BAND, "Humanoid Boogie"

Sergei Shutov's *Abacus* (2001) in the Russian pavilion of the 49th Venice Biennial International Exposition of Art (June 10–November 4, 2001) was a frequent subject of discussion during the press opening for the exhibition, which I attended in my capacity as a critic of the visual arts. *Abacus* consists of over forty crouching figures draped in black, which face an open door and pray in numerous languages representing a multitude of faiths while making the reverential movements appropriate to prayer. Nearby video monitors display the texts of the prayers in their many alphabets. People at the opening talked of the "performance" in the Russian pavilion; a journalistic colleague, knowing that performance is the main subject of my research and writing, asked me whether I considered the piece a performance. I blithely answered yes, realizing only later that I had taken a position I needed to consider further.

The reason for both my colleague's question and my own desire to think more about it is that the figures performing in *Abacus* are not human beings—they are robots programmed by a computer to engage in *dahvening* (Jewish prayer) movements accompanied by the recorded sounds of ecumenical prayer. Given that the figures are machines, not human beings, some might argue that the piece should be considered an animated sculptural installation, not a performance—it is described as an installation in the Biennale catalog.

(The figures could also be considered automata, or the whole system could be seen as a playback device, possibilities I will consider shortly.) I prefer to think of it as a performance, however, not just because I believe that machines can perform but also because to view a piece such as *Abacus* as a performance by machines yields rich possibilities for its interpretation.

At the most basic level, the question "Can machines perform?" can only be answered in the affirmative. After all, the primary meaning of the verb *to perform* is simply "to do." Inasmuch as machines (or human beings) do things, they perform. Moving from that basic level to the context of art practices, however, the definition of performance proves to be context-specific, not universal; it changes according to the particular aesthetic form and tradition under consideration. What it means to perform a piece of classical music is not the same as what it means to perform jazz, and neither musical definition of performance is applicable to the theater, dance, or performance art. One crucial area of difference is the assumed relationship of the performer to the text being performed: the relationship of a classical musician to the piece is not the same as that of a jazz musician to the music she performs, for instance, and the respective relationships of actors to dramas and dancers to choreography put still other variables into play.

If the definition of performance is context-dependent, so is the determination of what counts as a performer. To the question of whether the robots in *Abacus* should be considered elements in a sculptural installation, automata, parts of a playback system, or performers in their own right, I offer an inclusive response: they are all of these things. Credible arguments can be advanced for each of these identifications, and the categories are not mutually exclusive (an automaton could be an element in an installation or part of a playback system, for instance). How one chooses to describe the robots depends primarily not on their intrinsic properties but on the artistic tradition to which one wishes to assimilate them. In this essay, the artistic tradition in which I ultimately will place the robots is that of performance art.

Brief considerations of the *Abacus* robots as parts of a playback system or automata will help to shed light on what is at stake in my identification of them as performers. In his estimable study of musical performance, to which I shall refer repeatedly here, Stan Godlovitch discriminates the playback of a recording from a performance: "The playback is no more a performance than the photograph is the thing photographed. . . . In a recording, I hear an acoustic image of a performance given necessarily at some past time."[1] From a technical standpoint, *Abacus* is indeed an elaborate

playback device: the robots and sound system function to make the playback of the computer program apprehensible to an audience in a way analogous to a CD player's converting information on a disc into audible
music. But *Abacus* is not a playback device of the kind Godlovitch
describes because the actions of its robots do not re-create a prior performance: although *Abacus* is a representational work, it is not a record of a
gathering of black-garbed figures that took place at some earlier time. As a
playback device, *Abacus* is, in this respect, what I have called a technology
of production, not reproduction.[2]

Whereas it is easy enough to agree with Godlovitch that the playback of
recordings of prior performances is not a performance in itself, the question of whether *Abacus* generates a performance is not clear-cut even when
it's seen as a playback device. To define the problem, I propose the following test, which I admit is not scientific. Whereas one might wish to record
a performance, one would have little reason to record the playback of an
existing recording of a performance except to produce a copy of the source
recording. (A sound recording rerecorded during playback or a film or
video shot from the screen during projection or playback—one way in
which bootleg videotapes of films are produced—would be examples of
such copies.) If *Abacus* were a playback device of the kind Godlovitch
describes, one that provides access to a record of a prior performance, then
a recording of its playback would constitute only a copy of another recording. This clearly is not the case—a video recording of *Abacus* in action is
not merely a copy of the computer program it plays back. It is, rather, a
record of the behavior of the robotic figures made as that behavior
unfolded—the robots' real-time activity is the prior performance captured
on the video. A video recording of *Abacus* is therefore interesting and valuable for precisely the same reasons that a recording of any performance is
interesting and valuable. This suggests, albeit indirectly, that *Abacus* is
more like a performance we might wish to record than a device for playing
back a recorded performance.

Reproduction, then, is one of the issues at stake here, which I have
addressed by discussing the possibility that *Abacus* is a playback device.
Agency and its delegation are also central issues that can be broached by
discussing *Abacus* in relation to puppetry. In differentiating automata
from puppets, Steve Tillis argues, "The distinguishing characteristic of the
automaton is that its movement possibilities are 'closed.' With puppets of
all kinds . . . the nature and duration of each movement is open to the control of the operator."[3] Within these parameters, the robots in *Abacus* are

ertainly automata rather than puppets: they are not manipulated in real
.ime by an operator but controlled by a computer. All the operator has to
do is set the apparatus in motion by initiating the program. Tillis goes on
to say that automata should be considered "kinetic sculpture[s]" rather
than puppets, implying, I think, that automata should be excluded from
an artistic tradition associated with performance and assigned to a special
category within an artistic tradition associated primarily with static
objects. His underlying argument is that to qualify as a performance, an
event must be spontaneous rather than programmed. Performances, this
argument suggests, put human agency on display, even when the agent is
hidden, like some puppeteers. Automata, on the other hand, are cases of
what Jane Goodall calls "transferred agency," in which agency is delegated
to machines by human beings whose work is completed before the
machine undertakes its actions. Goodall suggests that cases of transferred
agency fuel "cultural anxiety" about technology's potential to usurp
human authority, perhaps even human identity.[4] Most traditional
definitions of performance reflect this anxiety in their emphasis on liveness and implicit resistance to the concept of machine performers.[5]

Before going any further, I want to make it clear that although I clearly
do wish to make a case for seeing machines as performers, I am not
proposing that machines can perform in all of the ways that human beings
can. One element common to most traditional definitions of performance
is an emphasis on the agency of the performer as the interpreter of a text of
some kind and an artist who expresses something of her own through
interpretation. In his discussion of musical performance, which he defines
as a skilled activity, Godlovitch makes a useful distinction between two
categories of skills a performer may possess: technical skills and interpretive skills.[6] Whereas "Technical skills [in the case of music] involve causing objectively determinable and (often) quantitatively measurable
acoustic effects. . . . Interpretive skills involve aesthetic effects for which no
obvious quantitative measure exists, and typically emphasize
'expression.'"[7] Although it may be difficult in practice to distinguish
moments in a performance that reflect the exercise of purely technical
skills from those that entail interpretive skills, especially from the audience
perspective, Godlovitch's distinction between the two is analytically valuable. Transporting Godlovitch's analysis from the musical context into the
present one, I would argue that the robots in *Abacus* possess technical skills
since their actions cause the effects that constitute the content of the piece.
(I realize, of course, that Shutov, the artist who created and programmed

the robots, is the root cause of their actions. Nevertheless, the robots themselves are the proximate cause—through their movements, they create the effects the audience sees.) Using a musical analogy, it might be tempting to argue that Shutov is the performer and the robots are his instruments. The problem here is that since Shutov is not present to play these "instruments," it is not his technically skilled physical manipulation of them that is the immediate cause of the piece's effects. In terms of the musical analogy, Shutov is more akin to a composer who depends on the technical skills of musicians to make his piece available to an audience.[8]

Although I insist that robots can possess technical performance skills, I will not claim that robots can possess interpretive skills. This, it seems to me, is the crucial distinction between robotic performers and human performers: although robots are capable of executing technical assignments, they lack consciousness, intelligence, and emotions—all the ingredients that presumably contribute to the development of interpretive skills. It is for this reason, more than because of technical limitations, that there is currently no machine capable of presenting a performance of the *Kreutzer Sonata, Hamlet,* or *Swan Lake* that would pass muster with the relevant audiences. And there probably will never be one.[9]

If machine performers are limited to a repertoire that requires only technical skill and not interpretive skill, that may be less of a limitation than it seems. Although the definitions of performance arising from the context of the traditional performing arts generally entail notions of interpretation and expression that exclude machines from being considered performers, the history of each of the performing arts yields examples in which human performers have been called upon to exercise their technical skills but not their interpretive skills. (I shall refer to this kind of activity as "technical performance.") In principle, such pieces could be performed either by human beings who are not using their potential interpretive skills or by machines that simply lack such skills but possess the requisite technical abilities. W.B. Worthen has analyzed the use of "modernist puppets and automata, and the more widespread machining of live performers in twentieth-century theatre,"[10] tracing the history of that impulse from Gordon Craig, the Italian futurists, and Vsevolod Meyerhold through to Antonin Artaud, Samuel Beckett, and Robert Wilson. The Tiller Girls dance troupes, founded in the 1890s by Manchester businessman John Tiller, who brought Taylorist methods of mass-production into popular entertainment, are an example of technical performance from the realm of popular entertainment rather than avant-garde art.

Something equivalent to Taylor's scientific selection, based on mea-surement, was involved in [Tiller's] choice of personnel. The four chil-dren who were to feature in the first showpiece were to be as near iden-tical as possible in height and build. In order to emphasize the idea of multiple copies, he gave them all identical dolls and choreographed a geometrical pattern of synchronized movements, in which they were drilled from morning until late at night.[11]

Eventually, multiple troupes of Tiller's interchangeable performers exe-cuting standardized choreography toured the world.

It is not difficult to find examples of performance in which human per-formers are employed primarily for their technical skills and asked to cede a substantial part of their agency to someone else without referring either to the modernist avant-garde or such distinctive phenomena as the Tiller Girls. The orchestral musician, as described by musicologist Christopher Small, is such a case:

The musical skills that are required of a professional orchestra musician are without question of a high order: in a good orchestra substantial mistakes in the notes are rare and breakdowns almost unknown. At the same time those skills are very specialized and fall within a limited range, consisting of technical dexterity, the ability to sight-read and to respond rapidly to the notations and to the conductor's gestures, as well as those of attuning one's playing to the ensemble. . . . Even longer-term musical thinking is left to the conductor. I remember my aston-ishment at being told by a respected orchestral double-bass player that when he played a concert he read his part measure by measure and often could not remember the measure he had just played.[12]

I have quoted this passage at length to emphasize that Small clearly describes symphonic musicians' performance skills as *technical* (dexterity, sight-reading, rapid response, coordination) rather than interpretive in nature. (If one thinks of interpretation as a hermeneutic procedure that involves relating parts of an object to the whole, then the bassist Small describes cannot be engaged in interpretation since he performs each mea-sure with no awareness of the previous measure or the next one.) As Small indicates, the meaning and expressiveness of the piece are left to the com-poser and the conductor; the musicians' task consists solely of producing the required sounds. Orchestral section players are similar to Tiller Girls in that they are asked only to execute someone else's interpretation of the musical text.[13]

Other conventional cases come still closer to the Tiller Girls than the symphonic musician because they include an invariant repertoire as well as the demand that the performers exercise only one set of skills. Classical musicians, whether soloists or section members, are not usually called upon to play the same music night after night, or even season after season, but the players in Broadway pit orchestras and Las Vegas show bands frequently are. Again, the emphasis is on technical skills—musical directors and conductors control the interpretations of the scores; the musicians' job is to replicate their instructions as exactly as possible at each and every performance. Like Tiller Girls, symphonic, pit orchestra, and show band players are asked primarily to use their technical skills to make someone else's aesthetic choices apprehensible to an audience.[14]

It is interesting in this context that Godlovitch describes performance skill, in part, as "the ability to produce and re-produce certain results on call."[15] Since a performer who does something only once and cannot repeat it is not of much value in the traditional performing arts—or in most realms of human endeavor—the ability to "duplicate a result" is a measure of skill. We ask of human performers the same reliability that we demand from machines and measure their skill in those terms. In that functional sense, the musicians I have been discussing are not very different from Shutov's robots, yet we would not normally refuse to call them performers.[16]

Even though technical performance is the bread and butter of professional performers in many categories, including actors who perform in long-running plays and the musicians I have been discussing, the fact that much of the actual performing in conventional, Western genres is highly routine and "machined" is often overlooked in favor of the individualistic, interpretive aspects of performance. "Perhaps," as Goodall suggests, "the performer and the machine have some strange affinity that draws out cultural anxieties about becoming automatic."[17] Godlovitch's description of how we define skill in performance may provide the key to that "strange affinity"—by equating performance skill with the ability to reproduce results reliably, we implicitly define performance skill in machinic terms. The fact that we also habitually emphasize the interpretive over the technical in performance may be a defense mechanism, a way of not having to confront the anxiety-producing possibility that because the very concepts of "performance" and "performer" often entail the ability to reproduce the same effects on demand, they implicitly blur the distinctions between human beings and machines.[18]

Thus far, I have discussed *Abacus* in relation to the traditional performing arts in order to examine the implications of identifying robots as performers. But since *Abacus* plainly does not belong to any of the traditional performing arts (that is, it is not a work of theater, dance, music, or even puppetry) there is no reason to continue discussing it in that context. The context of performance art, a constellation of performance genres pioneered largely by visual artists rather than performing artists, seems the appropriate one in which to consider a work that was presented as a sculptural installation in a major, international venue devoted to visual art, yet may also be a performance. In the aesthetic context of performance art, the definitional picture is quite different than in the traditional performing arts. Whereas the traditional performing arts emphasize interpretation and expressiveness as central characteristics of performance (even though that emphasis overlooks the realities of many performers' lives, as I've suggested) performance art can involve a multiplicity of types of performance ranging from those found in conventional music, theater, and dance to others in which expression and interpretation are much less important. Technical performance is a noteworthy theme in the ongoing history of performance art as its practitioners seek to distinguish it from theater and the other performing arts.

Writing about one of the earliest genres of American performance art, the Happenings of the late 1950s and early 1960s, performance theorist Michael Kirby coined the term "nonmatrixed performing" to describe a kind of performing he considered specific to Happenings and to distinguish it from acting. Essentially, nonmatrixed performing is a task-based, nonrepresentational genre of technical performance. The matrices to which Kirby refers are the contexts of fictional time, place, and character that frame conventional acting. In nonmatrixed performing, the performer does not represent anything other than herself, doing whatever she's doing, wherever, whenever, and in whatever situation she's doing it.[19] This performer is not called upon to interpret a role or be expressive in the ways that actors are: "he is not expected either to project the subrational and unconscious elements in the character he is playing or to inflect and color the ideas implicit in his words and actions."[20] The only thing asked of the nonmatrixed performer is "the execution of a generally simple and undemanding act" such as sweeping the stage.

In keeping with the idea that the Happening is a form of visual art,

Kirby suggests that the performer is used in Happenings primarily as an element in a visual composition that unfolds in time and space. The performer is asked to surrender his own agency to that of the artist who created the Happening: he "does not work to create anything. The creation was done by the artist when he formulated the idea of the action. The performer merely embodies and makes concrete the idea." In addition to stating that the nonmatrixed performer offers no interpretation of the act she performs, Kirby clearly describes the necessary skills as technical ones: "Nonmatrixed performing does not eliminate the factor of ability, however. Although the walking section of *Autobodys* [a Happening by pop artist Claes Oldenburg], for example, could be performed by almost anyone, the prone hopping of *The American Moon* [by Robert Whitman] would be difficult or impossible for many people to do well." Kirby also emphasizes the technical in his equation of the performer in Happenings with theatrical technologies: "the performer frequently is treated in the same fashion as a prop or a stage effect."[21]

Because nonmatrixed performing consists of the more or less mechanical execution of tasks designated by someone other than the performer and does not call upon the performer to interpret a text or be self-expressive, it models a kind of technical performance in which both human beings and machines can engage. Although the figures in *Abacus* are representational in that they depict human figures, those figures are not matrixed: they do not represent specific characters in a particular fictional time or place apart from the venue in which they are shown. Rather, they are nonspecific, black-clad bodies. Because it is not necessary that they actually pray (whatever that may mean), only that they appear to do so, their actions also may be treated as nonmatrixed and task-based. Human performers could produce the same effects as the robots simply by carrying out the artist's instructions—the piece does not require that they enact characters who are praying or that they actually pray themselves, only that they move in a certain way.

Two other pieces on exhibit at the Venice Biennale provide further examples. Max Dean and Raffaello D'Andrea's *The Table: Childhood (1984–2001)* is described by one of its creators as "a fully autonomous robotic table" capable of movement through a confined gallery space.[22] I will paraphrase the action for which it is programmed from the catalog and render it as an instruction: "Select a viewer and attempt a relationship with that person." The robotic table does this by following a chosen person through the space and performing movements that are meant to be ingratiating. Because a successful execution of the action that underlies *The Table* does not depend on factors like which spectator is selected and followed, exactly how the spectator reacts, and so on, the choices the table makes exemplify the kind of noninterpretive decision that can be taken either by a human being or a machine.

I am not saying, of course, that a hypothetical human performance of this piece would be similar to the performance of the robotic table, only that both robots and human beings are capable of giving performances that reflect the underlying programming. Expressed as a simple verbal instruction, this programming sounds very much like the score for a Fluxus performance, for instance, or a performance by Vito Acconci.[23]

The Table is a particularly interesting case because the performer, whether machine or human, is called upon to make certain choices—the exact shape of each iteration of the piece depends on which person the performer chooses to follow, that person's reaction to being courted, and so on. In this respect, the robotic table contributes much more to defining the performance than Shutov's praying figures. The case against seeing the table as a simple playback device is therefore even stronger than that for *Abacus*—not only is there no originary performance that the table's actions re-create, but each iteration of the table's performance is different.[24] The question this piece prompts in relation to my analysis here is this: Do the decisions the table makes transcend technical performance to become interpretive? To suggest that they do would be to impute interpretive skill—and therefore intelligence—to the machine; I shall argue that even though these choices determine what happens in a given performance of the piece, they are not interpretive choices.

Kirby points out that certain choices are left open to nonmatrixed performers in Happenings, but he describes these choices as insignificant: "If the action is to sweep, it does not matter whether the performer begins over there and sweeps around here or begins here and works over there. Variations and differences simply do not matter—within, of course, the limits of the particular action and omitting additional action."[25] He emphasizes the triviality of the performer's choices, even going so far as to say that because the scenarios for Happenings determine less of what happens in the performance than theatrical playscripts, "the differences in detail are greater between two successive performances of a Happening than between two successive performances of a traditional play, but, again, these variations are not significant." Despite Kirby's insistence on this point, he does not explain what he means, and his claim seems counterintuitive. Inasmuch as the performer's choices determine what the audience experiences in any given iteration of the piece, they certainly are aesthetically significant. Kirby does not deny this; he actually implies it when he allows that some performances of Happenings are of higher quality than others.[26] What Kirby seems to mean is that the decisions left open to the nonmatrixed performer yield variations that are insignificant because they fall within the range of action designated by the artist who constructed the Happening. As long as that is the case, the performer cedes agency to the artist and functions only to concretize the artist's intentions, not to interpret the piece. If a performer in a Happening were required by the artist to hammer a nail, certain decisions might be left open to the performer: what kind and size of hammer and nail to use, what position to assume while hammering, how forcefully to hammer, and so on. It is beyond doubt that the particular choices made would have a major impact on the audience's experience. Nevertheless, these are merely the decisions the performer needs to make in order to carry out the action at all, the same decisions needed to hammer a nail in "real" life—they do not constitute an interpretation of the action comparable to an actor's interpretation of a role or a musician's interpretation of a piece. To return to the musical analogy for a moment, the decisions left open to performers in Happenings are comparable to an instrumentalist's technical choice of fingering to play a particular note. Different fingerings produce different visual effects for the attentive spectator, but do not amount to interpretive decisions.

The kind of activity required of a human performer of *The Table* would be highly comparable to Kirby's nonmatrixed performance. The robotic table is programmed with a repertoire of movements from which it selects in response to input from the audience. Since it lacks consciousness, its choices are not interpretive, but functional. A human performer of this piece could be called upon to make decisions within a specified range, in the manner of Kirby's nonmatrixed performer. The human performer would be given a repertoire of movements analogous to those for which the table itself is programmed (categorized, as they are for the table, as attempts to get attention, salutations, pursuing and fleeing movements, etc.[27]) and told that she could use any or all of them in response to appropriate viewer behaviors but could not introduce her own movements. The performer would also be instructed not "to inflect and color the ideas implicit in his words and actions," to quote Kirby once again. Just as the table cannot leave the gallery space even if the object of its attention does, so too could a human performer be told not to do so. In such a case, even though the performer would make choices on the fly during the performance, the range of possible choices would be circumscribed in advance by the creator of the piece and therefore reflect the creator's interpretation of the situation, not the performer's. An audience might be inclined to view a human performer's act of ingratiating him- or herself to spectators and pursuing them as implying that the performer is doing more than just following instructions, but audiences are always free to infer whatever meanings they wish from the performances they see. Those meanings need have no direct relationship to the underlying causes of the performed images the audience interprets.[28]

Whereas *The Table,* performed at the Biennale by a robot, could be performed by a human being, Nedko Solakov's *A Life (Black & White)* (1999–2001), performed by human beings, could just as readily be undertaken by machines. The catalog description reads "Black and white paint; 2 workers/painters constantly repainting in black and white the space walls for the entire duration of the exhibition, day after day (following each other)." (One painter paints the walls black; the other follows and paints the same walls white, and so on.) Because all three of these pieces are based in simple, nonmatrixed actions that can be executed effectively either by machines or human beings and because their impact does not depend on decisions made by the performers (as Kirby indicates, the performers' actions are only concretizations of the artist's choices even when the performer is allowed some latitude in the selecting specifics), it is not necessary that the actions be carried out by human beings in order that the pieces be considered performances. Whether a person or a robot undertakes the actions, these events are recognizable as performances belonging to the tradition of performance art.

Having argued that the events discussed here are characterized by nonmatrixed performing, a type of performance that can be undertaken by both human beings and machines, and that it doesn't matter to their constitution as performances within the tradition of performance art which type of performer is involved, I hasten to add that it does make a substantial difference to the interpretation of the pieces. Far from suggesting that human agency makes such pieces richer in meaning, I propose that machine performance, acknowledged as such, provides the deeper object of interpretation. The reason is simple: because machines generally can be viewed as surrogates for human beings or metaphors for human concerns (indeed, what else could they be?), a piece performed by a machine usually can be interpreted in the same way as the same piece would be if performed by a human being. (This is true even for a performance featuring an apparently nonanthropomorphic machine such as The Table, which is subtitled "Childhood" because its creators see the object as reenacting the human developmental process.) The question of what it means to have the actions that define the piece performed by a machine provides for a further, enriched level of interpretation. In the Biennale catalog essay on *Abacus,* for example, Sergei Khripun reads Shutov's piece as a conciliatory gesture "bringing alienated and even confronting confessions together," while noting at the same time that religious belief both unites and divides people—"the paradox that humankind has faced throughout its history."[29] It is interesting that this humanistic interpretation makes no reference to the fact that the piece is actually performed by machines; Khripun treats the robots as transparent representations of human beings whose own ontological status and materiality are irrelevant. I am not disputing Khripun's interpretation; I am suggesting that acknowledging that machines perform the piece would add another layer of interpretation by inviting the critic to consider what it means to have machines serve as surrogates for human beings at prayer. What does the metaphoric use of machines signify in this particular context?[30]

In his catalog essay on Solakov's *Life (Black and White),* Daniel Kurjakovic suggests that the piece is "an allegory of the abysmal, Sisyphus-like futility of human action."[31] This interpretation is certainly available when human painters perform the piece, but I would argue that it is equally available if the piece were to be performed by robotic painters. The futility of the robots' actions would almost inevitably be seen as metaphoric for human existence. Addressing the further question of what it means to deploy robots in the senseless task of continually repainting walls would open up other areas of interpretation that might enhance or expand this reading. Is it just as ironic, in an existentialist sense, for a human being to program a robot to undertake futile and meaningless work as it is to assign that work to other human beings? Or does the use of a robot displace the futility of existence onto an entity that does not suffer from experiencing it, thus suggesting a path of liberation for human beings through a somewhat perverse use of technology? There are many possibilities for interpretation that arise from defining such a piece as a performance undertaken by machines and addressing directly both the ways in which the machines can be seen as metaphoric humans and the implications of using a machine in the particular context of the piece.

NOTES

A much shorter version of this essay was commissioned by *Art Papers* and appeared in volume 26, no. 1 (January–February 2002) under the title "Humanoid Boogie: Robotic Performances at the Venice Biennial." The epigraph to this chapter is drawn from lyrics from a song by Neil Innes as reproduced on the sleeve of The Bonzo Dog Band, *Urban Spaceman,* Imperial LP 12432 (1968).

1. Stan Godlovitch, *Musical Performance: A Philosophical Study* (London: Routledge, 1998), 128.

2. Auslander, "Live from Cyberspace, or I was sitting at my computer this guy appeared he thought I was a bot," *Performing Arts Journal 24,* no. 1:21. Strictly speaking, this statement should be limited to the visual aspect of *Abacus.* Since the sound of the prayers emanates from a conventional sound recording, the audio portion of *Abacus* functions entirely in the way Godlovitch describes and is exempted from the claims I make in this section.

3. Steve Tillis, "The Art of Puppetry in the Age of Media Production," *TDR* 43, no. 3 (1999): 192–93.

4. Jane Goodall, "Transferred Agencies: Performance and the Fear of Automatism," *Theatre Journal* 49, no. 4 (1997): 442.

5. David Z. Saltz's analysis of interactive computer art is a case in point, given that he defines performativity as a characteristic of "all art forms in which live human behavior constitutes the aesthetic object" ("The Art of Interaction: Interactivity, Performativity, and Computers," *Journal of Aesthetics and Art Criticism* 55, no. 2 [1997]: 119). Since I am arguing here that robotic figures whose behavior is not live, and who certainly are not human, can be seen as performative, I clearly disagree with that definition. Later in the essay, Saltz does imply that a computer can function as a performer (124), but says in a footnote that in such cases, the computer "enters into the dramatic scene with the [human] performers as an agent in its own right" (127 n. 21). Saltz's distinction between human performers and computer agents here echoes his earlier claim that performativity requires the presence of human performers. I am perfectly happy to use human behavior as the standard against which to define performance and performativity, but I am arguing here for seeing at least some kinds of performance as possible for both humans and machines.

6. Glossing Diderot and Meyerhold, Joseph Roach similarly breaks down theatrical acting into two internal processes that he calls habit and consciousness: "Habitualization of corporeal motion enables the actor to gain conscious control of the entire process and all its effects. Paradoxically, the feeling of spontaneity is achieved by the rigorous transformation of action and gesture into unconscious automatisms. The key here is the active retention of the alert consciousness—the administrative ghost in the reflex machine—as the sovereign creative executor" ("The Future that Worked," *Theater* 8, no. 2 [1998]: 24).

7. Godlovitch, *Musical Performance,* 54.

8. As Godlovitch (ibid., 102) points out, a number of modern composers have fantasized about technologies that would enable them to do without performers and thus allow them not to have to deal with other people's interpretations of their work. W. B. Worthen, "Of Actors and Automata: Hieroglyphics of Modernism," *Journal of*

Dramatic Theory and Criticism 9, no. 1 (1994): 3–19, discusses a parallel desire on the part of modernist theater directors.

9. To address the question of whether there will ever be a machine possessed of interpretive skills would be to venture into the artificial intelligence debate, an issue that lies outside the scope of my discussion here. I am assuming throughout this essay that the machines I discuss do not possess anything that could meaningfully be called intelligence.

10. Worthen, "Of Actors and Automata," 7–8.

11. Goodall, "Transferred Agencies," 450.

12. Christopher Small, *Musicking: The Meanings of Performing and Listening* (Hanover, N.H.: Wesleyan University Press, 1998), 69–70.

13. This analysis leads me to disagree with Noël Carroll, who seeks to distinguish live theatrical performances from film screenings by arguing that "it takes artistry and imagination to embody an interpretation, whereas film performances require nothing more than technical competence" (*A Philosophy of Mass Art* [Oxford: Oxford University Press, 1998] 213–14). Although I find Carroll's description of performers as embodying interpretations felicitous, my point here is that even in the traditional performing arts, such embodiment results more frequently than we are wont to admit from the exercise of technical competence, not artistry and imagination. I'm also emphasizing the idea that there are many occasions on which performers on stage do not engage in acts of interpretation but in technical performances embodying existing interpretations.

14. Most pop and rock musicians are also expected to present the same performances of the same songs night after night, perhaps for the entire length of their careers (think especially of those who work the oldies concert circuits). They are more like classical soloists than like pit band players in the sense that the interpretations they repeat are likely to be their own. But unlike classical soloists, most pop and rock musicians are not rewarded for offering fresh interpretations of their repertoire.

15. Godlovitch, *Musical Performance*, 18.

16. A possible objection to my argument is that since machines are designed and programmed by human beings, human agency always lurks behind machinic agency. Herbert Blau, "The Human Nature of the Bot," *Performing Arts Journal* 24, no. 1 (2002): 22–24, makes this point in response to Auslander, "Live from Cyberspace, or I was sitting at my computer this guy appeared he thought I was a bot," *Performing Arts Journal* 24, no. 1 (2002): 16–21. This situation is not reversible, at least not until a machine builds a human being! I am suggesting here, however, that there are performance situations in which human performers are "programmed" by other human beings such that the former's agency in the performance is not significantly greater than that of a machine.

17. Goodall, "Transferred Agencies," 442. This cultural anxiety may be compounded by the fact that audiences cannot deduce the inner life of performers from the external manifestations of their performances. As Godlovitch points out, "We certainly have no working theory of the inner mental side of artistic performance. . . . Performers at work may have their minds on any manner of things. In the spirit of professional entertainment, someone performing sensitively may simultaneously be bored to distraction." (*Musical Performance*, 127). There may be a lingering suspicion

that performance is always potentially deceptive, that what we take to be an inspired performance may actually be a rote, mechanical one.

18. Many theories of performance suggest that repetition is one of the characteristics that distinguishes it from other behaviors. Richard Schechner's definition of performance as "restored behavior" is a well-known example (*Between Theater and Anthropology* [Philadelphia: University of Pennsylvania Press, 1985], 35–116). In Schechner's account, however, performances need not re-create earlier behaviors exactly; his concept entails the possibility, even the probability, of repetition with difference when behaviors are restored as performances. I am suggesting here that many, but certainly not all, kinds of performance involve exact replication of behavior rather than repetition with difference. Those kinds of performance trouble the distinction between the human and the mechanical.

19. Michael Kirby, *Happenings* (New York: E. P. Dutton, 1965), is careful not to claim that all the performing in Happenings was nonmatrixed; he notes that character, interpretation, and "traditional acting ability" were all employed in some Happenings, sometimes alongside nonmatrixed performing (16).

20. Ibid., 14–16.

21. Ibid., 17, 19.

22. Max Dean, "The Table: Childhood, 1984–2001," in La Biennale di Venezia Esposizione Internazionale D'Arte, English version, ed. Harald Szeeman et al. (Venice: Electa, 2001), 1:82.

23. See Auslander, "Vito Acconci and the Politics of the Body in Postmodern Performance," in *From Acting to Performance: Essays in Modernism and Postmodernism* (London: Routledge, 1997), 89–97, and "Fluxus Art-Amusement: The Music of the Future?" in *Contours of the Theatrical Avant-Garde,* ed. James Harding (Ann Arbor: University of Michigan Press, 2000), 110–29.

24. Although the issue of liveness (Auslander, *Liveness: Performance in a Mediatized Culture* [London: Routledge, 1999]) is not central to my discussion here, I would argue that the table is not only a performer but also a live performer because it responds to its environment and makes real-time decisions. It is live in a way that the *Abacus* robots, for instance, are not. See Auslander, "Live from Cyberspace," where I argue that chatterbots, software robots that engage in conversation, should be seen as live performers.

25. Kirby, *Happenings,* 17. Kirby indicates that nonmatrixed performing frequently includes an element of indeterminacy, which he distinguishes from improvisation. For Kirby, improvisation demands that the performer make interpretive decisions on the fly, decisions that shape the performance in significant ways. Indeterminacy, by contrast, means that although the artist leaves certain aspects of the performance open-ended, the performer's decisions are neither interpretive nor significant—any decision the performer makes within the parameters established by the artist will yield an iteration of the piece that reflects the artist's intentions rather than the performer's own interpretation of those intentions.

26. Ibid., 19.

27. See Dean, "The Table," 82.

28. For example, Kirby notes in a different essay ("On Acting and Not-Acting," in *The Art of Performance: A Critical Anthology,* ed. Gregory Battcock and Robert Nickas

[New York: E. P. Dutton, 1984], 101) that the audience will perceive a group of people playing cards onstage during a theatrical performance as actors pretending to play cards in order to portray characters who are playing cards even if they make no effort at characterization and really are simply playing cards.

29. Sergei Khripun, "Sergei Shutov," in Szeeman et al., *Biennale,* 2:120.

30. The fact that the machines do not tire but can engage in perpetual prayer in a way that human beings cannot (machines are the ultimate "endurance artists") is a dimension of the piece that might be interesting to consider in this connection.

31. Daniel Kurjakovic, "A Life (Black & White): Nedko Solakov's Restrained Allegory," in Szeeman et al., *Biennale,* 1:104.

FIVE

Philosophy and Drama

Performance, Interpretation, and Intentionality

Noël Carroll

The Philosophy of Theater

The purpose of this article is to probe one of the central questions of the philosophy of theater, namely, "What is drama?" However, before broaching the issue of the nature of drama, there is a more basic question: how are we to understand the very notion of a philosophy of theater? For surely one's conception of the philosophy of theater will influence one's approach to answering the query, "What is drama?" So let me begin by saying briefly where I am coming from philosophically before we plunge into the more substantive topic of the nature of drama.

The brand of philosophy to be mobilized in this essay is often referred to as analytic philosophy. So a first step in clarifying what is involved in this sort of philosophy is to say what it is that analytic philosophers analyze. If one is a philosopher of theater, upon what aspects of theater does one focus?

Notice that the label—the philosophy of theater—is reminiscent structurally of the philosophies of so much else. It is the philosophy *of* something. What fills in the blank in the "philosophy of ——?" Usually the name of some practice—like the philosophy of law. Often these are practices of inquiry—for example, the philosophy of science or of mathematics or of history. But there may also be a philosophy of some practical activity or set of activities—like the philosophy of sport. The philosophy of theater is this sort of activity or practice—primarily a matter of making and doing, rather than one of pure inquiry.

Practices, moreover, have a conceptual dimension. That is, practices are organized by certain deep concepts that make the practice possible or, to put it differently, that constitute the practice as the practice it is. For instance, law is a practice. In order to conduct legal activities a whole set of often interrelated concepts are presupposed, including guilt, personhood, intentionality, and, of course, the very idea of law itself. The analytic philosophy of law takes as its fundamental task the analysis of the concepts that make a practice like the law possible.[1] A philosopher of law asks what constitutes legal personhood, guilt, *mens rea,* and, most importantly, what makes something a law. Is something a law in virtue of its relation to some transcendent morality, sometimes called natural law, or is it merely that which has been promulgated by a duly appointed body of legislators applying recognized procedures in the right way?

Just as the philosophy of law attempts to clarify the nature of the concepts that make the practice of law possible, similarly the philosophy of theater interrogates or analyzes the founding concepts of the art of theater. One such concept is that of drama. In this essay, I attempt to elucidate the notion of drama. One discovery about the concept of drama that I will attempt to defend is that it involves not one concept, but at least two. That is, the concept *drama* can apply to either a play text or play-plan, on the one hand, or to a play performance, on the other hand. I will then go on to try to illuminate the distinction between these two applications of *drama.* One conclusion that I will draw is that drama-as-performance differs in profound ontological respects from mass mediatized performances. This finding is at odds with the position recently and ably defended by Philip Auslander.[2] So the final section of this essay will address the kinds of objections Auslander raises to the type of analysis advanced of drama-as-performance.

What Is Drama?

One of the fundamental concepts that organizes the practice of theater is *drama.* According to Aristotle, the concept of drama was derived from a Greek word for "doing" or "acting."[3] Aristotle used this word to refer to the representation of action. But, of course, the action that concerned Aristotle could be represented in two ways: by means of the play text, as composed by a Sophocles, or by means of a performance of the play text by some ancient Athenian troupe or a contemporary one. This duality in the notion of drama is mirrored in our own usage. For example, if we want to find the play scripts in the bookstore, we will have to go to the drama section. On the other hand, if we want to take courses in acting, directing, stage designing, or lighting for the theater, we will enroll in what is often called the Drama Department or the Department of Dramatic Arts. Moreover, such departments may or may not have courses in playwriting, though they will always have courses in acting, reflecting the fact that their emphasis is on the performance of plays, rather than their composition.[4]

Though *drama* is one word, for the purposes of the philosophy of the art of theater, that one word applies to two distinguishable art forms: the art of composing play texts (or, more broadly, performance plans) and the art of performing them. Drama, in this respect, is a dual-tracked or two-tiered art form.[5] This duality, of course, is openly acknowledged by theater academics, who sort themselves under the headings of "stage" and "page." On the one hand, as typically practiced in contemporary Western theater, drama is a literary art; a drama is a verbal construction that can be appreciated and evaluated by being read, just as one might read a novel. On the other hand, drama is also a performing art; it belongs to the same family as music and dance, and, qua performing art, it can only be appreciated and evaluated through enactment.

Of course, the preceding distinction needs to be immediately amended and qualified somewhat. The way in which it has been stated is too parochial, tied, as it is, to contemporary Western practice. Not everything we may be disposed to call drama in the first sense need be associated with a literary or written text, even if that has become the standard case nowadays. The script, so to speak, of a performance may live in memory of the performers—who may be a troupe of actors or the members of some subculture enacting a ritual whose instructions have been passed down orally through the ages. Though we think first of a written text in this context, it may be more fruitful to think of this dimension of drama as a play plan or performance plan. The play or performance plan can be discussed and evaluated in its own right, that is, apart from its performance. This is perhaps most obvious in the case of the text of the well-made play. But an untranscribed harvest ceremony also has a performance plan, albeit unwritten, that can be analyzed and appreciated independently of its performance, just as a traditional folk dance has a design that can be scrutinized in isolation from any particular performance of it. Improvised theater, as well, also usually has a performance plan broadly construed—a set of scenarios, strategies, gambits, or riffs that the performers call upon and then elaborate on the spot.

The first step in developing a philosophical analysis of the notion of the art of drama, then, is to note that there are two concepts here. We might call them drama as composition and drama as performance. In order to elucidate the concept of drama as composition, let us use the example of the well-made play, and then go on to add the necessary qualifications for dramas that do not possess written texts.

The play as a literary work—our leading example of drama as composition—is created by a playwright (or playwrights) who is (are) the author(s). This artist or collaborative group of artists is a *creator;* the creator brings the play text or performance plan into existence, though in some cases we may not know the name or names of these creators. In contrast, there are another group of artistic functions involved in making the performance plan manifest. In contemporary theater, these roles include the actors, directors, designers, music directors, and so on, who literally embody the performance plan. Whereas the artist with respect to drama as composition is a creator, the artists with respect to drama as performance are *executors.* To simplify matters drastically: Edward Albee created *Who's Afraid of Virginia Woolf;* Uta Hagen, among others, *executed* it. The different kinds of artists here signal different arts of drama: the art of composition or creation, and the art of performance or execution.

Needless to say, the same person could be both the creator of a play, its author, and one of its executors—its director or a player, for instance. Shakespeare, in point of fact, was both an author-creator and a player-executor with respect to his artworks. However, the roles of creator and executor are nevertheless categorically distinguishable. As the choreographer is to the dancer troupe, and the composer is to the conductor-cum-orchestra, so normally the author of the play text is to the director, actors, designers, and so forth. In these cases there are two discriminable arts: the art of composition and the art of performance. The creation of the author—the play text—is fixed by her intentions. The art of the performance is variable. Just as we expect different violinists to bring out different qualities in a musical score, so we expect actors and directors to disclose different aspects of the relevant composition, at least in contemporary Western theater. We prize texts for the singularity of their design, but performances are valued for their variability and diversity.[6]

In this regard, we are really making a virtue out of necessity. No text, no performance plan, no matter how elaborate, is determinate with respect to every feature relevant to its manifestation or implementation in performance. There are always some questions unanswered by the text or performance plan about matters like how a character looks, how she speaks, how the performance space is shaped, what motivates a line reading, what gesture goes with it, and on and on. Different performances make different choices concerning these questions. In order to produce a performance, the executors must go beyond what is given in the play text or performance plan.

We evaluate performances in contemporary theater in virtue of the choices they make in this respect, noting their insight, profundity, and inventiveness—often comparing and contrasting the performance at hand with other variations on the same play text or performance plan. Though there are significant debates about the latitude or degree of compliance performers should respect in filling in the unavoidable indeterminacies of the text, no one can deny that all performances involve interpretations of play texts or play plans in the sense that dramatic performances must go beyond what is given in the text or play plan.[7] That is, there is always a latitude of *play*—some scope for invention in putting flesh on a performance plan. A performance plan needs to be filled out by performances; that is why performances are often called interpretations: they are interpretations of performance plans, or, in the typical case nowadays, they are interpretations of play texts.

As literary art, play texts (dramas-as-compositions) are types from which copies are derived. Moreover, your copy of *Middlemarch* and my copy are both tokens of the type created by George Eliot. These tokens are material objects that grant us access to the abstract type, the artwork *Middlemarch*. If my copy of *Middlemarch* is destroyed by fire, the novel by George Eliot nevertheless continues to exist. For it is an abstract object, a type, and it cannot be burned. Moreover, this type is complete. Save the discovery of a hidden manuscript by George Eliot that reveals her intentions on the matter, there are no new words to be added to *Middlemarch*.

It is true that the reader will have to presuppose certain mandated details that are not stated on the page—such as that Casaubon has a four-chambered heart. But otherwise the book is closed; the artwork is fixed. Likewise, a drama as a literary work—*The Master Builder*, for example—is fixed as the art type it is for all time in terms of the relevant aesthetic elements that constitute it as determined by the intentions of its author, Ibsen.

However, dramatic performances are variable. This is because when viewed from the perspective of drama as a performing art, play texts are regarded simply as recipes—semiporous formulas to be filled in by executors in the process of producing performance artworks—rather than as fixed artworks in their own right. They are blueprints rather than finished buildings, figuratively speaking. That is, they are sets of instructions to be elaborated upon—embroidered even—and executed by actors, directors, and so on. Play texts specify the ingredients of the performance—such as lines of dialogue, characters, and perhaps some props—as well as the range of global emotional tones or flavors appropriate to the work. But just as a culinary recipe calls for the cook to interpret how much vinegar a "dash" is, so the executors of the play text must exercise judgment in arriving at, for example, the precise tempo of a performance. However, this does not allow the executors of the play text to do anything they wish with the text, just as the cook cannot legitimately "interpret" a "dash" of vinegar as an instruction to add a pint of cream.

Nevertheless, the play text as recipe permits a robust space for variations and inventions—for *play*—as do recipes in the culinary arts and scores in music, though, of course, within the bounds of a set of indeterminate instructions. (Where those boundaries lie, needless to say, is subject to much dispute; for example, should performances be constrained by an author's, such as Chekov's, original intentions, or by the hypothetical intentions that we infer someone like Chekov would have had were he alive today, or are the constraints proffered by the text even looser still?) In order to be incarnated as a performance, every play text requires interpretive activity on the parts of the executors who must extrapolate beyond what has been written or otherwise previously stipulated (as in the case of orally transmitted performance plans).

Some play texts—like Megan Terry's script for *Comings and Goings*—permit a generous scope for improvisation, while others may attempt to exercise more authorial control. But inasmuch as any performance plan will be, necessarily, riven with indeterminacies to be filled in by executors, every dramatic artwork qua performance will be an interpretation. Moreover, it is because the play text is always inevitably somewhat indeterminate, in the way of a culinary recipe, that it makes sense that we savor different performances in the way that we do different preparations by different chefs of the same sauce. Each variation brings out different aspects of the recipe-type.

Both the dramatic artwork as composition and the dramatic artwork as performance are types. However, the manner in which tokens of these two types are brought into existence is notably different. Where the dramatic artwork is a literary work, nowadays tokens of it typically come to us in the form of printed matter. Generally, these tokens are mass produced by some mechanical or electronic system of replication. Moreover, if they are hand-made—done by quill as one supposes Shakespeare's folios were composed—I suggest that the manuscripts were still mechanically produced in the sense that ideally they were rote transcriptions where the scribe's penmanship was artistically indifferent (if a scribe refigures such a play type imaginatively, perhaps by adding illustrations or illuminations, then the writing becomes a singular artwork in its own right and is not merely a token of the pertinent type).

Tokens of Shakespearean dramatic compositions are generated mechanically. Either by anonymous scriveners striving to achieve the status of carbon paper or, nowadays, by machine processes; once the type is set, token copies of it are stamped out mechanically (or electronically). At this point, the tokens are generated by a series of sheer physical processes. A token of a particular play by Shakespeare—my copy of it—is an object, brought into the world by a sequence of brute causal events.

However, a token of a play by Shakespeare from the perspective of drama as performance is a very different affair. Because of the duality of drama, plays have as tokens both objects and performances. Considered as a literary work, a token of *The Libation Bearers* is a graphic text of the same ontological order as my copy of *Middlemarch*. But considered from the perspective of drama as performance, a token of *Libation Bearers* is something else again. It is an event, rather than an object. Indeed, it is a specific kind of an event; it is a human action. The production of a token instance of *Libation Bearers* by way of performance requires intentionality. It is not a consequence of a process of physical causation. It involves mentation (where the mark of the mental, as Franz Brentano proposed, is intentionality).

The production of my copy of *Libation Bearers*—which grants me access to the dramatic artwork as composition that Aeschylus created—required a template (either hot type or an electronic file); this template itself is a mere physical entity or process that unlike the type, *Libation Bearers,* is spatially situated and can be destroyed physically. The production of a performance token of *Libation Bearers,* on the other hand, requires something above and beyond mere bodies in motion, causally interacting. As we have seen, it requires an interpretation given the indeterminacies of the play text. For, as we have already argued, the play type by Aeschylus—when viewed from the perspective of performance—is akin to a recipe that must be filled out by executors, including actors, directors, and the rest.

This interpretation, moreover, is a conception of the play type, and it is this conception of the production that governs the performances from night to night. These interpretations, furthermore, may be performed in different theaters, consider touring companies; and they may even be revived after a hiatus. Thus, these interpretations of the recipe are themselves types that then generate performance tokens. The relation of the play type to its performances is mediated by an interpretation, suggesting, then, that an interpretation is a type within a type. What gets us from the play type qua recipe to the token performance of it is an interpretation that is itself a type. On the other hand, what gets us from the dramatic artwork qua composition to a token instance (my copy of *Libation Bearers*) is a template that is a token.

The action of the template token in the production of the token instance of the literary art type *Libation Bearers* is starkly a matter of physical causation. The action of the interpretation type in the production of the token performance of *Libation Bearers* is quite different. Not only is it the case of a type rather than a token in action, but the type in question involves, ineliminably, mental or intentional components. Indeed, not only is the interpretation that governs the performance itself intentional; to enact that interpretation, to instantiate it tonight onstage requires thought—requires an interpretation of the interpretation relevant to the immediate circumstances of the live performance.

So far then, we have argued that drama is a two-tiered or double-decker art form. There is drama as composition and drama as performance. Drama as composition involves an author who creates an artwork—a play text or performance plan. Drama as performance involves executors—performers who make the performance plan qua recipe manifest by way of an interpretation (or an iterated series of interpretations). Token instances of dramatic artworks as compositions are material objects generated mechanically by templates; token instances of dramatic artworks as performances are events generated intentionally by interpretive acts. Moreover, we call an art a performing art just in case it exhibits this duality.

Two possible counterexamples to our claim about the duality of drama are plays created with no intention that they be performed (Seneca's tragedies, for example); and works of pure improvisation, that is, improvisations with no previous production plan. For my own part, I am very suspicious of the notion of utterly pure improvisations—ones engaged without any previous planning or entered into with altogether no background repertory of strategies or tested response patterns to certain types of situations or challenges. Even the improv comic, asked to enact a scene on the spot, pauses for a moment to think out a plan (and, I suspect, to rummage through past skits for pieces for the new one). Furthermore, though some plays may be written with no thought of performance, that does not entail that they literally cannot be performed. And finally, if my rejoinders to these counterexamples strike you as too ad hoc, it might also be noted in favor of the duality thesis that the concept as such of drama may still be dual even if there are some dramas that are only dramatic compositions and others that are only dramatic performances.

What is drama? Drama is a two-tiered art form, an art form comprised of two kinds of artworks: creations, on the one hand, and performances, on the other hand. Drama, moreover, is a paradigmatic performing art, where a performing art is one marked by precisely this sort of duality.[8]

Can Dramatic Performances Be Mediatized?

If the preceding discussion of drama as performance is correct, then it follows that there is a categorical distinction between dramatic performance and what may be called the mass-mediatized arts of film, television, and computer-generated imaging. In order to see why this is so, let us quickly review again the way in which a performance of a token of a mass-mediatized artwork, like a film, reaches its audience versus the way in which a performance token, like the enactment of a well-made play, reaches spectators.

In many important respects, the story about how the token instance of the mass-mediatized artwork reaches its audience repeats what we have already said about the way in which the token instance of the drama type as composition is transmitted to its readers. Just as my copy of *Baal* gives me access to the type created by Bertolt Brecht, so the token performance of *Finding Neverland* (its screening), in my neighborhood cineplex, gives me access to the film type *Finding Neverland.* If my copy of *Baal* were torn apart or if the showing of *Finding Neverland* was canceled midway due to a bomb threat, neither event would imperil the existence of the relevant art types. These mishaps would be a matter of the destruction of token instances of the artworks in question; the pertinent artworks, as types, would continue to exist.

Mass-mediatized artworks of the sort that immediately concern us—fictional narratives—are types in the sense that they can be incarnated by an indeterminately large number of tokens. Unlike paintings and sculptures, they support multiple instantiations of the same artwork. Identical tokens of the same mass-mediatized artwork can be consumed simultaneously by people in different locales. Among other things, this is what makes a mass-mediatized artwork so potentially lucrative. You can show it—like a soap opera—all over the world at the same time, thereby commanding immense audiences.

But drama is also a multiple instance artform. There can be many token performances of *Cats*—indeed of the same production of *Cats*—in different places and yet at the same time. There may, for example, be touring companies. And perhaps with enough touring companies, *Cats* could reach comparably sized audiences across as many different locales as *Finding Neverland* does. This would be extremely expensive, but not literally impossible.

So it looks like mass-mediatized artworks and some theater performances might be on a par. Both examples are type artworks and, in some cases, the type in question can be exhibited simultaneously at different reception sites. This is what the WPA Federal Theater project attempted with its production in 1936 of *It Can't Happen Here,* which, after a movie company dropped out, opened in eighteen cities at once. Does this suggest that mass-mediatized art and drama as performance are in the same boat ontologically? I contend that they are not, because there are subtle, but important, differences between the delivery of mass-mediatized artworks to their audiences versus the way in which a token of a work of dramatic art as performance makes its way from the type to the stage.

Contrast how you get from the type *Finding Neverland* to its token performance (the screening) in my multiplex tonight with a token performance of *Baal* at the university theater down the road in the same neighborhood at the same time. To produce a token instance—a performance/showing—of *Finding Neverland,* you need a template, for example, a film print, which itself is a token of the type *Finding Neverland.* Once the film projector is adjusted properly, you run the template, the print, on the mechanism. You flip on the switch and certain mechanical and electronic processes take over automatically, generating a token performance of *Finding Neverland.*

But this is not how you generate a token performance of *Baal* nor, for that matter, even a token performance by one of the touring companies of *Cats.* These live performances are not generated automatically from a template. Rather, the performers have access to a script and perhaps to a set of directorial instructions that, in turn, constitute a recipe or blueprint—

rather than a template—which the executors go on to interpret in order to bring a token instance of the play to life.

The live performance—whether of *Baal* or *Cats*—is the result of the executors's intentions, beliefs, and desires, and not the mere consequence of fully automatic mechanical, chemical, and/or electronic processes. Live performance tokens of plays like *Baal* and *Cats* (and of all those other recipes here unsung) are the result, first and foremost, of *mental processes*—interpretive acts; whereas token performances of *Finding Neverland* are not—once the projector starts humming—immediately a matter of a series of mental acts, but a matter of brute, scientifically law-governed, physical processes. What the projector operator believes about the fiction has no impact on the unfolding of the celluloid story world frame by frame.

What gives rise to tonight's 7:30 P.M. performance of *Finding Neverland* is a mechanical-electronic apparatus engaging a chemically fixed, predetermined template in accordance with certain technical procedures and natural laws. The process can be completely automated; it's mostly pure physics. But what gives rise to tonight's token performance of *Cats* are continuous processes of judgment about how to interpret the production recipe on the part of the actors, dancers, singers, lighting crews, and the like.

If you ask yourself why you are seeing three characters screen left in tonight's showing of *Finding Neverland,* the answer has to do with the physical structure of the template; the images and the positions of the three characters are chemically fixed in the template. What you see in *Finding Neverland* is counterfactually dependent upon the physical structure of the template. Had the physical structure of the template been different, that is, the image would have been different. If there had not been three characters imprinted on the template, you would not be seeing their image. Had the three characters—contrary to fact (or counterfactually)—been on the right side of the image instead of the left, you would be seeing them screen right.

On the other hand, when you see three characters on stage left in *Cats,* that is because the actors in question have interpreted the production recipe in such a way that they *believe* that they should be on stage left at that moment. What you see onstage, in other words, is counterfactually dependent upon the beliefs of the performers. Quite simply, if they did not believe that they should be on stage left, they wouldn't be there, and, for that very reason, you wouldn't see them there.

What you see onscreen then is counterfactually dependent upon the structure of the template as it is processed primarily through a series of sheerly physico-causal processes. What you see in a live performance of a play, however, is generated by the interpretative acts and beliefs of the performers. The token performance of *Finding Neverland* is generated through mindless physical procedures, whereas the live token of *Cats*, as a dramatic performance, is generated intentionally—it is proximately mediated, moment by moment, by the beliefs and judgments of performers striving to interpret the production recipe. Call this the difference between generation by intentional systems (systems of mediation operating through intentional or mental states) versus generation by physical systems (systems of mediation operating through exclusively physical states).

This is an important ontological distinction. Put into a crude slogan—one that admittedly requires further refinement—it is the difference between mental properties and physical properties. Since mass-mediatized artworks are type artworks that rely upon templates to produce token performances, mass-mediatized artworks differ categorically from dramatic performances that rely on intentional states—interpretative acts—in order to be made manifest. It is the role of intentional states in the generation of token dramatic performances that I believe disposes us to call these events live. For, were *Cats* performed by zombies, I do not think we would be comfortable with calling the performance live nor the troupe a living theater. For, though zombies are supposedly animate, they have no intentions of their own.

But, in any event, the performance of the mass-mediatized token is almost exclusively an affair of matter in motion, whereas the token dramatic performance is ineliminably an artifact of mind. Or, mediatized-mass art tokens are to tokens of dramatic performance as matter is to mind. Thus, a token dramatic performance as a work of art in its own right cannot be a mass-media artwork.

One reason for this is that the token performance of a mass-mediatized artwork is not itself an artwork. Recall: a token performance of *Finding Neverland* is brought about by putting the template—a reel of film—on the projection mechanism and operating the machine strictly according to established routines. On the other hand, a token performance of a dramatic performance is an artwork in its own right, just because it depends on the mindfulness of the performers.

A successful token performance of *Finding Neverland*—the projection of the film or the running of a videocassette or DVD—does not command aesthetic appreciation, since it is not an artwork. We do not applaud the projectionist as we do a pianist at the end of a successful performance. We may complain when the film burns up in the middle of the screening and may even demand our money back. But we regard this as a technical failure, not an artistic failure. If we regarded this as a matter of artistry, then we would expect people to cheer when the film does not burn, but they don't. For the happy film performance only depends on operating the apparatus as it was designed to be operated, and, since that involves no more than often quite minimal mechanical savvy, running the template through the machine is not held to be an aesthetic accomplishment. The projectionist is, in other words, not an artist of any sort, let alone a performing (or interpreting) artist.

On the other hand, the successful delivery of a token dramatic performance involves a token interpretation of an interpretation type, and, inasmuch as that depends on artistic understanding and judgment, it is a suitable object of aesthetic appreciation. This is why the token *performance* of a mass-mediatized artwork is not an appropriate object of artistic evaluation, whereas the token dramatic performance is. For it is the mentation of the executors that merits praise or blame, not merely matter in motion.

Perhaps another, more scandalous way of putting this point is to say that the pertinent mass-mediatized art forms—notably film and television—are not performing arts in terms of the framework developed in this chapter. This may sound incredibly bizarre, since many of the people who contribute to the making of a motion picture are what we usually think of as performing artists—actors, directors, lighting and sound engineers, set designers, costumers, choreographers, fight coaches, and so on. However, it is essential to note that whatever the interpretive activities and performances that these artists contribute to artwork are indissolubly integrated into the motion picture type as constitutent parts in a way that is determinately fixed forever at the inception of the final version of the type. The acting is not adjusted or reinterpreted given the exigencies of different theaters or audiences. Once the motion picture has been edited and put in the can for good, there is no opportunity left for intentionality; token performances of the type will be as alike as two quarters, though token performances of the dramatic type *Baal* can be very different, because they are different inerpretations.

With respect to mass-mediatized art forms, a fixed interpretation of the script comes to be built into the very token template. The template is then run mechanically. There is no further interpretation of the script involved.

In this respect, the mass-mediatized artwork is not a two-tiered art form, but single-tiered, more like a novel than a performance. Consequently, since they lack the required duality, movies—whether film, broadcast TV, video, or CGI—are not works of performing art, though some of their contributors may have been trained as performing artists. Moreover, the person who is responsible for the performance of a movie—the projectionist—is not an artist, performing or otherwise. He or she is just a technician.

Undoubtedly, the hypothesis that movies are not a performing art will please neither the drama department or the cinema department. The drama folks will rue the loss of all those students who want to study acting in order to become movie stars; while the cinephiles will resent the loss of prestige they fear they will suffer, if they no longer sit at the same table with music, drama, and dance. However, neither money nor fame counts for much when it comes to ontology. And ontologically the mass-mediatized arts of narrative fiction are profoundly distinct categorically from drama qua performing art.

One theorist who has advocated the destabilization—even the deconstruction—of the distinction between mass-mediatized artworks and dramatic performances is Philip Auslander.[9] One reason that Auslander objects to the distinction is that he thinks it is motivated in contemporary circles by spurious political motivations.[10] He contends, for instance, that Peggy Phelan's characterization of live performance as a mode of disappearance—whose transience enables it to be politically resistant[11]—is false; Phelan's conception of live performance would not have the political ramifications she assigns to live performance even if her characterization of the difference between live performance and mass-mediatized art were compelling (which, of course, Auslander thinks it isn't).[12] However, even though I think that Auslander's objections to Phelan and to similarly disposed theater theorists are spot-on, I do not think that Auslander is correct in alleging that there are no significant ontological differences between mass-mediatized artworks and live dramatic performances.

For Auslander, there can be live, token dramatic performances that are functionally equivalent. That is, the token performance of the Disney staging of *Beauty and the Beast* in one city could be functionally equivalent to a counterpart token performance, enacted in another city, at precisely the same time of day. The actors playing the flatware, for example, would be made up in the same way, deliver the same lines, dance the same steps, and so on. From the orchestra pit, one might imagine, the performances will be pretty much perceptually indiscernible—presumably as indiscernible as the projection of two different prints of the same film template.[13] Auslander, in fact, suggests that the California producer Barrie Wexler's *Tamara* "franchise" is another such example.[14]

But I am skeptical. Mass-mediatized artworks, such as movies, are types that require templates that generate token performances through automatic processes of sheer physical causation. They are solely the result of the movement of matter in accordance with scientific laws. Once the lens is focussed and the machine is activated, the rest is pretty much blind nature grinding through its paces. But no live performance, not even one of the *Tamara* franchises, is like that. Token dramatic performances require actors, lighting crews, and so on, who generate the relevant performance tokens through processes of ongoing decisions—mental acts—comprised of beliefs, judgments, and interpretations. Token performances of *Tamara* are not automated physical processes; they are mind-mediated through and through.

Even if, *per impossible,* a movie of *Tamara* and its token performances looked indiscernible and were functionally equivalent in every way, that would not entail that there are no ontological differences between them. For these perceptual and functional congruencies are not ontologically bedrock. They are only superficial or surface similarities insofar as these phenomena have radically different, metaphysically significant provenances. These similarities, in other words, are only skin-deep. But there are deeper distinctions here. One token performance reaches us by way of mind and the other by way of matter.

Auslander attempts to elude this conclusion by maintaining that the distinction that I draw between generation-by-template and generation-by-interpretation is not as sharp as I suppose.[15] Actors' interpretations, Auslander argues, can be as mechanical as a physical template, like a film print or a DVD disk. I see no compelling reason, even if one is a materialist about what exists, to believe that mental properties are fully reducible to physical properties. Mental causation is ontologically different from sheer physical causation in pertinent respects (while, also, obviously being related to physical processes). And given these distinctions, the differentiation between mass-mediatized artworks and live performance falls out naturally.

Auslander may think that many of the actors' interpretations in the *Tamara* franchise are *mechanical,* but surely "mechanical" in such a context would probably mean something like "uninspired" or "unimaginative." It cannot literally pertain to the decision making and judgments of the performers in question. For, they are not machine-tables churning out mindless sequences of behavior.

As is well known, actors adjust their performances to live audiences; they assay the temper of the crowd, and reinterpret their lines appropriately. Tonight add a dash of irony; tomorrow, be a pound more serious. This is an important distinction between movies and live theatrical performances, one noted by Walter Benjamin in his discussions of mechanical reproduction.[16]

The Purple Rose of Cairo notwithstanding, the actor in a token performance of a motion picture cannot modify his approach to suit the sentiments of the spectators in the house. But this is commonplace in token dramatic performances. Even where the actor relies on so-called technique, rather than inspiration, to get through the evening, there are always subtle reinterpretations of the recipe to fit the occasion. This is why it makes sense to say that the actor's performance, no matter how reliant upon technique, was better yesterday than it was today. But it would be absurd to say that Johnny Depp's acting in a token performance of *Finding Neverland* was better yesterday than it was today. And this very absurdity marks the differentia between a token performance of a mass-mediatized movie versus a token enactment of a specimen of drama-as-performance.[17]

Conclusions

Drama is not one art form, but two: the art of dramatic composition and the art of dramatic performance. Moreover, the art of drama as performance, though perceptually very much akin, in many respects, to the mass fictions projected by movies, is nevertheless radically, categorically different. Indeed, even if there were a point-perfect motion picture replica of a token instance of a dramatic artwork as performance, that was, in certain circumstances, effectively indiscernible from the original, that would be only at best a *recording* of the dramatic performance token. Moreover, a performance of that document—a screening—would not be an artwork in its own right.

Why?

Because it would be mindless.[18]

NOTES

1. This characterization of philosophy is developed in Noël Carroll and Sally Banes, "Theatre: Philosophy, Theory, and Criticism," *Journal of Dramatic Theory and Criticism* 16, no. 1 (2001): 155–63; and Noël Carroll, *Philosophy of Art: A Contemporary Introduction* (London: Routledge, 2000), introduction.

2. Philip Auslander, "Against Ontology: Making Distinctions between the Live and the Mediatized," *Performance Research* 2, no. 3 (1997): 50–55.

3. Aristotle, *Poetics,* trans. Malcolm Heath (London: Penguin, 1996), 5–6.

4. Parts of what follows have been adapted from my article "Text" in *The Oxford Encyclopedia of Theatre and Performance,* ed. Dennis Kennedy (Oxford: Oxford University Press, 2003).

5. J. O. Urmson treats literature as this sort of art form. I disagree with his contention that literature is two-tiered; nevertheless, I think the idea of two-tiered art forms is a useful one. See J. O. Urmson, "Literature," in *Aesthetics: A Critical Anthology,* ed. George Dickie and Richard Scalafani (New York: St. Martin's Press, 1977).

6. These remarks pertain to contemporary drama. Ritual dramatic enactments may be evaluated primarily for their realization of some norm. I will attempt to take account of this in my analysis of the concept of drama as performance a bit further down the line in this essay.

7. An exception here might be improvisation, though I suspect that most improvisation involves a performance plan, albeit sketchy, that the performer has ruminated over, at least mentally. Of course, if there is pure improvisation, that would not show that there are not two art forms denominated by the notion of drama, but only that in some cases, some dramatic works only exist as pure performances.

8. This analysis follows the one offered in my "Defining the Moving Image," in *Theorizing the Moving Image* (New York: Cambridge University Press, 1996). See also my *Philosophy of Mass Art* (Oxford: Clarendon Press, 1998), esp. chap. 3.

9. Philip Auslander, *Liveness: Performance in a Mediatized Culture* (London: Routledge, 1999).

10. Auslander, "Against Ontology," 50–52.

11. Peggy Phelan, *Unmarked: The Politics of Performance* (London: Routledge, 1993).

12. Auslander, "Against Ontology," 50–53.

13. Philip Auslander raised these sorts of considerations in an untitled essay that was supposed to be published, along with a comment by me, in an issue of *Performance Research*. Unfortunately, the exchange was never printed.

14. Auslander, "Against Ontology," 50–53.

15. Auslander in the unpublished essay cited in note 13.

16. Walter Benjamin, "The Work of Art in the Age of Mechanical Reproduction," in *Illuminations,* ed. Hannah Arendt, trans. Harry Zorn (New York: Schocken, 1955), 217–51.

17. Unlike Auslander, I maintain that there are ontological differences between dramatic performances and mass-mediatized performances. However, I do not think that this disagreement ultimately compromises Auslander's work. For he has shown us many arresting ways in which recent live art has been influenced stylistically and

structurally by the mass media. His insightful observations do not seem to me to be undercut by the fact that there is an ontological distinction between mass art and dramatic performances. Borrowings can occur between ontologically discrete categories. Fashion designers can imitate foliage. Auslander's compelling comparisons between live performances and mass media do not require him to deconstruct or to abjure ontology. He can have everything he wants and some metaphysics too.

18. I would like to express my gratitude to Sally Banes for her help in the preparation of this chapter, though she is not responsible for any of the errors or infelicities herein.

SIX

Embodiment and Presence

The Ontology of Presence Reconsidered

Suzanne M. Jaeger

The following discussion addresses recent contentions in performance theory about the concept of *presence*. Two conflicting viewpoints are evident. First there are those for whom the lived phenomenon of presence still makes sense and is borne out in practical experience.[1] Presence is thought of as "the *lingua franca*" for many stage performers, acting teachers, critics, and audiences. Second are poststructuralist interpreters of performance art who reject the possibility of any singularly meaningful experience of self-presence. Experiences of presence are contested by solely linguistic explanations of the nature of meaning. The challenge, therefore, for a performance theory that aims to affirm the lived experience of presence is to address important poststructuralist correctives to traditional accounts of meaning as well as the arguments against the metaphysics of presence. I draw on the work of Maurice Merleau-Ponty both to circumvent opposing arguments and to give coherence and precision to the notion of stage presence. Merleau-Ponty's description of the body image or schema helps to explain the experience of presence in such a way that it is not inconsistent with poststructuralist claims about the indeterminacy of meaning.

Stage presence can be defined as an active configuring and reconfiguring of one's intentional grasp in response to an environment. It is to be aware of the uniqueness of a particular audience and of certain features of a theatrical event rather than performing a perfect repetition of a familiar and well-rehearsed pattern of behavior. This Merleau-Pontian explanation is useful for performance theory because it makes sense of the claim that certain performers, at certain "on" moments in their performances, are "present." Moreover, this account of presence does not attenuate the conditions of meaningful experience to either language or the productive nonpresence of differences. In support of this definition, I consider stage presence as a lived experience and a real phenomenon. I also examine both Jacques Derrida's arguments that cast aspersion on the philosophical concept of presence and Philip Auslander's criticisms of stage presence. Finally, building on Auslander's analysis and relying on Merleau-Ponty's work, I clarify the notion of stage presence in light of the deconstruction of presence.

Presence in the Context of Live Performances

Despite a fairly recent linguistic turn in acting theory, young actors continue to perform exercises that help them enhance their physical presence. Peter Brook's work has largely been developed around the idea of theater as immediacy and the actor's ability to be present to the spontaneity of events that occur only once. Joseph Chaikin has similarly focused on the immediacy of the actor's presence in live performances.[2] American drama critic John Lahr writes of his response to Tina Turner's "luminous presence" on stage: "'Hi, Tina!' we say, forgetting where we are. . . . People move toward [her] like moths to a light. Her energy is superhuman."[3] While presence is experienced by audiences as charisma, it is achieved by performers as a special capacity for spontaneity.

Performers, especially dancers, sometimes talk about "being in the moment" or having an "on performance," in the sense of being really on top of it, or in good form. Sometimes this sense involves both for the performer and for the audience an awareness of things uniquely coming together. One sees brilliance, a special communication between the artist(s) and the audience, a sensuously and perhaps emotionally heightened, lively awareness that unfolds within and is unique to a specific performance. The "on moment" occurs when the performer not only correctly repeats everything she rehearsed, but also has a keen awareness of herself, the other performers and the audience in the immediacy of a live performance. It is reported by performers as a feeling of being fully alive to the audience and other performers, a feeling of supreme control and power, but also paradoxically an openness to the contingencies of a live performance.[4] It is sometimes described as a kind of "flow" or "grace."[5] It is spoken of by some performers as a vulnerability or risk in the immediacy of live performance.

By contrast, Philip Auslander focuses on the rejection of theatrical presence by postmodern performance artists who integrate contemporary technologies of mass communication within live performances.[6] In a self-critical gesture and for disparate reasons, says Auslander, such artists ironically challenge the meaning of presence in theater art. However, given that many actors, directors, and innovators of theater techniques have developed their work by exploring features of human experience relating to presence, it still seems reasonable to ask how observable, peak moments of stage presence are explained. One answer can be found in Francis Sparshott's consideration of the distinctive features of elite forms of artistic expression.[7] He describes the extraordinary achievements of professional dancers as the mastering of a system of skills and related options to a level of refinement that amateurs never achieve. The professional artist has a fine-tuned, distinctively developed set of bodily powers. An *on performance* can thus be explained as the moment when the professional dancer comes closest to a perfect articulation of her style of bodily movement that makes full use of her skills in a distinctive way relative to the objective demands of the art form. Ballet dancers, for instance, strive to embody the aesthetic values of classical line and grace. Contemporary dancers similarly aim to embody qualities distinctive to a modern style of dance, such as rapid and dramatic flow, precise elocution and lyricism. Artistic perfectionism is an attempt to embody as perfectly as possible objectively determined aesthetic values or symbolic meanings. The *on moment* occurs when the dancer approximates that perfection.

This explanation corroborates Peggy Phelan's claims about stage presence for the actor as relating to his or her skill to create a believable self. Presence, according to Phelan, relates to a particular performer's ability to be "convincing," "commanding," and "captivating," and to trick the audience into believing the representation of the character portrayed.[8] The performance is believable because the performer has accurately reproduced the manner and actions of a recognizable character. The audience recognizes the presentation of a certain figure or set of actions that is familiar in some way. Or it may be unfamiliar in ways relative to experiences that are meaningful. According to this explanation of presence, an actor's stage presence, like a dancer's *on moment,* is related to her ability to more perfectly articulate, "in the moment" of a particular staged performance, meaningful characterizations or socially significant portrayals. What makes a character or social practice meaningful can be thought of as the rules of a game or as a structural system of habituated and therefore familiar actions. Stage presence is, according to this paradigm, an effect of a performer's "conforming to" or knowing and playing well the rules of particular social-linguistic games.[9] The performer employs with precise expertise the subtle rules of social practices that are recognizable if not by everyone, at least by audiences who are acquainted with the culture in which such words and gestures make sense.

This purely technical account of what makes a particular dancer's performance special has been challenged by those who draw attention to the differences between technically flawless, but nonetheless "empty" performances and "artistically animated" performances. The difference to the capacity for some dancers is to "invest" the dance with a "psychological reality." The difference is always concretely visible in features of the dance. A second reason why stage presence is not easily reduced to mastery or elite proficiency is because of a paradox concerning agency and the production of meaning. Performers are assumed to have the agency that enables them to master the art form, but they also subordinate themselves to the aesthetic values or meanings generated by their performances. There is a sense in which artists are not so much using the language of the art form to express themselves as being played by socially determined meanings and aesthetic values. Auslander brings out a different facet of this paradox. In a discussion of acting technique, he states that if an actor must be, as Roland Barthes put it, "a master of meaning," she is faced with a dilemma. The actor "must convincingly portray something that she is not" or something of which she has no firsthand experience.[10] The actor must become for example, a physician, lawyer, or perhaps the murderer of a spouse or child.

Stanislavsky, Brecht, and Grotowski confronted this dilemma, according to Auslander, by mistakenly grounding the actor's persona on not only the actor's life experience, but also on the presence of some authentic presentation of the actor's self. These three theorists believed that dynamic acting is based on real-life experience and that stage presence is fundamentally related to the presentation of the self. Their explanations of the self involve, among other things, an existential understanding that presumes the availability of more or less authentic feelings and choices made in response to socially determined meanings. Like other existential thinkers, the core of authenticity is freedom to choose one's self in response to inauthentic self-representations determined by mass culture. Actors trained in existentialist techniques were encouraged to obtain experiences beyond their limited worlds. This did not mean actually becoming a lawyer or killing a wife or child, but instead having experiences that enabled the actor to understand sympathetically the life-situation of his or her character. The actor's portrayal would then be based on authentic self-expressions. Auslander's criticisms of this notion of authenticity raise significant issues.

Like the existentialists, Auslander is concerned with questions of autonomy in relation to mass culture. However, he argues against notions of authentic selfhood as the origin of an actor's presence and supports his position by appealing to Jacques Derrida's claims regarding the linguistic origin of self-presentation.[11] Like Derrida, for Auslander language is the medium of self-revelation. The self, says Auslander, "is inseparable from the language by which it expresses itself: it is a function of and does not precede that language." Moreover, since all expressions, whether gestural or verbal, are a function of differences, their meaningfulness is "defined by the rules of language as a system of differences."[12] Artists may still think of their work in terms of self-expression, but in linguistic analyses the performer is no more than a cipher or zero point generated by the performance. She is a readable text determined solely by a socially and politically significant economy of aesthetic values. "The death of the subject" is one consequent refrain of poststructuralist theories of meaning. References to a performer's artistic intentions are subordinate to semiotic strategies of reading performances as polyvalent texts. The actors thus need only focus on the words rather than on their inner experiences to find compelling motivations. In the next section we examine more closely Derrida's criticism of the metaphysics of presence. Although his deconstruction of the concept also has difficulties, it suggests surprisingly the possibility of a more philosophically satisfying explanation for the phenomenon of stage presence.

Poststructuralism, Presence, and Embodiment

Derrida's criticisms of the concept of presence are best understood, I believe, in relation to a "representational theory" of meaning. According to representationalism, a word, image, or signifier is connected to a signified or referent. The referent is an object, either an actual physical object or an idea (mental object). Words are meaningful, according to representationalism, because a community of people shares the same signifiers for the same objects (both physical and mental). Signifiers, whether verbal, written, or gestured, are substitutes for objects that are not actually present. Thus we talk about signs or signifiers making present such mental objects as our shared concepts of love, justice, and friendship. Derrida, by contrast, argues against the mind/body dualisms presupposed in appeals to such mental objects as "ideas" in the mind.[13] Language, according to Derrida, is a system of materially marked differences. Verbal or gestured signifiers operate as perceptible marks in a system of perceptible differences with which we have more or less familiarity. A language user learns the system of differences. They become familiar with a complex, sophisticated economy of differences marked by signifiers. Meaning is thus a result of the play of differences. Our explanation of difference does not require, however, a presence behind or preceding the signifiers that mark the differences productive of meaning. Signifiers may be commonly understood to refer to or re-present objects, but their meaning is given in relation to other signifiers in each specific context in which they are repeated.[14]

The concept of repetition is important to Derrida's account of meaning. He uses the term *iteration* to refer to the condition for the possibility of communication. It refers to the function of language that both permits meaning and defers presence. In one sense, iteration is akin to that function of repetition mentioned earlier in regard to presence as the more or less perfect articulation of the rules (or economy) of a practice (or system of differences). One has truly understood a new word, for example, when one is able to use it correctly in a new context. Iteration is also, however, the condition for the impossibility of a pure meaning: a repetition of a word or gesture is always a *recontextualization,* says Derrida, and therefore slippages in meaning occur. New meanings are acquired by virtue of the repetition of a word or gesture in new contexts. Derrida's argument against presence is an argument against continuity in meaning. In a new context (and there is an infinite number of repetitions of words in new contexts) a new economy of differences is generated. Derrida uses the term *différance* to refer to the mark or trace of differences between repeatable signifiers generating new meanings, but *différance,* according to Derrida, is nothing in itself. Although signifiers and their referents make it seem as though our words and gestures have consistent meanings across contexts, Derrida's analysis focuses on the instability of language. He emphasizes the discontinuities in our intended meanings, and the multiplicity of possible meanings by virtue of recontextualization. His notions of *différance* and *iteration* have, moreover, been understood to apply not only to writing and verbal language, but to all human experience. His work has made possible deconstructive strategies that challenge normative receptions of cultural meaning. For example, performance theorists like Peggy Phelan claim that "the body is not coherent; only reading practices . . . make [it] beautiful, sick, well, living, or dying."[15] For Phelan, like others who have applied deconstructive semiotics, performances are texts to be read and interpreted. The words and gestures, the costumes, music, sets, actions, and so on, are all material marks of differences in the surface of the text. The audience will be more or less familiar with the system of differences in which these marks meaningfully function. There are, however, always new and different ways of interpreting texts given the many ways in which texts are reproductions of repeatable signifiers.

Différance and iteration refer to the mechanics of linguistic structure and therefore Derrida's explanation preserves a duality of form as a function of discourse or linguistic structure, and matter as the outside of language, being either formless and unstructured or inaccessible to the logic of language. Indeed his account has been criticized for being overly formalistic, and hence disembodied. As Joan Scott puts it: "It is no longer individuals who have experience, but subjects who are constituted through experience. . . . Experience is a linguistic event. . . . The question then becomes how to analyze language."[16] Auslander similarly concludes, in the context of his criticism of traditional accounts of stage presence, that "[p]ure self-exposure is no more possible on a physical level than on a verbal level because of the mediation of difference." Communication, whether of gestural or verbal expression, is "defined by the rules of language as a system of differences."[17]

Linguistic accounts of meaning, such as Derrida's, seem, at first glance, to preclude explanations of the phenomenon of stage presence as an "authentic" experience of one's self creatively alive "in the moment" and in dynamic rapport with one's surroundings. The subjectivity of the performer becomes a zero point in the production of meaning through gestured and other physical signifiers. Presence as the appearance of something real, here and now; the appearance of a self, an acting, physical body in the world, engaged reciprocally with other real bodies or other real features of the world; all of these ideas that relate to notions of stage presence and openness to the real world seem, from a semiotic perspective, impossible to philosophically defend. As soon as a person tries to express something about his or her nonverbal experiences, it is brought into the symbolic system of differences marked by signifiers. The difficulty is not only, however, that our self-understanding is constructed by the language we use to describe ourselves. Our bodily gestures, manner of dress, style of movement, posture, comportment, and facial and other expressions are all understood as socially conditioned aspects of human existence. As such they are habituated actions, repetitions, and therefore also meaningful signifiers in a socially determined system of possible meanings. Whatever we find meaningful in life is determined for us by social-linguistic conditioning beyond our control, and often beyond even our conscious knowledge. Our long-standing definition of human subjectivity as an independent, monological, and free consciousness is challenged by a linguistic explanation of meaning. The agency long thought to be at the core of subjectivity is ultimately at stake, hence, the refrain about the death of the subject.

Phelan contributes to this discussion by developing ontology of presence from Derrida's notion of *différance*. She defines the notion of presence that is attributed to live performances paradoxically as absence. "Performance's only life is in the present," says Phelan. "Performance cannot be saved, recorded, documented, or otherwise participate in the circulation of representations of representations: once it does so, it becomes something other than performance. . . . Performance's being, like the ontology of subjectivity . . . becomes itself through disappearance." According to Phelan, it is because performances occur "in the moment" of lived time that they have the potential to make present that which has not yet been signified. Just as, for Derrida, iteration is the condition for the possibility both of communication and of the indeterminacy of meaning, for Phelan, performance is the possibility of openness to that which is outside the text, that which is "unmarked."[18] It is the immediacy of temporally and spatially configured appearances that has special significance for Phelan. Unlike written language, live, fully embodied performances are never the same. The difference between two live performances, as well as the difference between a particular reading or interpretation of a performance and its fleshy actuality, is, like *différance,* not anything in itself, but the possibility of slippage in the assumed isomorphic relationship between linguistic meanings and our lived, fully embodied presence in the world. Thus, for Phelan, Derrida's deconstruction of presence does not necessarily preclude the possibility that linguistic meaning is transformed by the unmarked.

Although Auslander is sympathetic with the political role Phelan gives to presence in performance theory, he criticizes Phelan for not recognizing the significance of the pervasive integration and developmental influence of film, video, and computer technologies on live performance. His political concern, supported by the work of Walter Benjamin, is the entertainment industry's profit-driven manipulation of popular culture. Auslander also criticizes the notion of stage presence as based on spurious metaphysical assumptions. Following Derrida, Auslander claims that descriptions, for example, of stage presence are the nostalgic dreams of a lost origin for meaning. He contests claims about stage presence that appeal to the body as that which "transcends the play of difference that constitutes language."[19] In order to make his argument against Phelan, Auslander builds his case on Phelan's ontology of presence as disappearance as well as on Derrida's deconstruction of the metaphysics of presence to show how both live and mediatized performances are both predicated on ontology of disappearance.[20] He argues that the history of the concept of "liveness" shows little distinction between live and mediatized performances other than a historically contingent, romanticized notion of liveness as perceptually more authentic and temporally preceding mediatized performances. "Mediatized forms like film and video," says Auslander, "can be shown to have the same ontological characteristics as live performance, and live performance can be used in ways indistinguishable from the uses generally associated with mediatized forms."[21] Two examples illustrating his point include the integration of video recordings and canned music into live performances and the subsequent staging of "live" tours by rock musicians of their "original" recordings. Auslander is concerned in such cases with the commodification of presence and the privileging of one form over another on the basis of questionable assumptions. Nevertheless, he grants that although mediatized performances engage all of the same senses as live performances, they may well engage the senses differently.[22] He also states that differences in kind have less relevance than differences in magnitude. To admit, however, that the senses can be engaged differently allows that ontologies of liveness and presence are not superfluous differences. Auslander's dismissal of the possible significance of how the senses can be engaged differently disregards the importance of the body. Moreover, to say that ontologies of presence are only tenuous indications of normatively relevant differences between live and mediatized performances ignores the connections between our ethical commitments and our understanding of human experience.

The critical question is whether iterations in verbal language are the same as iterations in other mediums. That is to say, are iterations in written or spoken language the same as iterations in facial expressions, gestures, bodily movements, and posture? The repetitions of a gesture or body movement are surely different from the repetitions of written words. At the most simplistic or literal of levels, what it is for a musician to repeat a phrase of music on the keyboard while at a live concert is surely different from what it is to replay a DVD in one's living room. It may be correct to say that all of the senses are engaged in both experiences, but they may also be engaged quite differently. I am proposing here that the ontology of iteration is yet relevant. Derrida's notion of iteration is useful, but it has remained too broadly conceived and formalistic when applied to all experience. The different ways in which the senses are employed in different contexts is significant. I am not referring here just to the rapport between performer and audience, but to the differently constituted iterations that belong to the various mediums employed in the creation of performance art. How the senses are engaged is significant to the meaningfulness of the experience. The concept of iteration is a good starting point for understanding the structuring of human experience as meaningful, but it remains too abstract and mechanical to offer much in the way of an explanation of human experience as fully embodied.

Merleau-Ponty's Ontology of Presence

Philosophers interested in the ontology of experience turn to Maurice Merleau-Ponty's phenomenology of bodily being-in-the-world for its account of meaning rooted in not only language and cognition, but also in bodily powers of perception. In the *Phenomenology of Perception* Merleau-Ponty analyzes various modalities of perception, such as mobility, vision, hearing, taste, touch, smell, sociality, sexuality, and language. Although these various powers are distinct from each other, they also intertwine. He calls this interaction "synaesthetic perception." Touching, says Merleau-Ponty, resonates in certain ways with taste, smell, and language.[23] Our ways of moving, walking on two legs, the ways in which we use our hands, all influence cognition and the language we use, and language, too, affects the other modalities of perception.[24] For Merleau-Ponty, this transposition of our senses occurs within the limits of each modality as distinctive, material mediums through which we engage with certain features of the world. Such claims are relevant to the notion of presence.

Although the materiality of the organs of perception recedes in our instrumental engagement with the environment, each modality of perception is uniquely structured by its distinct, material constitution. We might experience our eyes, for example, as windows that look out onto the world without being conscious of the fleshiness of muscles, nerves, tissue, and so on that enable sight. Human eyes function, however, in ways that are unique to their structure and different from the way insect eyes and even other mammal eyes *see* the environment. Merleau-Ponty often describes the powers of perception as "gearings into" the world. They are intentional structures in the sense of being distinctive connections to particular features of the environment. He uses the terms *transcendence* and *reversibility* to describe these intentional structures. It follows from the bodily connectedness with the environment that our ways of moving are not only effects of internalized values inherent to social-linguistic systems. That is to say, I do not move in feminine ways only because I have internalized social values of femininity. I move in certain ways because I have a particular body with particular capacities to move, some very similar to other humans, some fairly unique to my own body and, moreover, because these distinctive bodily powers are geared into particular features of the world. A style of movement is not an effect of forces stemming only from our representational practices. It is also the effect of particular features of the environment, complexly adhering to the unique bodily powers that belong to the individual. It is intricately constituted by particularities belonging to both the individual's unique bodily powers of perception and species-specific characteristics as well as effects of synesthetic perceptions, or what Merleau-Ponty calls, in his later work, "criss-crossing" influences from the various other modalities of perception (including language) and from the particular features of the environment with which the individual is interacting.[25] In other words, a style of movement is complexly structured by many different contributing forces.

Merleau-Ponty describes the synthesis of the various aspects that together comprise perception as an intentional insertion of the individual in his or her world. He uses the term *intentionality* because, like Husserl, he understands the transcendent terminus of perception to be objects and actions in the material world. The object is the culminating synthesis integrating the bodily powers of perception. For example, my seeing, across the expansive depth of an auditorium, certain meanings arising from a particular dancer's movements is the culminating point of various forces and bodily powers. My eyes have a certain physical ability to focus light and to determine clearly the outlines of the dancer against the background of the proscenium stage, rows of other people sitting in the auditorium, the sets, lights, costumes, and other dancers. My "knowledge" of Western forms of art dance also helps me to focus on the meaning, as does the lighting and its refraction through my lenses, the materiality of the dancer and her environment, its changing contours, colors, the shades of light and dark, the changing configurations, the audience's reactions, and so on. Merleau-Ponty calls the unity of the object of perception a "symbolism" that links each sensible quality to the rest.[26] It is a symbolism in the sense that there are many aspects that comprise meaningful connections to objects in the world, some physical, emotional, social-linguistic, or cognitive, some unique by virtue of the uniqueness of our bodies, and, some general, more commonly recognizable ways by virtue of our similarities with others and the social nature of the human world.

In the context of his arguments against Husserl's solipsism and the assumption that reality is the thing in itself, Merleau-Ponty states that "what makes the 'reality' of the thing is therefore precisely what snatches it from our grasp." Here, Phelan's ontology of presence is suggestive of Merleau-Ponty's claim that the "aseity [independent existence] of the thing, its unchallengeable presence and the perpetual absence into which it withdraws, are two inseparable aspects of transcendence."[27] Perception of an object is always an incomplete process, and its reality for us is given in the incomplete character of perceptual experience. One never gets to the totality of what makes the thing what it is. One's perception is always limited by what one has not yet seen, what one no longer sees, what is absent from one's present vision. Intellectualism mistakenly conceives perception to be completed by an act of cognition. For example, "This is a dance about romantic love." Now I know. I know in an abstract, omnipresent sort of way over and above any particular perceptions because of the abstract concepts of "dance" and "romantic love." By contrast, Merleau-Ponty says that "we understand the thing as we understand a new kind of behavior. . . . A form of behavior outlines a certain manner of treating the world."[28] That is to say, the concepts of "dance" and "romantic love" contribute to a certain way of perceiving, but perceptual experience is always incomplete, partial, somewhat ambiguous, and never total. New understandings and insights are gained with further encounters with the object.

The epistemological significance of the incompleteness of perception together with his phenomenology of the complex bodily constitution of intentionality lead Merleau-Ponty to the claim that there is a "system of levels" orienting a person toward an optimal distance or *proximity* from which a particular object is best perceived. Proximity is the balance between clarity and richness when they are in inverse proportion to one another.[29] For example, if I want to see the expressions on a dancer's face and the details of her gestures, I need to go closer. However, I can also get too close so that the meanings of the dance given in the dancer's changing spatial relationships with other dancers will be lost. According to Merleau-Ponty, the system of levels that tends toward the optimal is constituted by the various bodily powers, features of the object as well as language or cognition, for example, certain concepts of dance. The unity or synthesis of these various factors is the achievement of a transcendent, incontrovertible connection or presence of an individual to an object in an environment. Another term Merleau-Ponty uses to describe this synthesizing intentional grasp on the environment is the *body schema*. It is the synesthetic complexity of this grasp that leads Merleau-Ponty to say that sensations are laden or "pregnant" with meanings that remain hidden until given representation.[30] One never fully comprehends the object or exhausts the field of perceptual experience in any particular environment. Thus, like Derrida, Merleau-Ponty emphasizes the instability and uncertainty of human knowledge, but for different reasons.

Merleau-Ponty's sense of the instability of meaningful experience is based on his phenomenology of perception. His argument with rationalism leads him to assert a mitigated realism with regard to the object as the *motivation* for the unity of perceptual experience.[31] Our actions or practices bind together the perceiver with the perceived or the person with the environment. This epistemology is not, however, entirely antithetical to semiotic accounts of meaning because of the incomplete and undetermined nature of perception. It is conceivable that there are other motivators of unity besides the object. It is also possible that ideas or abstract concepts, symbols, and feelings, rather than objects in the world, motivate the unity of perceptual experiences. Merleau-Ponty acknowledges the possibility of differently synthesized logics of perception in his comments on schizophrenia and mythological thinking as various expressions of spatial existence.[32] It is because there are different unifying motivations that Merleau-Ponty claims that the connectedness between a perceiver and the environment is not only the result of physical causality. Perception is not just the result of a physical cause partly because of its complex, synesthetic constitution, but also because of its active rather than passive nature. "To experience a structure is not to receive it into oneself passively: it is to live it, to take it up, assume it and discover its immanent significance."[33]

Observations of the world are motivated in varying ways. For example, the object of science is a function of measured relations of space, force, mass, and so on and presupposes detachment from subjective, hard-to-measure qualitative interests in the object. By contrast, poetic perceptions of objects are often motivated by feelings, memories, desires, personal metaphoric and metonymic associations, and so on. Thus, linguistic meanings can motivate certain ways of experiencing the world, but what distinguishes Merleau-Ponty's epistemology from other theories of meaning is the role that embodiment plays in meaning-making.

Linguistic accounts of meaning by themselves fail to acknowledge how aspects of the object and of the environment contribute to the synthesis of perception. They narrowly assume that only linguistic functions can be motivators of perceptual unity. For Merleau-Ponty, because we do, indeed, engage with objects in the world, because "my body is a movement toward the world and the world my body's point of support," perception is not a confusion of sensations that get synthesized in either an act of mind, the mechanics of language, or the values inherent in social practices.[34] Nor is perception entirely socially constructed to the extent that an embodied person is understood to be denatured and separate from the material conditions of the environment. The unity of perceptual experience is a function of the complex, active, embodied engagement with specific features of the environment. Practices are social, but they are also embodied and therefore connected to the environment in distinctive ways. For Merleau-Ponty, the structuring of experience as meaningful belongs to the nonhuman as well as the human. My consciousness of the world is influenced by sunlight, electromagnetic forces, interpersonal psychic energies, and other elements in the environment to which I respond, in ways often intractable to cognitive awareness.

In the context of a discussion of sensation, Merleau-Ponty states that the "subject is time itself."[35] Our intentional grasp on the world is, for Merleau-Ponty, both a temporal and spatial concept. The present moment, that is to say, my immediate perceptual experience, has a spatial-temporal depth. There are at least two different ways to understand the spatial temporality of intentionality. First, it is the constitution of an experience as a synthesis of the various bodily powers engaged in or connected to features of the environment. In the synthesis constitutive of perception, for example, a visual perception of an object, time passes not only as a series of distinct, equivalent, clocked intervals, but also as a rhythm unfolding in or as the perception of the object. A useful example of this nonlinear and spatial experience of time would be the sense one sometimes has of losing track of clocked time while absorbed in an activity. Rather than the regular intervals of clocked time, one is engrossed in rhythms arising from the activity itself, the ebbs and flows generated by material (bodily) connections to the particular environment in which one is involved. For example, it is easy to become immersed in the text appearing on a monitor screen. Without explicitly thinking about the muscles and coordination of the fingers, one types whole meaning on the keyboard that then appear on the screen. One performs actions with a click of the mouse that carry one along in a project defined, in part, by its electronic medium. The connections between oneself, the symbolic meaning of the text one is manipulating, and the electronic medium in which they are materially represented are gathered together into an experience of time that is distinct by virtue of the particular powers of perception engaged, particular features of the environment, the bodily powers particular to the individual and a myriad of other aspects that may be composite elements of the activity.

A second, related way in which intentionality can be described as both spatial and temporal is as a repetitive, habitual structuring of perceptual experience. Perception in the fullest sense, including all the various modalities of "being-in-the-world" that Merleau-Ponty discusses in the *Phenomenology of Perception,* involves habituated, anticipatory patterns of bodily connectedness to the environment. Merleau-Ponty uses terms such as *style, rhythm,* and *bodily schema* to describe the sedimented, underlying structures or syntheses of the various elements that constitute an individual's meaningful, interactive perception of the environment. Individuals have, for example, their own styles of walking, running, seeing, and even thinking. A style is a sedimented, recognizable pattern of engaging with aspects of the environment.[36] Similar to Derrida's claims about iteration, for Merleau-Ponty immediate experience or presence to an environment is conditioned by established patterns, repetitions, or habits of perception. These habits of perception can be understood as systems of differences; for example, the dancer's ability to make meaningfully complex and aesthetically beautiful gestures is a power to articulate her body in relation to gravity, the aesthetic values of the art form, other dancers, the stage environment, and so on in specific, controlled, hence repeatable ways. However, for Merleau-Ponty meaningful presence to what is unfamiliar and other than oneself is not thereby made impossible. Instead, habituated structures of perception are modifiable by virtue of their constitution as engagements with the environment. Habits of perception are modified in dynamic rapport with those anticipated features upon which they were first constituted as patterns of perception. Perceptions are holds on or connections with certain features of the environment constituting a style of being in the world. There are transformations of habituated structures because of the "there is" world that transcends and therefore affects the habits of perceptions structuring particular experiences.

According to Merleau-Ponty, the unity of the bodily schema is therefore open and limitless.[37] Although it may be true that meaningful perceptual experience is possible only because of an acquired style of perception or connection with features of the environment, our environments are never static, nor are the powers of the body. Bodies are transformed by further experiences and because of aging and other forces affecting their material conditions. Environments too are in continual flux. Moreover, since perception is partial and never total, the unity of perception, that is to say, the bodily schema or style of comportment constituted in connection with specific features of the environment, is also open to subtle shifts and accommodations.[38] An example of this shift is the transition a virtual reality user makes from a style of perceiving in the actual world to one geared into computer-generated images. Most virtual reality technologies, such as Head Mounted Displays (HMD), use direct light stimulation of the retina rather than reflected and refracted light (which is how we perceive actual objects in the real world). This shift in the intentional structures that gear a person into the world in specific, fully embodied ways explains why many HMD users experience the nausea of extreme disorientation and why the nausea dissipates with frequent use. Artificial environments require new ways of using the body, and a reconfiguration of the unity of a bodily schema that ties the person to the environment. The person is not, as is sometimes thought, disembodied by using technology, but reembodied in the experience of presence to a new environment, whether actual or virtual.

Herein lays the main point. Merleau-Ponty's epistemology provides an explanation of presence as a reconfiguration of the bodily schema. Presence is openness to alteration in the unity of a bodily schema, that fully embodied activity of synthesis and balance between richness and clarity which constitutes our perceptual experiences. This account of presence as a shift in the bodily schema connecting oneself to an environment does not essentialize the body, but affirms its fleshy and malleable constitution. Nor does this explanation exclude philosophical reflection on the nature of embodiment. Reflection is possible because cognitive powers and language are constitutive aspects of perceptual experience along with other modalities of perception. Furthermore, this explanation is compatible with semiotic interpretations of meaning without reducing meaningful experience to merely the functions of language.

Similar to Phelan's notion of presence as absence, presence as shift or change in the bodily schema implies a disappearance or absence. The absence entailed by a shift in the bodily schema is not, however, the empty or merely logical negation of a representation. Embodied presence as shift is the possibility of positive or content-rich change, in other words, the possibility of new truths. Modulations in the distinctive styles of embodiments, for example of femininity and masculinity, come about not just because of the formal function of recontextualization or the repetition of a representation in new contexts. Changes in meaning and in the habitual structures of perception also come about because of the constitution of these habitual structures as bodily connections to the environment. The emphasis here is on the word *connection*. Absence is not merely an empty negation of presence, but the experience of a shift in the bodily schema that connects a particular individual to a particular environment. The shift brings with it possibilities of new ways of connecting or new connections with different features within a familiar environment.

This latter point is relevant to Auslander's argument against the ontological distinction between live and mediatized performances. Experiences of mediatized performances are indeed like live performances in that all the same senses may be engaged, but they are engaged differently. For example, by virtue of their unique bodily styles of comportment, no two perceivers have exactly the same experience. Moreover, because bodily schemas are transformed by the particularities belonging to different environmental elements, the differences may be both artistically and ethically significant. For example, one may choose to communicate with others via telephone or email or in person. Each medium of communication will engage the various perceptual powers differently and contribute to a certain style of relating, constituted in part by the material conditions belonging to that medium of rapport. In the same way that we choose particular mediums of conversing in everyday life, sometimes for reasons specifically related to the style of communication afforded by one medium in comparison with another, artists too choose particular mediums of artistic expression because of the particular play of sensory perceptions made possible by the medium. Not only does language structure experience; our environments make a difference to our style or manner of being in the world (what might also be called consciousness). Meaning in human experience is thus even more radically indeterminate according to a Merleau-Pontian epistemology than it is in poststructuralist accounts that presume language to be the only medium for meaningful experience. According to Merleau-Ponty, meaning is subject to the continual fluctuations brought about by changes in the elements configuring our environments, our own bodies, and therefore also our grasp on the environment. Hence, it is important to make choices about the elements constituting our environments. We do so all the time, though, of course, the material results of these choices may be commodified.

To summarize, Merleau-Ponty's phenomenology of perceptual experience reminds us that any acquisition of a social practice presupposes a perceptual (or bodily) openness as, at least, a capacity to learn socially determined ways of structuring experience. Perceptual openness or presence to what is new, different and other must in some way constitute an individual's ability to experience a world. Presence is the possibility of transformation in familiar, habituated, and socially entrenched patterns through which one experiences the world. The "on performance" or moment of stage presence is possible because of this capacity to be open to what is other than a mere repetition of familiar ways of structuring experience. Being present requires having a recognizable style of being the world, but it also requires the power to concentrate on the singularity of the moment, ready for the shifts, accommodations, and adaptations belonging to the challenge of active, conscious, fully embodied engagement "in the moment." Audiences can see it. The performance is alive with that special quality some performers have and that we call stage presence.

NOTES

1. See, for instance, Ian Watson, "Reading the Actor," *New Theatre Quarterly* 5, no. 11 (1995): 135–46; Eugenio Barba, "The Fiction of Duality," *New Theatre Quarterly* 5, no. 20 (1989): 311–14; and Barba, *The Paper Canoe,* trans. Richard Fowler (New York: Routledge, 1995).

2. See Elleen Blumenthal, *Joseph Chaikin: Exploring at the Boundaries of Theatre* (Cambridge: Cambridge University Press, 1984), and Joseph Chaikin, *The Presence of the Actor* (New York: TCG, 1991).

3. See Robert Cohen, *Acting Power* (New York: Mayfield, 1978).

4. In 1997 and 1998 I conducted interviews with performing artists, many of them dancers, who verified this assertion of "flow." Among the interviewees was Peggy Baker, a modern dancer, teacher and choreographer, Dominique Dumais, soloist with the National Ballet of Canada, Evelyn Hart, prima ballerina of the Royal Winnipeg

Ballet, Rebecca Todd, modern dancer and choreographer, and Carmen Romero, flamenco dancer and choreographer living in Toronto.

5. See Mihaly Csikszentmihalyi, *Flow: The Psychology of Optimal Experience* (New York: Harper, 1990), and *Finding the Flow: The Psychological Engagement with Everyday Life* (New York: Basic Books, 1997), for information discussing flow, intelligence, and creativity.

6. Philip Auslander, *Presence and Resistance: Postmodernism and Cultural Politics in Contemporary Performance* (Ann Arbor: University of Michigan Press, 1994).

7. Francis Sparshott, *A Measured Pace: Towards a Philosophical Understanding of the Art of Dance* (Toronto: University of Toronto Press, 1995).

8. Peggy Phelan, *Unmarked: The Politics of Performance* (London: Routledge, 1993), 115–17.

9. I use the term *linguistic* in the broad sense here to refer to structures and patterns that are the basis of shared practices.

10. Philip Auslander, "Just Be Yourself," in *Acting (Re)Considered: Theories and Practices,* ed. Philip Zarrilli (London: Routledge, 1995), 63.

11. Ibid., 65.

12. Ibid., 64, 65.

13. I am relying primarily on Derrida, *Of Grammatology,* trans. Gayatri Spivak (Baltimore: John Hopkins University Press, 1976; *Writing and Difference,* trans. Allen Bass (Chicago: University of Chicago Press, 1979); and *Limited Inc.,* trans. Gerald Graff and Samuel Weber (Evanston, Ill.: Northwestern University Press, 1988).

14. For Derrida, *iteration* is a technical term to be distinguished from *repetition* (*Limited Inc.,* 127–28).

15. Peggy Phelan, introduction to *Ends of Performance,* ed. Peggy Phelan and Jill Lane (New York: New York University Press, 1998), 16.

16. Joan Scott, in *Feminists Theorize the Political,* ed. Joan Scott and Judith Butler (New York: Routledge, 1992), 34. Contemporary feminist philosopher Linda Martin Alcoff, "Merleau-Ponty and Feminist Theory and Experience," in *Chiasms: Merleau-Ponty's Notion of Flesh,* ed. Fred Evans and Leonard Lawlor (Albany: State University Press of New York, 2000), argues against this kind of epistemological skepticism that results from a conception of language as only a self-referring system (262). See also Judith Butler, *Excitable Speech: The Politics of Performance* (London: Routledge, 1997), for a criticism of Derrida's linguistic formalism.

17. Auslander, "Just Be Yourself," 65.

18. Phelan, *Unmarked,* 146.

19. Auslander, "Just Be Yourself," 66, 65.

20. Philip Auslander, *Liveness: Performance in a Mediatized Culture* (London: Routledge, 1999), 54–55.

21. Ibid., 159.

22. Ibid., 55.

23. Maurice Merleau-Ponty, *The Phenomenology of Perception,* trans. Colin Smith (London: Routledge, 1962), 230.

24. George Lakoff and Mark Johnson develop the relevance of this observation for cognitive science in their discussions of the influence of bodily experience on language, indicated, for example, by many of our common metaphors for thinking, feel-

ing, and understanding. See *Philosophy in The Flesh: The Embodied Mind and Its Challenge to Western Thought* (New York: Basic Books, 1999).

25. Maurice Merleau-Ponty, *The Visible and the Invisible,* trans. Alphonso Linis (Evanston, Ill.: Northwestern University Press, 1964).

26. Merleau-Ponty, *The Phenomenology of Perception,* 19.

27. Ibid., 233.

28. Ibid., 319.

29. Ibid., 318.

30. Ibid., 297.

31. Ibid., 364.

32. Ibid., 286–90.

33. Ibid., 258.

34. Ibid., 350.

35. Ibid., 241.

36. This understanding of style is similar to Pierre Bourdieu's notion of a bodily hexus, *The Logic of Practice,* trans. Richard Nice (Stanford: Stanford University Press, 1990), which is a disposition acquired gradually in the many seemingly mundane aspects of growing up (12).

37. Merleau-Ponty, *The Phenomenology of Perception,* 233.

38. I am indebted to Sam Mallin for this notion of shift, which he develops in *Art Line Thought* (Dordrecht: Kluwer, 1996).

~

SEVEN

Presence

Jon Erickson

You are standing waiting at an airport gate for the beloved's plane to arrive.[1] Air traffic has been heavy and the plane is late. Finally the plane arrives at the gate and passengers begin to emerge out of the tunnel. You search for her face among all the various faces of the people being greeted warmly by family and friends, or simply moving quickly to some connecting flight. You keep scanning but see no sign of her as more and more people get off. You are annoyed that none of these faces, which you glance at and then ignore, are hers, and worried that she missed her flight and she won't appear at all. It seems as if everyone has now gotten off the plane when suddenly you see her face. She doesn't see you at first, but then turns and beams at you. Suddenly the whole gate area seems to fill with her presence, the rest of the people disappear and all that exists is her. As you embrace and walk toward baggage claim, the rest of the world is gone and the only thing that matters is the two of you linked by flows of words punctuated by looks.

This is one way to look at the concept of "presence."

Other ways: the entrance into a restaurant, cafe, bar, of someone, male or female, whose beauty is so striking that no one can resist looking; a person whose personal charisma and authority prevents an angry group of people from hurting an individual; a stranger to whom you tell your troubles and who then can see deep into your soul and tell you exactly what the problem is, whether or not you want to hear it; a person, perhaps even yourself, who in the midst of a disaster or horrendous accident has the presence of mind to do the right thing to save or protect lives. All these things involve something we might call "presence." Despite the tendency of theater theorists to view with suspicion the power over audiences that performative presence has, it should not simply be relegated to a form of authority that we would call oppressive, but should also be recognized as a kind of authority that can evince wisdom and respect. It may indeed mystify us in a certain way, but not necessarily in an exploitative sense: it may simply be a mystery (not all mysteries are mystifications). But perhaps most of all it is related to the most positive aspects of human attraction and love.

This is not to deny that the power of personal presence can be used to seduce and manipulate others for evil or ideological purposes, or to intimidate. But to associate presence *only* with these things is to advance a rather simplistic idea of what presence means in human experience. And by extension, any animus directed at the quality known as presence in the theater that derives from a critique of theater's power for or over the spectator is likewise simplistic if it reduces the concept of presence to a purely invidiously framed notion of authority.

The problem with the critical animus against presence, character, and inevitability in dramatic performance is that its entire focus is on the presumed deleterious effects of these features on the critical capacities or potentials of the audience in their reception of a work. Methods for disrupting or subverting these features are deemed necessary for the critical awakening or political enlightenment of the individual spectator. But what is avoided is the question as to why these features are so important to the spectator and how they function in terms of his or her desire. Thus, disruption or subversion of these elements is really a frustration of spectators' desire. How is the frustration of desire supposed to lead to a critical awakening? Doesn't it actually tend toward its opposite—a *rejection* of the work precisely because of its intent? What spectator *wants* to be frustrated by a work? This is not the same as dealing with the difficulty of meaning that comes with the seductiveness of complexity.

The critical answer—as difficult as it is to accomplish—is that the performance should frustrate the spectator's typical desire in order to transform it into desire for something else. Thus, in Brecht it is the pedagogue's desire to transform the pure love for entertainment into the purer love for instruction. ("Instruction" here can mean, even if contradictorily, both initiation into the process of critical examination of the various sides of an issue, and *how* the critical examination is supposed to end up: acceptance of the Brechtian point of view.) But even Brecht knew—what often his followers did not—that the spectator's typical desire has to be fulfilled within the very scene of instruction. At the same time, the moment a spectator suspects he is being "instructed" is the moment he will turn against what he is seeing, and suspect the motives or goodwill of the theater artist. On the other hand, it is quite possible that the ones who relish the "instruction" are ones who are usually convinced by it already, and it is simply reinforcing their already-established beliefs or prejudices. This reinforcement is my particular definition of "entertainment" in its purest sense. For any political in-crowd, such a notion of politics *as* entertainment can certainly obtain, even as it takes a therapeutic form.

In March 1995 at the first Performance Studies International conference at New York University I presented a paper called "A Critique of the Critique of Presence," in which I took to task certain theories being put forward at that time about avant-garde performance and the necessity of such performance to undermine any sense or illusion of presence for the spectator as a kind of intrinsically political action. As I noted at the time, this was an attempt to wed conventional Brechtian alienation with a newer more vibrant Derridean deconstructive attitude—deconstruction demonstrating how any operative term such as presence is never absolute, but always inhabited by its concealed opposite—even as it seemed to have less to do with the content of performance than its formal presentation in general. The theorists I critiqued in this regard were Philip Auslander, Elinor Fuchs, and Michael Vanden Heuvel, well-known advocates of deconstructionist and poststructuralist critique.[2]

The problem as I viewed it at the time was that these critics had read Derrida as somehow indicating that there was a kind of moral imperative in avant-garde performance (whether the performers knew they were doing this or not) to "deconstruct" presence where it seemed to be occurring, so as to break the fundamental hypnotic hold of dramatic absorption on the spectator wherever possible. (In Fuchs's case, it was the literal demonstration to the audience that the performance was always already the product of writing and not the spontaneous speech of actors.)

My point was that Derrida was advancing no such agenda, since for him "presence"—or more exactly, "full self-presence"—wasn't possible in the first place. Derrida was primarily speaking (writing) about what he saw as the Western philosophical tradition's privileging of the immediacy, the "presence," of speech over writing.[3] Whether or not this is really the central problematic of Western philosophy, as Derrida would have it, his development of a "grammatology" that prioritizes a "generalized writing" incorporates both speech and writing as differential systems of meaning production, beginning at the level of the phoneme. However, if *différance*—his central concept that informs everything he has written since the sixties[4]—involves the play of absence and presence, even presence itself is not dismissed as illusory, but a necessary component in the process of signification itself. Derrida's critique is directed at the erasure of absence in the illusory affirmation of a signifying "fullness" that is also connected to a self-assured unity of being in the subject understood as "pure" or "full" "self-presence." In this regard it should be noted that Derrida never uses the simple word *presence* invidiously. It is always qualified by *pure, full,* or *self-*. I find nothing very controversial about this, nor would I doubt that most philosophers of a traditional stripe would either, especially those critical of Descartes (including Kant) from the time the *Meditations* were published until today (I include both continental and Anglo-American traditions). I suspect that Derrida derived some of this (unacknowledged) critical direction from Jacque Lacan, who at least ten years before him was reflecting on the split subject, whose speech is never fully to be counted his own and present to himself.

[margin note: Scale of Presence]

In any event, both Auslander and Fuchs were present to hear my paper, and I noticed that in their subsequent publications—Auslander's *From Acting to Performance*[5] and Fuchs's *The Death of Character*[6]—their previously more pointed remarks about the undermining of presence by performance were comparatively qualified and subdued. As time has gone by I have not encountered as many remarks by theorists about a necessary critique of presence as I did then.[7] At the most, there has been Auslander's critique of apparent privileging of presence in Peggy Phelan's *Unmarked*, in which the live event that resists reproduction and lasts only for the moment is somehow intrinsically politically progressive and resistant.[8] In fact I quite agree with Auslander's criticism of this position, even accepting his understanding of such events as always already conditioned by mediatization. As such, Auslander's critique of presence has shifted to his focus on the word *liveness* instead. Nonetheless, he claims his critique to be "against ontology," and so still includes an attack on presence. But being for or against presence involves being able to adequately define what you mean by presence. Auslander's critique, despite his attempts to couch it as purely historical (as if the historical is the antithesis of the ontological) is nonetheless itself ontological in a more refined sense, while at the same time de-essentializing the more typical ontological claims made about performance. And yet he hasn't had a great deal to say about the constitutive relation of presence to desire.

[margin note: Zing]

It is clear to me now that in my response to these presumed deconstructions I had ended up positing a "weak version" of a defense of presence by basically accepting the pure temporality of Derridean *différance* and thereby insisting that "presence" is not an ontological position at all, but only a figure of one's desire that is enticed by the play of absence and presence.[9] Of desiring to have and fearing to lose: presence is thus "invested" in something by the spectator, in the way that Benjamin perceived the "aura" as a product of a kind of psychic "social investment."[10] That is, I was describing presence as purely phantasmatic, depending upon the particularities of the desirer's desire, and having no intrinsic relation whatsoever to the object of desire. I could thus define presence in a way that seemed to avoid the ontological issue altogether. But as that stands, whatever is invested by desire could be seen as arbitrary and entirely personal, and its effects less likely to be shared and communicated collectively. I am no longer convinced by this, as I think it is true that there are individuals who have, for good or ill, more "presence" than others and elicit more fascination and attention from people than others do. What had been left out of my response were the characteristics (of the desired or respected performer or individual) that *elicit* desire or respect in the first place.

Thus in my attention to presence as a psychic investment that seemed defined primarily by absence, I discounted the possibility of any possible material psycho-physiological truth about personal presence that compels attention and resistance to absence; who "has" presence and who hasn't and why. That human beings can develop character over time and emanate experience or thoughtfulness may be a physical truth about what we call "presence" in a social setting. There is thus a recognizable material side to presence. It has to do with a certain kind of saturation of feeling or thought in the individual; it accrues according to age and to sensitivity (some can accrue presence at a very young age, others grow into it). This is a "strong version" of a defense of presence. Indeed, one of the reasons to "deconstruct," or more exactly, undermine presence in performance is the effects of performative charisma (Auslander has indicated as much, although he does not go into any detail about what charisma is or how it is constituted). This indicates that the opposition to presence accepts the strong version already, despite the references to the Derridean weak version (which is nonetheless misinterpreted as a moral-political agenda rather than a given of human experience and thought).

"Charisma," unfortunately, remains uncomfortably unanalyzed, if undefined. Those who take a strong antimetaphysical and materialist approach to things cannot explain it adequately, although they would love to be able to explain it away, through recourse to some purely comprehensible socio-semio-psychoanalytic structure of desire. Nonetheless, they clearly note its social power in resisting it. Even Max Weber, despite his studies in the history of what authorizes social organizations in particular ways, does not have much to say in the way of elucidation of what actually *produces* charisma, even though charisma is developed as one of his three central foundations of sociopolitical authority—the others being tradition and reason.

Of course, given what I have said so far, it would be an act of hubris to think that I am in any better position to definitely locate what the power of charisma is (although I do think it has to do with not just the person, but the time and place within which the person acts). I simply offer a modest and tentative idea, mentioned above, about a kind of saturation of feeling, of sensibility, a condensation of experience that in the right circumstances emanates from the person or performer. But perhaps what is most important for the performer is that it is not simply a condensation of experience, but of *practice* as well (one clearly gets this impression from reading the work of acting teachers and theorists like Eugenio Barba, for instance; that Stanislavsky drew from the being-present practice of yoga is not insignificant). Still, even this is not always clear, since teachers often recognize the difference between those who have to really work to develop a sense of presence and those for whom it seems to come naturally. I have nothing more to say about this, which may come as a relief to those semiotic materialists who want to discount the very idea of presence while they contradictorily seek to resist its power over others (and perhaps even themselves).

In terms of presence as an aim of practice, it could probably be found in two interdependent aims: that of directing and focusing the audience's attention in as strong a fashion as possible, and, as a performer engaged in performance, remaining as present as possible in one's concentration and being. In this there is not much difference between the strongest actor and the strongest athlete, for instance; great dancing represents the clearest medium between these two. I would insist that it is this sense of being present—despite all the temporal microdifferences that defeat our conceptions of "perfect" presence, and, in a good performance, are not significantly noticeable in any case—that absorbs our attention and has the ability to take us out of ourselves for the moment. In response to those who might reference Brecht over against the apparently authoritarian "directing and focusing" of audience attention, I would claim that Brecht asks his own actors to do exactly the same thing, even if for metatheatrical aims.

Presence and "Liveness"

I do not think that the experience of presence as a characteristic of a performer or individual is limited to co-present "live" performance, and thus the argument for mediatization or technical reproduction does not affect my characterization of it. That is, I do not think that a sense of presence is limited to a transitory event (although its limitations as an event might enhance one's experience through a greater focusing of attention and desire). One can detect an individual's presence on film and in television. In fact, an accomplished film actor can easily elicit more of a sense of presence than an unaccomplished live actor. Presence, or at least the presence shown in what one sees transpire, has to do with the being-present of the performer-actor to the material at the moment the performer is captured on tape, film, or digital system. (I do not, in this sense, think that all "acting-effects" seen in film are the results of editing—which is often a question of genre; otherwise, what is the point of acting awards?) Despite all the parodic references to it, for me Marlon Brando in *On the Waterfront* demonstrates just exactly this quality. It is often in the eyes, which is exactly why various performance training techniques in the East concentrate attention on the eyes, from India to Indonesia.

In all this I do not mean to abandon the "weak version" of my presence argument as the effect of the play of absence and presence on the desire of the spectator for its replacement by the "strong version" of it as a characteristic possessed or developed by an individual performer. Both are necessary and interdependent, although it is possible, even by certain technical means, to produce a strong effect of presence through concentrating primarily on the weak version. The following is an example, which also illustrates my point that presence can be detected within certain mediated uses themselves.

A few years ago I found myself fascinated by a music video: Alanis Morissette's "Head over Feet." The video consists entirely of a close-up of Morissette, her face filling the frame, except for moments at the end when she drops back, caught up in the song, but then returns to the screen. The real kicker in the video is the fact that at some point she reveals that she has been lip-synching to the song: she stops lip-synching—stops moving her lips—altogether, or, toward the end, seems to be singing something else not matched by the soundtrack. I have found this video to be far more effective than the most expensive computer-generated graphic music videos. It disorients the viewer in ways that the fanciest graphics cannot, and does it in the simplest, and no doubt cheapest, way possible. But it points to something else I sense in this disorientation—a sense of presence coming from Morissette, or maybe just the video as a whole. Apparently it should be just the opposite: the illusion of "presence" is to come out of a sense of total integrity and unity of effects. In fact, it is a Brechtian maneuver, showing the "mechanism" of illusion, and presumably such maneuvers undermine "presence." Now insofar as my reading of what "presence" is has not been primarily ontological as a critique of the infinitesimal present, and phenomenological only insofar that phenomenology is predicated on desire (or intention, in Husserl or Brentano's sense) and belief, the notion that one can undermine "presence" altogether by a form of alienation is itself an illusion. For what that alienating maneuver does is only displace presence (as site of desire and belief) to another level—that is, to the level of the one doing the alienating, the "source" of alienation (the framer, the psychic proscenium). This points to the site of presence as also the site of authority, which theatrical "deconstructors" always like to point to, while denying how the advancement of their own authority is implicated in the act. If it works, we *believe* the alienator, and insofar as we believe him or her, he or she has presence for us. This goes for what I said above about Brecht's actors, and it has been my experience of the Wooster Group as well as Richard Foreman's theater, both privileged in the literature as alienating deconstructors of presence.

But let's take this another step. Whatever his or her specific agenda or aim otherwise, every artist is, in the process of creation, an *animist,* imbuing or assuming a kind of autotelic or even autopoetic life (or "presence") for their material, whether physical, visual, aural, or verbal. Even speech acts by conceptual artists participate in this process. Given that point, I would take this still farther and say that every *theorist* participates in this animism, if they want their theory to gain currency, which means taking on a life of its own. This is why most theorists aim at the development of certain specific terms or neologisms that can be quoted and used by others (referencing the theorist of course, and perhaps making his or her name). As in the work of art, these terms then take on a relatively autonomous existence once their general reception is assured. One reason why the critique of essentialism (the idea that human beings have stable biological or metaphysical essences) in theory is interminable is that certain forms of language, even if—or precisely *because*—they are employed *against* the essentialisms of others (however construed) inevitably take on "essential-ist" features themselves in the process (if they are believed). This is one reason why I believe the critique of essentialism in theory is interminable. Interminable because certain forms of language, even if or precisely *because* they are employed *against* the essentialisms of others (however construed) inevitably take on "essentialist" features themselves in the process (if they are believed). This is why so-called strategic essentialism (speaking of animated terms) is not a *choice*, but an always already, or *a priori*, fact of theoretical life.

Presence and the Experience of Time

At the heart of the critique of presence, and the positing of a term like Der-rida's *différance*, is a denial that the present "exists." This is exemplified in the apocalyptic speech of the homeless autodidact Johnny to the night watchman in Mike Leigh's film *Naked*. He demonstrates the impossibility of the present by repeating the word "now" over and over: by the time he's said "now" the present is already "gone." This falls perfectly in line with the traditional Heraclitean viewpoint about reality having no being, but only becoming through perpetual change; or, according to Heraclitus's disciple, Cratylus, the river one never even steps in *once*. But then consider a distraught mother out of reach of her child who is about to touch a hot stove: she screams "Stop where you are right *now!*" Would we say that her use of "now" in the imperative would be pointless because the "now" does not exist?

I think that it is important, when examining the so-called critique of presence, to distinguish between an abstract, presumably "objective" view of temporality and the subjective experience of temporality. The first cor-responds to Derrida's "micrological" deconstruction of the metaphysics of presence—the *belief* in the reality of presence that corresponds with the stasis of Parmenides' idea of Being. That is, Derrida's is an (anti)ontologi-cal deconstruction of a *concept* of presence as informing logocentric phi-losophy, not a negation of the subjective experience of presence. This micrological analysis depends upon Derrida's notion of *différance* in lan-guage taken from Saussure: every term in a sequence differing from every other term, but every term also deferring its meaning within the ongoing chain of signification (based in the desire for meaning). In order to critique the personal sense of presence of anyone, one has to wholly identify themselves with the language they speak, as opposed to what they do with their bodies (despite the fact that Derrida's critique of the privileging of speech-as-presence has a distinct phenomenological caste to it).

The fact of the matter is that people do not experience presence "mistakenly" at this micrological level. Consider the physicist's "micrological" view that a tabletop is not solid but consists of an atomic structure that itself consists of mostly space between the atomic elements. Of course that is not going to make much difference for my level of reality if I bang my fist or head on the tabletop. Nor, I suspect, are the characteristics of this micrological analysis of presence very useful in thwarting a person's attraction to a charismatic figure of authority, whether it is a Hitler or a Martin Luther King or a Gandhi (or a Jacques Derrida!). The basic problem is that this micrological view of ontology, or the ontological problematic, is largely irrelevant to most people's practical experience of the world. The same, I expect, concerns any "microanalysis," including the "micropolitics" of Michel Foucault and the combined work of Gilles Deleuze and Felix Guattari, in which all levels of experience are flattened out into a rather subliminal experience of the microlevel. The totalitarian view of "the personal is *the* political" (as opposed to the practically important "the personal is political") operates along these lines as well, but inasmuch as the political operates in the real world at the conscious level of strategy and argument, any complete focus on the subliminal level of the micropolitical would be self-defeating or else merely function as it does in the academy, as a *pose* of being political through theorization, without ever dirtying one's hands.

This gap between a philosophically logical position and experience is nothing new: we can think of Hume's analysis indicating that any possible relation between cause and effect cannot be proved, but may simply be a variety of *post hoc ergo proctor hoc;* nonetheless Hume admits he cannot function at this level when he decides to play a game of billiards.[11] In opposition to this micrological (anti)ontological analysis that is for the most part outside the ken of the majority's experience (including my own), it makes much more sense, if we are going to connect the concept of presence with a temporal framework, to conceive of it in the terms Paul Ricoeur (drawing from Augustine's famous Book XI of the *Confessions*) has presented us in *Time and Narrative*.[12] His point is that human beings can have no direct experience of time. Human beings only experience time through three modes: memory, as constructing the past; attention, as constructing the present; and anticipation, as constructing the future. At the same time (this is my point, not Ricoeur's), the attenuation or exaggeration of any one of these features has an impact on the others. (This is clear when we examine the consciousness of Samuel Beckett's characters.) Our *experience* of time can seldom partake of Derrida's micrologic, unless one can attain some altered state, and even then, it is impossible to sustain. Our relation to time is fundamentally psychologically mediated, through memory, attention, and desire. So the sub-ontological critique of pure presence means very little to our actual experience of what we take to be presence, and how we interpret what is present before us at any moment. What's more, given the variable relation between the three states of mind in its relation to what is happening at any given moment, "presence" is experienced not merely in an "on-off" relation with absence, but can also be understood as experienced in degrees, more or less. (I believe the audition of music is a good example.)

Is this to imply that micrological analysis is useless or pointless? If we asked the same question about microphysics, the answer would be obvious: of course not. But the value of microphysics is only valuable (and instrumentally so) through the process of translation to a human everyday level of experience, a level of tangible effects. In like manner we could assume the same of micrological deconstructive analysis or micropolitical analysis—their value only consists of how they are translated from a microlevel to an everyday level of experience. The problem with most discourses that employ microanalyses is that this translation from one level to the next, with its subsequent distortions, is not taken into account. The possibilities of its particular process and their vicissitudes (since in translation something is always lost) are ignored when a simple assertion of the microlevel gives one the sense that that is all there is. The sole focus on one level of experience can have the effect of making any other level of experience disappear. A good example is Foucault's genealogical analysis of disciplinary power.[13] By viewing everything at that level, as it presumes to account for everything "above" it—the ethical and juridical humanitarian notions that appear to frame it discursively—it effectively dissolves those frameworks as valuable, intentional, effective, or justifiable.[14] Thus all systems of deliberative justice disappear, since the reversal strategy of genealogical analysis is designed to negate them as epiphenomenal to their ostensible effects—making punishment and coercive normalization the "source" of justice, just as Nietzsche makes weakness and resentment the source of morality. The reversal of priority is designed to make that which then is viewed as an effect instead of a cause disappear as a human value. But if there is any value whatsoever in micropolitical or genealogical analysis, it certainly cannot reside at this point, which is as nihilistic—if not more so—than the system it condemns. So the problem of translation remains. We need not—indeed, should not—remain with Foucault at his microlevel to utilize realistically his valuable analytical contributions to our understanding of social existence. Genealogical analysis rests on a simple reversal of a traditional binary (that of cause and effect, or motive and result), something Derridean deconstruction notes as incomplete, because it also leaves things as they are (although it is dubious that deconstruction itself could do more than that). The illusion of genealogy is that the mere act of reversal is enough to significantly weaken the power, if not destroy the binary, of the leading term. This is true as long as you do not *act* on your new view of the world, thereby reestablishing the force of the binary, which for Foucault, is simply leaving power relations as they are.

The question remains—how does one make the translation from the micrological to the everyday level? (N.B.: there is also a macro-logical level we are not addressing here, the level of history, whether cultural or natural, although I imagine the same questions apply.) To do this with the effects of Foucault's analysis means ignoring Foucault's willingness to remain on the microlevel and his assumptions about the nature of actual everyday-level political, legislative, and juridical processes. In Derrida's case, it is a question of translating what happens on the microlevel of his analysis of "pure temporality" or becoming to the everyday level of communication that functions, paradoxically, in both a cruder and far more effective fashion than he gives it credit for. In Derrida's case it means a translation from a microanalytical (anti)ontological level to a less narrowly focused (or even less obsessional) psychosocial level of communication and reception. Michael Polanyi has much to say about this as he describes the relation of the formal features of perception (or "subsidiaries") to the *matter* of perception (or "focus") and how concentration on the subsidiary elements (like *différance*) obliterates the meaning of the focus, even as this concentration pretends to locate the putative source (not origin) of their meaning.[15] The sociohistorical "how it is produced" becomes confused with the "meaning-as-use" itself at any given point— the genetic fallacy that lies at the heart of genealogical analysis as well. It is clear that this same confusion has occurred with the conjoining of Brecht and deconstruction with regard to the basic elements of the theater, regardless of the content of what is being performed.

It would seem that this microanalysis has been a staple of the avant-garde since the impressionist's experiments with optics and certainly since Henri Bergson's speculations about human consciousness and memory. Bergson's notion of *durée* is a micrological analysis of our relation to time that evades most people's social experience of it—that is, when it is not obsessively internal, as in Gertrude Stein's "continual presence." Any possible or potential experience of pure *durée* is dependent upon a largely solipsistic experience, not a shared social experience that one can call historical. To conflate these two levels is in fact a category mistake, a relationship, which if forced to be defined as a "political" one also ends up to be self-defeating. (This is clearly a problem whenever "the historical" ends up being reduced to "temporality" per se.) Where it has been most focused as the style of a unique consciousness, it has been labeled "high modernism" (Woolf, Joyce, and Stein). Where it has attempted to align itself with overt political provocation, it has retained the label of avant-garde: futurism (fascism), Dadaism (anarchism, communism), surrealism, Brechtianism (communism). The intellectual bases of the avant-garde and its attempts at translating the micrological into the everyday have failed to be communicated to the masses, and outside their reception by intellectuals only the cruder, more uncontrollable effects have been received. It might be said that certain high modernists, like Woolf or Joyce (not Stein) accepted the fact that micrological understanding only occurs at relatively rare epiphanic moments, moments to be extended and built upon in the course of writing, but unsustainable in everyday life. One might say that this problem is shared by mysticism (parallel with Joycean and Woolfian epiphanies) in which individual experience can touch upon regions that micrology speaks of but does not consciously account for in normal social experience. And, *pace* Derrida, for mystics the experience of "presence" would be a full and intimate experience of *pure temporality*—which he would see as nothing but difference—which involves the *loss* of self, of self-possession. His concern, on the contrary, is the condition of "pure *self-presence.*" But the fact of the matter is, mysticism is no basis for political decision-making. It may in fact operate beautifully in one-to-one ethical action, but how can it function collectively or administratively? (Indeed every instance of collective mysticism on the political level has proved disastrous, if not evil.)

An example of the problem of translation from the micro-ontological level of temporal analysis to our individual experiences of "real time," a problem of translation between the exactitude of physics and the inexactitude of the psychological framework of perception, can be found in Robert Wilson's foundational story (his equivalent of Cage's story of the anechoic chamber) of the slow motion film of a mother picking up her baby. He wants to maintain that there is a subliminal, underlying truth to the baby's presumed reaction of crying when the loving mother picks it up. Viewed in real time, we see a smiling mother bending down to pick up an infant, who then cries. Slowed down, we "see" the mother "lunging" at the baby, an action that presumably caused the baby to cry. Outside of the fact that this is a singular instance and that there are no other cases to test it against, one has to ask a couple of questions. Can a movement that is perceived even by us as simply a quick, but nonthreatening one, really be *revealed* as "lunging" when shown at a slowed-down speed? For surely the relative speed of the movement and the minutiae we miss in its trajectory has a great deal to do with how we interpret it. What *appears* to be a "lunge" at slow speed *isn't necessarily* a "lunge" in real time. The assumption that it is relies on the idea that we *do* actually notice all the minutiae of characteristics that go into making it not just appear as a lunge, but *be* a lunge, while somehow not noticing it at the same time. In other words, we automatically recognize and respond to the subliminal "truth" of the movement (even if the mother did not). I think this is a pretty untenable position to take, especially given the general debunking of the subliminal arguments made in regard to advertising tests. But if it is not likely for *us* to notice this was a lunge, how much *more* unlikely would it be for an infant, whose focus is not as acute? (Given the general state of the child's focus, all movement coming near it at any speed could be interpreted as a "lunge.") This is not to gainsay whatever rare beauty has emerged in Wilson's theatrical practice of slowing things down, only to dispute the deeper psychological truth he believes to have found as a result of slowing things down. Besides, consciously slowing down an actor's movement will produce quite different results from slowing down the real-time movement of a film.

The untenable nature of Wilson's idea can be seen clearly with regard to the Rodney King trial and verdict, where the defense slowed down the video of his being beaten by police to a frame-by-frame analysis. They did this to show that it was *King* who was attacking and was a real threat to the police, and not the other way around. Given time enough and interpretive use of ambiguous movements that are seen as ambiguous only when taken out of their actual temporal context, one could prove anything. This is not to say that slowing things down does not reveal hidden truths to us, but they can only reveal physical facts, not true psychological states. While slow motion can reveal the trajectory of a bullet, as in Zapruder's film of the Kennedy assassination, can it show that a smile is really a grimace? Even if that is only a flickering impression made in a microsecond of time on the way to a smile, and certainly not experienced as such by the person smiling or the person receiving it? Such are the vicissitudes of micrological or microphysical analysis when applied to everyday perception.

Conclusion

The senses of presence connected to individuals, with which I began this chapter, which were all to one extent or another positive (such as "presence of mind" in a disaster) indicate that presence (or "the illusion of presence," whatever that means) is not intrinsically related to domination pure and simple. Consider a perception of presence in relation to the following qualities of human experience whose authority we acknowledge often enough in our everyday lives (even when we resist): dominative power (physical, political, or economic), yes!, but also beauty, moral probity or justness, wisdom, intellectual skill, grace (physical and social skill), sexual prowess.

I always find it suspect and sometimes downright silly whenever someone decides that one particular form that human experience or cognition takes is intrinsically bad (just as when someone decides that particular parts of speech are bad, like determining that metaphors are always bad because of an abstract formal analogy that makes them appear "phallogocentric," while metonyms are good, for the opposite analogical reason, of course). Pertinent to our subject, the focus becomes "presence" or "the experience of presence" or, closely connected to it, "empathy," and to go even further, the concept of "authority" itself. To my mind this is a naive formalistic approach to reality instead of an understanding of the basic pragmatic role that certain forms or concepts of experience play—even in their idealistic sense—in human life. The question is not what the effect of "presence" or "empathy" or even "absorption" automatically results in, in and of themselves, and in all circumstances, but how it functions within a specific context, how it motivates, and to what end. It is then that we can estimate whether its use is abusive or manipulative or necessary for an ethical or compassionate (or politically just) relation to function in the first place. It would be patently absurd to say that because daytime television talk shows (Oprah, Montel, etc.) milk the capabilities of human empathy and compassion for sensationalist purposes and viewer ratings connected to the guru status achieved by the hosts, that this means that "empathy" and "compassion" are the "problem" themselves (just as it would be absurd that some of the issues they address on their shows should be simply dismissed as well—the real question is that of the *approach* and its relative sensibility or efficacy). I do not intend here to get into a defense of empathy from the Brechtian animus against it, only to note that the very basis of Brecht's theory is empathetic, even if he attempts to clear it away from the practice. That is, when Brecht claims we should not speak in the name of morality, but in the name of the victims, how more ideally empathetic can you get? In a way, Brecht is less concerned with undermining the presence of theatrical performance than he is with increasing the presence of mind of the spectators. But this need not be seen as a zero-sum game.

Micrological, microphysical, metaphysical arguments. Maybe true, maybe not. The issue is whether they have value for us on any other level. One of the reasons that the primacy of speech over writing has held such currency for centuries has to do with a commonsensical notion of presence that fits the needs or desires of a common human psychology, not because of its "empirical" truth. To deny people the pleasure of speaking about presence in theater may be like condemning people for saying, "The sun rises," instead of, "The earth turns," which in the relativity of space is less a matter of illusion than perspective anyway. While there may be something pleasurable in observing the self-reflexive paradoxes of theatrical illusion, such as are witnessed to in Pirandello, there is something strangely perverse in trying to—and believing one *can*—frustrate the pleasure of the spectator's desire to believe, for the moment at least, in what the theater can give them. In fact, given the atomistic nature of our relations to each other in the world, and the state of theatrical performance in general, I would argue for more presence, not less.

NOTES

1. Obviously, this was before the events of September 11, 2001, changed the nature of airport protocols.
2. See Philip Auslander, *Presence and Resistance: Postmodernism and Cultural Politics in Contemporary American Performance* (Ann Arbor: University of Michigan Press, 1992); Elinor Fuchs, "Presence and the Revenge of Writing: Re-thinking Theatre

after Derrida," *Performing Arts Journal* 9, nos. 2–3 (1985): 163–73; Michael Vanden Heuvel, *Performing Drama/Dramatizing Performance: Alternative Theater and the Dramatic Text* (Ann Arbor: University of Michigan Press, 1991).

3. See Jacques Derrida, *Of Grammatology,* trans. Gayatri Chakravorty Spivak (Baltimore: Johns Hopkins University Press, 1974).

4. See Derrida, "Différance," in *Speech and Phenomena,* trans. David B. Allison (Evanston, Ill.: Northwestern University Press, 1973).

5. Philip Auslander, *From Acting to Performance* (New York: Routledge, 1997).

6. Elinor Fuchs, *The Death of Character: Perspectives on Theater after Modernism* (Ann Arbor: University of Michigan Press, 1997).

7. In a recent instance, Jon McKenzie, in his quite ambitious and remarkable book *Perform or Else* (New York: Routledge, 2001), which tries to construct the most inclusive "general theory" of performance possible, claims that "[t]he critique of presence, and the reevaluation of values it entails, have become a signature event of French poststructuralism, itself a signpost bearing—rightly or wrongly—the names of Bataille, Baudrillard, Barthes, Bourdieu, Cixous, Clement, de Certeau, Deleuze, Derrida, Foucault, Girard, Guattari, Irigaray, Kristeva, Lacan, Levinas, Lyotard and Serres" (40). An initial reading of this sentence would lead one to believe that all of these thinkers are significantly engaged in a critique of presence, and I assume that this is the general impression to be left with the reader. However, I find it difficult to believe that some of these thinkers have been overtly concerned with such a critique and so the idea that that's what they are doing is largely a matter of a broad interpretation. I would maintain that presence certainly does matter for thinkers concerned with experiences that challenge easy reduction of human life to semiotization, which would include Bataille, the late work of Barthes, Foucault, and even McKenzie's favorites, Deleuze and Guattari. And yet note how McKenzie frames this sentence: the critique of presence has become "a signature event" of French poststructuralism, *itself a signpost bearing—rightly or wrongly*—the names of," etc. "Poststructuralism's" signature event is thus the critique of presence, but insofar as these thinkers are "rightly or wrongly" associated with poststructuralism, then those with no specific interest in a critique of presence as a "key event" in their own work can probably be "wrongly" associated with poststructuralism. But a quick reading of the sentence would seem to indicate that all these high-powered thinkers were fundamentally engaged in such a critique. McKenzie gives no indication of how any of these thinkers, besides Derrida, are engaged in this critique. What's more, what "presence" is supposed to mean in this context is never clarified.

8. Peggy Phelan, *Unmarked: The Politics of Performance* (New York: Routledge, 1993).

9. This is a position I took in *The Fate of the Object: From Modern Object to Postmodern Sign in Performance, Art, and Poetry* (Ann Arbor: University of Michigan Press, 1995), connecting it to the relation of physicality to voice. What this doesn't account for is the quality of presence in nonspeaking performance such as dance.

10. Walter Benjamin, "On Some Motifs in Baudelaire," in *Reflections,* trans. Edmund Jephcott, ed. Peter Demetz (New York: Harcourt Brace Jovanovich, 1978).

11. See Hume's *Treatise on Human Nature* (London: Penguin, 1985). I'd like to thank James Harding for pointing out the connection.

12. Paul Ricoeur, *Time and Narrative*, trans. Kathleen McLaughlin and David Pellauer, vol. 1 (Chicago: University of Chicago Press, 1984).

13. Michel Foucault, *Discipline and Punish: The Birth of the Prison*, 2d ed., trans. Alan Sheridan (New York: Vintage Books, 1995).

14. In both the analysis of narrative of Roland Barthes and the biological analysis of life forms by Michael Polanyi, what is central is that meaning is only obtainable in relation to a hierarchy of functions, so that any "microlevel" has no meaning in itself, but is entirely dependent for its meaning upon levels above it that make its function meaningful. See Barthes, "The Structural Analysis of Narrative," in *Image/Music/Text*, trans. Stephen Heath (New York: Hill and Wang, 1980) and Polanyi, "On the Modern Mind," *Encounters* 24, no. 5 (May 1965): 12–20.

15. See Michael Polanyi and Harry Prosch, *Meaning* (Chicago: University of Chicago Press, 1975).

EIGHT

Technique

Robert P. Crease and John Lutterbie

When techniques are broadly defined—as process-oriented and involving any systematic and goal-directed human action—one finds them in every creative human activity: in sports, painting, dancing, playing musical instruments, and acting; in physics, chemistry, medicine, and astronomy; in education, administration, and sex. Joseph Agassi argues that magic consists of techniques, though unscientific ones.[1] The swing-era ballad "Oh, Look At Me Now" mentions "technique of kisses." But techniques can also be much more narrowly defined to include only fully articulated and independently recognized practices that are specifically identified and studied as techniques (the "Alexander technique").

Whether broadly or narrowly conceived, techniques tend to inspire an ambivalent reaction especially among practitioners of artistic fields and especially in theater. Champions deny the existence of a sharp distinction between technique and artistry, seeing the former as enabling, liberating, and essential to the latter. Skeptics draw a sharp division between technique as involving the (teachable) mechanics of acts, and artistry as involving the (unteachable) aesthetics of acts, and then point out how frequently the former comes to dominate, smother, and disrupt the latter. Musician Charles Ives, a critic of technique, is famous for remarking, "My God! What has sound got to do with music!" Indeed, it is virtually a cultural cliché that technique is at least disconnected from true artistry. A cartoon in the *New Yorker* magazine once depicted a robber explaining to several other robbers how to use a new gun; "Sure, technique counts," ran the caption, "but at some point you've got to trust your criminal instincts." Between the two poles—of technique as enabling or disabling artistry— lies a spectrum of attitudes, in which technique is regarded as contributing to artistry in a variety of ways and with different degrees of importance.[2]

Perspectives on Technique

In theater, a long-standing difference of opinion about the relationship of technique and the artistry or emotional intensity of performance has played out among philosophers and theater scholars ever since Plato's reflections on the *technē* of acting, in which he found no "knowledge" but only seductive passions arising from blind inspiration—the inexplicable presence of the Divine. Shakespeare, marveling at the ability of passion and form to work together, has Hamlet chastise himself for failing to do in life what the player can do "in a fiction, in a dream of passion . . . his whole function suiting / With forms to his conceit." Diderot felt that the passions were preeminent in acting until he realized that David Garrick's technique allowed him to play consistently well night after night, while those who depended on inspiration could not sustain the depth of passion in subsequent performances. Stanislavsky found that the actors of his time were depending on technique at the cost of emotional verity, was impressed by Chaliapin's apparently spontaneously and self-taught "natural genius," and worked at devising a system for training actors that could be relied upon to bring emotional honesty to the stage, "to create on stage *a live life* of the human spirit."[3] Technique, in short, generally is seen as a set of skills (i.e., tools that can be acquired) that allow the performer to access the emotional contents demanded by a role, but needs to be supplemented—even as it sometimes interferes—with a charismatic intensity that demands attention, understood as an intangible derived from inspiration (in-spiriting), pure talent, or "presence," like Stanislavsky's "human spirit."

This long-standing ambivalence about the value of technique—as well as the broad spectrum of activities in vastly different fields said to fall into that category—suggests an essential conceptual unclarity of the sort that philosophers might be expected to address. One would expect a philosophical account of technique to do much to exhibit the domain and limits of technique, to indicate what is the same and what different in each of its diverse forms, to clarify how the often polarized spectrum of attitudes about it came about, and to reveal those conditions under which it is liberating and those under which it is stifling. But among philosophers, alas, we find a repetition of the same spectrum of attitudes. Philosophers, too, seem to be scattered between two poles in their attitudes toward technique. At the one pole are those who regard technique negatively as the defining manifestation of the crisis of modernity, while those at the other pole view it positively as an inseparable feature of human activity itself.

The critics who view technique negatively—including most notably Martin Heidegger, Jacques Ellul, and Lewis Mumford—argue that technique is a means for imposing our will on ourselves and on the world that detaches *technē* from *poiēsis* and distorts relations between ourselves and nature, and among ourselves.[4] For them, technique is more than mechanization, more even than a distracting and even subversive instrument; the search for technique, the quest for effective means to ends, becomes an all-absorbing and insatiable end itself, leading us to gain mastery over beings at the cost of our understanding of Being. Paradoxically, technique becomes our master instead of our servant. In *The Illusion of Technique,* for instance, philosopher William Barrett opposes technique—which for him is teachable, akin to decision procedure, and rule-governed—to genuine creation—which is unteachable, free, and un-rule-governed. "Every technique is put to use for some end, and this end is decided in the light of some philosophic outlook or other. The technique cannot produce the philosophy that directs it." The result is that *"technique presupposes freedom for its own meaning."* Thus Barrett is not claiming, of course, that one can become a Mozart without studying scales, or play competition tennis without working on one's backhand; the point is that technique serves ends that it does not itself choose or influence, and that the true creativity lies precisely in these ends. But technique absorbs us, Barrett says following Heidegger, causing us to lose interest in those ends, or transform the end into the search for technique itself.[5] As a result, technique "blinds" the vision of modern philosophy, as it tends to blind the vision of other creative fields. The project of true, unblinded philosophy (and artistry) runs counter to technique, for it would seek to reawaken our sense of genuine human existence, of the lived body and the lifeworld operating prior to the overlay of theories and techniques that distort and abstract from experience. This would give us a maximum ability to make contact with and respond to—a maximum "grip" on—the world.

At the other pole are those scholars who view technique positively and as inseparable from human experience, without which we would have little or no grip on the world. Marcel Mauss sees what he calls "bodily techniques" everywhere from singing and swimming to spitting and lovemaking. A careful look at concrete practices in these areas, he says, discovers not "the soul and its repetitive faculties" but "the techniques and work of collective and individual practical reason."[6] For Mauss, techniques are actions that are *"effective* and *traditional"* (for "there is no technique and no transmission in the absence of tradition") that are "felt by the author as *actions of a mechanical, physical, or physio-chemical order* and . . . pursued with that aim in view." For Freud, the application of the term extends still further, into the unconscious realm, for it, too, works through techniques (as in "the technique of the dream"). Numerous philosophers of technology, including most notably Patrick Heelan and Don Ihde, emphasize that the lifeworld contains not just "spin-offs" of scientific activity, like thermometers and microwaves, but all scientific phenomena perceptible through readable technologies, some accessible only via techniques.[7] Technique is thus partly productive of the lifeworld, intrinsically connected with what it is to be human.

On the one hand, then, technique is viewed as an activity of self-assertion and domination, which manifests itself in numerous forms in a variety of disciplines, through which we enable ourselves to achieve arbitrary ends (artistic or otherwise). It is the creation of means to ends, with the choice of these ends the product of a different kind of activity (acts of will or thought) that is or ought to be primary and more fundamental than the means. Technique presupposes freedom, in Barrett's words. The danger, according to this view, is that technique leads us to become more absorbed by it than by the ends it should serve, and thus blind us to artistry. On the other hand, technique is viewed as an indispensable aspect of human experience and productive of the lifeworld, including its artistry. Human beings are already "techniqued" from the start: To be is to be techniqued. Turning Barrett's remark on its head, one might say from this vantage point that freedom presupposes technique. What seems left out by the first view is an account of what is happening when technique operates creatively and productively in the lifeworld, and by the second view an account of what is happening when it impoverishes or subverts the very activity it is supposed to serve.

Toward a Philosophy of Technique

A philosophical discussion of technique will have to straddle the disciplinary fence; it needs to be addressed as something that occurs in both the arts and sciences, albeit with different dimensions in each area. To insist on addressing performance separately in the context of theater and science would be to impose a false disciplinary boundary. What is discovered about it in one area may help to shed light on another. The disciplinary fence between the arts and sciences, however, has so much of a hold on our thinking that purists may find such talk abstract or loose—yet to address technique across that fence requires no more abstraction or imaginativeness than is habitually practiced in either domain.

A philosophical discussion of technique, too, we claim, needs to involve both a hermeneutical account of the origin of technique and a phenomenological account of the body. By a hermeneutical account, we mean one that would look at how techniques evolve out of an already existing involvement with, and understanding of, a concrete situation, leading to transformations of those involvements and understandings, and thus of the situation and our understanding of it, and so forth, in an unending process.[8] By a phenomenological account of the body, we mean one that takes its point of departure from what is variously called embodiment, lived body, flesh, or animate form, the experiences of which are that of a unified being, and which cannot be understood apart from concrete human experience.

One way to begin an account of technique would be to regard it as the standardization of a performance ability. In *The Play of Nature: Experimentation as Performance,* Robert P. Crease argued that the structure of performance is essentially the same in the theater arts and experimental science.[9] Performance involves the conceiving, producing, and witnessing of actions in order to try to get something that we cannot get by consulting what we already have. A performance is thus more than a *praxis,* or a skill or ability that simply produces what it does, but is a *poiēsis,* a bringing forth of a phenomenon, something with presence in the world, something that can be returned to and that can appear in different ways in different circumstances, thus exhibiting some lawlike behavior. In the performing arts, this lawlike behavior is represented or "programmed" in part by texts, scripts, scores, and so forth, which are then correlated with techniques and practices so that a phenomenon appears—the work. The representation thus structures both the performance process and the work itself. A script, for instance, both structures the actions of the performers on the one hand, and describes what transpires onstage (the work) on the other. Expressed in phenomenological language, a representation read *noetically* (with respect to its creating) is something to be performed; read *noematically* (with respect to the product, the creation), it describes the object appearing in performance. The argument is that the same is true of the experimental activity of science.

Performance, therefore, is not a metaphor that is extended merely suggestively from the dramatic arts into science; rather, its structure is the same in each. In both, the representation (theory, language, script) used to program the performance does not completely determine the outcome (product, work), but only assists in the encounter with the new. The world is wilder and richer than we can represent; what appears in performance can exceed the program used to put it together, and even surprise and baffle us. A scientific experiment that has been planned and programmed on the basis of a certain theory, for instance, can disclose things that cause its creators to change the theory, while the activity of putting together a performance can take directions that were unanticipated by the performers and playwright. That's, in fact, *why* we stage performances—to get something we couldn't possibly get with what we have.

While this may appear to be simply what is commonly called "trial and error," the point is that the way in which trial and error functions in leading to a deepening and enriching of our engagement with the world—the *meaning* of trial and error—has a quite specific, tripartite structure whose features are characterized by the "hermeneutic circle."[10] One moment is the presence of an existing set of involvements and abilities with which we have a grip on the world, which we can bring to each new situation. A second moment is the sense, the suspicion, the expectation, that we can acquire more of a "grip" over the situation, provides more out of it than we already do. A third moment is the presence of a sense of how to begin to get that better grip with what we already know how to do. The hermeneutical point is that the process is not a stepwise affair in which one finds knowledge and then applies it, but a continuous motion in which all three moments are at work all the time. Each moment—even simple puttering around, jamming, tinkering, noodling, improvising—is already a movement of interpretation, a making-explicit of what I already understand that assures, enriches, and deepens my involvements and expectations.

This process exhibits itself, as well, in the case of technique. But before discussing the hermeneutic circle in the evolution of technique, a short discussion of technique in science is useful, where a technique is something that results in measurements or preparations of objects for measurement or further manipulation. A technique is to be distinguished from an *effect* on the one hand, and a standardized *technology* on the other. An effect can be defined as a characteristic, instructive, or useful consequence of a scientific phenomenon (Rutherford scattering, the Doppler effect, the piezoelectric effect, and so forth). When an effect is sensitive to some sought-after parameter of a system (Rutherford scattering is sensitive to charge and mass distribution, the Doppler effect to relative speed, and the piezoelectric effect can produce short, high-voltage bursts of electricity), the effect is potentially useful as a technique, because it can be used to alter, analyze, or measure that parameter, or it can be put to use in other performances. A technology can be thought of as a technique transformed to be sufficiently standardized to become a "black box," something whose principles do not have to be fully grasped by a user. A black box can be plugged in and used not only without understanding its insides but also independently of its context. A "Doppler gun," for instance, can be used to check the speeds of cars without understanding wave mechanics, and under many different kinds of conditions.

Techniques in science, therefore, can be thought of as part of a *trajectory* of increasing standardization and decontextualization in which effects are transformed into techniques and techniques into technologies.[11] It is not a final product, for we are not interested in it per se but rather in what new it enables us to do. But it is also not a black box, automatic, entirely mechanical, a mere instrumental means to an end, whose principles we have forgotten and do not need; for we still have to have some appreciation of what goes into it. A technique is the standardization of a performance ability—something we know how to do—such that it fulfills expectations reliably enough so that instead of using it to linger over and explore a phenomenon, we can put it in the service of some other performance, using it to deliver us to a situation where a new kind of performance ability—a new kind of interplay with phenomena—becomes possible. A technique can be thought of as something we use, but whose principles are still perspicuous to us, and thus still under our control. Techniques, unlike technologies, can be thought of as performance abilities that are still "thick," not transparent as a pane of glass is to the viewer of a garden.

In theater, the analogue of "effects" are spontaneous, self-taught, "natural" abilities to dance, play, or act; recall, for instance, Chaliapin's "natural genius" in the eyes of Stanislavsky, and the latter's desire to develop a technique that would enable actors who didn't have this "natural" ability to perform as though they had it. The analogue to "some other end" is the ability to use this technique outside of one specific context. The analogue to technologizing ("Doppler gunning") technique is to apply it indiscriminately, without worrying about applicability or context.

Phenomenology of the Body and Technique

A philosophy of technique, we said, requires a phenomenology of the lived body. The testimony that had motivated Cartesian dualism—experiences of mental activity seeming to act independently of the rest of the organism, or of physical conditions weighing on, interfering with, or constraining mental activity—are not symptoms of an underlying division within this animate form but instead are made possible by its primordial unity. The body is not a bridge or instrument that connects subject and world, but rather a primordial unity productive of there being persons and worlds at all.

To elaborate the significance of this for technique in the context of theater requires an investigation of a process that Maxine Sheets-Johnstone calls the apprenticeship to our bodies. Rejecting the Cartesian privileging of the mind and even the traditional phenomenologist's tendency to privilege adult bodies, Sheets-Johnstone argues that we require a genetic account of the apprenticeship that animate beings undertake in infancy, when they experiment with movement, gaining the skills necessary to engage the world in constructive ways: "infants move in relationally meaningful ways toward the world, developing understandings of others and of objects in the process."[12] From the very first hours of life, infants demonstrate an ability, for example, to imitate the mouth and tongue movements of caregivers. In exploring how their bodies move, the infant demonstrates three seemingly innate activities—imitation, joint attention, and turn taking—that are not given but learned. Citing specialists in infant development, Sheets-Johnstone argues that these activities help us acquire neuromuscular coordination through movement that, in turn, allows us to acquire the skills needed to cope with an increasingly independent existence. Through repetition we become more at ease with ourselves and develop confidence in our ability to perform tasks, gaining a sense of ourselves as subjects and learning appropriate ways of behaving.

> Skill-learning is rooted in the capacity of one bodily presence to be attentive to another and to pattern movement along the lines of the other, imitating the way in which the other performs something, but also selecting the occasions on which one will and will not perform according to the methods of another. Imitation may thus ground not just social but aesthetic practice.[13]

For Sheets-Johnstone, the development of an autobiographical self (a combination of a bodily awareness and memory) arises from explorations in movement prior to conscious thought during which we come to understand how to use our bodies, develop a memory of experiences, and engage objects actively and effectively, through "an expanding repertoire of 'I cans.'" By being attentive to others and to the "dynamics of our own movement" along the axes of time and space, we come to master ourselves as animate beings and begin to know ourselves in the world, as we come to know the world.

Combining cognitive research into how we learn with evolutionary science, Sheets-Johnstone creates a convincing argument for the primacy of the body explicitly in our constitution as subjects, and implicitly in our performing. Her work is a corrective to the postmodern overemphasis on performativity at the expense of performance, which throws us off the phenomenological track, emptying the body out into discourse or disciplinary technologies, leading us to think that we need understand the body only by examining that discourse or those technologies. But the body is hardly that transparent; there is a "kinetic body logos" the richness of whose ontogenetic and phylogenetic density of meanings we are tempted to overlook.[14]

> In short, there is a richly subtle and complex nonverbal world that is there from the beginning of all of our lives, a dynamic world that is neither mediated by language nor a stepping stone to language, but that is literally significant in and of itself and remains literally significant in and of itself, a dynamic world articulating intercorporeal intentions that, although clearly affective in origin, are enmeshed in "agentivity," in expectations, in consequential relationships, and thereby in the phenomenon of thinking in movement.[15]

In the process of learning to move our bodies, we give form to them. The activity of the muscles and our sense of self encourage a developing image of the body and the felt sense of how we move and express ourselves. The world and our own bodies are not things given once and for all, but are continually undergoing transformation via a complex hermeneutic involving methods and practices into which one is initiated (intersubjectively) and through which the world is known, methods and practices that are continually being handed down, refined, and replaced.

Sheets-Johnstone recognizes, but does not fully develop, the way this apprenticeship to our bodies is also an apprenticeship to society. While it is not necessarily the intent of the caregiver to impose socially appropriate behaviors on the body of the child, it is inevitable that the child, in imitating however roughly the actions of an other, learns ways of moving and vocalizing that are appropriate to the culture, lessons the adult has learned through interacting with the society in which they live. There is, therefore, a cultural element to the learning of the body that begins from the moment of, and perhaps even prior to, birth. The process of learning to move one's body in a social environment lays the groundwork for the transformation of the phenomena into techniques through repetition. Mauss provides an account of how the development of technique involves cultural practices in the definition of skills and qualities for animate form.

> What takes place is a prestigious imitation. The child, the adult, imitates actions which have succeeded and which he has seen successfully performed by people in whom he has confidence and who have authority over him. The action is imposed from without, from above, even if it is an exclusively biological action, involving his body. The individual borrows the series of movements which constitute it from the action executed in front of him or with him by others.[16]

Mauss argues that the acquisition of various specific techniques is based on tradition and efficiency, on ways of accomplishing an activity that make sense within the economic and social structures of the culture. "What emerges very clearly from them is the fact that we are everywhere faced with physio-psycho-sociological assemblages of series of actions. These actions are more or less habitual and more or less ancient in the life of the individual and the history of the society."[17]

Mauss's conception of technique, as we noted above, is extremely broad and covers many activities ordinarily classed as habits. A more usual definition would regard techniques as consciously acquired, and as being useful in accomplishing certain specific objectives; whereas by habits we tend to mean things that are not consciously acquired, and are not tied to a telos but which serve as aids or guides in navigating the lifeworld.

Mauss does not differentiate between the voluntary and involuntary learning of techniques. Some techniques are learned "through the pores," prior to the development of what neuroscientist Antonio Damasio calls extended consciousness, which, he says, "provides the organism with an elaborate sense of self . . . and places that person at a point in individual historical time, richly aware of the lived past and of the anticipated future, and keenly cognizant of the world beside it."[18] Techniques that can be learned without extended consciousness include vocal patterns, a way of walking, ways of eating, and the like. Other techniques are learned volitionally and generally have an identifiable end, such as learning to swim, to ride a bike, and birthing practices. In acting training, we are clearly talking about instances involving a will to learn techniques, though at the beginning we may not be aware that we are learning techniques or understand what kind of technique we are learning. One might take acting classes in college as an elective without thinking that it would become the focus of one's life, or even know that techniques were being learned through the various exercises.

The process of learning techniques from a professional acting teacher, though by choice, follows the pattern defined by Sheets-Johnstone and Mauss. Instead of being apprenticed to our bodies, we are apprenticed to someone in whom we invest authority as teacher and who teaches us a tradition of acting training. Through this process we learn to express the energy of the body along facilitated paths through defined patterns of movement, such as those that lead to good vocal production or an expertise in stage combat, in much the same way a child learns the techniques of crawling. Furthermore, this training alters our body image and enhances our sense of self and our abilities, while providing an increasingly complex identity (although this need not be the case, as there are teachers who are injurious to the self-esteem or physical well-being of certain students). In engaging a teacher and entering a course of instruction, we have an image of what we would like to become, recognizing only later that we cannot, perhaps, achieve that end, or the anticipated end may change from an idealized expectation to a more realistic appraisal of what is being taught and what we will be able to do as a result of the training.

The conscious acquisition of technique involves a more conventional exhibition of the hermeneutic circle, where the first moment consists of a tactile-kinesthetic experience and set of abilities in a situation, the second moment a desire and expectation to acquire more of a grip over the situation, and the third the presence of some sense of how to obtain that better grip from where one is. But the process is continuous, and all three moments are at work and changing all the time. Anticipations of what can be achieved in a technique thus emerge along with the development of the ability itself, not prior to it. Accordingly, it is almost always to misunderstand technique (either in the arts or the sciences) to think that its practitioners think of an idea or goal in advance and then bring it into being, even though the process may be portrayed that way for any number of reasons (it makes the creative process seem less amateurish and more the product of unalloyed genius and craft mastery, for instance) in accounts according to which the end was clearly in view first and then some "trick" was thought up to accomplish it. Nature, including even one's own body, is hardly that malleable. Whenever we are engaged in developing a performance, no matter how apparently straightforward and regardless of whether we are speaking about art or science, it almost never comes out precisely the way we plan. Something invariably takes over at some point, as if wanting to divert us from our original ideas. It may be something physical that we cannot do, or something that does not feel right, or something that runs counter to our overall conception. We are, that is, involved in an interactive process with something that responds, with something that is giving us something back, with something more complex than we can possibly represent.

When this happens, we have a range of possible options. One extreme would be to try to ignore the diversion, or try to work around it, and persist in imposing our will; we try to force the material, or a particular way of doing it, on ourselves, our collaborators, or our company. Another extreme would be to decide that one's ambition is unrealistic, abandon the attempt, and do something else. Usually what happens is neither one of these but something on the spectrum in between. We compromise, jiggle things around, adapt the material even as we coax and woo the performers to engage the material differently. We partially allow the material to take its own direction, compensating and clarifying to serve our aims—or we encourage the novel element to exhibit itself more in the process. For in hermeneutical activity, we apply everything that has been historically and culturally transmitted to us in interacting with the world; but in interacting with the world we inevitably wind up acting originally and with fresh involvements, allowing ourselves to be guided and transformed by the encounter with the novel.

The development of a performance ability into a technique occurs in this dynamic world and through the elaboration of this kinetic body logos, via a give-and-take in which I discover what I get when I do *this* and what I get when I do *that*, so that when I get "it"—when my abilities match my expectations—my performance ability has been adapted both to what the world is and to what I can do. In developing and learning the technique, I accommodate myself to my body and serve it as much as subordinate it.

Technē is not divorced from *poiēsis*. This is true regardless of whether we are speaking about a newly discovered technique or an already-developed one that I am learning for the first time.

A friend, for instance, was learning tap-dancing techniques in a master class taught by Honi Coles. Though highly accomplished herself, she grew frustrated trying to master a certain foot move. Coles came over to ask her what was wrong. She said, "Every time you do it the sound it makes is a *schouuuuuuuum*. But every time I do it the sound is a *schowwwwwwwwm*." Coles asked her to do the move, and she did. He asked her to do it again, and she repeated it. This happened one more time. Coles thought for a moment, then said, "It's OK. On you it's a *schowwwwwwwwm!*"

Transformations, Crossings, and Affects of Technique

One significant difference from being apprenticed to the body and learning an approach to acting is that the body already has technique when we enter the acting studio. Therefore, part of the training process is getting the student to "unlearn" ways of moving or speaking, as well as providing the opportunity to learn new ways of being that are appropriate for a life on the stage. As Herbert Blau reminds us in the *Eye of Prey*, Stanislavsky believed "that the hardest thing for an actor to do on stage, though he had been doing it all his life, is to walk."[19] The walking learned in everyday life did not appear "natural" on stage to Stanislavsky, requiring that the student be reconditioned through learning a different technique for walking that served the needs of the stage. This helps to explain why students of Eastern traditions of performance begin training at a very early age. As we grow older our bodies become settled in particular ways of being and moving, and it is more difficult to "forget" one way of behaving for another, regardless of the recognized value of the new technique. Children's bodies are not fully set in their ways, and the specific techniques of Noh, Kabuki, or the Chinese opera can be inscribed on the body before the techniques of everyday culture are completely ingrained. Therefore, the process of learning to act, while following the same structure as being apprenticed to the body, in the learning of everyday techniques involves an active forgetting and embracing a new way of moving. This is perhaps most clearly evident in classical ballet, where quotidian movement is anathema to the artistic form. Dance students spend considerable time acquiring flexible bodies with a degree of extension and precision very different from our everyday ways of moving.

The effects of learning a technique, such as in dance, not only affects the body but also alters the individual's body image both physically and psychologically. We come to perceive ourselves differently as the result of a different discipline. The effects of boot camp (physically as well as psychologically) are designed to alter the self-image of recruits in order to develop people who are willing to act as part of a team, depend less on an individual conception of self, and sacrifice themselves in order to achieve specific ends. The changing image alters our identity as we begin to see ourselves as a dancer, soldier, or actor. This may be the real value of the gender subversions Judith Butler offers as a means of disrupting cultural practices relevant to sexuality: we change the culture less than we change ourselves through practices that require iterations of the same or similar modes of behavior. In its most positive light, in practicing a set of techniques we create ourselves in relation to our own image of what we wish to become; in a more negative light, we become what the institution wants us to become, like it or not. Self-images are never, of course, self-creations, but reflect our ideological engagement in the world. Our values are in our muscles because the way we express ourselves physically bears a relationship to what we value. Therefore, to enter into a particular mode of training is, as Althusser reminds us, to embrace the ideologies of the organization. One positive value in deciding to learn a specific technique is that it can open new, creatively empowering, ways of expressing ourselves.

A technique is very difficult to be rid of, principally because, like ideology, turning away from it entails turning toward another. Jerzy Grotowski sought to minimize technique when he worked with the Polish Laboratory Theatre. Acknowledging the influence of the later Stanislavsky (who had shifted from an emphasis on emotional memory to the performance of physical actions) Grotowski was less sanguine about any debt to Artaud's theater of cruelty, with its desire for unmediated expression. Yet Grotowski's approach to training seemed to strive for precisely that, through an approach to training he called "via negativa." "Rather, we subtract, seeking *distillation* of signs by eliminating those elements of 'natural' behavior which obscure pure impulse."[20] "Natural behavior" for Grotowski generally referred to blocked or contracted behavior, which was the result not so much of nature but of naturalized modes of social behavior that have become habitual, or in Mauss's terms "techniques of the body."

Grotowski's desire to rid the body of everyday modes of behavior may be understood via Eugenio Barba's differentiation between the energy of performance and everyday energy. Quotidian energy, for Barba, is based on efficiency, the ability to accomplish the greatest amount with the minimum effort, while he describes performance energy as extra-daily; acting requires a supplement of energy in performance, making it more intense but less than efficient. By ridding the body of its resistances, Grotowski sought to increase the amount of energy in performance through creating a body that could express the available energy in a creative process. This required breaking down resistances to particular modes of expenditure, of releasing contracted forms of expression. "What resistances are there? How can they be eliminated? I want to take away, steal from the actor all that disturbs him. That which is creative will remain within him."[21] Of what the creative, that which remains for Grotowski, consists is not clear, unless it is presence that through the implementation of various techniques (i.e., facilitated pathways of expression) leads to the creation of a material form that expresses the intensities of the body. Developing new ways for expressing the artistry does not free the body of technique; rather it inscribes on the body new techniques that allow for a desired mode of expression.

The creative impulse is always already tainted by representation, the Apollonian, by form. It is impossible to bring the pure impulse to the stage. To do so would be destructive of the psyche, of the efficacy of the "I" in the performance of everyday life as well as on stage. What is performed is always inflected by technique. "Reflection shapes memory into an expressive illusion—an illusion of feelings spontaneously overflowing as if for the first time. This is not Nature, then; it is second nature."[22] What technique provides is not an obstacle to the expression of presence, but the controlled release of energy that gives the illusion of presence, the closest that we can get to the pure energy of being. To move beyond the representation of presence would be to make known the "nonrepresentable origin of representation," which would mean negating the materiality of the body. What we can strive for is to seek and perfect techniques so that we can improve the quality of our performance.

Eugene Gendlin emphasizes that the physical processes of the body involve, not a mass of unorganized id-energies or raw sensation, but a highly organized and demanding "felt sense" that takes in and is taken by the entire situation, intersubjectively and linguistically.[23] This felt sense is not switched on and off, but is involved in a process that is constantly "carrying itself forward" differently. This carrying forward is accomplished neither by novel terms nor by old terms in their old meanings, but by old terms that, in performing, can work freshly and thereby transform the situation and our bodily processes. In performance, carrying-forward can happen in several ways. One is in a rehearsal situation, where one is working collaboratively on a specific problem or situation. Another is the improvisational situation. In improvisation, something must be done. But without the guidance of a tight structure, the gestures of our performance come to us more like the way our moods and feelings come to us. Rather than come to us out of habitual pathways or thoughtfully considered patterns, these gestures befall us out of our entire being-in-the-world. For one can (though not always) have in play more than what one can explicitly master.[24] Still another way of using carrying-forward to create new movement possibilities is through the crossing of techniques with new situations that are the product of other techniques, as is illustrated by Baryshnikov's dancing of Twyla Tharp. Tharp began with classical training, then developed her own movement technique; when Baryshnikov crossed his technique with a work generated by hers, it showed how far her technique had moved in relation to classical technique, but also how productive it was. But there are numerous other examples: classical cellist Yo-Yo Ma's recordings of Appalachian country melodies, classical flutist Paula Robison's recordings of Brazilian folk and popular music, and so forth.

The aim of technique, we mentioned at the beginning, is to deliver us over to a situation where a new kind of performance ability—a new kind of interplay with phenomena—is possible. When successful, this results in a transformation of self and situation and is accompanied by a distinctive *Befindlichkeit,* or what Gendlin calls "moody understanding." The specific kind of moody understanding involved in successful technique acquisition is anything but the detached and impersonal triumph that accompanies success at a project of domination and control. Dreyfus and Dreyfus provide a good description of the affects involved in skill acquisition and use, up to and including expert technique.[25] And a celebratory joy is a natural concomitant to the specific context of developing a new kind of performance ability, forging of a new way of being-in-the-world. Samuel Florman has collected several selections, drawn from history and literature, illustrating this celebratory feeling in connection with engineering techniques. One of the most striking of these is from *The Woman in the Dunes,* by the Japanese novelist Kobo Abé. A young man has become trapped at the bottom of a deep sand pit and is forced to dig for sand by villagers who threaten to withhold drinking water if he refuses. There is no escape, and he falls into a deep depression. But at a certain point he discovers that he can use a technique involving capillary action to obtain fresh water from the sand himself. Abé writes, "He had to sit down for a moment and control his breathing in order to quiet the wild beating of his heart. . . . But he could not suppress the natural laughter that welled up in him. . . . The fact that he was still just as much at the bottom of the hole as ever had not changed, but he felt quite as if he had climbed to the top of a high tower."[26] The young man is still literally in the hole, still doomed. Nevertheless, he is still able to experience, through his tiny acquisition and application of a technique, the celebratory mood, familiar to all performers from those in dance companies to laboratories, that accompanies an increase in one's performance abilities and capacity for interplay with phenomena.

The Perils of Technique

The use of technique, of course, does not always provide the liberating experience Abé's antihero had, but potentially can also distance oneself from the world and disable one's grip over it. An account of how this happens would help explain the polarity in its interpretation that we mentioned at the beginning of this essay of how technique can be understood alternatively as operating creatively and productively in the lifeworld on the one hand, and as impoverishing and even subverting the very activities it is supposed to serve on the other. Techniques can become impoverishing if they deliver the performer to a place where the full interplay with the situation did not occur. Ironically, this is apt to happen not by the failure of technique, but by success. The success of a technique threatens two very different kinds of dangers.

A first is by tempting us to lose sight of the interplay, to not fully engage ourselves with the situation. Suppose that the technique relied on an effect related to but insufficiently sensitive to the interplay—for instance, as is the case with certain therapy techniques that call for the analyst to pay close attention to the motion of body parts such as the eyes. One could easily become distracted and preoccupied, letting the effect overshadow the situation, and lose sight of the full play of the performance in process. Or, a technique may provide the performer with automatic reactions that are relied on as a substitute for spontaneous response to the interplay. This occurs, for instance, in music when technique is taught at the expense of artistry, so that a performer ceases to bring all of herself to the piece, and the notes produced to not have a full relation to the interplay. Still another way that the success of a technique may cause us to lose sight of the interplay is by tempting us to try to apply it outside of the sphere in which it was generated—which, again, we might illustrate with reference to Stanislavsky's trajectory; his initial attempts to develop a technique to do what Chaliapin did worked with some material but failed with others, leading him to rethink and rework the technique. All these ways in which technique fails have to be understood, though, first through an account of how we learn technique and our ability to render it transparent so that the artistry of performance—Barba's extra-daily—can be expressed through an animate and techniqued body.

A second danger posed by the success of a technique is that it may cause us to forget that acquisition of a technique necessarily involves self-transformation. The acquisition of technique is not like donning a new set of clothes that one can take off at the end of the day; it has consequences for the way our bodies interact with the world. Acquiring a new technique reconstitutes and redirects our bodies, it rechannels our energy flow—and in the process, while certain ways of interplay become newly possible, certain others become more difficult or even impossible. The Baryshnikov-Tharp example is a productive and possibly even rare example of a fertile crossing between one technique and another, but one could easily imagine this kind of crossing resulting in artifice and pretension. One thinks of Leonard Bernstein's recording of *West Side Story* using opera singers (the vibrant earthy dimension is lost), or in general of opera singers who perform popular songs (such as often happens, say, in the party scene at the end of act 2 of *Die Fledermaus* in New Year's Eve performances), thinking that they are bringing out the true artistry of the material, while in reality the opposite happens and the result is excruciating. Another example is ballet performers who attempt popular dances like the Lindy Hop.

These two different types of dangers of successful technique can be a product of the way a technique was developed, or is taught or understood in either the individual or institutional level—this being a particular danger since the less a technique is related to the whole the more teachable it becomes. For in these processes ideologies and various types of political or economic interests (teachability to the maximum number of people at once being one) may intervene. But only within the context of a philosophical account of technique will we be able to clarify the nature of these dangers; only such an account, therefore, will make a genuine critique of it possible.

We have laid out, therefore, what we think are the key elements for a philosophical approach to technique. Many other questions remain: What is the relation between technique and what might be called "presence," conceived both as an aesthetic phenomenon and as the animating force of subjectivity? What is the nature of the continuing apprenticeship we have with our bodies as we age? What is the relation between technique, improvisation, and imagination? But we claim that the account we have provided offers a suitable framework for answering such questions.

NOTES

1. Joseph Agassi, "Magical and Scientific Technology," in *Technology: Philosophical and Social Aspects* (Dordrecht: Kluwer, 1985), 77–95.

2. For a discussion of dance, see Susan Leigh Foster, *Reading Dance: Bodies and Subjects in Contemporary Dance* (Berkeley and Los Angeles: University of California Press, 1986).

3. See Joseph R. Roach, *The Player's Passion* (Ann Arbor: University of Michigan Press, 1996), 204–17; and Konstantin Stanislavsky, *Selected Works*, trans. Olga Shatze (Moscow: Raduga, 1984), 166.

4. Martin Heidegger, *The Question Concerning Technology and Other Essays*, trans. William Lovitt (New York: Harper and Row, 1977); Jacques Ellul, *The Technological Society*, trans. John Wilkinson (New York: Knopf, 1964); and Lewis Mumford, *Technics and Human Development* (New York: Harcourt Brace, 1966).

5. William Barrett, *The Illusion of Technique* (New York: Anchor, 1979), 117, 243.

6. Marcel Mauss, *Sociology and Psychology: Essays,* trans. Ben Brewster (Boston: Routledge, 1979), 101.

7. Patrick Heelan, *Space-Perception and the Philosophy of Science* (Berkeley and Los Angeles: University of California Press, 1983); Don Ihde, *Technology and the Life-world* (Bloomington: Indiana University Press, 1990).

8. Martin Heidegger, *Being and Time,* trans. Joan Stambaugh (Albany: State University of New York Press, 1996).

9. Robert P. Crease, *The Play of Nature: Experimentation as Performance* (Bloomington: Indiana University Press, 1993).

10. Heidegger, *Being and Time,* no. 32; Crease, *The Play of Nature,* 64–65.

11. See Robert P. Crease, "How Technique is Changing Science," *Science* 257 (1992): 344–53.

12. Maxine Sheets-Johnstone, "Kinetic Tactile-Kinesthetic Bodies: Ontological Foundations of Apprenticeship Learning," *Human Studies* 23 (2000): 345.

13. Ibid., 358.

14. Maxine Sheets-Johnstone, *The Primacy of Movement* (Philadelphia: John Benjamin, 1999), 489.

15. Ibid., 504.

16. Mauss, *Sociology and Psychology,* 101–2.

17. Ibid., 120.

18. Antonio Damasio, *The Feeling of What Happens: Body and Emotion in the Making of Consciousness* (New York: Harcourt Brace, 1999), 16.

19. Herbert Blau, *The Eye of the Pray: Subversions of the Postmodern* (Bloomington: Indiana University Press, 1987), 164.

20. Jerzy Grotowski, *Towards a Poor Theatre,* trans. Eugenio Barba (New York: Simon and Schuster, 1968), 18.

21. Ibid., 209.

22. Roach, *The Player's Passion,* 163.

23. Eugene Gendlin, *Experiencing and the Creation of Meaning* (New York: Free Press of Glencoe, 1970).

24. Robert P. Crease, "The Improvisational Problem," *Man and World* 27 (1994): 181–93.

25. Hubert L. Dreyfus and Stuart E. Dreyfus, *Mind over Machine: The Power of Human Intuition and Expertise in the Era of the Computer* (New York: Free Press, 1986).

26. Kobo Abé, *The Woman in the Dunes,* trans. E. Dale Saunders (New York: Vintage, 1991), 143–44; Samuel C. Florman, *The Existential Pleasures of Engineering* (New York: St. Martin's Press, 1994).

NINE

Presenting Objects, Presenting Things

Alice Rayner

Theater habitually situates abstractions in material realities. If the philosophical debates over the meanings and functions of presence initially draw from theater, practice returns them there, materializes and frames not only the qualitative sense of heightened being or charisma and the temporality of disappearance but the occasion of perception and the paradoxes of its partiality. All these elements have been carefully and well discussed in the essays in this anthology by Philip Auslander, Noël Carroll, Jon Erickson, and Suzanne Jaeger. Instead of duplicating their efforts, I want to consider one way in which theater presents—not so much to examine what it presents or whether it presents presence, but how, in presenting, it offers up the very multiplicity of meanings, contradictions, and occasions for perceiving that the philosophical debates engage. While many philosophical discussions seek to set definitional boundaries on what is or is not performance, theater, liveness, presence, and so forth, my aim here is to watch theater's temporal processes by which it puts objects of perception (be they machines, human bodies, or things) into the play of perception between presence and absence, meaning and materiality.

To begin as concretely as possible, consider the matter of objects. From a purely linguistic standpoint, the word *object* stands for any "thing" that is thrown *(-jected)* in front *(ob-)*, suggesting not simply the thingliness of objects but their position in relation to a subject, like an obstacle or an object of study. They are thus relational and set a boundary for the subject. Objects presented on stage have a unique status. They participate in multiple dimensions: in the signifying, narrative, and stylistic fictions of a drama; in the material, aesthetic, and tangible reality of things in themselves. But they also have a third function, which mediates between these aspects, in the degree to which, as staged objects, they present themselves *as* representations. Staging, that is, creates the representation of representation that isolates the fact of representation. Stage props almost always have a concrete, utilitarian purpose within that range of functions, and it would require a detailed analysis of any one prop to indicate the full range of its possibilities. Here, I hope more generally to elicit from stage props an image and a mode for understanding the conditions by which objects appear in their phenomenological complexity. Stage props, as paradigmatic objects, constitute the worldliness of the stage and in a sense are owned by the stage; properties in all senses, they give their material attributes to an otherwise empty space and in turn populate that space, dominate it, "own" it.

Especially when they are sitting backstage or in the prop room, prior to their uses in a performance, bereft of text and performance, prop objects can seem suspended between worldly and fictional uses. Like items in a lost and found, they implicate a history without an obvious order, a disparate group of items that beg for a story and ask to be played with, touched, recovered, and owned. Precisely because they are in suspense between instrumental usefulness and an imaginary field, there is a certain pleasure in handling and discovering them. Like lost toys, they elicit the imagination, as fragments of one world lost and another yet to be constructed. Props enter the theater from an elsewhere and give themselves over to the pleasures of touch paired with fantasy. When objects enter theatrical space, however, peculiar things happen. They start to move and to lose touch. They can expand into meanings as signifiers with historical attachments and contexts, or contract into aesthetics as form, surface, and texture. They can turn elaborate as symbols of other things, like an abstract concept (the "wild duck" means nature or freedom) or an historical icon (the throne stands for the king); or they can contract into something close to pure image, as they do in a Robert Wilson opera or, reduced further, toward decay into pure matter, as they did in Tadeusz Kantor's stages. As it tends toward image or matter, the object has an obdurate stillness and inert refusal to become meaningful.

A prop object's function and appearance are generally tied to a theatrical style. Thus realism, taken famously to an extreme by stage director David Belasco, would take the object out of its mundane uses and bring it on stage not just to refer to that world but to duplicate it. As realism blends into symbolism, the object becomes larger than itself, signifying meanings beyond its materiality and lending itself to abstract concepts of history or culture. And as modernism and postmodernism divest objects of meaning and aim toward their performative possibilities in being rather than doing or meaning, the object contracts toward its materiality, where its mute substance refutes and exceeds any meanings, symbols, or functions that might otherwise attach. Throughout the range of possible cases, some ratio is at work, creating a tension between the object and its representational function. The tension of perception oscillating between the inert matter and its signifying possibilities can, in some circumstances, create a sense of the uncanny, like the uncanniness of the automaton or puppet, moving like a human (such as the figures in *Abacus* that Auslander discusses), or of a human moving like a thing. An object, in other words, might be said to have a life, or at least a life history, in which its motility and its inertia both reside.

Backstage on the prop table, however, an object takes on another kind of status. Usually covered in paper, the table lays out all the objects that come and go from the stage during a performance in the order of their appearance on stage. Each one is outlined and labeled, identifying what it is and when it is used: crown, act 3, scene 4, or umbrella, act 1. The prop manager can then account for anything that is missing before and after a show, track it down, and replace it if necessary. The actor always knows where to take and replace any prop. It is a mundane and efficient practice that keeps the flow of objects going smoothly on and off stage. But the prop table is also an image for another kind of flow that carries objects between different stages of use and meaning. It is a kind of inert space, a holding zone, between the making or finding of props and their delivery into the public space of the stage, where they will ground the actors in material reality and serve as messengers to an audience, both enacting and representing an era, a history, a place, a symbol, or a character. The outline that graphically marks their absence is a reminder that their function on stage is temporary; that while they are away being used, they are in some sense not where they belong. The table is a holding space in which their identities are meaningful only in reference to their future use. Yet at rest on the table, filling in the absence the outline defines, avoiding the fluidity of uses, references, and meanings, they are fully themselves, at home, but inert. The often odd collection of disparate items on the prop table serves as a silent archive of a production, marking its material history and its future. Though they are destined for the stage, for use, and for reidentification by an audience, it is at the point of stillness that they contract into their material specificity that is neither aesthetic nor representa-

tional, neither messengers nor message. Tadeusz Kantor has a notation on
"The Post Office" that articulates this status of the object on the prop table:

> It is a very special place
> where the laws of
> u t I l I z a t I o n
> are suspended.
> Objects—letters, packages,
> packets, bags, envelopes,
> and all their content—
> exist for some time
> independently,
> without an addressee,
> without a place of destination,
> without a function,
> almost as if in a vacuum,
> in between a sender and a receiver
> where both are powerless,
> with no meaning,
> bereft of their authority.
> It is a rare moment when
> an object escapes its destiny.[1]

Once put into a stage space, an object is destined to travel. Traveling, it
is subjected to the power and authority of users (performers) as well as of
"sender and receiver," with their often competing or contradictory invest-
ments of "content" in the object. But during its life on the prop table, that
investment is absent. Sent toward its "destiny," the prop object leaves
behind only the outline of its former self-identity, when it had no function.
The outline not only marks the absence of the object, it remembers the
placement of a self-identical object now lost to itself. The outline, in other
words, is an evacuated site that calls the body-object home.

The stage can employ objects in all the phases of exile, desire, and
attachment. It can exile or alienate objects from ideology, as Brecht did; it
can turn objects into meaningful representations of other objects, as the
Elizabethans did; it can reconnect objects to the pleasures of the senses, as
someone like Robert Wilson does; it can isolate objects as symbols of otherness, like a William Forsythe; it can shock them into reality; it can frame
them as "things-in-themselves" as performance does. By setting out the

prop table as a unique site for objects, I am suggesting there is a temporary, in-between space like Kantor's post office, where both their origins in attachment and their destinies in exile are in suspense, temporarily at rest but marked for sending. It is obviously not a powerful, effective, or enduring site. It's only a prop table after all. But it is a actual site, and it is only in actuality that phenomena gather their complexities.

The prop table is obviously not a site outside either history or representation. It is neither mythical nor mystical but highly pragmatic. It, too, like the stage, locates a temporary condition for the objects it holds. But as a site for the possibility of an in-between suspension, the table is also really *there,* an actuality, like a post office. While an object resides there, it is available to being recognized not as an object but as what Martin Heidegger called a "thing." In his essay called "The Thing," in *Poetry, Language, Thought,* he distinguished objects as whatever interests the empirical habits of science, as whatever is at a distance, or can be called "objective" reality. On the prop table, objects can be known as "things" in part because they are temporarily at rest "in themselves." At that point between the expansion into reference, history, and signification and contraction into materiality, however, they can (again in Heidegger's terms) dwell "poetically." Heidegger's formulation is not without its problems, but for the moment I would like to consider the way that the concrete and pragmatic action of a prop manager can be understood as acting out the distinction between object and thing from within the practices of theater.

The prop manager is charged to find or create, gather, store, distribute, and place the objects to be used on stage. She prepares the appearances of the performance package: folding, tying up, and sealing the material forms that will produce the space of performance. Those objects will concretely "shelter" the performance and constitute its dwelling place. More specifically, she must make them ready for the actor at the right moment in performance. It is a job that is almost inevitably in service to the vision of a director and constrained by the aesthetics and economics of a production as well as the pragmatics of actors who must handle the objects. By giving her story these terms—folding, tying up, and sealing, which are taken from Kantor's work on "emballage"—the work of the property manager suddenly appears in alliance with Heidegger's essays "The Origin of the Work of Art" and the "Thing": a making, gathering, and giving. The prop, in these terms, is a gift, free of specific economic exchange and therefore free of commodification. It is an offering to the stage that from the stage is an offering to a public, harboring its meanings and its uses in the sensory specificity of texture and form. Empty because of its liminality, it is also more itself: its uses more available to perception. That emptiness through which it reveals itself is what turns the object to a "thing."

In his essay "The Thing" Heidegger aims the reader toward identifying the "thingness" of the thing: toward discovering what a thing is in itself in distinction to what a thing is as an "object," which is something "we place before us" either materially or mentally. He continually offers possibilities for isolating the factors that make a thing a thing rather than an object, then continues to undercut those possibilities by saying they are insufficient. Yet Heidegger cannot quite say just what the "thingness" of a thing would be as he proceeds through the essay. He defies common sense and common language and seems to be trying to lead the reader to some essence of material or mental objects that at first glance would seem to be just what Plato was doing when he distinguished a material object from the idea (or mental representation) of the object, and both of those from the Form of the object (eidos). For Plato, he seems to claim, "conceives of the presence [of a thing] . . . in terms of the outward appearance" and as an "object of making" that first required an idea of the thing for the maker.

Instead of something that stands before, over against, or opposite us, a thing, for Heidegger is "what stands forth." The essay makes two claims about what "standing forth" might be. The first is the sense that the thing came from somewhere, which might be to say it has a history, that it is the result of a process, either of self-making or being made. The second is, more obscurely, that "standing forth" has the sense of coming "into the unconcealedness of what is already present."[2]

One problem in understanding this claim is that it seems to be identifying some essential nature of the thing, in the case of Heidegger's example, a "jug." But on a purely material basis, Heidegger points at the "holding nature" of the jug that becomes apparent when we fill it. The "thing" is existential, not ideal. The sides and bottom of the jug are nevertheless not what does the holding, even though they are "what is impermeable in the vessel" and allow it to stand. Rather, it is the empty space, the void that does the holding; in shaping the clay, the potter who makes it is also shaping the void. "The vessel's thingness does not lie at all in the material of which it consists, but in the void that holds."[3] This characterization defies the commonsense version of the jug that comes from scientific objectivity. Unlike a thing, an object, he says, is primarily a topic for science, suggesting it is something primarily created by science in a quest for rational understanding and public agreement. Objective knowledge is the compelling mode for understanding and therefore for creating things that can be agreed upon as standing outside the production of an imaginary. While objective knowledge seeks on the one hand to recognize the independence of things in the world, on the other it creates the criteria for that recognition, and can only take in objects from a materialist ground, defining the parameters of an object by the limits of its material body. The "thingness" of things, given the scientific experience of reality, has not yet "laid claim to thought . . . have never yet at all been able to appear to thinking as things."[4] With such a statement the difficulty remains: the "thingness" would seem be equivalent to either some essence or irreducible element that Heidegger wants to get to, and this would not really be any different from what scientific objectivity would aim at. The confusion of the writing, then, sets up obstacles to any such understanding.

A clue to an escape from the impasse comes with possibility that the question is not just about the "thingness" of the thing—about some objective essence—but about the mode of thinking that does not seek an objective essence and hence does not seek to dominate or subjugate the object to thought but to allow the object to enter thought as a "thing" in itself. In this mode, the thing is not a product of the mind but an otherness that is recognized as having its own, for lack of a better phrase, life process. In the case of the jug, this life process is manifold, consisting of the void being made (or "gathered") both to hold and pour out. Rather than reducing the jug to an essence, Heidegger expands its possibilities in terms of its giving out the gift of the liquid it was made to do. At this point in the essay, the jug becomes a site for a mythopoetic conception of its connection to origins and ends: its origins in the earth, through the clay that makes it, the wine that comes from earth, water, and sun, and its purpose, or gift, to humans, in giving out drink and to the gods, in consecration. It is easy to become disconcerted by the mythopoetic stance that seems to revert to some undefined, unsituated, possibly Greek, or at least primitive, cosmology:

> In the gift of the outpouring that is drink, mortals stay in their own way. In the gift of the outpouring that is a libation, the divinities stay in their own way, they who receive back the gift of giving as the gift of the donation. In the gift of the outpouring, mortals and divinities each dwell in their different ways. Earth and sky dwell in the gift of the outpouring. In the gift of the outpouring earth and sky, divinities and mortals dwell *together all at once*. These four, at one because of they themselves are,

belong together. Preceding everything that is present, they are enfolded into a single fourfold.[5]

Heidegger then resorts to language that is characteristically opaque and tautological: "How does a thing presence? The thing things. Thinging gathers. Appropriating the fourfold, it gathers the fourfold's stay, its while, into something that stays for awhile: into this thing, that thing."[6]

In its opacity, this language points toward a conception of a thing as that which stands outside the ordinary functioning of objects, as that which can only be apprehended poetically, which is to say by the *poiēsis* that is a human way of world-making that, on the one hand, is in excess of survival needs and, on the other, is a means of creating connections between the material earth and the human community and the mysteries of being. The thing harbors its past attachments at the same time that it foretells its future in exile, alienation, and decay. Both the objective jug and the conception of the jug, that is, dwell in the flux of time; neither is static or fixed. Grammatically, then, both the object and concept "dwell poetically" in verbal forms of nouns, the gerund or participle.

The "fourfold" of being, earth, sky, mortals, and divinities, presents itself through the "thinging of the thing." But there are translations of these terms that have rational forms: If "earth is the building bearer," it can also be called ground or materiality or nature, though such terms are even more loaded with history than the word *earth*. What is the best word for that combination of elements which bears life ("nourishing with its fruits, tending water and rock, plant and animal"), which is never outside representation, but also is never identical to its representations? Nature? Probably not. But: the "sky is the sun's path, the course of the moon, the glitter of the stars, the year's seasons" could also be called time, as measured by planetary motion, day and night, weather, which is to say, change measured by matter. If the "divinities are the beckoning messengers of the godhead," they could also be called the signs of the inhuman and the nonhuman that signal the limits of human knowledge. And if mortals are those who are "capable of death as death," it needs little translation to say we are those who can die because we know we will die, which means we can represent to ourselves the unrepresentable. As things, we also decay.

If the "thing" for Heidegger consists of bringing the fourfold being into presence, then the thing is that which gathers matter and time together with whatever is beyond human power to know within the context of mortality, namely that unity of being projected by the unity of perceptual experience. Stuff, change, mortality, the unknown: the crude translation for what every "thing" holds and gives out in its relatedness. Thingness is thus not an attribute of an object but something more like an event or a moment when a material object is recognized as belonging to more than its representation, to more than is knowable, but also belonging to time and to mortality. These are also the gifts of the thing, as opposed to an object, which withholds. The "more than" means the thing is not exhausted by whatever it may signify. The "more than" paradoxically stands independent of representation at the same time it might be representing. It means the thing is not eternal but stands momentarily within the temporality of becoming and disappearing. It is not, according to Heidegger, what Kant called a "thing-in-itself," which would be only "the object of a representing that runs its course in the self-consciousness of the human ego . . . an object that is no object for us, because it is supposed to stand, to stay put, without a possible before: for the human representational act that encounters it."[7] The thing, rather, is a gathering in time and a moment of "unconcealing" of a manifold being that is not limited to representation and does not endure. As a gathering the thing does not refer to anything beyond itself; as a gathering, there is no elsewhere. "[The sculpture] is not a portrait whose purpose is to make it easier to realize how the god looks; rather, it is a work that lets the god himself be present and thus *is* the god himself. The same holds for the linguistic work. In the tragedy nothing is staged or displayed theatrically, but the battle of the new gods against the old is being fought." Bert States glosses this passage: "What Heidegger means here is not a literal presence of the god, but a presence that makes it unnecessary to refer elsewhere *for* the god. It is the *truth* of the god that arrives on the stage and not the stage that refers to a *real* god beyond it, existing in some unavailable form."[8] More unsettling is the sense that "thingness," like the work of art, may not be generally or widely recognized, might not be shared between people, is not apparently subject to common knowledge, and most particularly cannot be argued for (only against). Because it is a gift, it may or may not be well received. The contingency of the material object on a void or absence thus leads to the chronic and open questions about whether something is or has "presence."

If I transfer his notion of "the thing" into the art of theater and to the story of those who produce the objects of theater, the pragmatism of theater and its objects are then haunted by the dimension of the sacred that has long been lost, like the outline of the object on the prop table. For the staging of things puts them in process, traveling between a gathering of objects from the world, showing them in the transit of performative present, and still allowing their embeddedness in signification to trail along. The sacred act is in the giving away of the object to misunderstanding and in maintaining faith in its sacrifice to the community gathering.

The history of theater is a history of gatherings, regardless of any particular religious context. That is not to say that its history relating to Greek worship or Christian mysteries is irrelevant. It is not just that theater has turned "secular" or "profane" and lost some religious context that was there at a mytho-historical origin but that the cause or source of community gathering itself has a sacred dimension in the losses that the living endure as a consequence of living. In the utter pragmatism of bringing together a community, in other words, the "sacred" appears not in some *thing* that is lost, but *as* loss—a loss of, in, and through time, which demands a certain awful reverence or respect. Gathering is an action in time whose movement has a coming, a duration, and a departure. One meets a "thing" in the mutual transit, the gathering and departure of the present. Theater gives power to this poetic formulation of the sacred by its utter pragmatism not by what it represents but by its gathering of time and space.

Pragmatic choices and actions characterize the transformative difference between the mental, conceptual, and theoretical dimension of ideas about theater, and theater itself. That obvious fact, so often left in the general terms of "practical theater," is rarely specified as the locus of theatrical transformation in spite of the fact that such practical considerations are decisive. The importance of the choices of objects is difficult to theorize perhaps because they are so decisive, so particular, that their place in the transformational *process* to the "thinging" of theater gets lost. That is, objects seem to be static, unified, and complete in themselves rather than in a mental projection upon them. By contrast, what might be called the thinking of theater things includes a temporal, active dimension that involves immediacy, duration, repetition, and disappearance.

Such thinking is of course a matter of perspective, but by including the prop manager in a broader theoretical story of theater I want to include the "vulgarity" of pragmatic actions as a decisive feature of its ability to give flesh to the uncanny, and to see theater itself as a "work of art" in Heidegger's sense of an unconcealing. That unconcealing that is not some latency belonging to objects, not some ontological category of essence, but an unconcealing that consists of a perceptual event in which something that is materially present is suddenly perceived as both new and always already there. Giving flesh to the uncanny does not mean simply investing some object or body with a spirit, ghostly or otherwise; it means exploiting the temporalities of theater as a temporal and material art, as an action and a process that invites a moment of meeting, which is an act that cannot be held, only given. The giving comes also in mundane terms, in the generosity of time and attention coming from actors, directors, technicians, and audiences. If it becomes signified as an object, it is only done so in retrospect. The gift of time in the gathering collapses the felt (and generally lived) boundaries between past, present and future, with the uncanny effect of perceiving something that was there all along. In fact, the giving occurs only on the occasion of its perception, and only on its perception does it come into existence. No one can guarantee that perception will occur, and no two members of an audience may agree that it is occurring or has occurred. Such is the elusiveness of presence. It is a fortuitous meeting and a rare experience, but when it happens, that audience member has the sense of having been prepared for and of having been met and known. The gift of the art "object" is an event that might be thought of as a kind of reattachment of the lost object, or at least a touching of the wound. It is brief because the gift only appears in the moment of giving; it thus also entails a memory of the first loss and a grieving.

In a class discussion of Heidegger's essay, a student described such a moment of perceiving the "gift" of the thing in Pina Bausch's piece *Nelkin.* The stage was full of deep pink or red carnations, and a man in a tuxedo was signing the words to "The Man I Love" while the song played, and a woman wearing black briefs, high heels, and an accordion walked across to the middle of the stage. The student said that, for whatever combination of reasons, he was stunned by a sense of revelation, and his thought was, "How did she know? How could she have known me and that I would feel this way about that image?" It was certainly a matter of his perception and his readiness to perceive. There was no object for others, necessarily, to perceive; yet his perception was dependent upon the image and its occurrence at that moment in relation to other moments. The flowers, qua objects, were not the thing, yet the thing was, so to speak, flowering. There was also a specific matter of Bausch and her dancers and the technicians who put the mass of flowers on the stage, who created an image-object in motion, who repeated it long enough to be perceived and reperceived and still not "understood" or signified (and hence murdered), who met him at that moment. They were presenting the thing. Together, they gathered, held, and gave that moving image to at least one audience member and the theatrical thing came home—or became present—just as it departed.

Objects on the prop table, suspended between their arrival and departure, also provide an image for a certain form of history and its loss of presence. The collection of things arrayed as disparate items belonging to a past, living context takes on the function of a memorial that testifies to both the reality of a past, its loss to the present, and imaginary possibilities. The pragmatism of an arrangement of objects also suggests a kind of formality to the display of history. Materialist history in the form of an array tends to defy the "grand recits" of the master historical narratives, to use Lyotard's terms. It is a new form, laid out in a formal order and ready to be recontextualized by more self-conscious use of narrative and labeling. History, memorialized by objects, takes on the form of an array, or arbitrary collection, suspended between times.

The testimony of objects, in other words, brings into the present not just *what* was lost but the tangible presence of loss, loss in the form of a thing. The recovery of history and its evidence is an imaginative and performative act. This is a fact often lost in the empirical presumptions of museums. The objects are not whole ("this is all that's left") and have lost the context in which they were used. Once staged—in the theater or the museum—they are no longer identical to themselves. Of course, in terms of a production, they never really *were* real because they are stage props; on the other hand, they *are* real because they are stage props. Both representing the real and undermining it, those objects circulate between their materiality and the reality of representation. They do not disappear into the usefulness of ordinary objects but testify to the reality of the ordinary. Both real and alienated, the status of the objects is not a matter of ontology but of perspectives and positions relative to the subject that are constantly in transition. Tangible, they mark their own disappearance from time past as well as their persistence into the present. In their double nature they are uncanny because one wonders about their reality even as they give sensory testimony. As Susan Stewart says of souvenirs, they are "traces of authentic experience. . . . We do not need or desire souvenirs of events that are repeatable. Rather we need and desire souvenirs of events that are reportable, events whose materiality has escaped us, events that thereby exist only through the invention of narrative."[9] What once belonged to someone else, like an heirloom, now belongs of "me" or, in the case of the museum, to a public. It connects me at the same time it reminds me of the loss. To "have" something that once belonged to another is concretely to feel the other. The object, however, becomes a possession in both senses of the word, in that to possess is also to be possessed. Ownership is founded in the fantasy of possession, but that is not to say that the fantasy is an unreal or a matter of pretending. It is rather what Slavoj Žižek calls a mediation between a "formal symbolic structure and the positivity of objects we encounter in reality."[10] He goes on to say that fantasy "provides a 'schema' according to which certain positive objects in reality can function as objects of desire, filling in the empty places opened up by the formal symbolic structure."[11]

Fantasy also relies on a radical (i.e., at its root) "intersubjectivity" in which the object is the means by which a subject forms a connection (and thereby an identity) with another. That is to say it is not necessarily the object itself but the object as it is identified with satisfying the desire of another that forms the character of fantasy. In touching the object, one touches time in the register of the senses, time that is not separate from the object (as in the effects of time) but incorporated *as* the object in its present. It is the aura of possession in which one is increased or expanded by including the object that belonged to another, in a kind of material version of metonymy. The rhetorical trope of metonymy, that is, has a material, physical grounding in the phenomenon of touch. As a phenomenon, touch perception engages with the dimension of fantasy that invests the object with a power that it would not otherwise have. It takes the sensate condition of a person who is alive to fantasy to give the object its aura and to "experience" the effects of the very aura she donates. Attention to the simultaneity of the sense perception and fantasy offers what Susan Jaeger noted in her essay here as "presence": "an openness to alteration in the unity of a bodily schema, that fully embodied activity of synthesis and balance between richness and clarity which constitutes our perceptual experiences" (137).

Tadeusz Kantor considered the nature of objects more thoroughly than most theater practitioners and made some of the clearest attempts to "bridge the gap between representation and things-in-themselves," in Brigitte Peucker's phrase. A significant aspect of that bridge is the material effect of time upon an object. Peucker discusses the eighteenth-century picturesque's interest in "'the effects of age and decay' . . . [which] . . . explains the overwhelming fascination of the picturesque with ruins, structures upon which time has wrought its texture-creating effects."[12] The aesthetics of texture in the picturesque not only replicate the processes of time in the object of representation, they make a direct appeal to the sense of tactility in the object. The tactility of an object, however, tends to deconstruct those significations by contracting history and its absences into the "thing itself," and to constitute a sensory dimension in which history is known. Kantor, in a modernist context, similarly found ways to employ the effects of time upon objects, not in terms of a representation of history but in terms of texture. In the surface textures of his objects he found a way to access a dimension that was neither realistic and utilitarian nor representational. He worked to erase the fictional contexts that stage the meaning of an object and instead to present them as autonomous phenomena that were nonetheless ghosted by use, history, and abuse. Explicitly rejecting the aesthetic movements of the early-twentieth-century avant-garde (constructivism, surrealism, cubism) and the progressive development of stage technology in the 1940s, he defined the "the poor object" as the "simplest, the most primitive, old, marked by time, worn out by the fact of being used."[13] He catalogs the objects in his 1944 production of *The Return of Odysseus* in a characteristically formal notation on the page:

A CARTWHEEL,
simple,
primitive,
smeared with mud.　　A BOARD,
　　　　　　　　　　old,
　　　　　　　　　　rotten,
　　　　　　　　　　with marks of
　　　　　　　　　　nails and rust.

A CHAIR,
simple,
a kitchen chair,
well worn.

　　　　　　　　　　A GUN BARREL,
　　　　　　　　　　iron,
　　　　　　　　　　rust eaten,
　　　　　　　　　　big, thick,
　　　　　　　　　　not on wheels,
　　　　　　　　　　but resting on

A TRESTLE
smeared with mud,
cement,
lime.　　　　　　　A METAL ROPE,
　　　　　　　　　　thick and
　　　　　　　　　　rusty.

A LOUDSPEAKER,
military,
imperfect,
hanging on a metal rope.
        PARCELS
        covered with dust,
        lime;
        the audience "members"
        sit on them.

WALLS
of the room
where the performance
takes place,
bombed
full of holes
bare bricks,
coats of paint on the floor   A FLOOR
        missing planks
        debris scattered all over.[14]

More than indexes or signs of time, the objects on Kantor's stage took on the affective sorrow of change and disintegration on their surfaces. His objects were not props made for the stage, as Michal Kobialka points out, but real objects that might once have been useful and instrumental in the world, which had lost their usefulness in the world. Entering his stage world, those objects were ghosted by their former uses. They were witnesses to the losses and their own decay, but as such they entered the stage trailed by the reality of time that is not "stage time." They did not enter the hypothetical sphere of dramatic fiction but maintained the real time of mortality and corporeality. That real time itself became an aesthetic that was quite specifically tangible. The texture of surfaces situated an aesthetic that mourned the loss but transformed that loss into tangibility. Because they were aesthetic, those stage things held the reality of time in a space of the affect. Kantor's love of old objects bespoke an aesthetic of loss as a real rather than an imaginary condition. For the aesthetic perception, recalling Kant, is a perception that has no regard for usefulness or instrumentality. The objects hold the tension between a former life and ultimate death. Kantor's objects "throw out"—that is, present—the connection of corporeal, material life to death, such that death itself is made present. Bereft of

usefulness and resisting the function of representation of some other reality, Kantor's objects insist on their own presence.

If Kantor's use of worn and broken objects has since become a definable
"look" for the stage as well as for certain kind of home decor, it was not initially as much to create an aesthetic as to respond to the reality of two
world wars and to postwar conditions. As Michal Kobialka writes:

> The object wrenched from war and from its technical and theatrical
> conventions was a "poor object"—for example, a rotten board, no
> longer able to perform its utilitarian function in life or theatre. This
> functionless object was, for Kantor, the source of his artistic inquiry
> into what Artaud called "nontheological space" and into the object's
> essence and existence. This rejection of the concepts of a traditional
> theatre space and of an "artistic object" controlled by imitation and
> representation had far-reaching consequences in Kantor's theatre,
> compelling him not only to eliminate the idea of a stage prop but also
> to redefine the role of stage design, costume, blocking, lighting, and,
> finally, stage action.[15]

Those poor objects in *The Return of Odysseus* were not stage props in
any conventional sense but, as Kobialka points out, means of creating a
specific kind of "site that produced its own space and its own commen-
tary."[16] Nevertheless, those objects, like his later use of the old pews in *The
Dead Class,* or his repeating motifs of the bicycle wheel or the umbrella,
come to constitute an aesthetic because they make an appeal to the senses,
and specifically to the sense of touch. In addition to their visual form of the
umbrella or the bicycle, the tactility of the object gives its theatrical presence a sensory dimension that exceeds its visibility. The tactile excess, I
suggest, is also the access to the alternative space that Kobialka argues cannot be designated by representational modes of signification. For in the
early work with poor objects as well as that in the 1950s and 1960s with
"emballages," Kantor is able to isolate the phenomenon of surfaces: or
more precisely, to bring surfaces to their phenomenological complexity.
The surfaces of an old object carry the traces of its use and history, just as
the human body does. But more importantly, the tactility of the objects
joins the container from the thing contained, turning the container into an
autonomous thing. "Emballage," meaning wrapping or packaging as well
as the practice of wrapping, is an outside surface that both contains and
conceals whatever object, or whatever lack of object, lies inside. In his

"Emballage Manifesto," Kantor writes that it "actually exists beyond the boundaries of reality. . . . It could thus be discussed [and here he simply repeats: "Emballage, Emballage, Emballage," suggesting there is nothing to be discussed] in terms of metaphysics. On the other hand, it performs a function that is so prosaic, so utilitarian and so basic."[17] The discarded and discardable wrapping of the object on display thus lies on the threshold "between eternity and garbage."

The theatricality inherent in this notion of emballage may need "unpacking." For implicit in this manifesto, as well as in Kantor's theater practice, is the sense of theater's spectacle as an expulsion. Spectacle is the element that has been discounted, if not discarded, since Aristotle decided to list it and then ignore it in *The Poetics*. That theater seems to be all surface, all spectacle, whose substance, if there is any, lies in dramatic action and character, is a longtime idea for devaluing theater practice. From this view, spectacle—visible surface—is quite specifically something that is thrown out, expelled from the numinous core of essence, meaningful content, or invisible substrate. The degradation of theatrical spectacle to *mere* appearance follows an assumption that truth is located in an unseen, absent substance that ghosts the material presence: the Edenic realm of origins from which the object is thrown. It has taken a long period of modernism, postmodernism, phenomenology, and a certain amount of deconstruction to bring about an inkling that the seen and the unseen coincide, that there is nothing hiding inside or beyond appearances, and that the spectacle is the substance whose unseen is simply, as Heidegger formulated it, another surface, further back. Emballage, like the gathering of the fourfold, beyond the boundaries of reality, *could* be discussed in terms of metaphysics, but is not metaphysical; it is, rather, prosaic, ordinary.

As spectacle, the material thing of theater is also transient, discardable, and "one should remember, it is performed with a full awareness of the fatal end."[18] With the change of a vowel from *o* to *a*, the object becomes the abject: the thing that is not thrown before but thrown away, discarded; and the object always carries within its "thrownness" its potential as garbage, which is to say, its own destruction and death. Surfaces carry the marks of time and of passage between coming and going. Those marks are furthermore not available only to sight but to touch. Kantor's use of old, worn objects increases the sensory dimensions of objects and thereby gives sense to history; that history is no less a matter of surfaces whose folds wrap themselves through time. His objects trace a history of expulsion. Their material surfaces wrap, or "package," that history in such a way that the container and the thing contained are identical. It is the package that matters because matter is the phenomenon. With a view on objects as folding time into their surfaces it is possible to see how objects then appear to shelter both past and future. They appear as dwelling places for the presence of losses.

In his notion of emballage, Kantor presents a sense of the stage object that echoes Heidegger's distinction between an object and a "thing." For the "ritual" of emballage—the creation of the wrapping—involves "folding," "tying up," and "sealing." This mundane set of actions, common to any packaging, is a way of explaining how, as Heidegger tries to do, a thing (as opposed to an object) can be understood as an act. This is clearest in Kantor's notation on the umbrella, which he "discovered" by placing one on a canvas:

> An umbrella is a particularly metaphoric Emballage; it is a "wrapping" over many human affairs; it shelters poetry, uselessness, helplessness, defenselessness, disinterestedness, hope, ridiculousness. . . . The actors in Mikulski's play *A Circus* [Cricot 2, January 13, 1957] used umbrellas as shields for their poor and deranged lives as well as for what was left of scraps of hope and poetry.[19]

The object as the dwelling place or shelter of poetry, uselessness, helplessness, hope and ridiculousness, is not an aesthetic nicety but a materialization of an action, with historical, political, and social as well as personal and affective consequence and context. An especially acute example of a sheltering object is the public work in San Francisco called *Defenestration* by Brian Goggin. It is a highly theatrical work. At the corner of Sixth and Howard Streets in a depressed, though increasingly lofty, neighborhood, Goggin and one hundred volunteers took over an abandoned tenement building in 1997. Coming out of its windows, crawling along the sides of the building, hanging precariously from the roof, old furniture is suspended as though just having been thrown out. Couch, chairs, tables, one with telephone, lamps, a grandfather clock, a bed, all emerge from the four-story building, seeming ready to fall. Calling up the sense of total eviction of people as well as the objects that constitute living space, the work is audacious, even ridiculous. It is a sheltering space for the "scraps" of lives where hope and poetry are held in the materiality of their expulsion. It is a site for the affect of loss and violence, at the same time exposing an audacious and ridiculous political and social system that throws out the poor while it builds expensive living spaces down the street. The objects are out of place, no longer, literally, at home; they no longer perform in an invisibly useful context. Furniture objects, especially sitting and lying places, are ghosted by the absent, human bodies that have left their impressions on the surfaces. Chairs follow the line of the body's bends at knees and hips; beds remember the length of the corpse. Having been turned into a work, the building becomes a poetic sheltering of the loss of shelter.

Like the things laid out on the prop table, the building gathers together objects that are suspended between an origin and a destiny, between function and pure materiality: the between that characterizes the poetic object thrown out of the context of usefulness. There, at Sixth and Howard, the poetic object is acutely political. The objects are things in transit (and they periodically change), yet held still with uncanny familiarity that makes one laugh even while recognizing that the helplessness of the objects and their ghosts, unable either to fall or retreat to the safety of a room. On the surfaces of the building, *Defenestration* exhibits the helplessness of the people-objects who are all the more emphatically absent from the building, yet filling the streets below with hustle and heartache. This building is a public gift and a site of gathering of past and future. It is a still life that makes the motion of the street all the more emphatic. Its objects, its monumentality, are a memorial to the losses being lived out below. The presence of the objects testifies to the absences that subtend them. The theatricality of this site suggests precisely how theater gives or presents objects of the world to the world; in a Heideggerian turn of phrase, presenting presences. In expelling the objects from the places of habit, the building "shows them forth," suspended between places, concretely showing off both the attachment and displacement of those specific objects and as well as of objects in general. Quite literally thrown out into the world, the objects appear in their abject sense: thrown out of place, they are things in themselves as well as things present for the world.

NOTES

1. Tadeusz Kantor, *A Journey Through Other Spaces: Essays and Manifestos, 1944–1990*, ed. and trans. Michal Kobialka (Berkeley and Los Angeles: University of California Press, 1993), 82–83.

2. Martin Heidegger, *Poetry, Language, Thought*, trans. Albert Hofstadter (New York: Harper Colophon, 1971), 168.

3. Ibid., 169.

4. Ibid., 170–71.

5. Ibid., 173.

6. Ibid., 174.

7. Ibid., 177.

8. Ibid., 43; and Bert O. States, *Great Reckonings in Little Rooms* (Berkeley and Los Angeles: University of California Press, 1985), 3.

9. Susan Stewart, *On Longing: Narratives of the Miniature, the Gigantic, the Souvenir, the Collection* (Durham: Duke University Press, 1993), 135.

10. Slavoj Žižek, *The Plague of Fantasies* (London: Verso, 1997), 7.

11. Ibid., 7.

12. Brigitte Peucker, *Incorporating Images: Film and the Rival Arts* (Princeton: Princeton University Press, 1995), 113.

13. Kantor, *Journey Through Other Spaces,* 74.

14. Ibid., 73–74.

15. Michal Kobialka, "The Quest for the Self/Other: A Critical Study of Tadeusz Kantor's Theatre," in Kantor, *Journey Through Other Spaces,* 275.

16. Ibid.

17. Kantor, *Journey Through Other Spaces,* 78.

18. Ibid., 79.

19. Ibid., 82.

PART THREE

Reception

TEN

Infiction and Outfiction

The Role of Fiction in Theatrical Performance

David Z. Saltz

According to the online art lexicon ArtLex, what distinguishes "performance art" from "theater" is that "theatrical performances present illusions of events, while performance art presents actual events as art."[1] This conception of theater has a long history, one that we can trace back at least as far as Plato. In particular, the assumption that theatrical performance presents illusory, as opposed to real, events was an orthodoxy in twentieth-century theory, from the Prague structuralists through existentialism and phenomenology and, most emphatically, semiotics and poststructuralist theory. The standard view is that a theatrical performance is a kind of text whose primary goal is to represent an absent fictional world, and the audience looks past, or through, the real events to the fiction. My objective here is to sketch a coherent alternative to this standard view. Specifically, I will argue that it gets the relationship between performance and fiction backward. Theater survives in an age of film and video precisely because the reality of the theater event matters. An audience comes to the theater to experience a real event, to see real, flesh-and-blood actors perform real actions. Fiction in theater is vitally important, but not as an end unto itself, and not merely as a content that the audience extracts from the performance. Fiction functions as a cognitive template that informs an audience's perception of reality on stage, structuring and giving meaning to the actual events that transpire on stage. When fiction functions in this way, I call it *infiction*.

The account that I will develop here is closely allied to a nondualistic understanding of representation that Wittgenstein initiated with his analysis of "seeing aspects." After briefly outlining the dualistic assumptions underlying the standard understanding of theatrical representation, I will provide an overview of the nondualistic tradition in the philosophy of art that has grown out of Wittgenstein's insights, and finally present my own theory in the context of that neo-Wittgensteinian tradition.

The Standard View: Theater as a Semiotic Vehicle

In Sartre's play *Kean,* the prince refers to Edmund Kean as a "shadow," and Elaine responds: "A shadow? Is Kean then not a man?" "Indeed no, madam," pronounces the prince. "He is an actor."[2] Not surprisingly, the prince's remark here echoes Sartre's own theory of theater. Sartre maintains that the collective act of the imagination that transforms the actor Kean into the character Hamlet *negates* the real man, rendering him as unreal as the character he portrays. Sartre writes, "The transformation that occurs here is like that . . . in a dream: the actor is completely caught up, inspired, in the unreal. It is not the character who becomes real in the actor, it is the actor who *becomes unreal* in his character."[3] Theater semioticians adopt a similar position. Marvin Carlson approvingly quotes Peter Handke's description of the stage as a place where every chair pretends to be another chair, and where even light is brightness pretending to be other brightness.[4] According to this view, the events that actually transpire in the theater assume significance only insofar as they apprise the audience of some other event, often fictional, always absent. The audience looks at the stage in order to look beyond the stage. In performance, actors cease to exist as or for themselves, and become instead the stand-in for an absent and perhaps nonexistent other.

Some theater semioticians such as Jean Alter and Andre Helbo have tried to accommodate the actuality of the theater event within their theories of theater. But the basic dualism between the "real" and the "unreal" that underlies Sartre's theory of theater remains: these theorists still conceive the performance event to be "real" only to the extent that it does *not* relate to the narrative. The "reality" of the theater event, according to this view, consists of the actor qua actor. When Helen Hunt performed Viola in *Twelfth Night* at Lincoln Center, Helen Hunt was a real presence in the theater; Viola was not. According to what has become the orthodox view, as a spectator I must choose whether to focus my attention on the real world, which contains Helen Hunt, or the represented world, which contains Viola. These two levels of reality are distinct and cognitively incompatible. Helbo is expressing this orthodox view when he asserts that "sign and desire, meaning and denial of meaning, meet in the actor, a real physical presence, and at the same time the signifier of a narrative concept which denies that presence."[5] Similarly, semiotician Jean Alter distinguishes sharply between what he calls the "referential" function of performance, that is, the performance's representation of a narrative, and the "performant" function, which encompasses the performers' display of physical and imaginative skills in the here and now of the theatrical moment, and even more basically, the sensual and erotic presence of the performers' bodies themselves. According to Alter, the performant function "de-semiotizes the performance when it turns signs into pure signifiers, stripped of the referential function. . . . Barring de-semiotization, everything on the stage refers in this system to its mirror-image in an imaginary space off-stage."[6]

The attempts by Helbo and Alter to acknowledge the presence of the performer within semiotic theories occurred just as the vogue for semiotics peaked in the late 1980s and early 1990s. Since that time, theorists have put increasing emphasis on the performative nature of performance rather than its communicative function. Most of these theorists, however, have focused their attention on nontheatrical forms of performance, such as protests, performance art, and gender construction in the "real" world, and have paid little attention to the phenomenon of theater.[7] There is still no clear alternative to the semiotic model to explain the relationship between performativity and fiction in theater.[8] The most stimulating and sustained attempt to grapple with the "eventfulness" of dramatic performance remains Bert O. States's phenomenological analysis of theater in *Great Reckonings in Little Rooms*. States rightly faults semiotics for "its almost imperialistic confidence in its product: that is, its implicit belief that you have exhausted a thing's interest when you have explained how it works as a sign."[9] States reminds us that "theater—unlike fiction, painting, sculpture, and film—is really a language whose words consist to an unusual degree of things that *are* what they seem to be. In theater, image and object, pretense and pretender, sign-vehicle and content, draw unusually close. . . . Put bluntly, in theater there is always a possibility that an act of sexual congress between two so-called signs will produce a real pregnancy."[10] Nonetheless, States continues to take for granted that the relationship between the theater event and the narrative event is a semiotic one. For States, phenomenology begins where semiosis ends. Spectators assume a phenomenological perspective when, for example, they see a child or an animal on stage. At such moments, "the floor cracks open and we are startled, however pleasantly, by the upsurge of the real into the magic circle where the conventions of theatricality have assured us that the real has been subdued and transcended."[11] Notice that States here maintains the fundamental dichotomy between the reality of the performance event and the fictional world those events represent. To the extent we attend to the fiction, the real world is "subdued" and "transcended," and to the extent we attend to the real world of the stage, we are distracted from the fiction. The assumption underlying all these views harkens back to Coleridge's notion that spectators willingly suspend their "disbelief" when they encounter works of fiction. By contrast, I will propose that a spectator need not, and typically does not, repress the reality of the theater event in order to attend to the fictional narrative. The fictional narrative is an integral aspect of the audience's perception of the actual events that transpire on the stage.

Neo-Wittgensteinian Theories of Representation

Aestheticians such as E. R. Gombrich, Virgil Aldrich, Richard Wollheim, and most recently Kendall Walton have developed theories of representation that challenge the dualism implicit in the semiotic view. Instead of viewing representational artworks as signs, these theories propose that such works give rise to a phenomenon similar or identical to one that Wittgenstein explores in the final section of *Philosophical Investigations* (and elsewhere): that of "seeing aspects," or "seeing-as." This simple paradigm shift has far-reaching implications for the theory of theatrical representation.

Wittgenstein's paradigmatic example of "seeing-as" is the classic rabbit/duck image, which one can see either as a drawing of a duck or of a rabbit.[12]

What exactly changes when one switches from one interpretation to the other? Certainly, Wittgenstein notes, not the actual lines on the page. Still, the change is not merely in what the lines signify. The image *looks* different depending on whether one regards it as a duck or as a rabbit. One's visual experience itself undergoes a transformation. The concepts "duck" and "rabbit" impose altogether different gestalts on the image; they provide schemes that allow us to organize the actual lines on the page in a different way.

Wittgenstein considers the case of a simple line drawing of a face comprised of a few dots and dashes enclosed in a circle. He observes, "In some respects I stand towards [the picture-face] as I do towards a human face. I can study its expression, can react to it as to the expression of the human face. A child can talk to picture-men or picture-animals, can treat them as it treats dolls."[13] Such a drawing is not a blank slate upon which I can project anything whatsoever. It is a *particular* face, with a *particular* expression. One could, of course, try to describe that expression. Wittgenstein himself offers a delightful description of a simple face-picture in *The Brown Book*.

"It looks like a complacent business man," he suggests, "stupidly supercilious, who though fat, imagines he's a lady killer."[14] However he insists that any such description can convey only an approximate impression of the face. Ultimately, the expression on the face is just *that expression.* Wittgenstein proposes, "What goes on here is an act, as it were, of digesting it, getting hold of [the expression]."[15] On Wittgenstein's view, then, when we see the picture as a face, we in no way "negate" the physical lines on the page. Neither do we impose an image over the lines, or translate the picture into some other image. In *Zettel* Wittgenstein observes that

> we don't have to translate such pictures into realistic ones in order to "understand" them, any more than we ever translate photographs or film picture into coloured pictures, although black-and-white men or plants in reality would strike us as unspeakably strange and frightful.[16]

"Seeing as" is simply a way of seeing, and all seeing, as Kant originally recognized, is necessarily infused with imagination.

C. S. Peirce stipulates that "The Sign can only represent the Object and tell *about* it. It cannot furnish acquaintance with or recognition of that

Object."[17] The force of Wittgenstein's analysis is precisely to demonstrate that the phenomenon of "seeing-as" *does* acquaint us with an absent object (for example, the expression on an absent face), and that it does *not* represent anything else. This point comes out even more clearly when we consider Umberto Eco's definition of semiotics, which follows logically from Peirce's definition of the sign: "*semiotics is in principle the discipline studying everything which can be used in order to lie.* . . . I think that the definition of a 'theory of the lie' should be taken as a pretty comprehensive program for a general semiotics."[18] In the case of seeing as, the concept of "lying" does not apply. Iconic images present whatever aspects to us that we can find in them. They are what they are. As Wittgenstein puts it, "'I am seeing this figure as a . . .' can be verified as little (or in the same sense as) 'I am seeing bright red.'"[19] Of course we can, and often do, put iconic images into circulation as signs in particular contexts. For example you might ask me: "How did Kathy take the news?" and I might respond by drawing a smirking face. And significantly, it would then make sense to say that I "lied" with the image; for example, I may have deliberately misrepresented Kathy's anguished reaction. The phenomenon of "seeing-as" itself, however, is presemiotic.

Seeing Aspects and Theatrical Representation

Obviously, the phenomenon of "seeing-as" is directly relevant to art forms such as representational drawing, painting, and sculpture. What's not so obvious is that this phenomenon—or rather, an essential component of it—is also integral to theater. Theater provides some cases that directly exemplify the sort of seeing-as that Wittgenstein discusses. For example, we might see jagged lines painted on a backdrop as a mountain range; we might see a row of chairs as a train or an airplane. In theater games such as those the Open Theater popularized in the 1960s, one might see each performer in a group as a different part of a single large machine. At one point in Richard Foreman's 1972 production of *Sophia = Wisdom Part III*, a curtain was removed to reveal a series of small models of houses. Through the hollow frames of the house's roofs, one could see performer's faces. Michael Kirby describes the effect of this image this way:

> Either the houses on the cliffs are accepted as life-size and the heads that
> fill them become gigantic, or the heads are accepted as life-size and the

houses become miniature. Like an optical illusion these relationships change, and the mind instinctively searches for information to support and confirm one choice or the other.[20]

Foreman has listed Wittgenstein as among his influences, and may well be making a deliberate allusion to him when he enjoins us, in an early manifesto, to "remember that structure is always a combination of the THING and the PERCEIVING of it."[21]

Wittgenstein himself does not explicitly discuss the relevance of "seeing aspects" to theater. At one point in *Philosophical Investigations,* however, Wittgenstein brushes against this issue when he contemplates "a game played by children: they say that a chest, for example, is a house; and thereupon it is interpreted as a house in every detail. A piece of fancy is worked into it." Wittgenstein then asks: "does the child now *see* the chest as a house?"[22] Wittgenstein leaves the question hanging. However, he provides us with another piece of the puzzle much earlier in the *Investigations* in the course of evaluating the proposition that "if you see [a] leaf as a sample of 'leaf shape in general' you *see* it differently from someone who regards it as, say, a sample of this particular shape. Now this might well be so—though it is not so—for it would only be to say that, as a matter of experience, if you *see* the leaf in a particular way, you use it in such-and-such a way or according to such-and-such rules."[23] Wittgenstein's analysis of the leaf example applies just as effectively to the chest example. If the children stop regarding the chest as a "house" and begin instead regarding it as a "pirate ship," the chest will not undergo the sort of visual gestalt shift that marks the transition between seeing the duck/rabbit drawing as a duck or as a rabbit. What it will undergo is a shift in the *rules* that dictate the object's *use.*

Wittgenstein's example of the children's game with the chest recalls Gombrich's famous essay "Meditations of a Hobby Horse," in which Gombrich proposes a child's hobbyhorse as a paradigmatic instance of representation in art:

> if the child calls a stick a horse . . . [t]he stick is neither a sign signifying the concept horse nor is it a portrait of an individual horse. By its capacity of serving as a "substitute" the stick becomes a horse in its own right.[24]

Gombrich does not explicitly invoke the Wittgensteinian notion of "seeing-as" here, but his proposal is neo-Wittgensteinian in reorienting our focus away from what the representation points to and back onto the representation itself. Moreover, like Wittgenstein, Gombrich emphasizes the particularity of the representational image, and conceives of artistic creation as an act of bringing objects into the world rather than imitating or referring to preexisting objects. To quote:

> When Pygmalion blocked out a figure from his marble he did not at first represent a "generalized" human form, and then gradually a particular woman. . . . So when his prayers were heard and the statue came to life she was Galatea and no one else—and that regardless of whether she had been fashioned in an archaic, idealistic or naturalistic style.[25]

The theory Gombrich would later advance in *Art and Illusion* does explicitly invoke Wittgenstein's concept of "seeing-as," but ironically ends up much further from the Wittgensteinian position. Indeed, Gombrich embraces a dualism much like Sartre's, insisting that as soon as one begins to perceive a painting as a representation, one can no longer perceive it as a canvas covered with paint, that is, as a real physical presence in the world.

Imagining-As

The most fully elaborated version of what I would call a neo-Wittgensteinian theory of representation is the theory Kendall Walton sets forth in *Mimesis as Make Believe.* Walton departs from Gombrich, and follows Richard Wollheim, in stressing a crucial point: when "seeing an image in a drawing or painting . . . one attends to the canvas as well as the picture's representational content," and "these are not two separable experiences but distinguishable aspects of the same one." For Walton, "This duality consists simply in the fact that one uses the picture as a prop in a visual game: one imagines seeing a mill, and one does so because one notices the relevant features of the canvas."[26]

Most importantly, Walton follows both Wittgenstein and Gombrich (and departs from Wollheim) in placing emphasis on the way that viewers *use* artworks. Walton's theory allows us to draw a connection between "seeing an actor as Hamlet" and "seeing a drawing as a duck" by subsuming the Wittgensteinian examples of seeing-as within the larger phenomenon of "imagining-as." The cornerstone of the theory is the proposition that works of art function as what he calls "props in games of make believe." Walton defines fictionality as consisting of "prescriptions to imagine," and locates the difference between various modes of representation (depiction, narration, etc.) in "the nature of the games that works of various sorts are to be used in and the roles they have in them."[27] A picture of a face does not denote a face, but invites me to imagine that I am seeing a face, to try to make each part of the picture fit within this framework, and to ask myself some of the same sorts of questions about the picture that I might ask myself if confronted with a real face. Walton fleshes out the theory Wittgenstein hints at in his description of children at play. More generally, of course, Walton's attempt to explain artworks by appealing to the games we play with them recalls Wittgenstein's attempt to explain words and sentences by appealing to their role in language games.

Significantly, Walton's governing metaphor—that of a "prop"—is theatrical. Yet Walton has comparatively little to say about theater as an art form. For him, actors are just another kind of prop in the games that audiences can play. Specifically, actors are what he calls *reflexive props,* like Wittgenstein's chest and Gombrich's hobbyhorse: the actor does not merely prompt us to imagine that we see a character, but to imagine that he or she *is* the character. As Walton writes:

> Spectators imagine of Sir Laurence Olivier, when he plays Hamlet, that he is Prince of Denmark; there is a real person before them who they imagine to be faced with the task of avenging his father's murder, to hesitate in carrying it out, and so forth. . . . The imaginings are made more vivid by the *presence* of the actors. My suggestion is that their presence is important only because they are objects of imagining.[28]

Walton's analysis of acting is useful as far as it goes, especially in its ability to acknowledge the basic consanguinity between acting and other representational art forms. But the theory does not do full justice to the differences. For example, Walton endorses Wollheim's substitution of the expression "seeing-*in*" for "seeing-*as*" to describe what one does when viewing representational images. As Walton observes, we do not, typically, see a drawing of a horse *as* a horse; it is more natural to say that we see a horse *in* a painting of a horse.[29] But observe that acting and painting are different in this respect. It is perfectly natural to describe the experience of seeing Helen Hunt play the part of Viola by saying, "I saw Helen Hunt as Viola," while the expression, "I saw Viola in Helen Hunt" suggests something altogether different, such as that I detected a similarity between the real-life Helen Hunt and the fictional character Viola. In general, seeing-in seems to apply more felicitously to nonreflexive art forms such as painting and drawing, and seeing-as to reflexive art forms, such as dramatic performance.

More significantly, Walton fails to distinguish theater from other art forms that employ reflexive props, such as sculpture. Unlike sculptures, actors are not merely props in other people's games of make-believe; they are themselves game-players. Consequently, most of what Walton has to say about the audience's interaction with representational artworks is directly applicable to the actor's own imaginative engagement within the theater event. To a large extent, actors usurp the role that Walton carves out for audiences of artworks.

What, then, is the role of a theater audience? Although different forms of theater invite the audience to participate in importantly different ways, what makes theater—or more specifically, mimetic theater—distinctive as an art form is that, in Walton's terms, the object the audience uses as a prop in *its* game of make-believe is *itself* a game of make-believe. In order for the audience to play its own game effectively, it must have some understanding of the rules of the game that the actors are playing. And in order to make sense of that game, the audience must have some understanding of the fictional framework within which the game is defined, of what Stanislavsky (following Pushkin) famously calls the "given circumstances" of the actor's make-believe world. Just as the concepts "duck" and "rabbit" provide schemes to organize our perceptions of the duck/rabbit drawing, the fictional narrative of a play provides a schema that organizes the audience's perception of the game the actors are playing.

Imagine a game called "anti-tic-tac-toe," which is just like tic-tac-toe except that the object is to *avoid* having three of your marks form a straight line. The first player who is forced to fill a row, loses. One can see any occurrence of anti-tic-tac-toe as an occurrence of tic-tac-toe, and vice versa. However, the more brilliant a game is as an instance of anti-tic-tac-toe, the more inept it is as a game of tic-tac-toe, and so if I were to come upon two people competently playing anti-tic-tac-toe, I would marvel at their extravagant ineptitude—that is, until I caught on to the rules of the game they were playing.

Similarly, imagine a scene in which a character, let's call her Jane, needs to get across a river, and must coax a man with a boat, let's call him Jake, to get her across. The river is represented by a strip of cloth on the stage; the boat is a piece of cardboard that Jake holds. Jane's desire to get to the other side of the stage (that is, "across the river"), and her failure, given that desire, simply to walk over the cloth to get there, will both be unintelligible to us if we do not understand the fictional context that structures the rules of the game. The same situation obtains with naturalistic plays: someone with no understanding of the game of make-believe that the actors are playing could make no sense of the emotional pyrotechnics that take place, for example, when an actor playing Walter Lee Younger refuses to sign a piece of paper at the end of a performance of *Raisin in the Sun*.

Infiction and Outfiction

Brenda Laurel, in *Computers as Theater*, proposes an extremely instructive parallel between acting and interacting with computers. Both computers and plays, she argues, create virtual spaces within which people act. The real issue in designing computer interfaces, she writes, is, "How can people participate as agents within representational contexts? Actors know a lot about that, and so do children playing make-believe. Buried within us in our deepest playful instincts . . . are the most profound and intimate sources of knowledge about interactive representations."[30] What dramatic performance, computer interfaces, and virtual reality have in common is that they all implement a metaphorical restructuring of reality. Consider for example the way the desktop metaphor structures the graphical interfaces of Macintosh and Windows computers. Once we have learned what counts in the Macintosh game as moving a file—that is, how to point to an icon and drag it with the mouse—and once we have identified the trash can on our computer screen, we can easily figure out for ourselves what counts as deleting a file, that is, "throwing it into the trash." Note that our interaction with the computer doesn't tell us a story about some fictional desktop that exists apart from the computer, but rather the desktop metaphor makes sense of our actual interactions with the particular computer that we are using. This, I am proposing, is precisely the function that the fictional narrative plays in governing the actors' actions onstage, and in allowing the audiences to make sense of those actions.

The conception of metaphor implicit in this analysis is what Paul Ricoeur describes as an "interaction" (or "tension") theory of metaphor, as opposed to a "substitution" theory. According to Ricoeur, metaphors operate in a way analogous to scientific models: "Things themselves are 'seen as'; they are *identified* . . . with the descriptive character of the model."[31] Note that the interaction model of metaphor draws a very thin line between metaphorical and literal meaning. Consider once again the example of the graphical computer interface. The terms *file* and *folder* assume new meanings, related to the old, when used with reference to computers. When we first start using computers, we may rely heavily on the old meanings to understand the new; the words have a strongly metaphorical quality. But as one becomes fluent with computers, the words lose their old connotations, and refer directly, or "literally," to their new objects. Similarly, in the course of a performance "Hamlet" takes on a new meaning; it becomes a label that affixes to the actor, who is metaphorically a prince in Denmark and literally a "prince" in the game played on stage.

Let's call the fictional schema that structures the performance event the *infiction,* which we can distinguish from the narrative content that we extract from the performance event, which I will call the *outfiction.* The infiction is the set of "prescriptions to imagine" that, according to Walton, constitute fictionality. For actors (as for children in games of make-believe and audience members in participatory theater), the act of imagining isn't merely a mental exercise, but assumes a tangible form: the infiction governs the actor's physical actions in the real world. Insofar as spectators use the narrative as an *infiction,* the primary focus of their attention is the performance itself. The fiction does not function as a third term that exists outside the performance; it inheres in the performance itself, just as the expression on Wittgenstein's face-drawing inheres in the drawing. Our *metaphorical redescription* of these actions is what I am calling the outfiction. Wittgenstein's *description* of the face, which I quoted earlier, is an outfiction. Similarly, the story of Hamlet as I read it off of a performance of Hamlet is an outfiction.

The act of spectatorial or critical interpretation that produces the outfiction transforms an artwork into a sign. Recall that Peirce describes semiosis as a "thirdness," that is, as an irreducible relationship between three terms: a sign, its object, and its interpretant. A sign, writes Peirce, "addresses somebody, that is, creates in the mind of that person an equivalent sign, or perhaps a more developed sign. That sign which it creates I call the *interpretant* of the first sign."[32] What I have defined as the outfiction fulfills precisely the role that Peirce lays out for the "interpretant." Insofar as spectators use the narrative as an *infiction,* the primary focus of their attention is the performance itself. The fiction does not function as a third term that exists outside the performance; it inheres in the performance, just as the expression on Wittgenstein's face-drawing inheres in the drawing. This phenomenon exemplifies what Peirce describes as a "secondness." It involves a relationship between *two* terms: the spectator and a particular kind of performance, such as an *Antigone*-performance or an *Endgame*-performance. The narrative and the performance join together here to form what Nelson Goodman calls an "unbreakable one-place predicate."[33] Only when spectators *extract* the narrative content *from* the performance, that is, only when they treat the narrative as an *outfiction,* do we have a triadic relationship between the spectator, the performance, and the fictional world. The spectator, then, experiences, not just an *Antigone-performance,* but a performance *of Antigone.*

What I am proposing is that the relationship between narrative and performance runs two ways: from narrative to performance (fiction in), and from performance to narrative (fiction out). Theories of theatrical representation, and indeed of representation in art generally, have tended to turn their gaze only in one of these two directions, concerning themselves only with the meaning we *extract from* artworks. This tendency is most obvious in semiotic theories. For example, Julia Kristeva demonstrates the semiotic impulse to reduce works of art entirely to their outfiction when she asserts that "the painting is nothing other than *the text that analyzes it.*"[34] Significantly, however, even so nondualistic a theorist as Walton falls into the semiotic trap. While Walton occasionally acknowledges the existence of nonpropositional meaning in art, his theory nonetheless assumes that the ultimate objective of the games we play with artworks is to generate a set of fictional propositions.[35]

By recognizing the two-way nature of the relationship between performance and narrative, and by allowing for the possibility that sometimes the fiction serves its most important function going in rather than coming out, we can steer clear of otherwise intractable theoretical quandaries. Walton identifies a class of what he calls "silly questions" about artworks, such as, why are all the apostles sitting on one side of the table in Leonardo's *The Last Judgment?* Significantly, Walton devotes most of his discussion of this problem to examples from the theater, though he rarely draws on theatrical examples elsewhere in his book. Specifically, he raises the following "silly" questions: "How did Othello, a Moorish general and hardly an intellectual, manage to come up with such superb verses on the spur of the moment?" and "How can it be fictional that Dickinson says all that she does [in *Belle of Amherst*] . . . yet fictional that she is not gregarious?"[36] Though Walton's discussion of this problem is subtle and provocative, his theory does not provide any clear solution. All he can offer is a series of ad hoc solutions: in some cases, an artwork may "disallow" certain questions, in others, it may "deemphasize" them, and in yet others "it may be best to accept and even emphasize fictional truths that clash with one another, but to mute the clash by disallowing the fictionality of their conjunction."[37] The theory never defines the criteria that spectators use to determine which of these various stances they should adopt toward any given question.[38]

Once we have recognized that the infiction alone is often sufficient to render a moment meaningful in the theater, the need to erect ad hoc defenses against silly questions vanishes. For example, imagine a theatrical production in which all the actors wear grotesquely exaggerated masks, with one actor sporting an enormous nose and a pair of eyeglasses that projects two feet out from either side of her face. Further suppose that none of the characters ever acknowledge this actor's exaggerated appearance. The exaggerated elements seem to function as comments on the character's personality or social type, not as a literal depiction of the character's appearance in the world of the fiction. So far, everything I have said about this hypothetical production would be simple to account for in a semiotic analysis. But now imagine that at one point in the play, the actor tries to exit through a door but the glasses are too wide and she does not fit. She tries to exit sideways, but her nose does not fit, either. She finally squeezes through by bending her nose down with both hands with manifest effort. As soon as she walks through the door, she lets go and her nose springs back into position with an audible "boing." What is the audience to make of this shtick? What is supposed to be happening in the fictional world? The actor's actions make no sense unless we imagine that the character really does have an impossibly large nose and glasses. And yet if she did, surely she or another character would make some reference to her grotesque appearance. An alternative interpretation would be to construe the play as representing a fantasy or science fiction world in which human anatomy is significantly different than it is in our own world. But such a reading seems far too literal.

Consider another example. In the musical *My Fair Lady*, Henry Higgins, Eliza Doolittle, and Colonel Pickering famously celebrate Eliza's success in learning to pronounce Queen's English with an extended song and dance routine, "The Rain in Spain." What is supposed to be occurring in the world of the fiction during this scene? A convention of musicals, of course, is that the performers often sing to represent the characters speaking, and they dance to represent their general emotional state. But the following song, Eliza Doolittle's "I Could Have Danced All Night," implies that the characters really did dance in the world of the fiction. So the question becomes: did they dance the same dance that the performers did? It seems implausible to ascribe that degree of choreographic and dance skill to these characters. So how exactly did they dance, and for how long? Moreover, the ambiguity of the dance throws the status of the musical accompaniment into question. While we normally understand that musical accompaniment is not a diegetic element in the fictional world—the play does not depict a magical reality filled with invisible instruments—the highly coordinated tango-style dancing is even more implausible if we imagine it without the musical accompaniment. And the ambiguity surrounding the dance and music complicates our interpretation of the performers' singing, which otherwise we could construe simply as a stylized depiction of spoken conversation. Are the characters really supposed to be singing the song that we hear? Or a simplified version of that song? There is simply no way to determine the answer to these questions.

Significantly, while these are all logical questions from a semiotic perspective, they typically do not worry spectators watching the musical, suggesting that semiotics, whatever its value as a critical tool, is not a good model of the way an audience experiences theater. Spectators do not always, or even usually, treat theatrical performance as a text from which to extract details about a fictional world. The focus of their attention is on the performance itself, and on the significance and force of the performers' actions within the world the performers have created on stage. To ask questions about exactly what a stylized mask or the music in a musical represents within the world of the fiction is precisely analogous to asking what the windows and scrollbars on the virtual desktop of a Macintosh screen correspond to on a real desktop. The conventions of performance and the fictional narrative work together to create a structure within which the director and performers make their choices and perform their actions. The interest of both the hypothetical scene with the mask and the scene from *My Fair Lady* lies in the extravagant and inventive way that the performers play the theatrical game. In other words, the narrative functions as infiction, not as outfiction.

One might accuse performances that privilege the infiction at the expense of the outfiction of indulging in a kind of ludic formalism. The musical comedy example is certainly vulnerable to such a charge, as, in a different way, may be some of the work of avant-garde directors such as Robert Wilson and Richard Foreman. However, to recognize the function of the infiction also allows us to appreciate more fully the potential power of performance as a laboratory for social change. Augusto Boal's "forum theater" workshops with nonactors empower members of various oppressed groups—such as exploited farmworkers and abused spouses— by providing a time, place and structure for participants to adopt new roles and to rehearse new strategies for their own lives. Psychologists have suggested that just such a function is served by children's role-playing games. The conception of theater that I have been advocating here—as the actual embodiment of alternate structures of reality—underlies Jill Dolan's notion of the "utopian performative" and provides a philosophical basis for her unabashedly idealistic contention "that performance—and not just drama—is one of the few places where a live experience . . . of utopia might be possible."[39]

NOTES

1. www.artlex.com.

2. Jean-Paul Sartre, *The Devil and The Good Lord and Two Other Plays,* trans. Kitty Black (New York: Alfred A. Knopf, 1960), 165.

3. Jean-Paul Sartre, *Psychology of the Imagination* (Secaucus, N.J.: Citadel Press, 1948), 278. Many theorists have objected to Sartre's contention that to see something as a representation entails *negating* the thing itself. See, for example, Hidé Ishiguro, "Imagination," in *British Analytical Philosophy,* ed. Bernard Williams and Alan Montefiore (New York: Humanities Press, 1966), 133–78, and Karen Hanson, *The Self Imagined: Philosophical Reflections on the Social Character of Psyche* (New York: Routledge and Kegan Paul, 1986), 48–63. A semiotic theory need not adopt Sartre's proposal that we negate the actor's presence. What semiotic theories *do* ask us to do is regard the actor as a signifier, which is to say, as means of cognitive access to something other than itself.

4. Marvin Carlson, *Theater Semiotics: Signs of Life* (Bloomington: Indiana University Press, 1990), 75.

5. Quoted and translated by Marvin Carlson in "Review Article: Theater as Event," *Semiotica* 56, no. 3 (1985): 312.

6. Jean Alter, "Meaning and Theatre: Reassigning Performance Signs," in *Semiotics 1985,* ed. John Deely (Lanham, Md.: University Press of America, 1986), 85. The term *desemiotics,* of course, is not original to Alter, but comes from Jean-François Lyotard, who calls for a theater of energies and libidinal displacements to replace a theater of signs and representational displacements (*Des dispositifs pulsionnels* [Paris: Union générale d'éditions, 1973], 95–96).

7. Jon McKenzie explains performance scholars' neglect of theater by suggesting that the field of performance studies has established what he calls a "liminal norm,"

valorizing the study of subversive, transgressive forms of performance. See *Perform or Else: From Discipline to Performance* (New York: Routledge, 2001), 50.

8. I have investigated the status of speech acts in the theater in a series of articles arguing, contra Searle and others, that speech acts can and often do retain their illocutionary force on stage. The view I develop in those articles complements the view I present here, but the arguments do not entail one another. See David Z. Saltz, "How To Do Things on Stage," *Journal of Aesthetics and Art Criticism* 49, no. 1 (1991): 31–45 and "The Reality of Doing: Speech Acts in the Theatre," in *Method Acting Reconsidered,* ed. David Krasner (St. Martins Press, 2000), 61–80.

9. Bert O. States, *Great Reckonings in Little Rooms: On the Phenomenology of Theater* (Berkeley and Los Angeles: University of California Press, 1985), 7.

10. Ibid., 20.

11. Ibid., 34.

12. Wittgenstein's discussion of the rabbit/duck image occurs in *Philosophical Investigations,* 2nd ed., trans. G. E. M. Anscombe (New York: Basil Blackwell and Mott, 1958), part II, sec. xi, 194–97.

13. Ibid., 194.

14. Ludwig Wittgenstein, *The Blue and Brown Books,* 2nd ed. (New York: Harper and Row, 1960), 162.

15. Ibid.

16. Ludwig Wittgenstein, *Zettel,* ed. G. E. M. Anscombe and G. H. von Wright, trans. G. E. M. Anscombe (Berkeley and Los Angeles: University of California Press, 1970), 44e.

17. Charles S. Peirce, *Philosophical Writings of Peirce* (New York: Dover, 1955), 100.

18. Umberto Eco, *A Theory of Semiotics* (Bloomington: Indiana University Press, 1979), 7.

19. Wittgenstein, *Philosophical Investigations,* 212e.

20. Michael Kirby, "Richard Foreman's Ontological Hysteric Theatre," in *The New Theatre: Performance Documentation,* ed. Michael Kirby (New York: New York University Press, 1974), 179.

21. Richard Foreman, *Reverberation Machines: The Later Plays and Essays* (Barrytown, NY: Station Hill Press, 1985), 222. The resulting shifts in "seeing aspects" represent a case of "exploding noema" in Husserl's sense, not merely a case of changing significations. We reidentify what the objects are; we interact with them in a new and startling ways. As Foreman proclaims: "Our art then = a learning how to look at 'A' and 'B' and see not them but a relation that cannot be 'seen.' You can't look at 'it' (that relation) because it IS the looking itself" (206). Foreman here is, probably self-consciously, echoing Wittgenstein's observation that "what I perceive in the dawning of an aspect is not a property of the object, but an internal relation between it and other objects" (*Philosophical Investigations,* 212).

22. *Philosophical Investigations,* 206e.

23. Ibid., 35e.

24. E. H. Gombrich, *Meditations on a Hobby Horse,* reprinted in *Aesthetics Today,* ed. Morris Philipson (Cleveland: World Publishing, 1961), 155.

25. Ibid., 116.

26. Kendall L. Walton, *Mimesis as Make Believe* (Cambridge: Harvard University Press, 1990), 301. Walton discusses the relationship between Wollheim's view and his

own in greater depth in "Seeing-In and Seeing Fictionally," in *Psychoanalysis, Mind, and Art: Perspectives on Richard Wollheim,* ed. Jim Hopkins and Anthony Savile (Cambridge, Mass.: Blackwell, 1992), 281–91. For a very useful comparison of Gombrich's, Wollheim's, and Walton's views of seeing-as and seeing-in, see Patrick Maynard, "Seeing Double," *Journal of Aesthetics and Art Criticism* 52, no. 2 (1994): 155–67.

27. Walton, *Mimesis as Make Believe,* 292.

28. Ibid., 26–27.

29. Ibid., 300.

30. Brenda Laurel, *Computers as Theatre* (New York: Addison-Wesley, 1991), 21. Unfortunately, Laurel's specific ideas about how to relate theater to computer interface design rely on a narrow and old-fashioned dramaturgical model rooted in Aristotle's *Poetics.*

31. Paul Ricoeur, *The Rule of Metaphor,* trans. Robert Czerny et al. (Toronto: University of Toronto Press, 1977), 242–43. The way metaphor functions in the theory I am proposing is also closely related to the function of metaphor in Lakoff and Johnson's theory. Lakoff and Johnson convincingly argue that metaphors provide cognitive schemes that structure people's understandings of and interactions with the world around them. George Lakoff and Mark Johnson, *Metaphors We Live By* (Chicago: University of Chicago Press, 1980).

32. Peirce, *Philosophical Writings,* 99.

33. Nelson Goodman, *Languages of Art,* 2nd ed. (Indianapolis: Hackett, 1976).

34. Julia Kristeva, *Language the Unknown: An Initiation into Linguistics,* trans. Anne M. Menke (New York: Columbia University Press, 1989), 312–13.

35. For example, Walton says of a novel that "its *job* is to generate fictional truths" (*Mimesis as Make Believe,* 104f.; emphasis added).

36. Ibid., 175, 176.

37. Ibid., 182.

38. "The specifics of how one chooses to treat these examples do not much matter," Walton is content to explain. "I have mentioned various possibilities mainly to show that plausible options are available" (ibid., 183).

39. Jill Dolan, "Performance, Utopia, and the 'Utopian Performative,'" *Theatre Journal* 53, no. 3 (2001): 456.

~

ELEVEN

Understanding Plays

James R. Hamilton

The Issue

Theatrical performances require time for their presentation.[1] Theatrical performances require time for their reception. The time in which theatrical performance is received by an audience is the same time as that of its presentation.

Theatrical performances consist of events arranged in a sequence. The sequence of events in which a given production of a play is performed need not always be the same from performance to performance. We can imagine a production in which the scenes are numbered and, upon arrival for each evening's performance, the company settles on the ordering of the scenes by drawing from a hat numbers corresponding to the scenes. Clearly, in this production one night's performance could be different from every other night's performance. Just as clearly, however, each night's performance will have been arranged and experienced by the audience in just that one particular order, albeit an order that was randomly, perhaps we may want to say arbitrarily, chosen at the outset of the performance.[2]

Unless the performers make a mistake, the sequence of events in theatrical performances are experienced by audiences in the order in which the events have been arranged. Moreover, the events are experienced at roughly and typically the pace the performers have arranged for them to be experienced. The qualifiers "roughly and typically" are required because the performers may, for a variety of reasons, perform the sequence of events, in whole or in parts, more slowly or more quickly than they had planned.

In all of these respects theatrical performance may be said to be a *tem-*

poral art form.[3] Here is another. Individual moments in a theatrical performance, "zero-duration-time-slices" so to speak, as a rule are not considered as something in the performance to which one attends in experiencing the events of which the theatrical performance consists. A theatrical performance could be filmed and as a result single moments of individual scenes could be pulled out to be observed and even appreciated as pictures in their own right. But these would be freeze frames of the *film* of the performance, and not "non-temporally extended parts" of the performance to be observed for their own sakes, for of a theatrical performance there is nothing that corresponds to that description.[4] This is not to deny that performers can stop the action in a play and allow, by means of the stopped moment, for something to register with the audience. Such "freeze frames," if that is what we want to call them, are not only possible, they may be very effective bits of theater. But they are not presented or experienced as moments to be understood on their own in isolation from the rest of the sequence of events comprising the performance. Indeed their value as bits of theater will be experienced precisely because of their connections to and contrasts with the remainder of the events.

A further pair of features of theatrical performances follows from those listed so far. First, there is no stepping back from a theatrical performance and taking it in as a whole in a single observation. Nor, second, is there any flipping backward and forward through the performance to check if one got it right the first time, to remind ourselves who the character now present to us really is or to discover what will later become of her.[5]

Reference to these practices or capacities, characteristic of what one can do with movies and novels but not with theatrical performances, respectively, may be thought useful for distinguishing theatrical performance from those other forms of art. I offer no opinion about that. I rehearse them here to raise a different question, namely, what is it to understand theatrical performances given that they have these temporally inflected characteristics?

The simple and obvious answer I will give is that to understand a theatrical performance is to grasp what is happening in the sequence of events that is presented as it is happening. This simple and obvious answer requires qualification and has deep and deeply interesting implications. The tasks undertaken in this essay are to work out this view in detail and to investigate its implications.

A Useful Model

In this essay I will focus on understanding plays, by which I will mean narrative theatrical performances. Not all theatrical performances are narratively structured. That is to say, not all theatrical performances aim to tell stories, are expected to tell them, or are taken as telling stories. Ordinarily, I suppose, we still call such nonnarrative theatrical performances "plays." But in this essay I will not have in mind that wider use of the term. Nor will I be using the word *plays* to refer to *scripts* for narrative theatrical performances. When I am talking about scripts, I will use the word *scripts*.[6]

Narrowing the scope in this way may seem an unjustified privileging of narrative theater over other modes and styles. This is far from my intention. One reason for dealing with narrative theatrical performances first is that they are likely to be the style most familiar to philosophical readers. But there is another, more substantive reason for beginning with narrative theatrical performances. If any form of theater seems most likely to exemplify theater art's dependency on, and subservience to, literary arts, it is that of the narrative theatrical performance, a form of performance whose values have often been taken not to exceed those of literary works and which has been regarded as little more than illustration or interpretation of literary works in performance medium. The view I propose of the understanding of even narrative theatrical performance undercuts the view of theater as dependent on literature. Moreover, I believe, if the view I develop here is right for plays, understood as I have proposed, it will be fairly easy to show how to generalize the account to help us get a grip on what is going on when we understand nonnarrative theatrical performances.

The view of understanding plays I will set forth is initially and partially modeled on an account, developed and defended by Jerrold Levinson, of how we understand musical performances.[7] Thinking about understanding musical performances is a natural place to begin our investigation because it seems obvious that what goes on in listening to music with understanding must be similar in some respects to what goes on when auditing a play with understanding.

Levinson bases his "concatenationist" account of what it is to understand and enjoy music on the writings of Edmund Gurney.[8] In its boldest form, Levinson writes, concatenationism is a conjunction of four propositions.

1. *Musical understanding* centrally involves neither aural grasp of a large span of music as a whole, nor intellectual grasp of large-scale connections between parts; understanding music is centrally a matter of apprehending individual bits of music and immediate progression from bit to bit.

2. *Musical enjoyment* is had only in the successive parts of a piece of music, and not in the whole as such, or in relationships of parts widely separated in time.

3. *Musical form* is centrally a matter of cogency of succession, moment to moment and part to part.

4. *Musical value* rests wholly on the impressiveness of individual parts and the cogency of the successions between them, and not on features of large-scale form per se; the worthwhileness of experience of music relates directly only to the former. (*MM*, 13–14)

Levinson's is a rich and varied account, and it is developed and refined in considerable detail over the course of his book. For the present purposes it will be enough to focus on certain features he discusses concerning the first and third of these propositions.

Levinson offers his account in order to counteract a prevailing alternative view holding that understanding a musical work when one hears it just *is* a matter of grasping its large-scale form by means of hearing "a large span of music" and hearing certain "large-scale connections between parts." Part of the argument against this alternative view consists of working out what it takes to demonstrate one is listening with understanding. Levinson offers the uncontroversial suggestion that "if a listener can track a piece of music aurally from beginning to end it can . . . be said to 'make sense' to him, whatever his evaluation of that 'sense' turns out to be." And he then argues that all that is required for a listener to track a piece of music—from the listener's side of the equation, so to speak—is that "the listener [be] focused on individual parts as they occur, and on the connections of such parts with immediately preceding and succeeding parts" (*MM*, 25). Levinson develops the account by sketching out a variety of marks of "basic musical understanding," where these "marks" are signs or evidence that musical understanding in the basic sense laid out so far is happening or has happened.

The marks of basic musical understanding . . . [are] these: present-centered absorption in musical flow; active following of musical progression; inward seconding of musical movement; sensitivity to musical alterations; reproductive ability; continuational ability; and grasp of emotional expression. . . . [to which may be added] pleasure in listening, at least when that pleasure is taken in the right thing, namely the quality of the musical substance heard in all its particularity. (*MM*, 32)

Levinson is careful to note three limits on the applicability of this idea of basic musical understanding: *(a)* such understanding, he writes, is "guided for the most part by ideals or norms of continuation, progression, development, evolution, and directionality"; *(b)* this view does not preclude "richer notions of understanding" where that understanding "may also supervene on an occasion of comprehending listening"; and, finally, *(c)* this idea "only truly constitutes an understanding of that music if it occurs in a listener appropriately informed and backgrounded as to the nature of the piece he is auditing, for example, its period, genre, and instrumentation" (*MM*, 34–35).

As a last step in sketching Levinson's account of basic musical understanding, let us turn to what he says of the objects of that understanding. Levinson holds there is no need for conscious apprehension of formal relationships in which the bits and the transitions figure in order for an auditor to perceive cogency within and between the bits. "The *real* form of a piece of music," he writes, "is in effect exhausted by the constitution of the smallest individual units, that is phrases and melodies, out of formless elements, and the specific manner in which each independent unit leads to the next. There is in no important sense an overall form to an extended piece of music; there is only formedness or cogency within and between bits that are successively apprehended" (*MM*, 9). And finally, "cogency of sequence . . . is each part—whether motive, phrase, melody, or paragraph—leading convincingly to the next, each consequent appearing, upon familiarity, to be the natural, even inevitable continuation of each antecedent" (*MM*, 7).

Levinson writes that part of what it is to be appropriately "backgrounded," in the sense required for basic musical understanding, may be to have "internalized norms for pieces of certain kinds" so that one is able, for example to "perceptually hear-as-sonata" (as opposed to "intellectually hear-as-sonata") (*MM*, 72). He suggests that this kind of backgrounded preparation for musical understanding be understood on analogy with knowing the terrain in a given location (*MM*, 73). Later he argues that, even though background reflection on large-scale phenomena may be useful for musical understanding, it must not be confused with understanding itself. "One can find cases . . . where large-scale reflection might plausibly be thought to foster attainment of basic musical understanding, or the aural synthesis at its core. [But] such facilitation is just that, and not an absolute prerequisite or sine qua non of aural synthesis" (*MM,* 128).

Initial Doubts about Applying the
Model to Theatrical Understanding

Plays involve human speech and physical instantiation or illustration of actions in ways that music does not. Recognizing verbal interchanges and actions is a different matter from recognizing sound patterns. But this seems to pose no serious problem for a roughly concatenationist view of understanding narrative theatrical performances. What is important in both cases, of musical and of theatrical performances, is that what is to be apprehended is sequences of bits, be they bits of sound patterns or bits of dialogue and action. The concatenationist view is that apprehension of sequences requires nothing more than attention to the bits themselves and the transitions between them on the part of suitably backgrounded auditors.

Some of the features of what must be understood in grasping a play might seem to require more resources than concatenationism affords. Narratives, whether literary, cinematic, or theatrical, may employ shifts backward and forward in time in a way that has no obvious counterpart in music. These shifts, and other "narrative devices," are understood by audiences, and if our account is to work, it has to explain how these phenomena are grasped. Once again, however, it is easy to see how a concatenationist view will work here. So long as we recognize that a concatenationist account can include references to an audience's memory of bits that have gone before, bits that include, for example, time markers of whatever sort, one need not attribute to that audience a grasp of the whole or even a grasp of very large-scale theatrical structures to account for audience's understanding of these devices and their significance in the moment for what is happening in the story.

One might insist the issue is how we understand sometimes long stretches of a performance, including such things as the connections between a bit of action in the first scene and a bit of dialogue in the last. One might think the fact we understand these kinds of things suggests that understanding the play does require us to have its large-scale form present to mind in the act of comprehending.

But precisely here is where the temporal features of theatrical performances get their bite. There is no such thing as "standing back" from either musical or theatrical performances in order to get the whole thing in focus in the way there can be with paintings and buildings. This of course would not by itself distinguish the experience of music or theater from that of movies or novels. But also there is the fact that the sort of going forward and backward in the way there can be with novels and poems is not typically available in theatrical and musical performances.

This remark may be taken to suggest I have in mind "merely a technological limitation of live performance."[9] The point is not that it is difficult to *stage* the kinds of flashbacks or premonitions that can easily be achieved in novels and movies. In fact I do not think that is particularly hard at all. The point is that there are characteristic patterns to our *reception* of music, movies, novels, poems, and plays. Among these patterns is the fact that going backward and forward is typically under the reader's control with respect to novels and poems, and that this is characteristic of how good readers read novels and poems. Going backward and forward is typically not under the auditor's control with respect to music, movies, and plays, and this is characteristic of the expectations of suitably backgrounded auditors of music, movies, and plays. So, whatever account we give of what we grasp when we understand long stretches and connections over time, we are pushed in the direction of a concatenationist view of how that grasp is attained.

In both music and theater there is the possibility of reflection both prior to and after auditing the performance, and there are practices of using scores and scripts to aid the study of large-scale forms. I make no judgment about the correctness of Levinson's claim that such reflection can only *facilitate* musical understanding in the moment and is "not an absolute prerequisite or sine qua non of aural synthesis" (*MM*, 128). I do suspect this feature of his view will hold in favor of a concatenationist account of theatrical understanding.

This suspicion is bolstered by consideration of what would count as the specific signs that someone has understood or is understanding a theatrical performance. A partial set of the primary signs that an individual has understood a play would include her ability to recount the story she has audited, to talk convincingly to others about the individuals whose lives form parts of that story, and to remember lines and their particular delivery (showing, perhaps, a grasp of the psychological depth, where present, of events and characterizations in the performance). An important sign she is understanding what is going on while watching a play is whether she seems ready for immediate uptake of events, even their anticipation, revealed, for example, in the manner in which she squirms in discomfort or leans forward in advance of a set of actions she sees coming.

This list of primary signs is not intended to be exhaustive. It is important to acknowledge that any of these is also defeasible as a sign of comprehension. For example, our auditor may be able to tell the story, but she may also have missed the fact the play was entirely satirical.

Even though collectively incomplete and individually defeasible, it is hard to see how these signs could fail to mark at least prima facie theatrical understanding. Yet none of them requires grasp of the structure of the whole play or its large-scale features. Perhaps prior knowledge of some genre-specific devices is required, and having some of such knowledge might be part of being appropriately backgrounded. Even in that event, it does not seem that the apprehension that a genre-specific device has been put into play requires more than familiarity with the convention and an immediate focus on the present scene and on the transitions from preceding, and toward succeeding, scenes.

What I have characterized as typical signs of basic theatrical understanding do not require global apprehension of large-scale structures and features of the whole play. But they do point to a fundamental difference between basic theatrical understanding and basic musical understanding. At the end of the piece of music we have no particular expectations of the comprehending listener, nothing we expect the comprehending listener to be able to do. In particular she need not have a story to tell, nor a story to tell about how her story fits all of what she has seen together. Yet the first of these at least is precisely one of the principal signs of basic theatrical understanding.

Provisional Statement of the View

An initial statement of a concatenationist view of what I will call "basic theatrical understanding" consists of the conjunction of the following five claims.

First, understanding a play as it happens, to paraphrase Levinson, is centrally a matter of apprehending individual bits of dialogue and stage action and the immediate progression from bit to bit.

Second, signs of basic theatrical understanding will include at least the ability to recount the story one has audited, the ability to talk convincingly to others about the individuals whose lives form parts of that story, the ability to remember bits of dialogue, their particular delivery and their importance in the story, and the immediate uptake of events on stage, even their anticipation.

Third, the objects of basic theatrical understanding, I shall say, are at the outset *(a)* the moment-to-moment bits of dialogue and stage action and the transitions between them and *(b)* those bits of dialogue and stage action prepared for and then delivered on in a manner available for recognition later in the play. But the object of basic theatrical understanding, as it comes to have a *developed* object over the course of the auditor's experience of the play, is a story.

Fourth, making sense of what is happening in the performance requires, again following Levinson, nothing more than being "focused upon individual parts as they occur, and on the connections of such parts with immediately preceding and succeeding parts."

Fifth, one assesses whether what is happening makes sense by sensing whether the bits and the transitions between bits are cogent, moment to moment.

The central thoughts behind a concatenationist account of basic theatrical understanding are these. First, grasping what is happening in a play when we are watching it in performance is not a matter of apprehending such phenomena as three-act versus five-act structure, overall plot structure, for example, whether the plot is episodic or "well made," having a problem-development-climax-denouement structure, or any other such large-scale formal features that can be correctly attributed to a play only upon reflection and, perhaps, further study of the play's script. Second, what is grasped over the course of the experience of the play is a story. (Here the account has diverged from the model Levinson provides.) None of this should be taken to deny that plays and the stories that they tell have such structures nor that grasping those large-scale features and structures is important for the crafting of a script or the production of a play. What is denied is that having a grasp of them is required for or even normally a part of "getting" a play.

In calling what can be gained upon an initial auditing of a play "basic theatrical understanding," I am following Levinson's terminological lead. The idea is that there is surely something that can be gained upon an initial confrontation with a piece of music performed that counts as an understanding of the music, but there are just as surely what Levinson calls "richer understandings" of that same musical performance. Levinson holds that the latter may "supervene" on the former understandings. Unfortunately, this point is not developed in Levinson's account. Moreover, serious problems might be encountered when attempting to carry whatever supervenience account can be developed over to the case of understandings of theatrical performances. But I will not have space to deal with these issues in the present essay. For the present purposes it is enough that we grant the present account of basic theatrical understanding does not rule out that there can be richer understandings of a theatrical performance in which the person who attains it simply sees *more* of what is there to be had than does the person who has only a basic theatrical understanding.

The second clause in the third proposition holds that the objects of basic theatrical understanding include not only the bits of dialogue and action and the transitions between them but also those bits of dialogue and stage action prepared for and then delivered on in a manner available for recognition later in the play. This should be understood much in the manner in which we understand how a punch line of a joke is prepared for and perhaps only much later delivered. This is, in fact, the link between the first clause, that the initial objects of basic theatrical understanding are the bits themselves, and the place at which we must diverge from the Levinson model, the idea that ultimately the object of basic theatrical understanding is a story.

On the matter of cogency, an initial position might be this, borrowed directly from Levinson: there is no need for conscious apprehension of formal relationships in which the bits and the transitions figure in order for an auditor to perceive cogency within and between the bits. We may also accept, subject to later revision, that the "real form" of a narrative theatrical performance consists, mutatis mutandis, only "of the smallest individual units, that is phrases and melodies, out of formless elements, and the specific manner in which each independent unit leads to the next," and the correlative claim that "there is in no important sense an overall form to an extended piece of music; there is only formedness or cogency within and between bits that are successively apprehended" (*MM*, 9).

But the ease with which a concatenationist account of musical understanding can be applied to understanding plays as they happen, even in the amended form we have so far adopted, stumbles over some important details: *(a)* we cannot accept a theatrical correlative to Levinson's claim that basic musical understanding is "guided for the most part by ideals or norms of continuation, progression, development, evolution, and directionality"; *(b)* as noted earlier, we may not be able to accept the view that "richer notions of understanding may also supervene on an occasion of comprehending [auditing]"; and, finally, *(c)* we cannot accept all of the theatrical correlative of Levinson's formulation of the basic test for cogency in the auditing of musical works, namely that "[c]ogency of sequence . . . is each part . . . leading convincingly to the next, each consequent appearing, upon familiarity, to be the natural, even inevitable continuation of each antecedent" (*MM*, 7). In what follows I will concentrate on the first and third of these points of divergence.

Motivating Revisions in the Account

Some familiar facts about theatrical performance push us to diverge further from a strict adherence to the model of concatenationism that Levinson provides. First, in a musical performance, attention to performers is optional for gaining musical understanding in a way that it is not for gaining theatrical understanding of a play. It is not just that the theatrical performers' voices and bodies are their instruments, although that seems right as far as it goes. More to the point, whatever is conveyed in theatrical enactment is conveyed by means of audience attention to the bodies and voices of the performers.[10] And it is a notorious fact about the theater that the bodies and voices of performers are distracting.

Second, what is taken in by various audience members may vary, even quite considerably, and yet leave them with the same basic theatrical understanding. Paul Ziff makes a similar point about both theater and dance, especially regarding what can be taken in at any one auditing. Consider the simple example of two people auditing the same performance but from different locations. In certain theater arrangements the position from which two people see the performance can make for many differences in what they take in. Even in an ideal case when most of that is under the control of the performers, depending on how different those experiences are, we may come to a point at which we say the experience is so different they cannot have understood it the same way. But the interesting thing is that this is *not* usually the case even though the auditors may have qualitatively quite different experiences of the performance.[11]

Third, even though performers of plays attempt to focus our attention only on those elements of their voice, appearance, line delivery, and action that are directly and solely concerned with getting the plot or getting the sense of the key characters, what we actually see in theatrical performances is still highly varied, and the control exercised by performers over what we see is fragile and tenuous. In attending to the performers one of us may find herself focused on the unusual hands of one of the performers and find herself tracking the events in the play as they are reflected in the movements and the stillnesses of those hands. At the same time another auditor may be attending only to exactly those features of the performers and the performance that the performers had anticipated the audience would track. Clearly, in the course of a performance there may be considerable slippage between what audience members register, both consciously and unconsciously, and their immediate and growing understandings of the play.

All this is the kind of thing that caused Nelson Goodman to assert the primacy of the literary text over the other features of performance. Goodman asserted that in the case of drama

> the work is a compliance-class of performances. The text of the play, however, is a composite of score and script. The dialogue is in a virtually notational system, with utterances as its compliants. This part of the text is a score, and performances compliant with it constitute the work. The stage directions, descriptions of scenery, etc, are scripts in a language that meets none of the semantic requirements for notationality; and a performance does not uniquely determine such a script or class of coextensive scripts. Given a performance, the dialogue can be univocally transcribed: different correct ways of writing it down will have exactly the same performances as compliants. But this is not true of the rest of the text.[12]

But this misses the point. Given the kind of slippage and variability I have been discussing, it is not to be expected that the dialogue of a play can be univocally transcribed from a performance. The most we can hope for is that auditors will come out with *substantially* the same story. Moreover these stories' inflections cannot be avoided. Nor should they be. Nor should we be concerned about it. It is simply enough to assert a common basic understanding that auditors come out with substantially the same story.

Fourth, theatrical conventions can be put forward explicitly to an audience by performers and either accepted or rejected on the spot as part of the immediate experience of the theatrical performance. At some point in time, I am not sure when, American and English theater companies began to perform Elizabethan and Jacobean plays in twentieth-century dress. Their audiences, upon first viewing such a thing, no doubt wondered what the point was to be. In some cases, I hope most, they were rewarded by being offered something in the rest of the performance choices that made sense of this new unconventional costume convention.[13] Whether in this fairly tame example or in those more radical that can be imagined or remembered, it is important to note that when a convention is sufficiently unfamiliar to the audience, its significance may not completely register with them even if they accept it in the context of a particular performance. And they may still understand the play in the basic sense I have been describing.

Finally, our orderly and coherent everyday sense of "what follows what" in human action is frequently exploited but also frequently subverted in plays, by both authors and performers. This is another way in which theatrical performance can be a temporal art form. Theatrical performance allows for playing with time: the time of events in the story may be altered and shifted around, the time of the performance may itself be referred to and played against, and the time it takes to do a single action can be stretched or made unnaturally quick.[14] But for all that, such subversions still allow us to get the drift of things pretty well sorted out. Indeed the effectiveness of such exploitation and subversion usually depends on our ability to do so.

Deeper Reasons for Revising the Account

Rehearsing the foregoing familiar facts may help us see the usefulness of some remarks of Ludwig Wittgenstein in which he draws connections between dreams and dream reports and our understanding of certain plays. In one of these passages, Wittgenstein draws our attention to a particular way that Shakespeare's plays might strike someone.[15]

Shakespeare and dreams. A dream is all wrong, absurd, composite, and yet at the same time it is completely right: put together in *this* strange way it makes an impression. Why? I don't know. And if Shakespeare is great, as he is said to be, then it must be possible to say of him: it's all wrong, things *aren't like that*—and yet at the same time it's quite right according to a law of its own. (*CV*, 83e)[16]

In another remark Wittgenstein speaks of *recounting* a dream as a "medley of recollections" that "often form a significant and enigmatic whole." Then he adds, "they form, as it were, a fragment that makes a *powerful* impression on us (*sometimes* anyway), so that we look for an explanation, for connections" (*CV*, 83e).

At the outset of another remark (*CV*, 68e–69e), Wittgenstein observes that a Freudian dream analysis "dismantles" a dream so that the "original sense" of the dream is "completely" lost. This process of analysis he likens to watching a play on stage "with a plot that's pretty incomprehensible at times, but at times too quite intelligible, or apparently so," and then having the plot "torn into little fragments and each of these given a completely new sense." Using a different figure, that of a picture folded up so that it forms a new one, Wittgenstein remarks that it is not difficult to imagine the dream "unfolded" in Freudian dream analysis striking someone as "the solution," the content of the dream "minus the gaps." Wittgenstein observes that "this would then be the solution precisely by virtue of [the dreamer's] acknowledging it as such" much in the way that, in cases where you are searching for a word, "your acceptance [of the word you use] certifies the word as having been found." Wittgenstein goes on to stress that "what is intriguing about a dream is not its *causal* connection with events in my life, etc., but rather the impression it gives of being a fragment of a story . . . the rest of which remains obscure." In fact, Wittgenstein thinks, in contrast to the original dream *story*, the dream *analysis* is somewhat disappointing. The dream story, he says, is "like a painting that attracts and inspires us. . . . The dream affects us as does an idea pregnant with possible developments." It is hard not to think that the connection suggested by these remarks, between the impression of the *dream* as a story "fragment" and the dream *story* as having an attraction that occurs because of the sense of possibilities not spelled out, could have some implications for the view of basic theatrical understanding presented in the previous section.[17]

These remarks of Wittgenstein's can be used to suggest some ways we might articulate the difficulties we have in deploying the account of concatenationism Levinson provides for musical understanding as a model for developing a concatenationist account of basic theatrical understanding.

The experience of trying to track the theatrical performance can be like the experience involved in following a dream, filled with gaps, while still seeming to be completely comprehensible. A sort of "double tracking" experience can happen in several ways. The familiar fact regarding slippage between what we experience in attending to the voices and bodies of the performers and our sense of tracking the story can make us aware we are, simultaneously, both tracking pretty well and missing things. The familiar fact that we are engaging some new convention or an unexpected use of a known convention can make us aware, simultaneously, of negotiating with the convention and of tracking the story in such a way we may feel we are getting the story but still missing or stumbling over something.

The initial attempts we make to say what we saw may start as little more than a medley of recollections that pick out what was significant and powerful in the experience. Because we attend to performers' voices and bodies, the features of the performers themselves may register with us more directly than does the story we are to get by attending to them. The stories we tell have gaps for another important reason. We cannot tell all that we have seen. Yet, for all this, the stories often seem complete as we tell them, even when we know material we saw is being left out.

In many cases we are driven on to further reflection on our experience in the theater precisely because what is left out, what we saw but have been unable so far to tell, seems to us as significant and powerful as what we can immediately recount. That significance and power motivates us to look for connections, for something like a metastory about how we came to tell the story of the play we have seen. The connections for which we are looking may not be present nor entirely within our grasp; and yet we may feel they must be there, just beyond our grasp.

Finally, the analysis we provide, upon reflection and when we try to explain what we saw, is often a construction we put on the story to give us the content of the play "minus the gaps," so to speak. But the analysis can seem, in contrast to the sense of the understanding we experienced in the theater, denatured and disappointing.

All this can be overstated. I am not proposing we liken the theatrical experience to dreaming in all respects. I am pointing out that certain precise features of dream experience and of the recounting and analysis of dreams are, or can be, similar to our experience of a theatrical performance when we understand it, that these similarities reflect themselves in at least some of the signs we have understood the performance, and that these similarities appear as well in the later reflection we engage in about at least some of the performances we have seen. And my main point is that these possibilities force us to modify Levinson's version of concatenationism in order to obtain from it a satisfying account of basic theatrical understanding.

Revising the View

The fundamental idea in the initial account I have given of basic theatrical understanding is that understanding a play as it happens is centrally a matter of apprehending individual bits of dialogue and stage action and the immediate progression from bit to bit. This idea is connected to, and is supported by, reflections on what kinds of behaviors can be taken as signs of basic theatrical understanding. None of those signs of basic understanding seems to require that basic understanding involves apprehension of large-scale structural features of plays. What is understood, *at least at the onset,* are just the bits, the events that make up the sequence that is the performance and the transitions between bits. This account can be economical in this way in part because it allows for the fact that uptake on some, perhaps many, bits will require memory of earlier bits.

Even in this initial and relatively unmodified form, the present account has required one important divergence from the model Levinson provides us. While it remains true that making sense of a play requires nothing more than focusing on the bits and the transitions and making assessments as to whether the bits themselves and the transitions are cogent, moment to moment, what is built up in the process of such focusing and assessing when we understand theatrical performances of plays is a story. There is nothing corresponding to this in Levinson's concatenationist account of musical understanding. So far, Levinson's account of musical understanding is adopted as a model for theatrical understanding with only this one, albeit fairly major, revision.

In addition, however, Levinson's version of concatenationism makes substantive claims about *(a)* how conventions of expectations guide basic musical understanding, *(b)* how richer understanding of a musical performance is related to a basic understanding of it, and *(c)* how cogency of bits and transitions is determined. And here we find that the transfer of the detailed model of concatenationism Levinson provides for musical under-standing to the case of understanding theatrical performances runs into stiff resistance. The resistance, as we have seen it develop, has come in the form of recognizing some familiar facts about theatrical performances and of subsequent reflection upon how those facts contribute to a sense that the experience of theatrical performances in some specific ways can be like that of dream experience.

We now have before us, I conclude, reason to doubt we can think that basic theatrical understanding is "guided for the most part by ideals or norms of [some theatrical equivalents of] continuation, progression, development, evolution, and directionality" (*MM*, 34). Where there are such norms for theater they do not guide or control understanding in the same way such norms function for basic musical understanding. This is shown in the fact that we can still understand a play even when we are not entirely certain we have grasped all the temporal locations of the events in the sequence that comprises the performance. We can, for example, find comprehensible the kind of production involving random ordering of scenes, such as that described at the outset of this essay, even though its time sequence, on all but one of the possible performance occasions, vio-lates standard expectations "of continuation, progression, development, evolution and directionality."[18]

For similar reasons, tests of cogency cannot be the same for basic the-atrical understanding as may be required for basic musical understanding. Cogency of musical sequence, in Levinson's account, is "each part . . . lead-ing convincingly to the next [and] each consequent appearing . . . to be the natural, even inevitable continuation of each antecedent." The first thing to notice here is that there are two elements in Levinson's analysis of cogency, the bit about each part *leading convincingly* to the next and the bit about each subsequent part *appearing to be the natural or inevitable contin-uation* of the preceding part. The view of basic theatrical understanding I have been sketching suggests there is far more room for apparent incoher-ence in a cogent bit or transition in theater than may be allowable in music. So, it would be useful to my view if these two elements could come apart.

That they can and should is shown by the following considerations. First, if a transition from sequence to sequence is "convincing" to some audience member of a theatrical performance, then (1) that audience member does not object in some way to the transition, (2) that audience member can tell the story of that region of the play without being blocked at that transition, and (3) that audience member, upon being queried, is able to trace at least some connections, possibly only thematic or imagistic, between the preceding and the succeeding sequences. The audience member may also feel something, *feel* convinced, and perhaps that is even typical; but I am not sure such a feeling must be present in order for the audience member to *be* convinced.[19] In contrast, if an audience member sees one sequence as the "natural or inevitable" consequence of its predecessor, she must be able to trace, upon inquiry, not just some connections, but particular kinds of connections between the sequences. She must be able to trace, or at least think she can trace, causal, reasoned, or rule-governed connections, the kind of connections that entail naturalness or inevitability.

Consider two productions of *Hamlet,* one in which the company sees itself as giving nothing more than a reasonably straightforward illustration of the text and the other in which the company seeks to stress the sense of alienation the character Hamlet experiences and, to some extent, brings upon himself. In the latter, as a device to underscore the thematic stress, the company performs "the closet scene" (act 3, scene 4) as follows: from the outset of the scene through the moment that Hamlet sees that he has slain Polonius there are six performers onstage; each of the three—Hamlet, Gertrude, Polonius—are doubled; the performers playing the characters are bathed in light at separate spots on the stage, saying their lines; the other three performers each stand or kneel near the performer whose character she or he is doubling and makes appropriate, perhaps "stylized," gestures of listening, waving a sword about, holding a mirror away in horror, stabbing, falling, dying, and so forth. The company's hope, perhaps, is that seeing each character as isolated from the others and separated physically from her or his own actions will help underscore with their audience the psychological isolation that is the thematic underpinning of this production. The example is imaginary (and incomplete), the conception of the play in the example may not be inspiring, but the example is plausible. That is enough. For, if an audience member were to be convinced by the transitions from sequence to sequence in such a performance, clearly this would not be because in all ways each event appears naturally or inevitably to follow from its preceding events in a series of such transitions.

I conclude that while cogency, on my view, will still require that each part lead convincingly to the next, it will not require the sense that each sequence of dialogue and action, each event, seem to be a *natural or inevitable consequent* of the sequence or sequences it follows. For, although

some of the room for the lack of inevitability in cogent transitions in theatrical performances arises because that condition for cogency may also
fail more generally as a cogency condition for narratives, as the illustration
shows, it may also be due to the role of our perception of other people in
the understanding of plays and of the ways our perceptions of others can
be played with for us by performers and, even when not played with, can
be quite crude and distracted while still allowing us to get the gist of things
sorted out. So I think this is not merely or only a feature of the fact that we
are talking about plays, theatrical performances in narrative traditions, but
is a feature of theatrical performance considered in its own right.

It may be worth adding, quite independently I believe, that while the
view of basic theatrical understanding does require an appropriate background, here again there is a significant difference. The appropriately
backgrounded audience member for a play need not always possess specialized knowledge of such things as "the nature of the piece he is auditing,
for example, its period, genre, and instrumentation" or their theatrical
equivalents (even when equivalents do exist). Instead, for the most part,
what is required is general knowledge of human beings and their conduct.
In any case, if there is specialized knowledge required in this context, it is
far more likely to be knowledge of *cultural and social* norms than knowledge of norms of theatrical convention or narrative form.

Objections and Replies

I have focused exclusively on what it is to understand a play while it is happening. In so doing, one might think, I have overplayed the importance of
the momentary in theater so far as to render an account of our appreciation of theatrical performance impossible. Appreciation of a performance
depends upon some level of understanding, of having a concept of what it
is that one is experiencing.[20] But the account of theatrical understanding I
have offered here may well seem too thin to support the idea one has a
concept of what one is experiencing and, hence, too meager a kind of
understanding to support much by way of appreciation. Put this another
way. I have argued that one need not have a grasp of large-scale structures
of a play in order to have understood the play as it was happening. But to
appreciate a play, one might argue, does require having an understanding
of how the play works. And surely that could—must?—require having a
grasp of some of its large-scale features.

I think this is an interesting line of thought, but I doubt it poses any more of a problem for the view I have been sketching than does the fact that, at present, we stand in need of a careful analysis of the relation between basic theatrical understanding and richer understandings. If there can be richer and basic understandings, as I believe we must agree there can be, then it is possible too to have richer and basic appreciation. In fact, is it not a commonplace that some people may have richer appreciation of some art, people, or situations than others do? And is this not more or less directly a result of their having richer understanding of the relevant matters? One line of reply to this objection then is just that what it points out as a weakness is in fact a strength of the view, namely that it requires different kinds of appreciation that are based upon different kinds of understanding, even if we have not yet worked out the full story of how the richer and more basic understandings of a play are related to each other.

A second and more interesting line of reply is this. The thought behind the objection here could be that any feature of a work that is not present to consciousness in an understanding of that work cannot be said to be part of what is appreciated by one who appreciates the work based on that understanding. If, for example, I am unaware of some convention *as a convention,* then if the presence of that convention is responsible for some aesthetic features that are present to be appreciated, I simply cannot appreciate that work, at least not for those features.

Again, this is pretty interesting, but I do not think it is decisive.[21] Consider the example of conventions in more detail. What makes conventions useful in artworks generally and theater in particular is that they are ways of giving a particular focus on certain content or of giving rise to reactions that support a particular way of apprehending some contents.[22] In many cases, audiences are completely unaware of the conventions that are so used. In some cases, where the conventions are aimed at inducing unconscious reactions in audiences and where success of the performance depends on audiences having those reactions, appreciation is undermined by audience awareness of the deployment of the conventions. A simple case will suffice. Audiences are generally unaware of naturalistic conventions of the movement and positioning of sets and actors that are aimed at inducing a passive acceptance of the stories performed. Indeed, were audiences to become aware of the fact, they would react quite differently and the plays would go unappreciated, or at least would not be appreciated as the authors and performers intend them to be.

This much of what is true of conventions is also true of other large-scale features of theatrical performances. While it may be the case that failure to apprehend the presence of some large-scale feature in a play as it is happening can limit what an auditor can appreciate in that play, this is not always a limitation that matters. In many cases, audiences are completely unaware of the large-scale features that are deployed. And in some cases at least, where the features are deployed so as to induce unconscious reactions in audiences and where success of the performance depends on audiences having those reactions, appreciation is actually undermined by audience awareness of the deployment of the large-scale features in question, whether they are appropriately analyzed in traditional literary critical terms or in terms of some postmodernist view about how to "read" the play in performance.

NOTES

1. This essay is one in a series I have been developing that explores what it would mean were theatrical performance to be regarded as an art form in its own right rather than as a species of merely illustrated literature. I will not belabor this point for the most part in what follows, but it should be clear that, working from the alternative perspective, most of what I write here would be pointless.

2. The example is not, in fact, imaginary. Robert Corrigan, in discussion, has described to me just such a production of *Woyzeck*.

3. This list is not intended to be exhaustive. There are other respects in which time plays a role in various art forms, including theatrical performance. The most recent systematic discussion of these, on which I have drawn heavily in this section of the chapter, is that of Jerrold Levinson and Philip Alperson, "What is a Temporal Art?" *Midwest Studies in Philosophy* 16 (1991): 439–50. The first five claims about theatrical performances in this essay reflect four of the time-related characteristics of arts that Levinson and Alperson discuss. See also comments on temporal features of some art forms in Stephen Davies, "Is Architecture Art?" in *Philosophy and Architecture*, ed. Michael H. Mitias (Amsterdam: Rodopi, 1994), 41–43.

4. The phrase is from Levinson and Alperson, "What is a Temporal Art?" 443.

5. To be sure, performers may choose to play some scenes out of sequence, repeating from earlier in the sequence or playing a scene that will be played again later, and this may allow an audience to be reminded of someone or to discover something in advance. But this is under the control of the performers and not the audience and, so, is not the same set of phenomena.

6. For reasons of space I will usually not distinguish between performances, which are dated particular events, and productions, which may take performances as instances. Little that I write hangs on that distinction. For the most part, however, it may be useful to take what I write here as being about performances qua instances of productions.

7. Jerrold Levinson, *Music in the Moment* (Ithaca: Cornell University Press, 1997). All further references to this work, abbreviated *MM*, will be given in the text.

8. Edmund Gurney, *The Power of Sound* (1880) (New York: Basic Books, 1966).

9. The suggestion is made by John Dillworth in commenting on an earlier version of this essay, presented at the Annual Meeting of the American Society for Aesthetics in Minneapolis, October 2001.

10. James R. Hamilton, "Theatrical Enactment," *Journal of Aesthetics and Art Criticism* 58, no. 1 (2000): 23–35.

11. Paul Ziff, *Antiaesthetics: An Appreciation of the Cow with the Subtile Nose* (Boston: D. Reidel, 1984), 87.

12. Nelson Goodman, *Languages of Art: An Approach to the Theory of Symbols* (Indianapolis: Bobbs-Merrill, 1968), 210–11.

13. Theater historians can probably also tell us when the practice of producing these plays in "period costume" first began. That too is a convention that has a history and a point. The appearance of twentieth-century costumes is only the offering of a new convention against the background of another.

14. Some of these possibilities for playing with time can be achieved more convincingly in film than in theater, but the theatrical performance is open to some of them at least. See Levinson and Alperson, "What is a Temporal Art?" 443–44.

15. Ludwig Wittgenstein, *Culture and Value*, ed. G. H. von Wright, trans. Peter Winch (Chicago: University of Chicago Press, 1980). All further references to this work will be in the form *CV*.

16. In another remark, clearly related, Wittgenstein writes, "It is *not* as though Shakespeare portrayed human types well and were in that respect *true to life*. He is *not* true to life. But he has such a supple hand and his *brush strokes* are so individual, that each of his characters looks *significant*, is worth looking at" (*CV*, 84e). Unfortunately, I do not have space to trace out the implications of this remark in this essay.

17. It is pretty well known that Wittgenstein opposed Freudian theory. In *CV* that opposition was applied to Freudian analysis of dreams. "It might be regarded as a basic law of natural history that wherever something in nature 'has a function,' 'serves a purpose,' the same thing can also be found in circumstances where it serves no purpose and is even 'dysfunctional.' If dreams sometimes protect sleep, you can count on their sometimes disturbing it; if dream hallucination sometimes serves a *plausible* purpose (of imaginary wish fulfillment) count on its doing the opposite as well. There is no 'dynamic theory of dreams'" (*CV*, 72e).

18. And I probably need not add for readers familiar with the play, *Woyzeck*, that even in Büchner's original sequence, the title character of the play exhibits none of the kind of development that would seem to be alluded to here.

19. Conditions (1) and (2), by reference to time frames that may follow the experience of the performance, invoke the fact that what may feel convincing at a given moment may come to be reevaluated. A transition that does not immediately feel convincing may, upon the later discovery of one's ability to tell the story without stumbling over the transition, come to be revealed as convincing after all. And, correlatively, a transition that feels convincing at the time may, upon later reflection, come to be revealed as false with respect to its convincingness.

20. I accept in rudimentary form at least this much of Roger Scruton's account of aesthetic experience in *Art and Imagination: A Study in the Philosophy of Mind* (London: Methuen, 1974), part II.

21. See Brian Baxter, "Conventions in Art," *British Journal of Aesthetics* 23, no. 4

(1983): 319–32; and Mark Debillis, "Conceptions of Musical Structure," *Midwest Studies in Philosophy* 16 (1991): 378–93 (especially 387). I am not persuaded by Debillis's psychological account on this point. I do think Baxter is convincing, but the little argument I offer here is independent of the line he takes on this issue.

22. See Carolyn Wilde, "On Style: Wittgenstein's Writing and the Art of Painting," in *Wittgenstein and Aesthetics,* ed. Kjell S. Johannessen, Skriftserien no. 14: Proceedings of the Skjolden Symposium (Bergen: Department of Philosophy, University of Bergen, 1997), 136–60.

TWELVE

Perception, Action, and Identification in the Theater

Bence Nanay

My endeavor in this chapter is to examine the ways in which the general structure of perception is modified in the case of the reception of theater performances. First, perception in general is examined. I will then argue that a basic characteristic of perception is that it is sometimes interdependent with action. Next I turn to the special case of the perception of a theatrical performance—what I call *theater perception*—examining the role of perception for the possibility of action in the case of watching a performance. I contend that theater perception cannot be sufficiently analyzed without taking into consideration the action-oriented character of perception per se. For instance, if we perceive a gun on stage, we perceive it as the possibility of an action affording certain everyday actions. There is a significant difference, however, between the way action characterizes our perception in the theater and in everyday life. While in the everyday case we perceive objects as affording actions *for us,* in the case of theater perception we observe objects as affording certain actions *for another agent* (that is, for one of the characters on stage). This difference, which will be crucial for understanding the classic question of "identification" and character engagement, is analyzed in the last section of the essay.

Detached Perception

Before analyzing theater perception, some remarks are needed about perception in general. Theater perception can be examined only in comparison with the general characteristics of perception outside the theater; in this analysis I emphasize the connection between perception and action. According to the "classical" view, perception is independent from action; action has no constitutive influence on perception.[1] According to this picture, perception leads to beliefs; these in turn may or may not result in actions.[2] The connection between perception and action is unidirectional: what action an agent is inclined to perform (at time t) does not have any substantial, constitutive influence on her perceptual experience (at time t).

The advocates of the classical view would, of course, agree that the action I perform at t_1 does influence my perceptual experience at t_2 if t_2 follows t_1. For example, the action of turning my head at t_1 does influence my perceptual experience in the next moment. What the advocates of the classical view deny is that there is any constitutive influence of the action one is inclined to perform at t_1 on one's perceptual experience *at the same time*. The classical view of perception has been criticized considerably; it has been argued that the connection between perception and action is not unidirectional. What action an agent is inclined to perform (at time t) does have substantial, constitutive influence on her perceptual experience (at time t).[3] This last sentence, however, can mean many things. I will argue in this section that one's perceptual experience sometimes (but not always) depends counterfactually on the action one is inclined to perform. Perceptual experiences of this kind I will call *action-oriented perceptual experiences*. If a perceptual experience is not action oriented, that is, if it does not depend counterfactually on the action one is inclined to perform, then I call it *detached perceptual experience*. My claim is that some (or, arguably, most) of our perceptual experiences are action oriented. In the next section, I provide a short outline of an account of perception that takes into consideration the rich connection between perception and action. Then I turn to the relation between perception and action in the case of theater perception.

It ought to be emphasized that sometimes we do perceive the world in a detached way. Sometimes perception and action are indeed independent from each other. It would be a mistake, though, to infer from this that they are always independent, that is, that perception is always detached. Still, I do not want to claim that the theory of detached perception has to be discarded and completely replaced by another theory that takes into consideration the mutual interdependence between perception and action. My claim is that perception is not always detached; therefore, no general account of perception can be given based solely on the model of detached perception. Nevertheless, perception is detached *sometimes;* therefore, no general account of perception can be provided ignoring detached perception. I therefore favor a "pluralist theory" that allows for both detached and action-oriented perception.

Action-Oriented Perception

I define action-oriented perception as seeing the possibility of action in the stimulus: the agent perceives the stimulus as affording a certain action. It is important to emphasize that seeing the possibility of an action does not necessarily mean that the agent (the subject) acts—this would be true only for reflexes. More frequently, the agent only perceives the possibility of action; the action itself is not performed. The agent might recognize different potential actions in the same object under different circumstances. I attach different possibilities of action to a newspaper, for example, when there is a fly in my room that I want to get rid of and when I want to know the election results.[4] As we have seen, in the case of humans, the action involved in the definition of action-oriented perception is not necessarily an action that is in fact performed. Furthermore, it is not necessarily motor action, either. For example, when I solve a mathematical problem, I may recognize the abstract action of addition in the plus sign.

Action-oriented perception connects perception and action directly, without the mediation of abstract categories and inferences based on these categories. This analysis, however, does not imply a behaviorist account of perception and action, whereby perception causes action, because again, in the case of action-oriented perception, an agent may see the possibility of an action even if she does not perform that action.

When I say that I see the possibility of an action in a stimulus, it is not the case that I first categorize the stimulus and then from the fact that the things in this category can lead to a certain action infer that I can (or could) perform the action. If I see the possibility of eating in the stimulus of an apple, this does not mean that I first subsume this stimulus under the category of apple, and then, since apple is edible, infer that this stimulus affords the action of eating. The abstract category of apple is not needed at all for recognizing the possibility of eating in the stimulus of an apple. When one is very hungry, one sees the world as containing two kinds of entities: those that afford the possibility of eating and those that do not. Whether these entities are apples, books, or laptops does not matter; these distinctions play a role only on a far higher level of cognitive processes.

In action-oriented perception the possible action the agent might perform organizes what she sees: she distinguishes those features of the visual field that are relevant for the successful completion of the action she is inclined to perform. The other features are irrelevant. In other words, the connection between perception and action is not unidirectional: perception may lead to action, but the readiness to perform a certain action also influences what and how we perceive the world.

Action-oriented perception is more basic from an evolutionary and developmental point of view. Some animals and young children probably have only action-oriented perceptual abilities, and detached perception appears at a relatively late stage of both evolution and child development.[5] More importantly, the appearance of detached perception does not make action-oriented perception obsolete. We still use these early and simple ways of perceiving the world; furthermore, we arguably use them far more frequently than our detached perceptual capacities. When I am running on the street to catch my bus, it is very unlikely that I perceive the lamppost in my way in a detached way. I do not recognize it as a lamppost first, and then perhaps make inferences whether it influences my momentary purpose of catching the bus. If I decide that it does, I might act on this information: I might try to avoid bumping into it.

We perceive the world primarily in an action-oriented way. When I am running to catch the bus, I see the street as containing several entities, among them those I might bump into (people, phone boxes, lampposts, cars, trees, etc.) and those I might not bump into, allowing me to run toward the bus stop. When I sense the stimulus of the lamppost in my way, I directly recognize the possibility of the action it affords (or hinders) without contemplating what concept may apply to it. I see it as an obstacle and threat to my action, as something I may bump into. I do not classify it as a lamppost, and then infer that I may bump into it. This, however, does not mean that on another occasion I cannot see the lamppost in a detached way, when, for example, I sit on a bench in front of it without any particular need to perform any action.

These two notions of perception—object in the way of my action, and object in itself—are not exclusive. It is not the case that we have either action-oriented perception or detached perception. We are capable of both; we may see the world as affording a certain action, but we may see the world in a detached way, without seeing the possibility of any action associated with it. The question, however, is how these two perceptual capacities are related in the case of theater perception.

Perception in the Theater

I now turn to the specific case of theater perception and examine what is the role of the perception of the possibility of action in seeing a performance. I demonstrate that theater perception cannot be sufficiently analyzed without taking into consideration the action-oriented character of perception.

The prima facie intuition might be that theater perception is detached, since there is no action we are inclined to perform while sitting in the theater. In normal cases we are not disposed to perform any action during the performance. This is what is so unique about the reception of theater performances: no matter what happens on stage, we do not move. It would be a mistake, though, to infer from this that theater perception must be detached. If we perceive a gun on stage we do in fact perceive it as affording certain actions.

There is a significant difference, however, between how action characterizes our perception in the theater and in everyday perception. While in everyday perception we perceive object as affording actions *for us,* in the case of theater perception we perceive the object as affording certain actions *for another agent* (that is, for one of the characters on stage). For example, a scene from *Hamlet:* when in the last act the queen picks up a cup and toasts with it, we (the audience) know that the cup contains poisoned wine, which is meant for Hamlet, but Gertrude does not know that it is poisoned. The question is what the person watching this scene in the theater perceives. Is the cup affording any action for us? Are we worrying for our life? Or, alternatively, do we perceive this sequence in a detached way, not recognizing any action the cup might afford for the characters? I think neither of these is the case. We do see what action the cup affords, namely killing someone. However, we do not see the danger affording this action for us, but rather for the fictive character on stage, Gertrude. An even clearer and simpler example is provided by one of the all-time popular puppet show scenes, wherein we see a puppet who does not notice another puppet approaching with a weapon of sorts (a frying pan) from behind. The children in the audience react to this situation vigorously: they shout at the first puppet trying to warn him of the danger.

Thus, we see the space of the performance as affording a certain action for one of the characters on stage. What affords the action, however, is very often neither a gun nor a poisoned goblet nor a frying pan. More frequently, what we see is not a motor action afforded by an object, but a more sophisticated, sometimes verbal action afforded by a person. For example, in Bertolt Brecht's *Three Penny Opera,* Mack the Knife is in prison and does not see any means of escaping prior to the entrance of Lucy, the daughter of the police captain. What the audience recognizes is that Lucy symbolizes hope for Mack provided he convinces her that it would be a good idea for her to set him free, despite the fact that earlier he rejected her several times. Again, as I sit in the audience watching this performance, there is no action I would be inclined to perform in connection with Lucy. Nor do I see Lucy in a detached way, ignoring how her advent might influence Mack's future. If I am engaged with Mack the Knife, then my perceptual experience depends counterfactually on the very complex action Mack is inclined to perform with Lucy; I see her as a potential facilitator of Mack's action of escaping. In other words, I see Lucy as affording a very complex action, though not for me: for Mack.

These examples suggest that theater perception resides in an interstitial stage between detached and action-oriented perception. It is more detached than action-oriented perception, since it is not our life that is at stake, but only the life of a fictive character on stage. However, it is more action-oriented than detached perception, since we do see the space of the performance as containing actions, though not for us but for someone else. This is the core idea of theater perception, which I will spell out with the help of the notion of identification and character engagement in the next section.

Identification

The phenomenon just described is closely related to one of the oldest philosophical questions about the reception of theater performances, namely, that of identification.[6] Murray Smith summarizes this phenomenon as follows:

> [T]he illusion [is] that I (the spectator) am a character in the story world, faced with the dilemmas and experiences of [one of the characters]; or, more cautiously, that I am brought to imagine "from the inside" the character's experience. In more common parlance, I may be said to emphasize with the character.[7]

As this quotation shows, identification is usually interpreted as "imagining from the inside." The standard view of identification with a character in the theater (or in a painting or film) is that this process is a version of "imagining from the inside." Kendall Walton expresses this very idea: "Of course we identify with . . .fictional characters. My not very surprising suggestion is that this . . . involves imagining oneself in the shoes of the person identified with."[8] Gregory Currie coins the term *secondary imagining* (to be contrasted with primary imagining, which constructs the fictional world of a work of art) to refer to this phenomenon:

> It is when we are able, in imagination, to feel as the character feels that fictions of character take hold of us. This process of empathetic reenactment of the character's situation is what I call secondary imagining. As a result of putting myself, in imagination, in the character's position, I come to have imaginary versions of the thoughts, feelings and attitudes I would have in that situation.[9]

Prior to Walton and Currie, Richard Wollheim made use of the idea of imagining from the inside to describe the process of identification. Wollheim makes the explicit claim that "the person centrally imagined—if there is such a person—is imagined *from the inside.*"[10] What he means by central imagining is the following:

> When I visually imagine, or visualize, an event, there are two modes of doing so. I can imagine the event from no one's standpoint: it unfolds frieze-like, across a divide. Or I can imagine it from the standpoint of one of the participants in the event, whom I then imagine from the inside. This latter mode I call *centrally imagining.*[11]

Following Wollheim, I will use the terms *central imagining* and *imagining from the inside* interchangeably. But what does imagining from the inside or central imagining mean? At first approximation, imagining from the inside is to imagine having the experiences of another person. Kendall Walton analyzes the concept of imagining from the inside at length in book *Mimesis as Make-Believe.*

> Imagining from the inside is . . . a form of self-imagining characteristically described as imagining *doing* or *experiencing* something (or *being* a certain way), as opposed to imagining merely *that* one does or experiences something or possess a certain property.[12]

In other words, when I imagine A from the inside, then I imagine having the (perceptual) experience of A. Gregory Currie also expresses a similar idea: in the case of secondary imagining, "what we are primarily to imagine is the experience of a character."[13] Imagining from the inside (or, central imagining, or secondary imagination) means that one imagines having the experiences of another agent. In other words, in such cases, I imagine having the same, or similar, experiences the other person is having. This aspect of the imagining from the inside is quite problematic. First, it is not clear to what extent these experiences are supposed to be similar. Second, some clear cases of identification (or character engagement) do not follow this scheme. Some clarification or modification of imagining from the inside is needed.

My suggestion is that central imagining (and therefore, identification) should be conceived along the lines of the account of theater perception I outlined in the last section. In contrast, "acentral" imagining would correspond to detached perception, whereby we do not see the possibility of any action in the stimulus. We imagine a situation centrally, however, if we see (or imagine) the situation as affording a certain action for someone on stage.

Acentral imagining means that the spectator does not identify with any of the characters in the play. This is equivalent to saying that the spectator does not observe anything (or anyone) on stage as affording actions for one of the characters. Arguably, seeing the space of the performance as not affording actions for any of the characters in a performance is very rare when there is someone (not even necessarily a human being, as the puppet show example shows) on stage. This, however, does not mean that acentral imagining (which would be the equivalent of detached perception) is not possible in the theater. Furthermore, some performances include a lot of scenes where nothing we see concerns any action for anyone. Slow, stylized scenes of the theater performances exemplified by the works of Robert Wilson provide clear examples of this audience state.

Directors such as Wilson can, in fact be characterized very well based on how they apply and try to trigger central and acentral imagining. Puppet shows and slapstick scenes also provide the most obvious cases of central imagining whereby the scene affords simple easily recognizable motor actions. The Polish director Jerzy Grotowski and the British director Peter Brook are the two principal examples of very complex and subtle application of central imagining. In contrast, the theaters of Tadeusz Kantor, Ingmar Bergman, and Wilson present the audience with situations and characters where it is difficult to see anything or anyone on stage as a possible object of an action. What I wish to suggest is that the difference between central and acentral imagining does not mean quality difference of any kind: acentral imagining is no less specific to theater than central imagining. What makes the reception of theater performances interesting is precisely the interplay between these two modes of audience reception toward what is happening on stage.

We have observed that everyday perception is a diverse phenomenon: sometimes it is detached, while at other times it is action-oriented. In order to account for perception in general both of these forms of perception have to be taken into consideration. Theater perception is equally diverse: sometimes we imagine the situation centrally (that is, sometimes we identify with one of the characters), but sometimes we do otherwise. Therefore, a general account of theater perception has to absorb both central and acentral imagining. Nevertheless, it happens to be the case that in everyday perception and in the theater most of what we see is connected to the possibilities of action, suggesting that detached perception (or acentral imagining) is far less frequent.

Conclusion

Theater perception cannot be analyzed without taking into consideration its connection between perception and action. The most significant difference in comparison with everyday perception is not that theater perception is detached from action, but that my perception is connected to someone else's action. I see the objects (and sometimes the other characters as well) on stage as affording actions for someone else. This outline or sketch of theater perception does not aim to provide a general, all-encompassing theory for describing every aspect of the audience's experience in the theater. The crucial question, for example, as to which character we are identifying with has been avoided. Instead, the focus here has been the space of the performance as affording certain actions to one of the characters. But an important question remains: who or what decides who this character (this focal point) will be? In the Brecht scene with Mack and Lucy previously described, do I see the situation as affording a certain action for Mack, or for Lucy? Is it possible that I identify with one character at the beginning of a scene, and with another at the end? What exactly triggers identification with a character? In order to settle these questions, another and likely higher-order cognitive processes have to be taken to consideration. What I have endeavored to do in this essay is avoid a totalizing theory, but in a tantalizing way analyze the basic characteristics of theater perception, providing the groundwork and explicating the possibilities for further examinations of audiences' experiences in the theater.

NOTES

I presented earlier versions of this essay at the Annual Meeting of the American Society for Aesthetics, San Francisco, October 1–4, 2003, the Annual Conference of the British Society of Aesthetics, Oxford, September 12–14, 2003, the American Society for Aesthetics, Pacific Division Meeting. Asilomar, California, April 2–4, 2003, and the American Philosophical Association, Eastern Division Meeting, Atlanta, December 27–30, 2001. I am grateful for my commentators (Amy Coplan, Anna Christina Ribeiro, Julie van Camp) and the comments of Jerrold Levinson on several earlier versions. I am especially grateful for the comments, help, and encouragement of Richard Wollheim in the entire project.

1. A good historical summary of how theories of perception traditionally ignored action and how theories of action ignored perception can be found in Bernhard Hommel, Jochen Müsseler, Gisa Aschersleben, and Wolfgang Prinz, "The Theory of Event Coding: A Framework for Perception and Action Planning," *Behavioral and Brain Sciences* 24 (2001): 849–931.

2. Susan Hurley, one of the most devoted critics of this classical view, describes it as the "input-output model," which is implicitly present in most theories of perception and action (*Consciousness in Action* [Cambridge: Harvard University Press, 1998], 1–2, 6–7, 288–89). The input-output model identifies perception with the input from world to mind and similarly, describes action as the output from mind to world.

3. Just a few references: Gareth Evans, *The Varieties of Reference* (Oxford: Oxford University Press, 1982), 143–204; and John Campbell, *Past, Space, and Self* (Cambridge: MIT Press, 1994), 5ff., 13–16. See also John Campbell, "The Role of Physical Objects in Spatial Thinking," in *Spatial Representation*, ed. Naomi Eilan, Rosaleed McCarthy, and Bill Brewer (Oxford: Oxford University Press, 1993), 65–95; Christopher Peacocke, *A Study of Concepts* (Cambridge: MIT Press, 1992), chap. 1; Christopher Peacocke, "Scenarios, Concepts, and Perception," in *The Contents of Experience*, ed. Tim Crane (Cambridge: Cambridge University Press, 1992), 105–35, 106–9, 128–31; Hurley, *Consciousness in Action*, 1–2, 6–7, 288–89. A few examples from similar approaches in cognitive science: Gerald M. Edelman, *Neural Darwinism: The Theory of Neuronal Group Selection* (New York: Basic Books, 1987), and especially James J. Gibson, *An Ecological Approach to Visual Perception* (Boston: Houghton Mifflin, 1979). On Gibson see Jerry A. Fodor and Zenon Pylyshyn, "How Direct is Visual Perception? Some Reflections on Gibson's 'Ecological Approach,'" *Cognition* 9 (1981): 139–96; Shimon Ullman, *Against Direct Perception* (New York: Macmillan, 1980).

4. This example was given by David Marr in *Vision* (San Francisco: W. H. Freeman, 1982).

5. This view would be consistent with the recent theories of child development

and primatology. See, for example, Anette Karmiloff-Smith, *Beyond Modularity: A Developmental Perspective on Cognitive Science* (Cambridge: MIT Press, 1992).

6. Recently, this question is sometimes replaced with the following one: what are the mental processes that make it possible for me to *engage with* Hamlet? The notion of identification was repeatedly criticized by Noël Carroll in *The Philosophy of Horror, or; Paradoxes of the Heart* (New York: Routledge, 1990), 88–96, and in *Beyond Aesthetics* (Cambridge University Press, 2001), 306–16. Carroll's main objection is that this notion has the connotation that the spectator is somehow in identical (or at least similar) emotional states as the character she is identifying with. Thus, identification implies that there is symmetry between the experiences of the spectator and those of the fictional character. But as Carroll points out, in fact there is asymmetry: for example, if I identify with a fictional character who feels pain, I do not feel pain; I feel pity. Carroll also points out that the notion of identification is very ill defined; it is used in half a dozen different senses. Sometimes we say that we identify with a fictional character when we are just like her, or when we empathize with her, or when we sympathize with her. It is not clear which of these notions identification encompasses. For simplicity, I will use the notion of identification in this section, but everything I say here could be rephrased in terms of character engagement.

7. Murray Smith, "Imagining from the Inside," in *Film Theory and Philosophy*, ed. Richard Allen and Murray Smith (Oxford: Oxford University Press, 1997), 412.

8. Kendall Walton, *Mimesis and Make-Believe: On the Foundations of the Representational Arts* (Cambridge: Harvard University Press, 1990), 255.

9. Gregory Currie, *Image and Mind: Film, Philosophy, and Cognitive Science* (Cambridge: Cambridge University Press, 1995), 153.

10. Richard Wollheim, "Identification and Imagination," in *Freud: A Collection of Critical Essays,* ed. Richard Wollheim (New York: Anchor Press, 1974), 187. Wollheim used the term *imagining from the inside* years before Walton wrote about the topic. He warns against possible misinterpretations of equating central imagining and imagining from the inside right after having made this claim: "I could not trust that phrase [*imagining from the inside*] so abused in philosophy" (87).

11. Richard Wollheim, *Painting as an Art* (Princeton: Princeton University Press, 1987), 103.

12. Walton, *Mimesis and Make-Believe,* 29.

13. Currie, *Image and Mind,* 153. It has to be noted that according to Currie, the fact that "what we are primarily to imagine is the experience of a character" is not sufficient for identification. He writes: "Further, identification, if it is a notion with any content at all, would seem to require the one who identifies to have, or to imagine having, some concern with or sympathy for the values and projects of the one with whom she identifies" (175).

~

THIRTEEN

Empathy and Theater

David Krasner

Le coeur a ses raisons que la raison ne connaît pas.
—Pascal

A good empathy does not prevent understanding.
—Augusto Boal

In this essay I examine "empathy" insofar as it is a possible audience response in live theater. In particular I attend to empathy not merely as an emotional response but as something possessing cognitive function as well. My main concern will be with the idea of a theatrical experience that evokes empathy, that makes use of empathetic responses as part of the mechanism of artistic comprehension, and that emphasizes emotional responses as a unique, as well as a rational, activity. The subject of emotion in fiction and art has been the central focus in several recent studies, but less has been said about emotion in the theater.[1] Even less has been said about empathy in the theater. Notwithstanding Bertolt Brecht's critique of empathy, a philosophical analysis of empathy in theater has not yet been undertaken. I will attempt some preliminary explorations of the subject in hopes of eliciting further discussion.

Because of the multiple meanings and connotations that shroud the term *empathy*, it is important to set forth precisely the kind of empathetic experiences that concern us here. I will avoid analyzing acting and focus solely on audience responses. Acting theories that stress an actor's empathetic relationship to a role are important, having to do with Stanislavskian techniques and their derivatives. However, the empathy examined here concerns audiences independent of acting or acting training, which I make no effort to evaluate. More importantly, I examine empathy not as a timeless term, but rather as a contemporary concept relevant to the way in which theater operates. While I will provide a brief review of the history of empathy, my aim is to examine its current efficacy and define its present parameters. Given the fragmentary nature of the early-twentieth-first-century world, with varying ethnic groups and other diversities represented onstage, it is increasingly important that the concept of empathy be understood. Its significance is in the notion of how audiences respond to plays and stories that are alien to their own experience.

Empathy, I contend, *allows us to transcend the limits of our own world.* Although my feelings exist in a different temporal and spatial consciousness than that of the actor, empathy nonetheless inspires my imagination, intuition, and observation in an act of comprehending another world. A spectator might watch a play about people whose lifestyles are different, but through a process of empathetic imagination the spectator is brought into contact with what for her is a vastly different living circumstance. This is empathy's potential: it allows us to cross the boundaries between us, boundaries that are especially evident in this moment of world history. In *Literary Theory and the Claims of History,* Satya P. Mohanty asks a salient question: "How do we negotiate between my history and yours?" Without empathy the task is most likely insurmountable; we are left with a mere disembodied abstraction lacking immediacy to our lives. If I do not reach out, Mohanty says, "I cannot—and consequently need not—think about how your space impinges on mine or how my history is defined together with yours."[2] We remain isolated in our individual spaces. Empathy might serve as a bridge connecting alternative social spaces.[3] Even though we are unfamiliar with particular backgrounds, cultures, and ideas as they unfold onstage, empathy aids our understanding. One can identify with someone else's preferences and, as Brecht might have it, still maintain that the other is misguided or even foolish. Empathy entails, in addition to identification, grasping the values inherent in the other's experience without blindly endorsing that experience or action.[4]

Empathy enlists possibilities rather than certainties. Audiences may experience empathy in multifaceted ways, and each may be associated with varying levels and degrees of interest.[5] There is no uniformity in audience responses, nor is this to be expected. Quite the contrary, theatrical experiences benefit from mixed responses. This chapter considers empathy's multiple functions as a way of understanding theater that is outside solipsistic experience.

Toward a Definition of Empathy in the Theater

For our purpose, the term *theater* will be understood as an experience between performer and audience. Theater takes the form of performance, where an actor embodies a role (fictional or autobiographical) and conveys a story or action through gesture and voice. The actor may portray a particularly attention-grabbing and dynamic human being, who is neither simply the actor nor the character as such, but rather, as Michael Goldman observes, the "actor-as-character, to whom we relate to in a special way." The "extraordinary personage" called the "actor-as-character," Goldman says, "will be more interesting than people usually are in ordinary life" and will be different, too, in that the actor-as-character will "*command* our interest more; he will be more definitely projected."[6] Audiences agree beforehand to accept the actor-as-character within the unfolding fiction or ritual.

For empathy to occur in theater, three things must generally happen: first, the audience must be made aware of whom, or where, attention must be placed (even if the attention is multiple and spread among characters or people); second, some substantial understanding of the action or character must take place (even if abstractions occur); and third, the audience must have a grasp of the narrative (even if the narrative is disjointed, fragmented, and illogical).[7] Philosophically, the occurrence of "empathy" is rooted in the question of other minds: namely, how are we to know what someone else thinks or feels.[8] The *Oxford English Dictionary* (1989) defines it as "the power of projecting one's personality into (and so fully comprehending) the object of contemplation." However, one of the difficulties in defining the term *empathy* (in the theater or otherwise) is its ambiguity: it may mean an "affective reaction," whereby the observer shares a similar (though not entirely the same) feeling with the object of contemplation; or, it may mean a "cognitive reaction," whereby the observer comprehends the object in order to enhance understanding.[9] The first implies fellow feelings, while the second suggests a way of knowing without necessarily shared feelings. In the theater empathy is to be understood as an audience experience in response to an action, emotion, feeling, or circumstance occurring onstage. It is typically characterized by an increased excitation, associated with some connection to another (character, actor, circumstance, or all three). It is an affective response to a narrative, actor, or character, reflecting involvement, identification, understanding, or complicity of feelings.

Empathy in the theater, I contend, builds outwardly rather than drawing a line somewhere and excluding those outside the boundary of oneself. This view of empathy was not always the operative case (as we will observe shortly). Furthermore, it is important to repeat that audience responses vary, and not everyone will experience empathy in the same way (if they experience it at all). Still, commonly understood, empathy in the theater arises when the audience enters into the action of the play imaginatively, inspired either by the narrative, actor, or character. It therefore is, as a matter of course, more embracing of others. One of the powers of theater is its ability to heighten awareness of how life is experienced by others.[10] While books, poems, films, art, and architecture may reach across the boundaries of individual minds, the theater has the immediate power of a living being engaged in behavior, action, and expression before an observing audience.[11]

Empathy in the theater is achieved by spectators through intuition, imagination, and memory, whereby audiences associate certain feelings or observations with personal experiences. However, empathy is not, I would suggest, a merging with another (though some have described it as such), because an empathetic response assumes the distinction of self and other. It allows one to admit the existence of another being, or consciousness, within one's cognitive purview, without losing oneself in another. The effect and degree of empathy varies according to individual predilection and personal interaction. Still, my analysis of empathy is fundamentally based on a need for exercising the capacity for human communication, fruitful cooperation, and reciprocal interchange of values and ideas. Defining the term categorically, we can say that audiences empathize in the theater in at least four ways: identification, compassion, sympathy, and understanding. These functions, or subsets, operate at several levels, and may occur independently or overlap. These four categories are interchangeable and fluid, and are presented in no particular hierarchal order:

1. *Identification* implies believing that I could find myself in a similar situation as the actor-as-character. I need not agree with the actions or behavior of the actor, but given the circumstances I imagine that I do. Kendall L. Walton describes identification as allowing "the appreciator a kind of empathy with the characters, an ability to look at things more purely from their point of view, from a perspective relatively uncontaminated by his own personal concerns."[12] Carl Plantinga favors the expression "character

engagement" as opposed to "character identification," because engagement "allows for empathy and antipathy, sympathy and indifference, and certainly implies no melding of minds or identities" between viewers and actors.[13] His preference makes sense only if one thinks of identification as a *totally emulating experience;* identification, however, may enhance a connection without emulation or complete loss of self.

2. *Compassion* implies that I feel in some way that the character has been unfairly treated. Furthermore, I feel a sense of justice is necessary to correct the situation. By justice I mean fairness and moral circumspection. Compassion is therefore bound up with justice and judgments of value.[14]

3. *Sympathy* implies that I feel that the pain of a character, which elicits a feeling or desire to help, assist, or aid him or her. This differs from compassion in that I might be unconcerned with justice or fair play. My feelings are in line with the actor's, and his or her plight is what moves me.

4. *Understanding* implies comprehension of the actor's feelings or the character's situation. I might feel something for (or against) the actor and character, but I retain my critical judgment. I may, in fact, completely disagree with the actions taken by the actor. Consider, for example, the chess player: A good chess player must anticipate the moves of her opponent; the further ahead she can anticipate possible moves, the better she is. A good chess player therefore needs to empathize with her opponent in order to win. Empathy here is a mental act of putting oneself in the adversary's shoes, not in order to wear them as her own (as might be the case with sympathy) but in order to have some understanding of them (though not necessarily approving). The chess player projects her thoughts into the other's point of view for the purposes of conquest.

Brechtian Distancing

The contrast between disaffected audience and empathetic participation forms the basis of Brecht's rejection of empathy. According to Brecht, empathy is a superficial emotional response. For him, emotions in the theater, although not entirely undesirable, have minimal utility in affecting social change. He makes clear his objection in *The Messingkauf Dialogues:*

"Neither the public nor the actor must be stopped from taking part emotionally"; however, "Only one out of many possible sources of emotion needs to be left unused, or at least treated as a subsidiary source—empathy."[15] Empathy for Brecht is the least desirable emotion because it obfuscates logical analysis and cool-headed observation, pollutes reason, arises from parochial interests, and clouds judgments required to assess social conditions objectively.

Brecht's view of emotion and empathy varied. It would be unfair to describe him as entirely opposing empathy. In a *Journal* entry of 1941, he writes that empathy can be used in rehearsal *(Probe)* that might provide "the *arrangement* of the role" *(das Einrichten der Rolle)*. In another entry, he states that in reality the actor's "inexact copy" of life "can be swallowed when two differing methods are applied: the empathetic technique *(Einfühlungstechnik)* and the estrangement technique *(Verfremdungstechnik)*."[16] Toward the end of his life he even had some use for empathy in the theater.[17] But generally he distrusted it. Brecht viewed empathy as manipulative; the theatrical narrative, unchecked and uninterrupted, creates a stream of consciousness that can undermine reason and clear insight. The business of theater requires keeping passions under control lest spectators be led astray; the narrative therefore has to be interrupted in order to minimize the emotional flow. His theories are undeniably important: they foster cool, unemotional spectatorial distancing, providing breathing room for the kind of reflection essential to critical evaluation. However, at times he carried his rejection of empathy to extremes.[18]

Brechtian theory is important but misguided on two accounts: it credits audiences with little if any understanding of theatrical illusion, and it dogmatically assumes that empathy is an obstacle to critical judgment. First, however much we may empathize with the play, role, character, or actor, many spectators are not so naive as to assume that the events onstage are "real." Audiences are by and large not as simple-minded as Brecht supposes. The events onstage may have concomitant relations to reality, but we are not so easily duped. We accept the artifice and choose whether or not (and to what degree) we accept the events unfolding onstage as correlative to the real world.

Second, empathy, according to Brecht, substitutes miasma for judgment. He accepts an unambiguous divide separating emotion and reason, favoring reason as an implementation for social change. Emotions, especially empathy, "wear down the capacity for action,"[19] and sap the spectator's desire to pursue political action. Figures portrayed onstage ought not to be "matter for empathy," but rather "they are there to be understood." Feelings "are private and limited," he says, while "reason is fairly comprehensive and to be relied on."[20] Brecht emphasized didactic rather than emotive theater, noting that "the greater grip on the audience's nerves, the less chance there was of its learning. The more we induce the audience to identify its own experiences and feelings with the production, the less it [the audience] learned."[21] His dualism assumes that involvement and empathy on the one hand, and judgment and reason on the other, are separately operating mental procedures. According to Brecht, once empathy takes hold, reason takes leave. His strongest objection to empathy is its alleged capacity to cast a spell over an audience, a trancelike state that he termed "gapping" *(Glotzen)*. Actors, he said, "go into a trance and take the audience with them." He regarded this trance as contrary to didacticism; if the trance condition is successful, "nobody will [learn] any lessons."[22]

Yet Brecht's assumptions are unverifiable; he makes the unsubstantiated claim that when spectators empathize, they cease to think. Paul Woodruff is taken by Brecht's rejection of empathy because its use of identification occludes the spectator's critical freedom to judge. Woodruff correctly points out, however, that it is "not clear that identification inhibits this freedom."[23] For Brecht and the poststructuralists, narrative and its attendant empathetic emotions exert a power over the spectators, blinding their ability to question the narrative's direction and think through its intention. The incipient spectator, devoid of autonomy, functions properly as a critical spectator only if actors reveal the narrative to them as ideological manipulation. However, if we consider empathy *and* Brecht's demands for objective reason as functioning simultaneously, then the ability to identify with, and simultaneously distance from, the object of contemplation may provide a more forceful response. In fact, it may add to Brecht's "call to action" theater.

Some critics suggest that Brecht's position on empathy was not entirely dismissive. Angela Curran's essay "Brecht's Criticisms of Aristotle's Aesthetics of Tragedy" attempts to rehabilitate Brecht's approach to empathy. She points out that in his play *Mother Courage and Her Children*, Brecht "does allow the audience to sympathize with Mother Courage." Brecht, she claims, uses "sympathy and empathy with Mother Courage as a means for the audience to reflect further on the specific social and economic factors that brought about this loss and what might be done to change it." Curran, however, ultimately defends Brecht's approach to empathy and sympathy (she conflates the two terms into one meaning), saying that his "central concern about empathy is that by identifying with the protagonist and sharing his feelings, the viewer is locked into the perspective of the character." In order to counteract this rigidifying perspective, theatrical engagement "should be used in conjunction with dramatic devices that reveal the connection between individual action and social context."[24] Curran adopts Brecht's presupposition that empathetic identification with the character ultimately nullifies social perspectives, and is in itself insufficient to establish social context because empathy cannot induce social change. Social conditions have to be rendered explicit by some overt theatrical device (placards, estrangement effect, actors commenting on their characters, and so forth) so that reason can decipher the play's circumstances as they relate to real-world conditions.[25] Yet, if spectators fail to care about the actions, events, characters, or actors, why should they be moved to act? Why would demonstrating social contexts without empathy ipso facto inspire social change?

I hold that empathy enhances our comprehension of social conditions, provides a greater awareness of others, and works in conjunction with reason to evoke social action. We do, in fact, empathize with Mother Courage, even while we simultaneously understand and critique her misguided obsession with business and profit. We empathize with her despair, her desire for a better life, and her limited options, even as we distance ourselves from her reckless obsession for profit that costs the lives of her children. The audience relates to Mother Courage by way of an "empathetic connection"; we understand her social as well as personal situation—and might even be moved to feel that we would do the same thing in her circumstances—suggesting that empathy holds a cognitive as well as emotive capacity. We empathize with Mother Courage because we feel for her plight (she might starve if she acts otherwise), yet at the same time we criticize her for her blindness and avoidance of the larger picture. Our reasoning and feelings work simultaneously as an organic whole, operating conterminously as we observe events onstage.

Empathetic Connection: How Emotions Work

Empathy, I maintain, works in conjunction with reason, rather than in opposition to it. While empathy is generally regarded as a matter of emotions, subject to vicarious feelings and appetites, it has received less attention as an inducement to cognition. Yet empathy *enters understanding by way of emotion.*[26] Empathy, according to Arna Johan Vetlesen, "contains a cognitive dimension by virtue of which it, and it alone, *discloses* to us something about another person—namely, his or her emotional experience in a given situation." While it is often necessary in order to understand another's emotions, it is "not the same as sharing the other's feelings." Instead, it facilitates what Vetlesen calls "the reaching out" process, enabling us to walk in someone else's shoes without sacrificing critical reflection.[27] This connecting process enhances rather than diminishes our understanding. To "reach out" and connect empathetically is not necessarily a loss of identity, self, or judgment; as Martha C. Nussbaum contends, empathy "involves a participatory enactment of the sufferer, but is always combined with the awareness that one is not oneself suffering."[28] We can observe the tragic or humorous circumstances of the character; we can even find ourselves sharing similar experiences; but this does not mean that we have abandoned our ability to criticize the actions of the character. In empathy, according to David Woodruff Smith, "I 'identify' with the other, appreciating her experience *as if* I were going through it, but the boundaries between myself and the other, between my own experience and hers, remain clear to me."[29] As we observe action onstage, we do not compartmentalize our perception; rather, we perceive the events as an organic whole. We think, feel, reason, and empathize simultaneously. Emotions, in turn, provide a framework from which to view the world. Robert C. Solomon asserts that emotions "already 'contain' reason, and practical reason is circumscribed and defined by emotion." Our emotions "situate us in the world, and so provide not so much the motive for rationality much less its opposition but rather its very framework."[30] Emotions help designate a conceptual structure of our world, enabling one to find efficacious responses to given situations.[31]

A common view of emotions states that it is a function in a cognitive state requiring a belief in something. Ronald de Sousa provides an example: the object of my fear is the belief that a lion is charging. The lion may be real or imaginary; in either case the response is fear because *I believe the lion is coming.*[32] But how can the audience believe that a lion is charging the character, knowing full well that it is fiction? Real fear experienced when a lion charges and fictive fear when responding to a play are not quite the same, but there is an overlap bridged by the imagination. Emotions, therefore, do not always require belief; they can encompass a manifold experience, one that includes not merely beliefs, but also what Noël Carroll terms "thoughts and perhaps even patterns of attention."[33] Thought patterns can lead us to such diverse beliefs as that the woman on stage *might* be Medea, that events occurring to her *might* be happening, and that her actions *might* occur. We know she is not Medea, and we know she has not actually killed her children, but through the *imagination* the experience becomes one where the events take on real consequences. The imagination bridges the gap, connecting real and fictional realities.[34]

Imagination, then, is fundamental to audience awareness and inducement to emotion in theater, encouraging our feelings to accept fiction *as potentially actual.* Susan Feagin suggests that we empathize in the theater because we believe that "something may happen to *him* [the actor]" that in turn "affects me emotionally as if I were him." The beliefs required for audience empathy in theater, says Feagin, will be "slightly different" than the experienced emotions I feel for someone in life or for myself. Empathetic connection in a theatrical situation derives from the *imagination as well as belief,* and involves what Feagin calls "higher order beliefs."[35] In other words, empathy in theater is a means by which we adapt the feelings of another by way of imagination as well as belief, creating a "higher order" of our acceptance of the action.[36] These feelings may take the form of sympathy or empathy, but these two experiences are not necessarily the same.

Empathy is a translation from the German term *Einfühlung,* which literally means "feeling into." *Sympathy,* a much older term, is translated as *Mitfühlung,* meaning "feeling with." Empathy and sympathy have often shared definitions, creating a surplus of meaning and adding to the semantic confusion. In his effort to clarify the terms, Charles Edward Gauss maintains that empathy "supposes a fusion of subject and object, while sympathy supposes a parallelism between them in which I am aware of distinction between myself and the other."[37] Along similar lines, Rudolf A. Makkreel claims that empathy "allows the self to identify intuitively with the other," while sympathy "represents a more disinterested imaginative response to the other." Makkreel considers sympathy superior to empathy because sympathy "can range more widely" since "there is no claim of entering into others or identifying with them in sympathy."[38] Sympathy for Gauss and Makkreel implies a distancing that enables one to function unencumbered by identification.

I submit that empathy, not sympathy, implies the ability to identify with, and simultaneously distance from, the intended object of contemplation. I concur with Lauren Wispé, who maintains that *sympathy* "refers to the heightened awareness of the suffering of another person as something to be alleviated," giving rise to two levels of consciousness: awareness of suffering and desire to help. *Empathy,* by contrast, means "the attempt by one self-aware self to comprehend unjudgmentally the positive and negative experiences of another self," depending on "the use of imaginal and mimetic capacities." In empathy, "the self is the vehicle for understanding, and it never loses its identity." As a consequence, empathy evokes two levels of consciousness somewhat differently than sympathy: identification and judgment. The first requires imagination and emotion, and the second requires critical thought and contextual assessment. Sympathy is concerned with "communion rather than accuracy," and in sympathy "self-awareness is reduced rather than augmented."[39] Wispé clarifies the distinction (contra Gauss and Makkreel) between empathy as epistemological (a way of knowing) and sympathy as communal (a way of relating). While they may overlap—empathy may be communal and sympathy may provide a form of understanding in respect to another—sympathy, not empathy, can lead to "emotional distortion."[40] Although both have as their objects the emotions of another, they are different processes. Wispé characterizes sympathy as more passive, while empathy is a strategy for understanding. Sympathy is therefore an "agreement in feelings," while empathy entails identification of the feelings and thoughts of another person where agreement is unnecessary. Empathy, then, may range over a wider area than sympathy because, unlike sympathy, *it does not imply a corrective.* In empathy, the goal is what Thomas Natsoulas calls "empathetic accuracy";[41] the empathizer does not take the position of a pitier who then tries to alleviate suffering. Rather, empathy assesses the predicament of the other with possible sympathy, but it also seeks accurate clarification.

Genealogy of Empathy

While "sympathy" in Western philosophy is a result of Aristotle's examination of "pity" and extended elaboration by eighteenth-century philosophers David Hume and Adam Smith,[42] the English word *empathy* is (according to the *Oxford English Dictionary,* 1989) less than a century old. The psychologist Edward Titchener coined the term *empathy* in English in 1909 as a translation of *Einfühlung,*[43] by way of the Greek εμπάθεια (*Empatheia*), which signifies the ability to project one's emotions into an object of thought. The following will examine three categories of empathy roughly corresponding to its chronological development in Western philosophy and aesthetics during the nineteenth and twentieth centuries: the unifi-cation or merging approach, the phenomenological approach, and the embodied approach.[44]

The unification approach evolved during the nineteenth century as a study of aesthetic responses in psychology and art theory. It basically claims that the observer merges, or unifies, with the object of contemplation; audience and performer become one and the same. In his *On the Optical Sense of Form: An Aesthetic Contribution* (*Das optische Formgefühl: Ein Beitrag Aesthetik,* 1873), Robert Vischer (1847–1933) considered empathy as an affect on muscular and emotional consciousness during the viewing of an art object. He described this experience as a "contractive feeling" (*Zusammenfühlung*), which produces mental images stimulating emotions.[45] Empathy was regarded as an experience that merged subject and object through identification, a view of empathy that has since dominated descriptions of the term. Vischer described three stages of this type of empathy: first the sensory, or immediately feeling; second the kinesthetic, understood as a physical response; and third and most significantly, "empathy" as a deepening awareness of the object by a viewer, crystallizing into "empathetic sensation" (*Einempfindung*).[46] This third form insinuates itself when the art object incorporates the first two forms, the sensory and the kinetic, creating synthesis of the body and the will with the object of contemplation. Vischer argued that such a synthesis is based on a "pantheistic urge for union with the world." Empathy occurs, for instance, when the viewer has a kindred sensation (*Mitempfindung*) for the object, which expands to encompass a broader vision of the event. For example, we may pity the sight of a wounded soldier, but empathy broadens our scope beyond the event. It creates in the imagination "a more profound emotional experience" than the soldier's suffering because empathy includes one's view of the "sympathetic self" as a "general human self." The lone suffering of one soldier becomes part of a larger experience, one that envelopes the spectator. This is especially true in art forms, Vischer maintained, where the suffering can be choreographed for sentimental value. "The barbarity of enmity, the powerlessness of the individual, the whole sense of resignation," Vischer observed, "is written on the soldier's face."[47]

It is unfair, however, to characterize Vischer's view narrowly. He and others changed opinions on the subject frequently. The German psychologist Theodor Lipps (1851–1914) shared Vischer's view of empathy as the unification of subject and object, although he, too, changed views often.

Generally speaking, after arguing that empathy is not merely "a sensation in one's body," but rather "feeling something, namely, oneself, into the esthetic object,"[48] Lipps asserts that empathy was a complete dissolution of the subject and the object of contemplation, so much so that the subject may even imitate the object, what he called an "inner imitation" *(inner Nachahmung).* For example: we might tense our muscles when we see someone under stress. Empathy for Lipps creates a vicarious feeling that overtakes the spectator.[49] The perception of an object and the emotional response are united instinctually, as one's own conscious experience merges into the bodies of another.[50] A child, for instance, responds immediately to a smile without relying on some past experience of smiling. Lipps maintains that empathy existed as a positive and negative force: the former elicited a feeling of "harmony" *(Einklanges),* and the latter a conflict between one's "natural drives" *(natürlichen Bestreben)* and what is "a stimulus hostile to me, directed against me."[51] He concludes that empathy is an innate process generated in human experience, where another being or object may coexist with and functionally join in a single perception.[52]

The investigation of empathy *(Einfühlung)* by Edmund Husserl constitutes a significant shift in the term's meaning. The Husserlian concept of *Einfühlung* rejected the merging-unification theory that, according to Husserl, characterized Lipps's view; instead, empathy for Husserl was based on the notion that we know others not because we merge with them, but because we know them as "flesh and blood" variants of ourselves.[53] If, for example, I observe someone else in pain, I know the experience to the degree that I know pain can occur to me as well. It is not my pain per se, nor is it an illusion of pain, but rather my understanding of pain facilitates my comprehension of the pain of another. For Husserl, self-awareness provides the ingredient required to know others; I can perceive phenomena in others and consider correlative experiences in myself.

Husserl in *Ideas* asserts that we are individual subjects encased in our own consciousness. In other words, I cannot feel what you feel. However, in communicating and living in the world with others we experience what he termed "intersubjectivity"; that is, we relate to "an indefinite plurality" of various subjects in the world. The intersubjective plurality of experiences—the give-and-take of living communication—is "mediated through empathy."[54] By way of empathy, I can understand to some degree what an actor in a play is going through; I will not know the *precise* feelings, but I can grasp intuitively the character's thoughts and emotions.

Empathy here is the process whereby we attempt to comprehend another by comparing the actors' experiences with my own. In *Ideas II* Husserl describes the empathetic process as one in which we encounter in the surrounding physical world other "bodies," and through "empathy" I recognize these other bodies as "an Ego-subject" that is similar but not the same as my own.[55] We recognize and grasp the other being only, as he says, "in empathy," as analogous of ourselves. This analogous relationship does not overtake my consciousness, because, the other body is "there" spatially and temporally, and not "here" in my mind and body.[56] This is obvious; I am here, not there. But Husserl raises this point because he wants to insist that empathy never permits the ego to be absorbed by the other: "my appearances belong to me, his to him."[57] Only through the phenomenon of what he calls "appresence" *(Appräsenz),* or "apperception," which means a position of intuition and understanding, can we comprehend "the entire psychic life and psychic being [of the other] in a certain sort of unity of apperception."[58] In other words, I comprehend the other person not as me, but as someone who might be me given similar conditions and circumstances.

Husserl draws a complicated pattern for his notion of empathy, and he is not always consistent. Suffice it to say that in empathy, he contends, objects are not presented to us directly, but are grasped by our observations via "apperception" *(appräsentation).* Apperception, Husserl asserts, "is not inference, not a thinking act." Rather, it points to a "primal instituting," whereby the object is constituted by an "analogizing transfer," as the object is absorbed and appreciated but never merged.[59] For example: we can calculate the form and shape of the rear of a structure by viewing it from the front. We cannot "know" for certain what the rear of the building looks like, but we can, given our past experience, imagination, and intuition, form what Husserl might call an analogical conception. Similarly, although we cannot immediately grasp another's thoughts, feelings, or emotions, we can apprehend another through the analogical employment of apperception, forming conjectures and judgments through our intuition and past experiences. For him, imagination, intuition, and experience form a unified "apperception."

Husserl refers to this empathetic process as "pairing" *(Paarung).* He claims that this pairing, or the "phenomenon of coupling," is a *"primal form of that passive synthesis* which we designate as '*association,*' in contrast to passive synthesis of 'identification.'" Simply put, I associate rather than identify with the actor or character. Through the input of observation and

association, we (the actor and I) find "a unity of similarity,"[60] a common-
ality whereby I can understand and empathize. In pairing, the subject analyzes the object and, by way of empathy, establishes reciprocal experiences.
Husserl's concept of pairing goes a long way in developing empathy.
Empathy now becomes useful in increasing the audience's imagination.
Audiences can use their imagination by asserting an "as if" condition to
the stage action: I am not there onstage, but I might be *if* certain conditions
were to happen to me. As a member of the audience I am here, in my seat,
watching and not participating. But, through my imaginative use of projection, intuition, and empathy, *I could be there* onstage. I perceive the
events onstage as "potential" experiences of my own, but I am not swept
away by the action. I retain my thoughts, objectivity, and judgments, yet
still am moved by events onstage.[61]

Still, Husserl's emphasis on the solipsistic ego (the individual isolated in
his or her own mind), what he called a "sphere of ownness" *(Eigen-
sphäre),*[62] fails to adequately explain *how we actually achieve cognitive
understanding through empathy.* How is it possible to cross the boundary
of myself in comprehending another world if, as Alfred Shutz observes, I
constitute the world just for myself "and not for all other transcendental
egos as well?"[63] If another being never, in Husserl's own words, produces
"something novel over against the self,"[64] that is, something that trumps
my way of thinking and presents to me something new, how can I claim to
"understand" another if the other is experiencing something alien to me?
If we are not "possessed" by the other or merge with the other's experience, what have we learned and how might we cross the boundaries that
separate us? Husserl never satisfactorily explains how empathy as a phenomenon of knowing another within my consciousness can succeed in
comprehending or even approximating another's thoughts, meanings,
and intentions. If my ego fails to lose its self-contained singularity, personal immanence, and encased "sphere," then full understanding of
another hardly seems possible.

One way out of this problem of solipsistic enclosure—"I'm in my own
world, you are in yours"—is through an embodied approach: the ability to
empathize kinesthetically rather than merely as a mental inducing process.
Here theater and dance can take their place in the field of empathy where
other arts cannot; theater and dance present a "body" as the object of contemplation. The other body performing (entertaining, enacting, or
embodying a character) is flesh and blood, and, by virtue of its being (existence), shares similarities. I can therefore imaginatively and cognitively

remove myself (without losing my sense of self) when observing an actor. Along these lines, Maurice Merleau-Ponty and Emmanuel Levinas examine Husserl's conundrum of the self-enclosed ego unable to break out of its enclosure. They have developed an embodied approach to intersubjectivity. Merleau-Ponty raises the same question regarding the problem of solipsistic encasement: "how can the word 'I' be put in the plural," yielding "other I's?" In other words, how can I break free of my own self-enclosed world: "how can consciousness which, by its nature, and as self-knowledge, is in the mode of I, be grasped in the mode of Thou, and through this, in the world of the One?"[65] His opinion is that consciousness is not merely in the mind but "embodied," and to understand another we need to know how "an intention, a thought or a project can detach themselves from the personal subject and become visible outside him in the shape of his body, and in his environment which he builds for himself."[66] Husserl's intersubjectivity occurs within the context of isolation, or what might be called "Cartesian solipsism" (meaning I exist in my own mind and cannot escape my world), because Husserl's "sphere of ownness" is primordial, basic, and unyielding. Merleau-Ponty amends Husserl's position by emphasizing the transference of "corporeal" (embodied) existence in which my psyche and my awareness are "not a series of 'states of consciousness' that are rigorously closed in on themselves and inaccessible to anyone but me." Rather, my consciousness "is turned primarily toward the world, turned toward things; it is above all a relation to the world."[67] Outward relations to the world form consciousness, and the give-and-take of life influences who I am and how I think. Within the context of what he calls "synergetic sociability,"[68] the ebb and flow of social life, I absorb others into my consciousness by dint of the fact that they live in my environment. The "body" for Merleau-Ponty is not only visible in the world, but is also a "spatiality of situation," an existing entity that shares space with me, and not, as Husserl would have it, hidden within a private sphere. The lived body *(le corps vécu),* as Merleau-Ponty puts it, experiences structures in various situations. Fundamentally, the perception of structure for Merleau-Ponty "is to live it, to take it up, assume it and discover its immanent significance."[69] We "rub elbows" in life, and in the theater we extend this idea of social interaction further.

The lived body has significance for theater. The actor onstage is not an abstraction, but a living organism expressing emotions, actions, gestures, movements, and sounds. The actor evolves, too, allowing audiences to gauge the changes of experiences through the course of the play. I exist in the audience as observer, but I also exist as a body reflecting on the actions and movements of another body. Neither of us is a machine, programmed accordingly one way or another. We are in communication; actor and audience are living forms that adapt and adjust to the environment, the circumstances of the play, and the spaces we inhabit ("spatiality of situation"). I empathize with actors not in order to lose myself in them, or allow myself to be manipulated by them, but to absorb their experiences that in turn assist me in comprehending and enlarging the full meaning of the play and, in turn, the meaning of my life as well. The synergy between us is neither one-dimensional nor one-directional, but rather a dynamic give-and-take that allows experiences and consciousnesses to communicate across the footlights.

Levinas, along with Merleau-Ponty, considered Husserl's phenomenology too abstract. Concrete life for Levinas is not a solipsistic enclosure. Intersubjectivity is part of the essence of reality, not something "apperceived," that is, closed off in my mind and inaccessible to interaction. If we remain ego bound, the other becomes an empty abstraction. We must, he says, complete "the work of the philosophical intuition of subjectivity" in recognizing the other, by accepting our presence in the world as cohabitants.[70] The presence of our face-to-face encounters with others is without borders or enclosed egos. As observer, I take the actions of another as the material for standards or criteria of selfhood. In doing so, I place myself imaginatively in another situation. As an audience member, the experience of empathy involves a shaping of my self-presence as an experience of living with others.

Conclusion: Empathy and Caring

The embodied approach widens the use and definition of empathy by incorporating a borderless sense of community and strengthening the audience's ability to "care" about the events onstage. "To care" as an emotion can be a meaningful inspiration for social change, and not, as Brecht would have it, a force of inertia and incapacitation. Without some degree of empathy and care for the actor or character, mental activity performs in a void. Empathy places audiences in the position where they might care, and in doing so potentially reorients their perspective and increases their understanding. Jill Dolan maintains that the actor's "willing vulnerability perhaps enables our own and prompts us toward compassion and greater understanding." Such sentiments, she claims, "can spur emotion, and being moved emotionally is a necessary precursor to political movement."[71] Care and empathy are inextricably bound up with social action and heightened cognition, which are essential components to critical awareness and objective assessment.

Empathy, as this chapter has endeavored to explain, cannot be reduced to a simplistic dichotomy between reason and emotion, nor can it be summarily dismissed as loss of self leading to stasis. It is part of a complex, interactive theatrical experience that functions along with (and adds to) reason, understanding, and analysis and that in turn assists in social awareness. Without some concern and care for the character in a play (regardless of whether we are carried along with the narrative or not), social context devoid of empathy is little more than dull propaganda. Empathy informs our understanding in the theater, creating a multifaceted response that broadens our cognitive functions and widens our theatergoing experience. We cannot therefore accept a one-sided critique of empathy without taking into account empathy's history, varied approaches, and wide-ranging value.

NOTES

I want to thank Professor Juliet Koss, art historian at Scripps College, for her close reading and insightful critique of this essay.

1. See Jack Katz, *How Emotions Work* (Chicago: University of Chicago Press, 1999); Ronald de Sousa, *The Rationality of Emotion* (Cambridge: MIT Press, 1997); Richard Wollheim, *On the Emotions* (New Haven: Yale University Press, 1999); Mette Hjort and Sue Laver, eds., *Emotion and the Arts* (New York: Oxford University Press, 1997); and Derek Matravers, *Art and Emotion* (Oxford: Clarendon Press, 1998).

2. Satya P. Mohanty, *Literary Theory and the Claims of History* (Ithaca: Cornell University Press, 1997), 130, 131.

3. According to Frans B. M. de Waal, the motivation to empathize is not restricted to humans. Rats, Waal notes, "will deprive themselves of food when they notice the suffering of another animal, and will work to reduce the other's stress" ("Do Humans Alone 'Feel your Pain?'" *Chronicle of Higher Education,* October 26, 2001, B7–B9).

4. See Joel Kupperman, "Ethics for Extraterrestrials," *American Philosophical Quarterly* 28 (1991): 316, 319; and Amy Coplan, "Empathetic Engagement with Narrative Fictions," *Journal of Aesthetics and Art Criticism* 62, no. 2 (2004): 141–52. Coplan writes that in empathy, "I maintain a clear sense of my own separate identity. . . . [A]lthough I am deeply engaged in what he or she—the target of my empathy—is undergoing, I never lose my separate sense of self" (143).

5. I borrow the definition of *audience* from George Dickie, *Art and Value* (Lon-

don: Blackwell, 2001), who writes that an audience is "a set of persons the members of which are prepared in some degree to understand an object which is presented to them" (28).

6. Michael Goldman, *The Actor's Freedom: Toward a Theory of Drama* (New York: Viking Press, 1975), 6.

7. A similar position is taken by Peter Goldie, *The Emotions: A Philosophical Exploration* (Oxford: Clarendon, 2000), who raises the point that we do not "catch" empathy from another in a way we catch a cold. Rather, empathy for Goldie requires a more sophisticated use of imagination by the audience.

8. On the question of other minds, see J. L. Austin, "Other Minds" (1946), in *Philosophical Papers* (Oxford: Oxford University Press, 1979), 76–116.

9. For discussions of the two definitions, affective and cognitive, from a psychological point of view, see Mark A. Davis, *Empathy: A Social Psychological Approach* (New York: Westview Press, 1996), esp. 9–22; Arnold P. Goldstein and Gerald Y. Michaels, eds., *Empathy: Development, Training, and Consequences* (Hillsdale, N.J.: Lawrence Erlbaum, 1985); and William Ickes, ed., *Empathetic Accuracy* (New York: Guilford Press, 1997).

10. Philip Auslander claims the distinction between the live actor and other media is exaggerated. According to Auslander, we can and do experience similar emotions, feelings, and thoughts when watching a play as when watching other media. Auslander, *Liveness: Performance in a Mediatized Culture* (London: Routledge, 1999).

11. For two noteworthy studies of empathy in film, see Dolf Zillmann, "Empathy: Affect from Bearing Witness to the Emotions of Others," in *Responding to the Screen: Reception and Reaction Process*, ed. Jennings Bryant and Zillmann (Hillsdale, N.J.: Lawrence Erlbaum, 1991), 135–67; and Ed S. Tan, *Emotion and the Structure of Narrative Film*, trans. Barbara Fasting (Mahwah, N.J.: Lawrence Erlbaum, 1996).

12. Kendall L. Walton, *Mimesis as Make-Believe: On the Foundations of the Representational Arts* (Cambridge: Harvard University Press, 1990), 237.

13. Carl Plantinga, "The Scene of Empathy and the Human Face on Film," in *Passionate Views: Film, Cognition, and Emotion*, ed. Plantinga and Greg M. Smith (Baltimore: Johns Hopkins University Press, 1999), 244. Plantinga builds on Murray Smith's book *Engaging Characters: Fiction, Emotion, and the Cinema* (Oxford: Clarendon Press, 1995). John Deigh, *The Sources of Moral Agency: Essays in Moral Psychology and Freudian Theory* (Cambridge: Cambridge University Press, 1996) has observed that in order for empathy to advance beyond egocentrism, "it is necessary to distinguish it from emotional identification." Identification reduces the observer's ego to mere imitation; but the distinction of empathy, writes Deigh, is "that it entails imaginative participation in the other's life without forgetting oneself" (157).

14. Martha C. Nussbaum, "The Cognitive Structure of Compassion," in *Upheavals of Thought: The Intelligence of Emotion* (Cambridge: Cambridge University Press, 2001), 304–27, describes three cognitive elements of compassion: *size* (the seriousness of the event); *judgment of nondesert* (the object did not bring on the misfortune); and *eudaimonistic judgment* (the person is part of the good of the world).

15. Bertolt Brecht, *The Messingkauf Dialogues*, trans. John Willett (London: Methuen, 1965), 57.

16. Bertolt Brecht, "Journal Finnland," January 11, 1941, and February 1, 1941, *Werke: Journale I* (Frankfurt am Main: Suhrkamp, 1994), 454, 463.

17. Bertolt Brecht, "Conversation about being Forced into Empathy," in *Brecht on Theatre: The Development of an Aesthetic*, trans. John Willet (New York: Hill and Wang, 1964), 271.

18. According to Carl Plantinga, "Notes on Spectator Emotion and Ideological Film Criticism," in *Film Theory and Philosophy*, ed. Richard Allen and Murray Smith (Oxford: Clarendon Press, 1997), Brecht's bifurcation of reason and emotion considers involvement and judgment as "mutually exclusive" because Brecht "embraces a traditional Western perspective in his distrust of 'soft' emotion" (373, 374).

19. Brecht, "The Modern Theatre is the Epic Theatre," in *Brecht on Theatre*, 37.

20. Brecht, "Conversation with Bertolt Brecht," in *Brecht on Theatre*, 15.

21. Brecht, "On Experimental Theatre," in *Brecht on Theatre*, 132–33.

22. Brecht, "A Dialogue About Acting," in *Brecht on Theatre*, 26.

23. Paul Woodruff, "Engaging Emotion in Theater: A Brechtian Model in Theater History," *Monist* 71, no. 2 (1988): 242.

24. Angela Curran, "Brecht's Criticism of Aristotle's Aesthetics of Tragedy," *Journal of Aesthetics and Art Criticism* 59, no. 2 (2001): 173, 175.

25. This view stands in opposition to the Humean view that "reason alone can never be a motive to any action of the will," and that reason "can never oppose passion in the direction of the will" (Hume, *A Treatise of Human Nature* [1739; New York: Penguin, 1969], 460, 461).

26. In art, emotions may enter when the observer is moved, engaged, or otherwise involved on a personal level. This contrasts with postmodernist approaches, which dismiss free will emotions and actions, and generally favors a view of human beings as embodied motility subjected to action and reaction. The position taken here is that "empathy" is not so much an act of transcendental intentionality (where beings transcend social conditions and external power relations) as it is a functional intentionality (where beings are conditioned by social forces yet fully aware of their functioning intentions and acts) that operates in embodied communicative practices. (The term *intentionality*, taken from phenomenology, means the theory of consciousness that allows for the notion that a state of consciousness is directed at an object. Intentionality assumes that there is an immanent domain belonging to acts of consciousness, which is accessible to reflection. This reflection, in turn, is available to conscious reflection independently of objects that they are about.) The self is neither an autonomous agent indifferent to contingency and alterity, nor a being responsive solely to external forces, like a falling rock. Humans live between autonomy and heteronomy; we are volitional beings who also are conditioned by external events.

27. Arne Johan Vetlesen, *Perception, Empathy, and Judgment: An Inquiry into the Preconditions of Moral Performance* (University Park: Pennsylvania State University Press, 1994), 204, 205.

28. Nussbaum, *Upheavals of Thought*, 328.

29. David Woodruff Smith, *The Circle of Acquaintance: Perception, Consciousness, and Empathy* (Dordrecht: Kluwer Academic, 1989), 117.

30. Robert C. Solomon, "Sympathy and Vengeance: The Role of the Emotions in Justice," in *Emotions: Essays on Emotion Theory*, ed. Stephanie H. M. Van Goozen et al. (Hillsdale, N.J.: Lawrence Erlbaum, 1994), 294.

31. Noël Carroll argues that emotions "may serve reason in general by effectively guiding our attention to important information." As a consequence, there are "no

grounds for worrying that emotions, such as the emotions elicited by art, will necessarily subvert reason [as Plato would have it], since, among other things, reason or cognition is an ineliminable constituent, indeed a determining force, of the emotions" ("Art, Narrative, and Emotion," in Hjort and Laver, *Emotion and the Arts,* 198; reprinted in Carroll, *Beyond Aesthetics: Philosophical Essays* [Cambridge: Cambridge University Press, 2001], 215–34).

32. de Sousa, *The Rationality of Emotion,* 40.

33. Carroll, "Art, Narrative, and Emotion," 208, 209.

34. Abstract theater such as the works of Richard Foreman and Robert Wilson creates a somewhat different environment, where reality is obfuscated. But empathy can still function in these situations, since the actor's body and experience are still eliciting our response and awareness.

35. Susan L. Feagin, "Imagining Emotion and Appreciating Fiction," *Canadian Journal of Philosophy* 18 (1988): 489, 490. See also Alex Neill, "Empathy and (Film) Fiction," in *Post-Theory: Reconstructing Film Theory,* ed. David Bordwell and Noël Carroll (Madison: University of Wisconsin Press, 1996), 182–84.

36. Empathy permits us, as Margo Jefferson points out, "to see others as the others might see themselves" ("The Critic in Time of War," *New York Times Book Review,* October 28, 2001, 35).

37. Charles Edward Gauss, "Empathy," in *Dictionary of the History of Ideas,* ed. Philip P. Weiner, vol. 2 (New York: Charles Scribner's Sons, 1973), 87.

38. Rudolf A. Makkreel, "How is Empathy Related to Understanding?" in *Issues in Husserl's Ideas II,* ed. Thomas Nenon and Lester Embree (Dordrecht: Kluwer Academic, 1996), 203, 211. I thank my coeditor, David Z. Saltz, for alerting me to this book.

39. Lauren Wispé, "The Distinction Between Sympathy and Empathy: To Call Forth a Concept, a Word is Needed," *Journal of Personality and Social Psychology* 50, no. 2 (1986): 318.

40. Ibid., 319.

41. Thomas Natsoulas, "Sympathy, Empathy, and the Stream of Consciousness," *Journal for the Theory of Social Behavior* 18, no. 2 (1988): 179.

42. Sympathy can be considered derivative of Aristotle's definition of pity *(pathos).* "Let pity then," Aristotle argues in *The Art of Rhetoric,* "be a certain pain occasioned by an apparently destructive evil or pain's occurring to one who does not deserve it, which the pitier might expect to suffer himself or that one of his own would, and this whenever it should seem near at hand" (Aristotle, *The Art of Rhetoric,* trans. H. C. Lawson-Tancred [New York: Penguin, 1991], 163 [2.8]). See also Hume, *Treatise of Human Nature;* and Adam Smith, "Of Sympathy," in *The Theory of Moral Sentiments* (1759) (Washington, D.C.: Regnery, 1997), 1–8.

43. Edward Titchener, *Experimental Psychology of the Thought Processes* (New York: Macmillan, 1909), 21.

44. One important work that will not be referred to is Wilhelm Worringer's early-twentieth-century book *Abstraktion und Einfühlung (Abstraction and Empathy).*

45. Robert Vischer, *Über das optische Formgefühl: Ein Beitrag zur Aesthetik* (Leipzig: Hermann Credner, 1873), 4. For a translation of *On the Optical Sense of Form,* see *Empathy, Form, and Space: Problems in German Aesthetics, 1873–1893,* ed. and trans. Harry Francis Mallgrave and Eleftherios Ikonomou (Santa Monica, Calif.: Getty Center, 1994), 89–123.

46. Vischer, *Über das optische Formgefühl*, 16.

47. Ibid., 29, 30.

48. Theodor Lipps, "Empathy, Inner Imitation, and Sense-Feelings," ed. and trans. Melvin M. Rader in *A Modern Book of Esthetics: An Anthology* (New York: Henry Holt, 1935), 302.

49. Lipps was a follower of Hume; he in fact translated a great deal of Hume into German. Hume argued that "Reason is and ought only to be the slave of the passions, and can never pretend to any other office than to serve and obey them." Hume, *Treatise of Human Nature*, II.iii, 3, 462.

50. See Lauren Wispé, "History of the Concept of Empathy," in *Empathy and Its Development*, ed. Nancy Eisenberg and Janet Strayer (Cambridge: Cambridge University Press, 1987), 19.

51. Lipps, "Einfühlung und ästhetischer Genuß," *Die Zukunft* 54 (1905–6): 106, 107, trans. Karl Aschenbrenner as "Empathy and Aesthetic Pleasure," in *Aesthetic Theories*, ed. Karl Aschenbrenner and Arnold Isenberg (Englewood Cliffs, N.J.: Prentice-Hall, 1965), 403–14.

52. Aesthetic theorist Vernon Lee (neé Violet Paget), *The Beautiful: An Introduction to Psychological Aesthetics* (Cambridge: Cambridge University Press, 1913), described the feeling one has in observing mountain vistas: the mountain takes on the appearance of rising before us, even though the object is motionless. This illusion, she maintains, is empathetic. The German *Einfühlung*, she adds, derived from "a verb to feel oneself into something ('sich in Etwas ein fühlen')" (66).

53. According to Rudolf Bernet, *An Introduction to Husserlian Phenomenology* (Evanston, Ill.: Northwestern University Press, 1993), Husserl "took the term 'empathy' over from Lipps but never accepted it in the Lippsian sense of an instinctive projection of one's own immanent experience into bodies outside of one oneself" (155).

54. Husserl, *Ideas: General Introduction to Pure Phenomenology*, trans. W. R. Boyce Gibson (1913; New York: Collier, 1962), sec. 151, 387.

55. Husserl, *Ideas Pertaining to a Pure Phenomenology and to a Phenomenological Philosophy: Book II, Studies in the Phenomenology of Constitution*, trans. Richard Rojcewicz and André Schuwer (Dordrecht: Kluwer Academic, 1989), chap. 4, 172.

56. Ibid., [168] 176.

57. Ibid., [169] 177.

58. Ibid., [169], 177–78.

59. Husserl, *Cartesian Meditations: An Introduction to Phenomenology*, trans. Dorion Cairns (1931; The Hague: Martinus Nijhoff, 1960), 111 (5.141). Alfred Schutz offers a noteworthy distinction between "inference" and "empathy." In inference, we discover the other's thoughts "by a process of reasoning by analogy, inferring from the Other's 'expressive' bodily gestures his state of mind." This is supposedly analogous to our state of mind if "we perform the 'same' gesture." Conversely, the theory of empathy "is not an explanation of the origin of our knowledge of the Other, but just a hypothesis which explains the reasons of our belief in the Other's existence." In Schulz, *Collected Papers*, ed. Maurice Natanson, vol. 1 (The Hague: Martinus Nijhoff, 1967), 159, 160.

60. Husserl, *Cartesian Meditations*, 112 (51.142).

61. Edith Stein, Husserl's assistant and author of the dissertation (under Husserl's tutelage), *On the Problem of Empathy*, trans. Waltraut Stein (1917; Washington, D.C.:

ICS, 1989), defines empathy as "an act of perceiving [*eine Art Erfahrender*] *sui generis*," 119. Like Husserl, she rejects empathy as a commingling of subject and object, emphasizing instead that "empathy is not a feeling of oneness" with the object per se, but rather one can experience, for instance, "joy while I empathetically comprehend the other's [joy] and see it as the same [as mine]" [17] 17.

62. Husserl, *Cartesian Meditations*, 92–94 (44).

63. Alfred Schutz, "The Problem of Transcendental Intersubjectivity," *Collected Papers*, vol. 3, *Studies in Phenomenological Philosophy* (The Hague: Martinus Nijhoff, 1966), 76.

64. Husserl, *Ideen II*, quoted in Makkreel, 200.

65. Maurice Merleau-Ponty, *Phenomenology of Perception*, trans. Colin Smith (London: Routledge, 1962, 2000), 348.

66. Ibid., 348–49.

67. Maurice Merleau-Ponty, "The Child's Relations with Others," in *The Primacy of Perception*, trans. James M. Edie (Evanston, Ill.: Northwestern University Press, 1964), 116, 117.

68. M. C. Dillon, *Merleau-Ponty's Ontology* (Evanston, Ill.: Northwestern University Press, 1988, 1997), 118.

69. Merleau-Ponty, *Phenomenology of Perception*, 100, 258.

70. Emmanuel Levinas, *The Theory of Intuition in Husserl's Phenomenology*, trans. André Orianne (1963; Evanston, Ill.: Northwestern University Press, 1998), 150, 151.

71. Jill Dolan, "Performance, Utopia, and the 'Utopian Performance,'" *Theatre Journal* 53, no. 3 (2001): 459. Daryl Koehn, *Rethinking Feminist Ethics: Care, Trust and Empathy* (London: Routledge, 1998), maintains that empathy "not only allows us to enrich our moral discourse but also to assess our own efficacy as moral agents" (57).

⌣

FOURTEEN

The Voice of Blackness

The Black Arts Movement and Logocentrism

Mike Sell

We know who we are, and we are not invisible, at least not to each other. . . . The light is black (now, get that!) as are most of the meaningful tendencies in the world.

—LARRY NEAL, "And Shine Swam On"

We are, if one wants to put it this way, environmentalists of the arts.

—ROBERT MACBETH

In "And Shine Swam On," his most incisive description of the cultural, political, and philosophical imperatives of the Black Arts Movement (BAM), Larry Neal asks us to "listen to James Brown scream. . . . Have you ever heard a Negro poet sing like that?" He answers, "Of course not, because we have been tied to the texts, like most white poets. The text could be destroyed and no one would be hurt in the least by it."[1] At least, no one committed to the overthrow of political and economic powers reeling from the shocks of India, Ghana, Cuba, the Suez Canal, Vietnam, Watts, Detroit, Birmingham, and Bandung. These larger geopolitical— more specifically, nationalist and internationalist—events are inseparable from the critical, philosophical, and material implications of Neal's call for a mighty Black voice. That kind of situatedness is a basic concern of my essay, though my concerns are more philosophical, as might be expected in an anthology such as this. As I hope to show, Black logocentrism— which we can define initially as an emphasis on voice and speech in ethical, metaphysical, and critical thought—is intertwined with the concrete, localized project of nation building. In poems, plays, novels, and essays, the Black voice—as scream, shout, signifyin' inversion, science-dropping soapbox crusade, Negro spiritual, tragic dramatic cry, street-echoing cackle, and a myriad of other vocal modes—is understood to be the crucial lever to unhinge the spiritual and material hegemony of whiteness.

As Jacques Derrida has shown, logocentric modes of thought tend to marginalize and devalue writing, perceiving it to be impure, and an obstacle to truth. That seems to be the case for the BAM. The antitextual bias carried by the trope of the mighty Black voice is also a basic concern of this essay. The Black voice was emphasized by many BAM theorists as capable of shattering the chains of a cultural imperialism based on the imposition of textual literacy and all its correlative effects. Rejecting the text and restoring the voice would allow for the ontological grounding of philosophy, economy, culture, and identity in a post-Western moment. The Black voice, it was argued, would undermine to the point of collapse the most stubbornly institutionalized conceptual categories of Western thought.

A more detailed description of Black voice theory—and the productive contradictions in this theory—can be found in other essays.[2] To sum up those essays, significant numbers of BAM critics and artists, including key theorists and writers, saw the situated, communitarian, and traditionalist implications of the spoken word as the best way to articulate a critical philosophy anchored in everyday activism, Tricontinental liberation (i.e., of Africa, Latin America, and Asia), and a commitment to folk and popular culture. The focus on vocality gave the movement as a whole a decidedly performative emphasis, as I and others have shown. Considered a cultural strategy that unites the local and the global in a peculiarly effective manner, Black Arts vocal theory and practice can be viewed as part of a larger critical tendency, a tendency that worked to destroy whatever threatened the commodification of the Black body, of Black creativity, of Black culture—in short, an effective response to the theories and practices of slavery and colonialism.

The BAM is notable for its sophisticated and politically inflected drama, theater, and performance. This is important because drama, theater, and performance can be politically effective only to the extent that they're able to link the local, situated, singular experience of theater to a credible and persuasive vision of community. The BAM attempted this and, for the BAM, the vision was global. According to Robert J. C. Young, Tricontinental praxis "mediated and continued to develop the Marxism of the liberation movements whose particularity of cultural location operates dialectically within the general paradigm of the world systems theory," a dialectical operation that "has emphasized what one might call the untranslatability of revolutionary practices, the need for attention to local forms, and the translation of the universal into the idiom of the local."[3] Young's formulation also describes the Black Voice; he seems to be describing the timbre produced when concept rubs against the socially situated body. In this regard, the BAM shared much with other contemporary "grassroots" movements, which also emphasized face-to-face encounters in political work. The BAM artist—whether poet, playwright, editor, dancer, or painter—understood his or her expression as an event in a thickly layered cultural environment, an event that would unite praxis (the embodiment of theory in technique) and locality (the particular tones, dialects, acoustic quirks, and linguistic history of the performance location). Thus, it makes perfect sense to discover that Larry Neal and Askia Touré—to name only two—spent summers door-to-door canvassing for their political organization, the Revolutionary Action Movement: spreading the word, activating volunteers, getting the lay of the land, hearing the voices of the masses.

Black Voice sounds in singular, transformative spaces. These spaces are both theatrical (created out of the stuff of the stage) and actual (the neighborhood, the auditorium, the spectator's body). This combination of a space produced during performance and the actual space in which that production occurs can be illustrated by Sonia Sanchez's play *Sister Son/Ji*. *Son/Ji* is a monodrama whose character systematically transforms her appearance and voice over the course of the play. Every change occurs on stage, from elderly woman to "Negro" college girl to Black Nationalist to revolutionary to elderly woman again. The transformation at the end—a return to Son/Ji's first identity—brings with it a timbre that Son/Ji didn't possess four scenes earlier; yet, oddly, it's not a quality that can be pinned down. The elderly Son/Ji asks, "Anybody can grab the day and make it stop. can u my friends? or may be it's better if i ask: will you?"[4] The call to the audience at the end of the play literally resonates with ideological certainty and the wisdom earned as the protagonist struggles and survives. It's a tonal shift, an augmentation of the first moments of the play, a shift in the character's *position,* a shift that is temporal (Son/Ji speaks to us from a not-too-distant future) and ethical (she now speaks as an authority).

The demands on the performer's voice in this play are quite heavy. Not only does she have to modulate through five distinct moments in Son/Ji's life, but she must demonstrate persuasive fluency in the dialects and rhetorical modes of several African-American communities, fluency demonstrated by changing tones, tempos, and vocabularies that stand out vividly against the minimalist set and severely simplified costume and makeup stipulated by the script. Recalling Robert Macbeth's claim that Black artists are "environmentalists of the arts," Sanchez creates a role for a talented performer who creates set and setting through speech and motion, literally speaking the nation. However, Sanchez's emphasis on voice is inseparable from her clever play with textual conventions. Three of the most popular dramatic genres of the BAM are in play here: the drama of politicization (the "Negro" becomes "Black"), the drama of madness (Son/Ji goes insane as a consequence of race war, the death of her children, and adultery), and agitation-propaganda (the call to action). The BAM's performative sensibility was keenly attuned to the singularity of the per-formance situation and rigorous critical demands. However, it was also keenly attuned to textual registers that enabled certain kinds of communi-cation to occur.

Conventionalized in the poetry and drama of the period, soul mani-fested itself in bold emotional through-lines, dramatic confrontations that resonated with centuries-old cultural archetypes, in hip banter, emotional fluency, sexual tension, contemporary speech conventions, naturalistic detail, and in an audible understanding of the community orature—and all centered on a fundamental tension between life and death. Voice acti-vated, transformed, and anchored, producing explosive potential in the soulful dialectic of local and national, the past, the present, and the future. This potential is described by Student Non-Violent Coordinating Com-mittee field secretary Charlie Cobb in the concluding lines of "Ain't That a Groove":

> Play James Brown on a Black block anywhere.
> Play it loud. No matter what our folks are doing, his sound gets
>   included. People can dig our leaflets, but it's not the same. Not the
>   same.
> . . . .
> Let's use it.
> Our sound.
> Out [sic] beat.
> Against the problem of the Local White Motha-fuckers.[5]

He skillfully moves from the imperative based in an implied "you" to the explicit "we" of the collective imperative and possessive form of the last three lines, enacting the classic blues call-and-response on the grammatical level. In addition to relying on oral patterns in his manifesto, he denigrates the very textuality he's using; he trumps leaflet with loudspeaker. Earlier in the piece, Cobb describes organizers discussing ideology with those children playing hopscotch, youths hanging on a corner, and the African-American masses at a Fourth of July James Brown concert: "Energy, Music, Motion. Twenty thousand Blacks erupt into a finger popping of dance and rhythms."[6] After this poetic evocation of an actual Atlanta concert, Cobb modulates into speculation, "Street motion begins to take on the rhthms [*sic*] of the music," and a white cop gets jumped. This modulation from poetic journalism to fictional speculation shows a similar impatience with the generic limits of textual forms as was shown by *Sister Son/Ji* and forecasts the semantic transformations and denigration of text found in the concluding lines.[7]

Despite its focus on sound, textual objects permeate Cobbs's piece: leaflets, memorized songs, graffiti, and newspapers. The BAM's attack on the text was carried out in the name of "soul" and in the form of screams, shouts, theatrical climaxes, song (amateur, professional, live, and recorded), sermons, street corner debates, and stand-up routines. Yet these vocal attacks used the text as vehicle, whether in the physical sense (plays, song scores, pamphlets, and manifestos) or the conceptual (i.e., social text, or what Neal describes in his essay on the blues as an "encounter [that] takes place against a specific symbolic text . . . the world is . . . text").[8] Moreover, and unlike most logocentric movements, they were often quite conscious of the contradictions of their textualized anti-textualism. The Black voice is a peculiarly self-conscious voice.

Consider drama, seen by many Black activists as especially capable of presenting and interrogating the dynamic, often conflicted relationship between text and voice. In the most basic terms, drama is nothing but such a relationship, a textual form that categorically assumes vocalization. Many BAM artists self-consciously explored this relationship, for example Bullins in his early play *How Do You Do?* Bullins subtitles the play a "nonsense drama."[9] In it we find the absurd dialogue of Roger and Dora Stereotype, backed by the cries of a struggling, idealistic Black poet. The play demonstrates the effects of the voice's precedence over the text in the BAM as Bullins systematically wrecks a range of African-American identities in bits of silly, banal verbal shtick. Bullins wrecks the theatrical experience, too, through a slow, inexorable ramping up of dramatic tension, an intensification that slowly reveals an active, elusive, and decidedly Black consciousness lurking behind the masks. Paul: "Make him think that you don't know anything about language. That you can't logically think because you say: 'I ain't never done no nothin' . . . DESTROY HIS INSTITU-TIONALIZED, STRUCTURED LOGIC THROUGH ILLOGIC . . . YAWHL!"[10] The play arranges and rearranges a dozen or so modes of vocal expression into an unstable architecture of self-loathing, irony, aggressively entertaining pro-fanity, and self-reflexivity. The performers of this play must carefully han-dle its subtle, insistent, and vocal modulation of bourgeois pretension and revolutionary cliché into something else—the drama resides in this trans-formation. Through this modulation of voice and gesture, Bullins system-atically modulates his characters from ridiculous, simplistic, and loqua-cious kowtowers into courageous explorers of the thrilling, threatening gap between sense and sensibility. Through this modulation, a conscious-ness is revealed lurking behind the clichés, a resolute spirit insistently manifesting itself in tone, inflection, and tempo, an audio assassin in tex-tual disguise.

The way Bullins inspirits the deathly pale text spoken by his characters recalls both Sanchez's Son/Ji and Federico Garcia Lorca's aged flamenco dancer in "Theory and Practice of Soul," published in the Black National-ist *Liberator* magazine in 1966:

> Years ago, in a dance contest at Jerez de la Frontera, an eighty-year-old woman, by the solitary act of lifting her arms, throwing back her head, and striking the platform with her heel, defeated beautiful women and girls whose bodies flowed like water, simply because, over that gather-ing of angels and muses, a moribund soul had lifted its rusty wings.[11]

The text is merely a vehicle. The voice transcends because it is a form that is "perpetually coming to life and passing away, . . . configur[ing itself] over an exact present," yet remaining "liberated from time."[12]

This transcendent but vocal urge is at least partly the source of the BAM's tenuous place in literary, political, and theater history, and one of the reasons why the movement has been scorned by, among others, Stan-ley Crouch, Henry Louis Gates, Jr., Houston Baker, and, in a more nuanced and ultimately positive fashion, Amiri Baraka.[13] However, though the BAM can be viewed as logocentric, nationalist, and essentialist, it can also be viewed as a mode of writing, as internationalist, and constructivist. Not surprisingly, this instability is due to the movement's focus on that peculiarly difficult genre, drama, which as in dance requires "the interpretation of a living body."[14] Though the BAM on one level (i.e., the level of textual discourse) seems to represent the apotheosis of Western metaphysics as described by Derrida (i.e., necessitating systematic exclusion of various kinds of "others" such as whites, feminists, homosexuals, and Jews in order to constitute a purified Blackness), on other levels (i.e., the level of performance and theater), it seems to implement exactly the kinds of critical, deconstructionist tactics used by Derrida himself to subvert the Western metaphysical tradition.

The contradictory qualities of the movement (at once essentialist and deconstructionist, both European and Tricontinental) places the movement in an odd position vis-à-vis Young's complaint that "[w]hereas postcolonialism has become associated with diaspora, transnational migration, and internationalism, anti-colonialism is often identified exclusively, too exclusively, with a provincial nationalism."[15] This is indeed a general tendency, one with especially devastating effects when it comes to the BAM, a movement that has, until recently, been ignored by most scholars and critics. This is not to say that provincialism wasn't a significant factor in the movement; rather, that it is only part of the picture. That said, Baraka's rejection of the cultural nationalist position in 1974 as a "bourgeois-nationalist, reactionary-nationalist kind of trend"[16] and the rise of Black Feminism are both evidence of the diverse kinds of criticisms of the movement that were generated *within the movement itself,* criticisms that accurately assessed the movement's shortcomings without abandoning the movement's core concepts and methods.

As accurate as they may be, accusations of chauvinism have tended to overshadow the powerful forms of hybridity invented within the BAM that allowed artists and critics such as Sanchez, Alice Walker, Toni Cade Bambara, Nikki Giovanni, and Julian Mayfield—to name only a few—to excel. Theater and performance helped to create the spaces and languages that enabled such success. As an anticolonial movement that attempted to unite communities dispersed across great geographical spaces, and did so without benefit of technologies like television or the Internet, the BAM put into place a geographically broad, trans-American articulation of hybridity that was indeed "a revolutionary mixture of the indigenous and the cosmopolitan." A significant aspect of this articulation was performance, which put text into context, theory into praxis. The soulful sounding of Black voice across the Americas in the 1960s and 70s was enabled by a complex dialectic of performance and text. The voice mediated this dialectic.

The Black voice *theatricalizes* and *dramatizes* the spaces in which it sounds, defining at once the scene and its seers, the Black voice disciplining the Black eye, configuring itself, to recall Lorca once more, over an exact present. *Sister Son/Ji* captures the contradiction well. Voice is at once the vehicle of the individual, of the self, diversity, and locality, but is also the guarantor of ideological homogeneity and community coherence, which we see in the play vis-à-vis its repetitive scapegoating of white academics, white female radicals, philandering Black men, and those in the audience who do not affirm the revolutionary perspective. Soul reflects and is reflected by the diversity of African-American history, its long defense of individual style, culture, and location; yet it is also a transcendental signifier that mercilessly judges those who are signified or not signified by it. Son/Ji dramatically transforms into an embodied icon.

Contra Sanchez, Joyce Green argues that chauvinism—particularly sexism—is due to the omnipresent presence of the term *soul* in the discourses of the BAM and, the corollary of soul, to the emphasis placed on the expressive potential of the local. She writes, "American society has created a technology which by its very existence denounces any divine being, and the Black man has come to realize that He Who Never Prays Has the Power. Therefore, increasingly, with each generation of Blacks, atheism is becoming the creed. However, because the Black man is innately spiritual, with religion rooted in his life style, it becomes a constant task to renounce it."[17] Green correctly argues that sexism—and by implication the uncommon but pungent moments of anti-Semitism and homophobia that peppered the movement—is linked both to the BAM's politicization of everyday life and to a deeply rooted metaphysical sensibility that justified the exceptional status of African America within the African diaspora.

However, such romanticism is hard to pin down when it comes to the antitextual bias of the BAM, especially when we understand that the text was an emblem of a more general socioeconomic tendency: the reification of culture, the separation of text from context. The antitextual bias of the BAM was aimed toward *antimetaphysical* ends. Neal writes,

In the gallery or the salon, [African sculpture] is merely an objet d'art, but for your ancestors, it was a bridge between them and the spirit, a bridge between you and your soul in the progression of a spiritual lineage. It was art, merely incidentally, for it was essentially functional in its natural setting.[18]

Along these lines, Etheridge Knight argues for a revised understanding of the notion of publication, an understanding that would relegate print genres to a supporting role as part of a larger set of "public utterances,"[19] a set in which spoken word is preeminent because it is anchored to a body both localized and responsible for what it says and hears. It's no accident that Knight developed this theory while serving as editor of his prison's newspaper. Knight had to deal with readers who did not accept the notion that a text was distinct from the person who wrote it; in Knight's case, to express oneself was to place oneself quite literally into the public arena: cafeteria, shower room, yard, library. In similar fashion, Bullins utilized the textual practice of editing to situate plays, journals, and debates in a variety of theatricalized—and thereby *politicized*—contexts.[20]

As is already apparent in the discussion of Black romanticism, the problems and possibilities of Black voice surround categories that were the object of intense political and artistic debate. When we consider issues of voice in the work of writers like Neal, Bullins, Cade, James T. Stewart, Maulana Ron Karenga, Marvin X, Giovanni, and Knight, we find self-critical, incisive, innovative, *and consistently theatricalized* celebration of the Black voice as the embodiment of historical necessity and individual audacity—because theater was the one practice in which text, performance, and theory were the most provocatively related to each other. Neal often argued that the embodied qualities and necessities of theater and performance enabled a direct understanding of Black history, community, and selfhood. Theatricality, for Neal, is inextricable from the developmental innovations of African-American being. This explains why, in "The Black Arts Movement," Neal focuses on drama rather than poetry, despite the fact that poetry and the essay were the media he most often used as a writer. Recalling the eloquent rage of Baraka's *Dutchman*—recalling specifically Clay's fatally honest, resonant outburst at its end—Neal argues that theatricality in general and theater specifically are "inextricably linked to the Afro-American political dynamic. And such a link is perfectly consistent with Black America's contemporary demands. For theater is potentially the most social of all of the arts. It is an integral part of the socializing process."[21] Neal concludes by claiming that theatricality is the crucible in which body, voice, community, and time are fused; theater marks the movement of "Black men in transition."[22] In sum, Black Arts theater is a foundational *philosophical* gesture in this reconstitution and revision of Black identity, ontology, and organizational theory.

The fact remains, however, that the sanctification of the voice places the

Black Arts Movement and its philosophico-politico-aesthetic program, the Black Aesthetic, in troubling territory. In *Of Grammatology,* Jacques Derrida writes that voice-centered discourses have "always placed in parenthesis, *suspended,* and suppressed for essential reasons, all free reflection on the origin and status of writing, all science of writing which was not *technology* and the *history of a technique,* itself leaning upon a mythology and a metaphor of natural writing."[23] Derrida convincingly argues that efforts to erase writing and establish transcendent, unqualifiable truths lead to the marginalization and victimization of those "marked" as different on both the social level (chauvinism, homophobia, colonialism, etc.) and the epistemological level (the failure to acknowledge the "play" of textuality in the knowing of Being).[24]

That said, we should not forget a central point of Derrida's critique: the critique of logocentrism is inseparable from the cultural and intellectual *habitus* of the thing it critiques.[25] Very much a part of the generation of '68 and very much a part of the Western philosophical tradition, Derrida's critical practice persistently roots out the erasure of difference and the promotion of naturalized, autonomous self-identity, tendencies visible in a range of ideologies and identities, including those that claim to evade and undermine it. Derrida, rather, is in line with the argument posed by Theodor Adorno and Max Horkheimer that Nazism was the apotheosis rather than the negation of the Western philosophical, aesthetic, and ethical tradition.[26] The influence of Martin Heidegger is also legible in Derrida's writings: Greek philosophical constructs built on the differentiation of subject and object, spirit and matter, set into motion a history we are unable to escape, and hardly able to criticize.

Deconstruction does not attempt to mark such an escape—the dualistic thinking underwriting the idea of an "inside" and an "outside" is also a legacy of the Greeks—but it certainly troubles, if not completely de-legitimizes, essentialist thinking of the sort that enabled the Nazis to justify and promote the most catastrophic forms of anti-Semitism, misogyny, homophobia, and racism. Perhaps more troubling to his critics is the fact that Derrida's critique of logocentrism also troubles those ideologies that, historically, have opposed fascism; specifically, liberalism, and left-wing nationalism. This has raised the ire of those who insist on the importance of a positive alternative to the minuet of fascism and liberalism, not "mere" wordplay.

Rather like those in the BAM, Derrida confronts a tortuous critical question: How does one maintain the openness of deconstructive method in the limited confines of situated political action? David Wood argues that *Of Spirit* attempts to carry through a number of interrelated projects: to answer the charges of apoliticality/crypto-fascism by locating the "site of the political" in Heidegger's writings, to practice a viable reading of Heidegger (sorely lacking in the uproar surrounding Farias's book),[27] and to trace the destiny of a term of singular importance to the Western philosophical tradition, *spirit* (a term that carries with it nearly as much baggage as that preferred by Black activists: *soul*).[28] Derrida addresses Heidegger's failed efforts to link his project of metaphysical destruction to the political practices of the German Nazi party, noting in particular his efforts to articulate a notion of the *Volk* that was, in fact, antiracist. The rejection of Heidegger's philosophy by the Nazi party serves as an example of how the concept of spirit "cannot be opposed to [biologism, naturalism, and genetic racism] except by reinscribing spirit in an oppositional determination, by once again making it a unilaterality of subjectivity, even if in its voluntarist form."[29] This is precisely what he attempted when he took over the rectorship of Freiburg University in 1933 and announced a position critical of the "vulgar Nazism" he saw taking over Hitler's project.

Derrida makes a troubling move with this information, using Heidegger as an emblem for antifascist thinking in general. Derrida asks, "[B]y thus inverting the direction of determination, is Heidegger alleviating or aggravating this 'thought of race'? Is a metaphysics of race more or less serious than a naturalism or a biologism of race?"[30] Unexpectedly, Derrida doesn't answer the question; rather, he chooses to leave the question "suspended" due to the fact that Heidegger's work is emblematic of "a program and a combinatory whose power remains abyssal. . . . It leaves no place open for any arbitrating authority. Nazism was not born in the desert. We all know this, but it has to be constantly recalled."[31] In short, any effort to critique fascism "in the name of an axiomatic—for example, that of democracy or 'human rights'—. . . comes back to the metaphysics of *subjectivity*" and, by extension, to the myth of Logos.[32] Derrida would certainly agree that Blackness is such an axiomatic, an axiomatic firmly grounded in the metaphysics of "soul" and the voluntarism of avant-garde esprit de corps.

Significant objections can be—and have been—raised to Derrida's reading of antifascist critique, objections that are germane to the critique of Black voice and the being of Blackness. One objection concerns theater and performance in movements advocating essentialist/universalist positions. Logocentric discourses rarely accept performance, voice-centered or otherwise, except in the most carefully monitored and deindividualized forms (i.e., the Nuremberg rally), so the complementary presence of the ater and essentialism in the Black Arts Movement would seem paradoxical. Where fit cultural movements such as the BAM that are based on meta physics of subjectivity as described by Derrida, yet determined by the situ ational singularities of performance? A performance of a preexisting text—the favored mode of Black Art, a legacy of its origins in avant-garde jazz—for example, is close ontologically and epistemologically to the "sig nature," a key trope for deconstructive practice. Derrida's "Signature Event Context" argues that performances of written texts are inherently problematic, a paradoxical, unsettling mode of singular repetition that subverts the distinction between writing and performance and, with it, the system of metaphysics in which the signature functions. He writes, "The sign is born at the same time as imagination and memory, at the moment when it is demanded by the absence of the object for present perception."[33] The consequence is that, "[a]cross empirical variations of tone, of voice, etc., eventually of a certain accent, for example, one must be able to recog nize the identity, shall we say, of a signifying form. Why is this identity paradoxically the division or dissociation from itself which will make of this phonic sign a grapheme?"[34] This unstable dynamic between unifi cation and dissociation is characteristic of the global radical movements of the 1960s, of which the BAM was a significant part. The logocentrism of whiteness was undermined by the logocentrism of Blackness.

What Made the Difference? Location— Lorca's Exact Present—*Place*

The BAM far exceeded the American regionalist movement of the nine teenth century in its celebration of the specificity of place. This may be due to a particular cultural and economic logic described by Wahneema Lubiano, who notes that cultural nationalist orientations such as the BAM effectively supplement a lack of actual owned space with the imagination of place. Lacking both its own real estate (with some notable exceptions, such as Teer's theater, which is now a sizable Harlem real-estate venture) and a sure foothold in the strategically important, property-owning, mid dle-class communities of African America, the most advanced segments of the Black Arts Movement chose ephemeral, situational, performative forms of avant-garde poetry and theater in working-class neighborhoods and lumpenproletarian hangouts. African-American communities were dispersed and surrounded. If they were to unify into a truly revolutionary nation, they needed to devise a theory of culture and cultural leadership that could effectively respond to the violent economic, political, and cultural shifts of their times, and do so with a highly nuanced understanding of the local. As Neal puts it, "[T]he context of the work is as important as the work itself."[35]

However, the focus on place was not simply necessity. James Spady argues that the Black Aesthetic was the invention of young intellectuals seeking a communicative ethos that could capture the diversity of African-American culture along the lines described by Cobb. Speaking to Neal's youth in North Philadelphia, Spady writes, "Whether Columbia or Ridge or Susquehanna [streets], they crisscrossed through Nations."[36] Supporting this interpretation, former BAM canvasser Neal writes, "[T]he function of artistic technique and the Black aesthetic is to make the goal of communication and liberation more possible. Therefore, Black poets dig the Blues and Black music in order to find in them the means of making their address to Black America more understandable."[37] The unstable dynamic of unification and dissociation described by Derrida is fully manifest in Neal's statement; the address is always individualized, always diverse, a case, as Julian Mayfield puts it, of one Black Aesthetic touching another.[38]

The cultural nationalists of the BAM went local, creating a "haven" in which Blackness could be sounded without in any way being determined by white expectations.[39] Neal's description of the salutary effects of life in such a haven is worth quoting at length, especially since he emphasizes inner-directed "spirituality":

> The tension, or double consciousness, is most often resolved in violence, simply because the nature of our existence in America has been one of violence. In some cases, the tension resolves in recognizing the beauty and love within Black America itself. No, not a new "Negritude," but a profound sense of a unique and beautiful culture; and a sense that there are many spiritual areas to explore within this culture. There is a kind of separation but there is no tension about it. There is a kind of peace in the separation.[40]

If the voice gives Blackness its body, the spirit gives it its autonomy. Neal perfectly embodied this inspirited materialism. Spady memorably describes him:

Before Larry opened his mouth, he had already asserted the elements of style. Taste setter. He was to the Black Arts Movement of the 1960's what Nelson Boyd was to the Beboppers of the 1940's: the tailored conscious, carrier of the . . . style to those who sought it. For those too crass to recognize Larry's style, he would immediately acknowledge their unhipness: their lack of urban modern civility.

He was, Spady concludes, "Immediate presence and prescience."[41] This is an interesting way to describe *style,* which depends on an absolute poise between community approval and individual transgression, between repetition and difference, the situated and the transcendent. Presence is decidedly other-oriented; presence is self-consciously *performative.*

Black artists saw themselves as leading their communities, but they saw such leadership as fundamentally structured by a relationship of mutual education and transformation manifested most crucially in strict codes of visibility politics (today, we would describe this relationship as "hybrid" or "transcultural"). Their collaborative spirit was as much pulpit-and-pew as it was Maoist, an effort to construct a more situated, embodied "intimacy with the people" by doing things as simple as talking with their neighbors about the sculpture exhibit they installed on a street corner, investigating the politics of racial separatism as both an offshoot and a line of flight from the West, and promoting creativity throughout the African-American community, even recruiting sixteen-year-old playwrights such as Herbie Stokes. Rather than lead the people with exemplary actions (e.g., Huey Newton marching up the stairs of the California capital building with rifle in hand) or codify the image of Black militancy to ensure national news coverage (e.g., the Black Panther "look"), the BAM organizations sought to work in radically democratic fashion inspired by Mao, Antonio Gramsci, and the long-lived tradition of African-American resistance, promoting grassroots political and philosophical activism based around existing cultural structures, particularly those that promoted the gathering together of Black artists and Black and/or soon-to-be-Black audiences. Black voice—Black logocentrism—mediated an explosive dynamic of unification and dissociation. "Blackness" is at once the dreaded transcendent signifier of logocentrism—a universal category that could account for all particular manifestations without in any way being determined by them—but it is also processional, contextual, situational, performative. Neal writes that the BAM had to "create another cosmology springing from [its] own specific grounds, but transcending them as your new world realizes itself."[42]

To further understand the complexity of the movement's logocentrism, we need to understand it both explicitly and tacitly as aiming a blow against nascent forms of reactionary hybridity that in no way threaten the rule of historically oppressive powers in Europe and the United States. Such weak forms of hybridity—not to be mistaken for the strong forms of hybridity theorized in recent critical race theory—sought out by such powers after the legal destruction of racial categories in the 1950s and 1960s, have enabled difference to be at once affirmed and exploited, but without having to substantially address local conditions of poverty, violence, and hopelessness.[43] From this perspective, the reliance of Black Arts activists on essentialist categories can be read as a tactically effective complement to its use of performance; however, even as it empowered Blackness through site-specific manifestation, Black theater also worked to expose and destroy those within the community who supposedly threatened the autonomy of Blackness (as we see in *Sister Son/Ji* or in Neal's sartorial savvy).[44]

This double edge is typical of nationalist movements, which often depend on clear geographical and ethnic boundaries that inevitably victimize those who straddle such boundaries. As Michael Hardt and Antonio Negri note, although deprived as it is of any territorial definition, Black Nationalism presents the "two fundamental progressive functions" of all nationalisms: "the defense and unification of the community."[45] That said, the nationalism of the Black Arts Movement shouldn't be simply equated with the form of Black nationalism described in *Empire*. As Cedric Robinson teaches us, the history of Black radicalism cannot be elided by the Western radical tradition. He suggests to us that the Black voice echoes in tones and in spaces not everyone can hear.[46]

The theorization of soul by Black artists and critics was part of an attempt to define a particular cultural temperament, a common set of experiences and criteria that manifests the diverse social, economic, sexual, geographical, and ideological conditions of African-American community. The Black Arts Movement took this effort to a new level, bringing soul out of African-American neighborhoods and into the public debate on race, colonialism, imperialism, and social justice. The debate over soul significantly impacted the larger debate over the structure and status of the "Black Aesthetic," a philosophical system that not only defined a specific, long-lived set of criteria for producing and recognizing the validity of art, but also encompassed the time- and space-specific cultural, economic, and political demands of the revolution. This is not a contradiction—rather, this robust interplay of transcendent critical principles and highly aware, contextually anchored violence against various kinds of "others" marks the boundaries of an historical "problematic," a set of ideological questions, practical concerns, and popular style codes whose successful instantiation would be judged meticulously by a community that was partly formed by such instantiations.

The Black Aesthetic covers diverse cultural questions and places; for example, the relationship of the intellectual to the masses, the ideological validity of the blues, the diversity of African-American cultural sites and traditions (did Birmingham, Watts, and Howard share the same Blackness?), and the tactical and strategic potential of cultural politics in a period that witnessed the explosive growth of mass media and a concurrent easing of the price and accessibility of text. The question of logocentrism can hardly be addressed in purely philosophical-literary terms. Any effort to understand Black logocentrism must be anchored to these kinds of highly problematic situations.

This is, perhaps, why the theater played such a significant role in the enunciation of Blackness. The Black Aesthetic's critical articulation by Black theater demonstrates how philosophical traditions are structured by the forms of praxis that attempt to negotiate and ultimately resolve hugely complicated political problems. As Peggy Phelan has persuasively argued, the intertwining of politics and theater inevitably raises the question of visibility and the possibility of forms of political resistance that will remain, either by choice or by force, invisible.[47] This opens radical cultural activity to a complicated set of questions and problems. One of the most effective ways to control a community's oral culture is to control its performance practices. If you ban a dance, you effectively ban not only a way of moving, but also a form of communication, and a mode of thinking. Given the highly localized, performative nature of theater, it's no surprise that it has been perceived as inherently disruptive of authority. Theater for the BAM was the front line of an organizational revolution that sought to wrest away from white power the control of artistic experience and a wide range of performance techniques. If theater (and poetry) could be broken free, a fundamental goal had been achieved. And yet, at the same time, Black theater served to effectively police its own borders.

When Robert Macbeth declared Black cultural activists "environmentalists of the arts," he was declaring a total revolutionizing of cultural production, but also, I think, raising awareness of the way such a revolution could turn ugly when turned inward (a lesson he surely learned when the

New Lafayette was burned to the ground in '67 and threatened with bombs a year later). For those who wish to consider the interrelationships of text, context, and theory—exactly the project I'm pursuing here—the question of *how* difference is articulated in specific locations is the fundamental question. The local conventions of difference play out into all kinds of highly reticulated sociopolitical structures that threaten even deconstruction's capacity to describe (for example, intense forms of nationalism or chauvinism like those found in the works of the otherwise exemplary philosophers Martin Heidegger and Paul de Man). What is the difference in logocentrism that it is itself unable to reflect?

The BAM demonstrates a characteristically postmodern organizational strategy, the consequence of its participants' practical and theoretical experience with social realism, site-specific art, trade unionism, and (precocious achievement!) the work of Italian Marxists such as Gramsci. Ernesto Laclau and Chantal Mouffe, also influenced by Gramsci, would most likely agree with the description of the BAM as an effective response to "the transition towards a new situation, characterized by the essential instability of political spaces, in which the very identity of the forces in struggle is submitted to constant shifts, and calls for an incessant process of redefinition."[48] As Leandre Jackson notes, the Black Aesthetic is "a position and stance that views an apprehension of symbol, historical context, and informed critical philosophy as absolutely key" in comprehending the structure and impact of Black art.[49] The soul is not only a transcendent signifier (and it is definitely that), but also an historical tradition and an organizational strategy. Moreover, it is the only signifier that rivals the dollar as the leading ideological icon of the West (is the soul expressed in jihad or in profit?).

Laclau and Mouffe's *Hegemony and Socialist Strategy: Toward a Radical Democratic Politics* directs us to think of cultural leadership by vanguard groups as occurring on a terrain beyond the categories of traditional bourgeois-liberal thought and its radical alternatives. They write that "behind the concept of 'hegemony' lies hidden something more than a type of political relation complementary to the basic categories of Marxist theory. In fact, it introduces a logic of the social which is incompatible with those categories."[50] They systematically demonstrate that we can no longer "maintain the conception of subjectivity and classes elaborated by Marxism, nor its vision of the historical course of capitalist development, nor, of course, the conception of communism as a transparent society from which antagonisms have disappeared."[51] Derrida's discussion of spirit in *Specters of Marx,* which enthusiastically notes Laclau and Mouffe's book, is intended to define a global politics that doesn't fall prey to this unilaterality.[52] Such a politics constantly redefines itself; it is a politics. The spirit of Marxism is revolutionary because it is a practice that operates within a changing tradition of memorialization and mourning.

As has been noted by many scholars, the theater has always played a significant role in the examination, ratification, and critique of its society's most basic beliefs about ontology, identity, and community. Anna Scott's point is relevant here; she identifies the movement (the "Black arts makers") with those individuals who "identify the process at work rather than solidify the codes into a fixed 'read,' thereby destroying their potential to traverse time, space, language, and national boundaries."[53] Of particular significance is her recognition that in performance communities "recollection is purposeful and productive."[54] Spirit is not a transcendent entity running roughshod over earthly difference, but an immanent quality of action best manifested in those arts that rely on a close congregation of artists and audiences. Soul is not a transcendent state of being, but rather a coherent, situated expression of culture, a realization of difference that can enable both separation from the dominant culture and oppression of heterogeneous elements within the African-American diaspora. It is this paradoxical quality that enables even a sensitive, tolerant critic like Julian Mayfield to proclaim, "I cannot—will not—define my Black Aesthetic, nor will I allow it to be defined for me," and yet to assert that it is exactly such a self-transforming aesthetic that can most efficiently destroy "this land of faggotry."[55] The purposeful and productive delineation, criticism, and instantiation of Afrocentric commitment—this was both the power and the Achilles' heel of the Black Arts Movement.

James Stewart links the BAM's separatist philosophy to a profoundly ephemeral material base. His critique of the covertly linear, qualitative logic of white-capitalist cultural production begins by addressing the question of cosmological models. He writes, "It is imperative that we construct models with different basic assumptions" than "white paradigms or models," which "do not correspond to the realities of black existence." "Our models," he writes, "must be consistent with a black style" reminiscent of West African worship systems, which do not differentiate between the art object and the process of making art.[56] He argues that Black art must be like the legendary temples of mud "that vanish in the rainy seasons and are erected elsewhere."[57] "Revolution is fluidity," Stewart argues.[58] Black art is the latest in a long, continuous line of cultural moments that links Asian mystical traditions, Afro-American blues riffs, the Black Baptist church, New Jazz, and Voudoun. In its paradoxical engagement with and separation from the West, the line is best characterized as a genealogy of "misfits estranged from the white cultural present."[59]

Fred Moten has noted that current critical and artistic representations of "soul" must inevitably tangle with the question of totality, that great bugbear of postmodern philosophy and great hope of nationalists:

> This question [of soul] is all bound up with the . . . question of soul's relation to black identity and to the question of whether or not that identity can be properly understood as totality. If it is, what is the nature of that totality? Or, rather, how is [B]lackness situated in the oscillation any totality instantiates between singularity and multiplicity? Is [B]lackness univocal, and is soul the true marker of that unity? Given the arguments regarding the constructedness or essentiality of identity, the question of soul is vexed. Is it a function of blood or of historical contingency? And if it is the latter, how fundamentally is soul tied to [B]lack pain even as it is figured as both a product and producer of [B]lack pleasure?[60]

This series of questions marks, for Moten, an unbridgeable conceptual gap at the heart of Black studies; however, Moten will attempt neither to bridge nor to deconstruct this gap. He sees this emptiness as a source of questions and as a tonal model (blood, history, pain, pleasure) for the instantiation of Blackness.

Moten neither deconstructs nor stabilizes the distinction between interiority and exteriority; rather, it is put into critical *play* (as, say, an aesthetic principle or a historiographical concept). We see this in Bullins's *How Do You Do?* as character and dialogue twine and untwine, as if in a masque. Likewise, we see it in *Sister Son/Ji*, as the performer transforms idiom and identity fluidly. Moten comprehends both Derridean and African-American aesthetics and ethics. Moten, like Derrida, is interested in soul as a difference that is a "condition of possibility constituting unity and totality and, at the same time, their essential limits."[61] But Moten is also interested in the immanent aesthetic practice of the most advanced trends in Black music. He notes in jazz composer Cecil Taylor's work an impossibility that is not literary at all: "No reading because the understanding of literary experience which (a) reading implies is exceeded in the enactment of what [Taylor's 1988 composition] *Chinampas* is and what *Chinampas* demands:

improvisation. . . . Words don't go there. Is it only music, only sound, that goes there?"[62] Moten, just as Neal does, reflects on the *nonbeing* at the heart of soul grounded in forms that exist somewhere between the ideal and the material. Soul is a foundational—and for that reason not conceivable—difference, a differentiation-in-situation between the totality of African-American history and culture and its idiosyncratic, singular manifestations. Thus, we find here yet another subtle but significant difference between Black voice and Western spiritual and philosophical traditions, traditions we normally associate with notions of fullness and "presence."

In the Black Aesthetic, we find a vision of the nation that is close in shape to what Moten calls "ensemble." A term borrowed from the aesthetic/organizational tradition of post–World War II jazz, Moten defines it as "the improvisation of and through totality and singularity in and as both phenomenological description and morphological prescription." The nation is like that poised, ephemeral, memorial community of players, listeners, and critics that exists in the performed moment of the jazz composition. It is "an extension and improvisation of the tradition of a singularist and differentiated thinking of the ensemble, most particularly as that tradition—at its highest level of intensity and internal tension—begins to be articulated through calls for its dissolution or continuance in the impossible language prompted by the incommensurable conjunction of community and difference."

The terms of the Black Aesthetic cannot, finally, be defined in such a way that we can cleanse them of chauvinism, just as surely as Derrida has proven incapable of dealing with the concrete, instantiated political activities of Heidegger. The belief that community exists beyond the fragility, misprisions, and insufficiencies of writing can justify the demonization of difference. It can also affirm, articulate, and revolutionize the differences between the oppressor and the oppressed and highlight differences *within* the community that are empowering and progressive. The relative significance of these positions is, in the end, undecidable outside of their instantiation in context and on view, undecidable outside the theater of Blackness.

NOTES

My thanks (once again) to David Krasner for his criticisms and suggestions.

1. Larry Neal, "And Shine Swam On," *Visions of a Liberated Future: Black Arts Movement Writings*, ed. Michael Schwartz (New York: Thunder's Mouth Press, 1989), 653. Qtd. in Peter Bailey, "The Black Theater," *Ebony* 24 (August 1969), 132.

2. See Mike Sell, "The Black Arts Movement: Performance, Neo-Orality, and the Destruction of the 'White Thing,'" in *African American Performance and Theatre History: A Critical Reader,* ed. Harry J. Elam, Jr. and David Krasner (New York: Oxford University Press, 2001); and "[Ed.] Bullins as Editorial Performer: Textual Power and the Limits of Performance in the Black Arts Movement," *Theatre Journal* 53, no. 3 (October 2001): 411–28.

3. Robert J. C. Young, *Postcolonialism: A Historical Introduction* (New York: Blackwell, 2001), 171, 169.

4. Sonia Sanchez, *Sister Son/Ji,* in *New Plays from the Black Theatre,* ed. Ed Bullins (New York: Bantam, 1969).

5. Charlie Cobb, "Ain't That a Groove," in *Black Fire,* ed. LeRoi Jones and Larry Neal (New York: William Morrow, 1968), 524.

6. Ibid., 522.

7. Ibid., 523.

8. Larry Neal, "The Ethos of the Blues," in *Visions of a Liberated Future,* 107–17.

9. Ed Bullins, *How Do You Do? A Nonsense Drama,* in Jones and Neal, *Black Fire,* 595–604.

10. Ibid., 602.

11. Federico Garcia Lorca, "Theory and Practice of Soul," trans. Ted Jones, *Liberator,* May 1966, 13.

12. Ibid.

13. See Stanley Crouch's typically tendentious "The Incomplete Turn of Larry Neal," in Neal, *Visions of a Liberated Future,* 3–6; Henry Louis Gates, Jr., "Black Creativity: On the Cutting Edge," *Time,* October 10 1994, 75; Houston Baker, *Blues, Ideology, and Afro-American Literature: A Vernacular Theory* (Chicago: University of Chicago Press, 1984), 74ff.; and Amiri Baraka, interview by David Barsamian, *The LeRoi Jones/Amiri Baraka Reader,* ed. Williams J. Harris (New York: Thunder's Mouth Press, 1999), 250–51.

14. Lorca, "Theory and Practice of Soul," 13.

15. Young, *Postcolonialism,* 2.

16. Baraka, *Jones/Baraka Reader,* 249.

17. Joyce Green, "Black Romanticism," in *The Black Woman,* ed. Toni Cade (New York: Mentor Books, 1970), 139.

18. Larry Neal, "And Shine Swam On," *Visions of a Liberated Future: Black Arts Movement Writings* (New York: Thunder's Mouth Press, 1989), 16.

19. Etheridge Knight and Sanford Pinsker, "A Conversation," *Black American Literature Forum* 18, no. 1 (1984): 12.

20. See Sell, "Bullins as Editorial Performer."

21. Neal, "The Black Arts Movement," *Drama Review* 12, no. 4 (1968): 68–69.

22. Ibid., 69.

23. Jacques Derrida, from *Of Grammatology,* in *Critical Theory Since 1965,* ed. Hazard Adams and Leroy Searle (Tallahassee: Florida State University Press, 1986), 103.

24. For an exemplary text, see Derrida, *Dissemination,* trans. Barbara Johnson (Chicago: University of Chicago Press, 1982).

25. For discussion of the notion of *habitus* in relationship to Heidegger, see Pierre Bourdieu, *The Political Ontology of Martin Heidegger,* trans. Peter Collier (Stanford: Stanford University Press, 1991).

26. Theodor Adorno and Max Horkheimer, *The Dialectic of Enlightenment*, trans. John Cumming (New York: Continuum, 1989).

27. Victor Farias, *Heidegger and Nazism* (Philadelphia: Temple University Press, 1989).

28. David Wood, introduction to *Of Derrida, Heidegger, and Spirit*, ed. David Wood (Evanston, Ill.: Northwestern University Press, 1993), 2–3.

29. Jacques Derrida, *Of Spirit: Heidegger and the Question*, trans. Geoffrey Bennington and Rachel Bowlby (Chicago: University of Chicago Press, 1991), 39.

30. Ibid., 74.

31. Ibid., 109.

32. Ibid., 40.

33. Jacques Derrida, "Signature Event Context," in *A Derrida Reader: Between the Blinds*, ed. Peggy Kamuf (New York: Columbia University Press, 1991), 88.

34. Ibid., 94.

35. Neal, "And Shine Swam On," 22.

36. James Spady, *Larry Neal: Liberated Black Philly Poet with a Blues Streak of Mellow Wisdom* (Philadelphia: PC International Press, 1989), 5.

37. Neal, "Any Day Now: Black Art and Black Liberation," *Ebony*, August 1969, 56. Stewart, senior member of the Muntu group, had been part of the social realist art movement in Philadelphia centered in Beacon Hill, was conversant in the Mexican muralist tradition, and had been an activist in the trade unionist movement. After reading Harold Cruse's "Revolutionary Nationalism and the Afro-American," *Studies on the Left* 2, no. 3 (1962), he became a cultural nationalist. See Spady, *Larry Neal*, 11–12.

38. Julian Mayfield, "You Touch My Black Aesthetic and I'll Touch Yours," in *The Black Aesthetic*, ed. Addison Gayle, Jr. (New York: Anchor, 1972).

39. Neal, "And Shine Swam On," 15.

40. Ibid.

41. Spady, *Larry Neal*, 29.

42. Neal, "The Black Writers Role, II: Ellison's Zoot Suit," in *Visions of a Liberated Future*, 53.

43. Concerning "weak" and "strong" forms of hybridity, Michael Hardt and Antonio Negri write, "The affirmation of hybridities and the free play of differences across boundaries . . . is liberatory only in a context where power poses hierarchy exclusively through essential identities, binary divisions, and stable oppositions. . . . In fact, Empire too is bent on doing away with those modern forms of sovereignty [i.e., those based on essential identities such as racial biologism] and on setting differences to play across boundaries." Hardt and Negri, *Empire* (Cambridge: Harvard University Press, 2001), 142.

44. Diana Fuss argues that the privileged nature of the category of essence allows it to be "deployed effectively in the service of both idealist and materialist, progressive and reactionary, mythologizing and resistive discourses." *Essentially Speaking: Feminism, Nature, and Difference* (London: Routledge, 1989), xii.

45. Hardt and Negri, *Empire*, 108.

46. Cedric J. Robinson, *Black Marxism: The Making of the Black Radical Tradition* (London: Zed Press, 1983).

47. Peggy Phelan, *Unmarked: The Politics of Performance* (New York: Routledge, 1993).

48. Ernesto Laclau and Chantal Mouffe, *Hegemony and Socialist Strategy: Towards a Radical Democratic Politics* (New York: Verso, 1985), 151.

49. Leandre Jackson, "Conjuring New Text for Context: Spady's Neal Essays," in Spady, *Larry Neal,* 18.

50. Laclau and Mouffe, *Hegemony and Socialist Strategy,* 3.

51. Ibid., 4.

52. Derrida, *Specters of Marx: The State of the Debt, the Work of Mourning, and the New International,* trans. Peggy Kamuf (New York: Routledge, 1994), 180 n. 31.

53. Anna Scott, "It's All in the Timing: The Latest Moves, James Brown's Grooves, and the Seventies Race-Consciousness Movement in Salvador, Bahia-Brazil," in *Soul: Black Power, Politics, and Pleasure,* ed. Monique Guillory and Richard C. Green (New York: New York University Press, 1997).

54. Ibid., 20.

55. Mayfield, "You Touch," 27, 25.

56. James T. Stewart, "The Development of the Black Revolutionary Artist," in Jones and Neal, *Black Fire,* 3–4.

57. Ibid., 3–4.

58. Ibid., 6.

59. Ibid.

60. Fred Moten, "Review of *Soul: Black Power, Politics, and Pleasure,*" *TDR* 43, no. 4 (1999): 169.

61. Rodolphe Gasché, *The Tain of the Mirror: Derrida and the Philosophy of Reflection* (Cambridge: Harvard University Press, 1988), 88.

62. Fred Moten, "Sound in Florescence: Cecil Taylor Floating Garden," in *Sound States: Innovative Poetics and Acoustical Technologies,* ed. Adalaide Morris (Chapel Hill: University of North Carolina Press, 1997), 213.

~

FIFTEEN

Theatricality, Convention, and the Principle of Charity

Michael L. Quinn

One of the crucial words that remains in the vocabularies of both the practical theater and theater theory, though in a fairly unexamined state, is *convention*. From the sociological standpoint of Elizabeth Burns the "theatrical metaphor" generated conventions that served as constitutive agreements for knowledge.[1] Yet this metaphor is also, for her, a "mode of perception," a basic phenomenological category like those described by Ernst Cassirer or Susanne K. Langer, which produces the social concepts that make theater—and any other concomitant forms of analogical "theatricality" in other contexts—possible.[2] Theater for Burns, then, is not a kind of knowledge but a perspective on knowledge, grounded in a convention that is comparable to other conventions of philosophy.

The conventional theory of theatricality enabled not only the construction of American dramaturgical sociology, as in the work of Erving Goffman and Raymond Cohen, but also a number of other, more artistically oriented kinds of discourse.[3] So, for example, the idea of conventional theatricality has provided a premise for arguments about spectatorship and authenticity in painting for art historians like Svetlana Alpers and Michael Fried.[4] In terms of Marxist literary criticism theatricality amounts to the imagination, for critics like Terry Eagleton, of a history that is conceived outside, or logically prior to, ideology.

The parallel I am pursuing, then, may be schematized as follows:

history/ideology → dramatic text → dramatic production
history → ideology → literary text

The literary text, that is to say, produces ideology (itself a production) in a way analogous to the operations of dramatic production on dramatic text. And just as the dramatic production's relation to its text reveals the text's internal relations to its "world" under the form of its own *constitution* of them, the literary text's relation to ideology so constitutes that ideology as to reveal something of its relations to history.[5]

The presence of such an analogizing concept of convention may be most pervasive of all in the thought of Saussurean structuralism, in which the premise of an arbitrary sign often leads to the assumption that "unmotivated" signs, and even tenuously motivated ones, are consequently aspects of the conventional structure of language that are historically negotiated.[6] In its more extreme forms this attitude about the negotiability of conventions, such as the psychoanalytic version employed by Coward and Ellis in *Language and Materialism,* results in a hopelessly conflicted account of human action and judgment.[7]

Deconstruction has only deepened the widespread conviction that conventional signs are negotiable, and in this case the relativist critique of signs is sometimes extended—though not by Derrida—to the concept of truth itself, a view that even in its most persuasive constructions can make no sense.[8] I propose to explore the very idea of a conventional theatricality, for the interpretive process of taking conventions for granted seems to me to be very suggestive for semiotic theater theory, and particularly for the understanding of some rather extreme challenges to the possibility of truthful communication.[9]

Quince, Questions, and Coordination

David Lewis defines conventions within a larger field of what he calls "coordination problems," or "situations of interdependent decision . . . in which coincidence of interest predominates," that is, in which people "have a common interest in all doing the same of one of several alternative actions."[10] Coordination—that is, mutual understanding—might be reached tacitly, through a process of thought that converges in a unique, commonly conceived, salient action. Most often, though, coordination problems are solved through precedents. Fictional precedents, and those negotiated through language, are as good as experience. And the more precedents for a situation, however various or analogical, the more likely that a "regularity of behavior" will emerge.[11] This regularity, then, is what

Lewis calls a convention. In relation to Burns's sociology of knowledge, a theater and its theatricality are thus matters of precedent and common understanding; they are what they have been and what people think they are, and they amount to however people treat them.

What are some of the problems in this view of convention? Firstly, the question of common interest is crucial; how do we know which interests people have in common in a complicated social situation like a supposed theater performance? What sorts of conventional steps, such as contracts, will be necessary to secure a common understanding? How can this sociology of knowledge admit a definition of the theater that will not be historically nonsensical if the objects of its definition should radically change? Conversely, can there be theatricality without normative precedent? Or if theatricality's conventional definition is so purely normative, how many conventional theaters might there be? I would like to argue that it is a simple idea of the theater that makes the idea of its negotiated organization possible. This argument rambles a little, but I hope that eventually it stands on its points.

One classic example of the sorts of communication problems that theater artists try to solve through convention comes in questions Quince fields from his fellow mechanicals, as they arrange their court performance in *A Midsummer Night's Dream*. J. L. Styan touched on this topic in an antisemiotic defense of Shakespeare's theatrical mystery when he asked, "When does a convention cease to be a convention[?]" so I will add Styan's question to Quince's, while trying not to get too involved in the interpretation of Shakespeare.[12] What *kinds* of questions do the mechanicals ask, and what are their solutions?

In act 3, scene 1, Quince sets the woodland stage: "This is a marvelous convenient place for our rehearsal. This green plot shall be our stage, this hawthorn brake our tiring house; and we shall do it in action, as we will do it before the duke." These decisions assume the precedent of a theater, for which Quince finds resemblances in the natural scene. Bottom then remarks, "There are things in this comedy of *Pyramus and Thisbe* that will never please; First Pyramus must draw a sword to kill himself; which the ladies cannot abide. How answer you that?" Snug has a similar concern about his part, "Will not the ladies be afeared of the lion?" The players are anxious about the coordination of their effects with their audience; the idea of fiction, strange to them, may be strange to others—especially to gentlewomen; no precedent is assumed. Consequently, Bottom prescribes a prologue, which still sounds like a good idea later on when Quince must resolve "two hard things; that is, to bring the moonlight into a chamber," and to show "a wall in the great chamber," through which the lovers talk. So as it turns out, rather than depend upon any less certain coordination of their actions, the mechanicals resolve all their difficulties through narrative exegesis; that is, they translate their stage images into explanations. Quince supposes that Moonshine "must come in with a bush of thorns and a lantern, and say he comes to disfigure or to present the person of moonshine." In performance, act 5, scene 1, a lunar icon alone is not judged sufficient, and so poor, heckled Moonshine is at pains to explain himself to his wisecracking crowd: "All I have to say is to tell you that the lantern is the moon; I, the man in the moon; this bush my thorn bush, and this dog my dog." Bottom's idea for the wall's chink is equally simple and charming when performed as he suggests through Snout's fingers (though it can also be slightly more comic and ridiculous if staged, as it sometimes is, with that hand between the player's legs).

This modest court performance, strangely enough, meets all of Lewis's requirements for conventional communication. The players have an interest in common; if all goes well, the ambitious group of "hard-handed men" can expect royal favor, with Bottom topping the list as "six-pence-a-day" (act 6, sc. 2). The prologues serve as contracts to secure a common understanding of the performance. But the range of precedents available to the mechanicals is vastly different from the competence of their audience; so in their attitudes toward the agreements—e.g. in matter like genre—the audience and the players find their greatest difficulties of coordination. As Theseus notes straightaway (act 5, sc. 1):

> A *tedious brief scene of young Pyramus*
> A*nd his love Thisbe; very tragical mirth.*
> Merry and tragical! Tedious and brief!
> That is hot ice and wondrous strange snow.
> How shall we find the concord of this discord?

The difficulty of the players comes not in their failure to communicate, but in that they communicate so much more earnestly than the situation requires. Conventions are not usually arranged situations of understanding; they are assumed understandings, and the amateur players assume too little in the context of a play by Shakespeare in which very much—mistaken identities, fairies, magical transformations, and more—is merely taken for granted despite its real-world implausibility. Quince's "negotiated" rehearsal hall in the wood actually *is* a stage, so his perceptions of similarity are only half-completed recognitions of identity; in a theater he makes believe a glade is that theater. When shortly faced with the less explicable "Bottom translation," Quince can only cry "O monstrous! O strange!" and flee the stage; he has no coordinating precedents to help unravel this reversal of impersonation.[13] To answer Styan's question, then, a convention stops being a convention when it stops facilitating coordinated understanding, and Quince's questions, however quaint, have lost none of their theatrical relevance through time.

Evident Conventions and Communicative Action

Yet there must be some conventional alternative to the labored explanations of Shakespeare's clowns, and it seems to me that there may be such a potential in another kind of clown, Bill Irwin. In his dramatic compositions, Irwin tends to let the conventions form as the action is performed— sometimes with explanations, but most often relying solely on the evidence of repetition.[14] In *Largely New York* Irwin's remote control establishes the way precedents for the unique conventions of the performance are constructed throughout his work. Whether or not the engineering of a remote control is understood by an audience, and whether or not the audience has ever seen a remote control in operation before, Irwin's opening sequence clearly establishes the remote control as a semiotic "index," as a pointing device that seems to raise and lower the curtain, and generally to control the stage however Irwin wishes.[15] Yet this constructed convention, which operates not through agreement but through the repeated demonstration of its working, functions as effectively as any prologue for the establishment of precedents that can then go comically awry; soon the remote is pointed, pressed, and the wrong things happen— swamping a confused Irwin in velour or lifting him marvelously into the fly-space.

In his first evening-length entertainment, *The Regard of Flight,* part of the fun in Irwin's dramaturgy was a comic "laying bare of the device."[16] Such effects as his miraculous antigravitational illusions, sweeping an upright body beyond the limits of possible balance, would subsequently be explained by the stage manager as conventional effects of the "lean-heel shoe." Irwin's drama doesn't explain *everything*, like the mysterious force that repeatedly threatens to suck him under the curtain into apparent oblivion, or the inexplicable power of invoking "Shakespeare" while brandishing a volume of the plays—a ploy that keeps the play's pesky formalist critic at bay for quite a while. Many of the performance's conventional tricks are so difficult that only a clown as accomplished as Irwin could do them well. Yet even the best devices, like the minitrampoline that Irwin uses to elude the critic in a chase scene, seem to wear out over time (until eventually he gets caught). Irwin, who dramatizes the construction of conventions, and makes a theme of explaining them, also dramatizes their apparent dissolution, as they become "too conventional" to be of interest.[17] Only academics, like the inquisitive, robed chorus in *Largely New York,* are sufficiently stimulated by the ordinary theater to consider its investigation and take a plunge into its structure—or as Irwin's scholars do, into its orchestra pit.

There seems to be some difference, then, between conventions that sustain the theater as such, the sorts of conventions—like writing or impersonation—that Heideggerians call "primordial," and the temporary set of devices that the formalist concept of convention implies.[18] In *The Regard of Flight* Bill Irwin mostly just wants to be able to dance—to perform movement that is not about anything in particular so much as it is about dancing itself, performing the intuition that one might have an idea of the dance before a dance about anything in particular could even be conceived. Accordingly, Herbert Blau, one of Irwin's first directors, proposes that "what is universal in performance is the consciousness of performance."[19] Rather than view this profundity as a tautology, it might be better to consider this idea of performance as something like a logical simple, to which point an analysis of theatricality must return from time to time if only to remember what the thought is about.

Yet consciousness alone is not quite a convention. For Blau's theory to be a universal of performance, consciousness of performance must somehow be shared, that is, communicated, even if only for the ritual purposes of confirmation.[20] Successful communication has not been a popular topic in the age of deconstruction, which is predicated on an argument about the failure of representations to be the things they represent (even in the case of a performer like Bill Irwin who says to his critic, "No, I'm not the other one. You see, it's modern. I'm not anyone.")[21] In terms of the development of theory, it's time now to pay some attention to the shadow side of the failure of representation, that is, to the concept that makes the very supposition of failure possible.

There is an inside-out to deconstructive arguments about truth that is brought out by the extent to which people agree about them; that is, at some level of understanding deconstruction communicates to people in a convincing way, and its arguments about the impossibility of representing truth have themselves been accepted as true.[22] Deconstructive writing quite rightly argued against cultural preferences for different kinds of signs, against specific exemplary definitions of truth like the cogito or the presence of the voice that worked as epistemological rhetorics to distribute power unevenly.[23] Yet deconstructive discourse analysis, which suggests like W. V. O. Quine that truth may be exemplified in different conventional patterns, still ultimately depends for its coherence on Alfred Tarski's primordial "convention T," an utterly banal, "pre-theoretical" concept of truth that is simply the comparison of a sign's claims to its objects, however those might be constituted.[24] Truth is not singular by relational, a judgment of coherent correspondence that assumes nothing like empirical objectivity. Tarski's may be the sort of dull theory that produces statements like "Snow is White" is true if and only if snow is white, but such basic making and matching must still be an aspect of truth-judgments in any context of semiotic activity if successful communication is conceivably to occur.[25] Since this idea—of similarity—may seem strange to those who have learned that its cognitive partner, that is, that signs are systems of differences, I'll digress in a moment into a couple of examples.

Donald Davidson takes the argument one step farther, asserting, "In sharing a language, in whatever sense this is required for communication, we share a picture of the world that must, in its large features, be true."[26] Without this basic assumption, and without successful communication, the world would simply be unintelligible. Even so politically cautious a theorist as Terry Eagleton has recently endorsed this view.[27] But how, then, do we work out the political problems of sharing this language? And must it be a natural language, as Davidson suggests, or might it not also be some other sign system that works "like a language?"

Israel Horovitz has dramatized at least two possible outcomes of the problems of language sharing. In one play, *The Indian Wants the Bronx*, two young New York men meet an East Indian, Gupta, who needs directions to his son's house. Rather than help the Indian by reading the directions on his note or calling his son, the two torment him, making him a pawn in their own masculinity games by deriding him as a "Turk." The Americans make no effort to understand his language. When one man goes off, the less aggressive of the two begins to speak more sensibly to Gupta, who recognizes some of his words and tries to understand him;

they almost become friends. But the young man, Joey, is ultimately too suspicious, afraid that the Indian will reveal his kindness to his friend, who would interpret it as weakness; when the other man returns he torments Gupta a while longer, calling the Indian's son and then severing the phone line, punishing the stranger because Gupta doesn't understand their American games, and eventually even cutting Gupta's hand with a switchblade. The short play ends with Gupta alone on stage, holding the telephone receiver—with its dangling wire—out to the audience while repeating the only English words he knows, "Thank you."[28] There is no "coordination," no common interest, in Gupta's experience with the young men, though precedents are established for his later judgments, which are likely to be inspired by fear. Yet beyond the violence, there is another political problem to consider. Though Lewis doesn't consider it an ethical problem, the coordination of behavior may be an ethical imperative, even if the agreement of both subjects is to work separately. The absolute refusal to attempt to share languages, which is the bully's position in *The Indian Wants the Bronx,* is one of the crucial concerns of communicative action theory, for sincerity and access to communication are the foundations, for theorists like Karl-Otto Apel, of a new a priori ethics that makes the exchange of thought a new kind of virtue.[29]

Horovitz has written another play, *The Primary English Class,* in which issues of translation and language sharing remain fundamental.[30] None of the five students in the class speak the same language; their American teacher speaks only English, the janitor is Polish, and consequently they are so little able to coordinate their behavior that they can scarcely convene. Nevertheless there are moments of comprehension, points of contact like the moment when the characters learn that they are all named, coincidentally, with words like *La Poubelle* and *Patumiera* that all translate as "wastebasket." The drama of this comedy is the difficulty of translation, the way simple dangers, like choking on a raisin, might be avoided if people could talk. Most of the characters in *The Primary English Class* give up, but at the play's end Debbie Wastba, the teacher whose family shortened their name, has discovered a new commitment to communication. Teaching and translating, which constitute community, exemplify the sort of communicative politics that Jürgen Habermas has advocated to transform contemporary social theory.[31] And Horovitz changes his own attitude toward translation in the two plays; in *The Indian Wants the Bronx* Gupta's lines are translated only for the actors, in the stage directions of the text, while in *The Primary English Class* an invisible translator speaks key lines to the audience in English, so that the spectators can understand the specific problems and the scope of the missed communications on stage.

Translation between relatively similar languages is not such a difficult problem; different webs of belief may not match up exactly, but both webs are largely true, and that largess should allow sufficient contacts between the two for semantic equivalences to begin to be constructed. This is not to say that poetries can be so easily translated into poetic equivalents, but rather to argue that the difficulties of equivalence can be explained, and that this explanation proves their cognitive translatability, however awkward the text itself might be. Ordinary translation, like tacit thought, becomes a scene for the coordination of behavior, for establishing the regularities that enable collective actions like the making of theater.

Flora, Interpretation, and the Principle of Charity

More difficult, from Donald Davidson's standpoint, is the problem of "radical interpretation," the understanding of strange communications. These might come within a language or between languages, so translation often involves radical interpretation, too. And such judgments also inform attempts to understand communications that function like language, such as the gestural acrobatics of Bill Irwin. In any case the simple theory of truth is basic to the conduct of understanding; rather than truth being a concrete specific of a single given language or behavior, it is a convention, variable in time, place, and expression, assumed by all communications. Radical interpretation, then, for Davidson, tries to hold

> belief constant as far as possible while solving for meaning. This is accompanied by assigning truth conditions to alien sentences that make native speakers right when plausibly possible, according, of course, to our own view of what is right. What justifies the procedure is the fact that disagreement and agreement alike are intelligible only against a background of massive agreement.[32]

Interpretation then involves building up an understanding impression of beliefs like those known to us that are expressed in a communication, "whether or not we agree about them."[33] Strange communications are only more difficult cases for an interpretive attitude that Davidson, Quine, and others call, after Neil Wilson, "the principle of charity."[34] Such a principle assumes that the beliefs of a speaker are mostly true and coherent, and that consequently the listener is justified in lending to that expression his or her own background of beliefs. I should make it clear that the politics of this position are not condescending, despite the charity of listeners like Theseus in *Midsummer;* rather, the assumption is that everyone is making sense, probably making sense differently, and so strange speech deserves a hearing. The truth convention will eventually prove, through the contradictions and incoherences of irrationality, whether the strange speech is mistaken or deceptive; in other words, suspicion takes a little longer than generosity, and complete validity is not necessarily prior to—or even necessary for—understanding.

This model of interpretive charity and understanding clearly applies to a wide range of human problems.[35] One of the ways to test its extent, then, is to move outside of strictly human concerns, to cases of even stranger communication; enter Flora the Elephant. In Martha Clarke's *Endangered Species,* the choreography plays out several important human problems, like racial politics and sexuality, but the most compelling communications on stage come from the strange presence of several unusual animals: Bert the miniature goat, Tony the Capuchin monkey, and especially Flora, a young female African elephant from the circus of the same name. Given Davidson's assertions that animals are rational, though lacking in coherent beliefs because of their lack of a language, I would like eventually to reconsider a question of access to theatrical conventions that was raised by Bert the phenomenologist, that is, Bert States.[36] Nor do I quite agree with Davidson's perspective; true, animals lack, by and large, a language of their own, yet intelligent animals, like Flora, may be charitable enough to borrow the languages of people. In relation to language, animals are mostly listeners and interpreters, talking back by other means.

Martha Clarke, I should probably add, loves Flora and the animals. The conception and title of her piece come from a conviction about their value, and their interest in performance—a kind of exaggerated charity. Bert States, on the other hand, assumes that the dog on stage is a dog-in-itself, charming because it doesn't know it's in a play, "blissfully above, or beneath, the business of playing, and we find ourselves cheering its performance precisely because it isn't one."[37] There is something to States's argument that the principal interest of the dog is its dogness, but I also think that this *epochē* makes the dog too isolated; dogs, if they are anything like the labrador I know, are interested in communication. If the dog doesn't know it's in a play, part of our delight might come from its bewilderment as it sincerely tries to understand the situation; canine indifference might come later, then, once the dog gives up, or the actors begin to ignore it. The dog probably *does* know how to play, might have its own precedents for play, and consequently might actually need to be *cast,* as a specially competent dog (like the one that inspired Goethe's resignation from the Weimar Court Theater).

This more particular, engaged, and charitable attitude toward individuated animals is the one adopted by Martha Clarke toward her friend the elephant:

> Flora is pre-adolescent. She's patent leather shoes and white ankle socks. She still likes dolls. Even though she's an elephant, she knows she's on the cusp; she's maturing. She opens suitcases and throws clothes around. She has a party. Some of it's fanciful. She's trained.[38]

Contra States, I think from Clarke's description that Flora knows about play, and knows she's being watched; she meets Blau's basic convention for universal play, and might even get Kendall Walton's premise of "make-believe" as a universal of representation.[39] The difficulty is that Flora doesn't seem to know quite *which* play she's in, or *whose,* or *what* to represent. Like the monkey, whose part was eventually cut because he tended to improvise (i.e., "couldn't take direction"), the secondary conventions are the ones that baffle Flora; says Clarke, "When she knows a routine too well, she starts to play."[40] Consequently, carefully controlled in a few moves, including tricks like closing some large doors with her tusks on cue, Flora's performance in *Endangered Species,* according to Frank Rich, "earns the audience's raptest attention and warmest applause."[41] Maybe it was Flora's bio in the program that helped the audience toward this charitable interpretation of Flora's "fetching if enigmatic" presence, since the play itself was a critical failure.

Because animals are often so charitable, they may give us the idea that we know exactly what it must be like to be one of them; one of Shklovsky's best examples of a formalist convention is from Tolstoy's story told through the eyes of a horse. But this kind of complete transformation is not quite possible, as Thomas Nagel explains in "What is It Like to Be a Bat?":

> It will not help to try to imagine that one has webbing on one's arms, which enables one to fly around at dusk and down catching insects in

one's mouth; that one has very poor vision, and perceives the surrounding world by a system of reflected high-frequency sound signals; and that one spends the day hanging upside down by one's feet in an attic. Insofar as I can imagine this (which is not very far), it tells me only what it would be like for *me* to be a bat. But that is not the question. I want to know what it is like for a *bat* to be a bat. Yet if I try to imagine this, I am restricted to the resources of my own mind, and those resources are inadequate to the task.[42]

On the other hand, understanding is a production of communication, not of commutation between bodies, and it may be sufficient just to understand the bat, however vampirical your ambitions, without insisting upon anthropomorphism as a necessary condition of knowledge. Clarke, in all her sympathy for Flora, cannot *be* Flora and still love her.[43]

If animals can communicate with one another or with people, and like Thomas Sebeok I can think of no convincing argument why they can't, then they must also have access to some basic conventional understandings.[44] They can learn rules, even others' rules, and act rationally through some basic tests of truth. More importantly, from the coherence theory of knowledge that Davidson supports, the perceptions of similarity and difference that construct coded contact in situations of radical translation and charitable interpretation are only possible for beings with complex, integrated minds; unlike older positivist notions of "conventionalism" that still haunt sociologists like Burns or empiricists like Nelson Goodman, this matching of signs to concepts through basic conventions assumes that subjects have a complete consciousness rather than a tabula rasa.[45] To think otherwise is to make an error in the theory of minds and knowledge that is something like Quince's assumption—that a play has to be built from the ground up every time.[46] As Irwin's work shows, building from the ground up still requires some basic, logically simple conventions, as well as a complex history of more specific, sophisticated procedures. In contrast to Horovitz's people, Flora's "creaturely" performance shows that it may be easier to share the most rudimentary, sustaining conventions of play with animals than it is to communicate more seriously and specifically, across languages, with other human beings. The bigger the differences between communicators, the more likely we are of telling the forest from the trees. Tarski's Convention T provides us with a minimal theory of truth that works, but perhaps more importantly for the theater it can also inspire a convention "t" of theatricality, which does not try to derive its definition from some essential part of any historical theater, or from some specific cultural agreement that forms it into an institution. Nor does it serve as an ad hoc metaphor to be deployed at whim, unless some others are let in on the joke. This second convention "t," the shared consciousness of performance, is too basic to communication to be derived from anything other than the shared, perhaps even tacit, conventional assumption that performance is the case.

NOTES

1. Elizabeth Burns, *Theatricality: A Study of Convention in the Theatre and in Social Life* (New York: Harper and Row, 1972).

2. For a fascinating recent use of these two major figures in the philosophy of symbolic forms, see Eli Rozik, *The Language of the Theatre* (Glasgow: Theatre Studies Publications, 1992).

3. Goffman's classic study is *The Presentation of Self in Everyday Life* (New York: Penguin, 1971), first published in 1959. For Cohen see *Theatre of Power: The Art of Diplomatic Signalling* (New York: Longman, 1987).

4. For Svetlana Alpers, the relation to theater is usually a question of subject matter, as in *Rembrandt's Enterprise: The Studio and the Market* (London: Thames and Hudson, 1988), though in questions of authorship and subject the theater serves as a general criterion for judgments of authenticity. In Fried's work theatricality has, until recently, been a more metaphorical concern, as in *Absorption and Theatricality: Painting and Beholder in the Age of Diderot* (Berkeley and Los Angeles: University of California Press, 1980).

5. Terry Eagleton, *Criticism and Ideology: A Study in Marxist Literary Theory* (London: New Left Books, 1976), 68–69. I have tried to clarify the metaphysical basis of this analogy in my essay, "Imagining Semiosis in Material Terms: Concretization and Theatrical Production," *Ĉeskos-Slovensky Ŝtructuralizmus a Viedensky Scientizmus (Czecho-Slovak Structuralism and Scientism of Vienna)*, ed. Ján Bakoš (Bratislava: Stimul, 1992), 270–89.

6. See, for example, Roland Barthes, "Myth Today," in *Mythologies,* trans. Annette Lavers (New York: Hill and Wang, 1972), 109–59, with its delirious displacement of truth in myth's meaning onto the rhetoric of figurative representations.

7. See, for example, their remarks on Frege in *Language and Materialism: Developments in Semiology and the Theory of the Subject* (London: Routledge and Kegan Paul, 1977), 138, in which his theories of logically simple concepts are made nonsensical by their contextualization in a theatricalizing Freudian mind. A recent application of this model to "theatrical" culture studies is Joseph Litvak, *Caught in the Act: Theatricality in the Nineteenth Century English Novel* (Berkeley and Los Angeles: University of California Press, 1992).

8. For a survey of such arguments see Hilary Lawson and Lisa Appignanesi, eds., *Dismantling Truth: Reality in the Post-Modern World* (New York: St. Martin's Press, 1989). Compare these to the sketch of a simple truth theory in Paul Horwich, *Truth* (Boston: Blackwell, 1990).

9. My model in this regard is Donald Davidson's paper "On the Very Idea of a Conceptual Scheme (1974)," in *Inquiries into Truth and Interpretation* (Oxford: Clarendon Press, 1984). I have already played out some basic intersections between Davidson and theater semiotics in an unpublished paper presented at the Semiotics Society of America annual meeting, University of Maryland, 1991, called "Davidson, Theatricality and the Method of Truth in Semiotics."

10. David Lewis, *Convention: A Philosophical Study* (Cambridge: Harvard University Press, 1969), 24.

11. Ibid., 51.

12. J. L. Styan, "Quince's Questions: The Mystery of a Play Experience," in Michael Issacharoff, *Performing Texts* (Philadelphia: University of Pennsylvania Press, 1988).

13. Jan Kott, however, has explanations rich in precedents and effects in his title essay for *The Bottom Translation: Marlowe and Shakespeare and the Carnival Tradition* (Evanston, Ill.: Northwestern University Press, 1987), in which this "exchange of signs" become the key trope of the play.

14. For a survey of Irwin's early work, see Mel Gussow, "Clown," *New Yorker,* November 11, 1985, 51ff.

15. The index is one of Charles Peirce's types of semiotic connection, equivalent to a proposition, as outlined in "Logic as Semiotic: The Theory of Signs," in *Semiotics: An Introductory Anthology,* ed. Robert Innis (Bloomington: Indiana University Press, 1985), 1–23. The constructive communicative implications of this idea are developed by Karl-Otto Apel, *Charles S. Peirce: From Pragmatist to Pragmaticism,* trans. J. M. Krois (Amherst: University of Massachusetts Press, 1981), 99.

16. My assumption throughout this section is that what Victor Shklovsky calls "device" or, in some translations, a "technique" is a kind of convention, however innovative. See Shklovsky, "Art as Technique," in *Russian Formalist Criticism: Four Essays,* ed. and trans. L. Lemon and M. Reiss (Lincoln: University of Nebraska Press, 1965), 3–24.

17. This emptying out of conventional meanings is traced most effectively by Roman Jakobson in "On Realism in Art," in *Readings in Russian Poetics: Formalist and Structuralist Views,* ed. and trans. L. Matejka and K. Pomorska (Ann Arbor, Mich.: Michigan Slavic Contributions, 1978), 38–46.

18. Compare two books by Peter McCormick, *Heidegger and the Language of the World* (Ottawa: University of Ottawa Press, 1976) and *Fictions, Philosophies and the Problems of Poetics* (Ithaca, N.Y.: Cornell University Press, 1988), the second of which integrates the second order of poetic tropes or conventions within a larger phenomenological view. The philosophy of symbolic forms might fall somewhere between the two.

19. Herbert Blau, "Universals of Performance, or Amortizing Play," in *The Eye of Prey* (Bloomington: Indiana University Press, 1987), 171.

20. This notion of truth as performance is the argument of Gertrude Ezorsky, "Truth in Context," in *Pragmatic Philosophy,* ed. Amelie Rorty (New York: Doubleday Anchor, 1966), 495–520.

21. This widespread mistaking of questions of representations for questions of truth has become a recent focus of Richard Rorty's work; see, for example, "Representation, Social Practice, Truth," in *Objectivity, Relativism, and Truth,* vol. 1 of *Philo-*

sophical Papers (Cambridge: Cambridge University Press, 1991). The Irwin quotation is from a fragment of text reproduced in Ron Jenkins, *Acrobats of the Soul* (New York: Theatre Communications Group, 1988), 160.

22. One of the first people to comment incisively on this state of affairs is Derrida's leading English exponent, Christopher Norris, in "On Not Going Relativist (Where It Counts): Deconstruction and 'Convention T'," in *The Contest of Faculties: Philosophy and Theory after Deconstruction* (New York: Methuen, 1985).

23. This critical philosophical practice has of course found its most effective political influence in the hands of contemporary Marxist culture critics, following the contours laid out by Michael Ryan in *Marxism and Deconstruction: A Critical Articulation* (Baltimore: Johns Hopkins University Press, 1982) and extended by Gayatri C. Spivak, *In Other Worlds: Essays in Cultural Politics* (London: Routledge, 1988).

24. See W. V. O. Quine, "Truth by Convention (1935)," in *The Ways of Paradox ad Other Essays*, 2nd ed. (Cambridge: Harvard University Press, 1976), 77–106; and Alfred Tarski's 1936 essay "The Concept of Truth in Formalized Languages," in *Logic, Semantics, Mathematics* (Oxford: Clarendon Press, 1956), 152–278.

25. Quine's recent definition of truth as disquotation, which refers to the removal of quotation marks in the second part of a truth statement, is in fact a communicative theory, since it argues that the removal is allowable by agreement; see Quine, *The Pursuit of Truth* (Cambridge: Harvard University Press, 1990).

26. Donald Davidson, "The Method of Truth in Metaphysics (1977)," in *Inquiries into Truth*, 199.

27. Eagleton, *Ideology* (London: Verso, 1991), 9–10; Eagleton wants to leave considerable room for the analysis of what Habermas calls "systematically distorted communication," but I think Habermas's distinction between communicative and strategic action reorients even rhetorical statements toward a coherent hermeneutic perspective.

28. Israel Horovitz, "The Indian Wants the Bronx," *Famous American Plays of the 1960s*, ed. Harold Clurman (New York: Dell, 1972), 275–309.

29. See Apel, "The *A Priori* of the Communication Community and the Foundations of Ethics: The Problem of a Rational Foundation of Ethics in the Scientific Age," *Towards a Transformation of Philosophy* (London: Routledge and Kegan Paul, 1980), 225–300.

30. Horovitz, *The Primary English Class* (New York: Dramatists Play Service, 1976).

31. Habermas's comprehensive theory is outlined in the mammoth *The Theory of Communicative Action*, trans. Thomas McCarthy, but a careful study of Chapter 3 in vol. 1, *Reason and the Rationalization of Society*, reveals most of his categories for his distinctions between communication designed to build community and communication designed for deception. This not to deny that communicative action has ulterior motives; see Davidson, "Communication and Convention," in *Inquiries into Truth*, 272.

32. Davidson, "Radical Interpretation," *Inquiries into Truth*, 137.

33. Ibid.

34. Neil Wilson, "Substance without Substrata," *Review of Metaphysics* 12 (1959): 521–39.

35. See, for example, the extensions supplied by Robert Feleppa, *Convention, Translation and Understanding: Philosophical Problems in the Comparative Study of Culture* (Albany: SUNY Press, 1988).

36. Donald Davidson, "Rational Animals," in *Actions and Events: Perspectives on the Philosophy of Donald Davidson,* ed. E. Lepore and B. McLaughlin (Oxford: Basil Blackwell, 1985), 473–80; see also the follow-up essay, which answers some of Davidson's doubts about animals in friendly terms, Richard Jeffrey, "Animal Interpretation," 481–87.

37. Bert O. States, *Great Reckonings in Little Rooms: On the Phenomenology of Theater* (Berkeley: California UP, 1985), 34.

38. Hilary Osterle, "Alas, No Giraffe," *Dance Magazine,* 64 (Oct 1990), 49.

39. Kendall Walton, *Mimesis as Make-Believe: On the Foundations of the Representational Arts* (Cambridge, MA: Harvard UP, 1990).

40. Eleanor Blau, "On the Boards in Brooklyn: An Ark's Worth of Animals," *The New York Times,* v. 140, 9 Oct 1990, C13.

41. Rich, "Clarke's Beastly Humans and Beguiling Beasts," *New York Times,* v. 140, 9 Oct 1990, C13.

42. Thomas Nagel, "What is It Like to Be a Bat?" *Mortal Questions* (Cambridge: Cambridge UP, 1979).

43. On the increasing relevance of this consideration, see Martha Nussbaum, *Love's Knowledge: Essays on Philosophy and Literature* (New York: Oxford University Press, 1990); I should acknowledge here my debt to the best Martha Clarke scholar I know, Diane Quinn, whose essay is in *Critical Survey of Drama,* vol. II, ed. Frank N. Magill (Pasadena, CA: Salem Press, 1994), 468–78.

44. Among Sebeok's many works on "zoosemiotics," see " 'Talking' with Animals: Zoosemiotics Explained," in *The Play of Musement* (Bloomington: Indiana University Press, 1981), 109–16.

45. Even a correspondence theorist like Nelson Goodman agrees on the astonishing impact of contacts with strange but coherent intelligences; see *Ways of Worldmaking* (Indianapolis: Hackett, 1978), 131.

46. See the careful response to Rorty's material mind, and an attempt to move Davidson's philosophy toward the theory of consciousness, in John Searle's *The Rediscovery of the Mind* (Cambridge: MIT Press, 1992).

Contributors

Philip Auslander is a Professor in the School of Literature, Communication, and Culture of the Georgia Institute of Technology. His books include *Presence and Resistance: Postmodernism and Cultural Politics in Contemporary American Performance; From Acting to Performance: Essays in Modernism and Postmodernism; Liveness: Performance in a Mediatized Culture;* and *Performing Glam Rock: Gender and Theatricality in Popular Music.* He received the prestigious Callaway Prize for the Best Book in Theater or Drama for *Liveness.* Professor Auslander is the editor of *Performance: Critical Concepts,* a reference collection of eighty-nine essays in four volumes, and, with Carrie Sandahl, coeditor of *Bodies in Commotion: Performance and Disability.*

Noël Carroll is the Andrew W. Mellon Professor of the Humanities at Temple University. His most recent books are *Beyond Aesthetics* and *Engaging the Moving Image.*

Robert P. Crease is a Professor in the Department of Philosophy at Stony Brook University. He is the author of numerous books and articles on the interface between the sciences and the humanities, and he writes a monthly column, entitled "Critical Point," on the social dimensions of science for the international magazine *Physics World.* His books include *The Prism and the Pendulum: The Ten Most Beautiful Experiments in Science* (2003) and *The Play of Nature, Experimentation as Performance* (1993). His edited books include *Hermeneutics and the Natural Sciences* (1997), and his translations include *American Philosophy of Technology: The Empirical Turn* by H. Achterhuis (2001), and *What Things Do: Philosophical Reflections on Technology, Agency, and Design* by P.-P. Verbeek (2005), both translated from the Dutch.

Jon Erickson is Associate Professor of English at Ohio State University. He is the author of *The Fate of the Object: From Modern Object to Postmodern*

Sign in Performance, Art, and Poetry and numerous essays on theater, theory, and philosophy.

James R. Hamilton received his Ph.D. in philosophy from the University of Texas at Austin in 1974. His research is in aesthetics, especially the aesthetics of theater. He has published articles on theater and other performance arts in the *British Journal of Aesthetics, The Journal of Aesthetics and Art Criticism,* and *The Journal of Dramatic Theory and Criticism.* He has entries on Brecht and on Theater in the recently published *Oxford Encyclopedia of Aesthetics* and *Routledge Companion to Aesthetics,* respectively. He is currently working on a book project to be published by Blackwell Publishers on theatrical performance as an independent art form. He teaches courses in logic, philosophy of art, and aesthetics. He has been a participant in an NEH Summer Seminar on theater and is a recipient of an NEH Fellowship and a Big XII Fellowship.

Suzanne M. Jaeger is an Assistant Professor at York University, Toronto, Canada. Her published work focuses on philosophies of embodiment and the nature of meaning-making in the contexts of art dance aesthetics and also health care ethics. Prior to receiving her degrees in philosophy, she was a professional ballet dancer and teacher.

David Krasner is the author of *American Drama 1945–2000: An Introduction,* and editor of *Theatre in Theory, 1900–2000,* an anthology of dramatic theory and criticism. He is the coeditor with Rebecca Schneider of the University of Michigan Press series begun by Enoch Brater, "Theater: Theory/Text/Performance." He is currently writing *A History of Modern Drama* in two volumes for Blackwell Press and teaches theater, drama, and performance at Yale University.

John Lutterbie is an Associate Professor of Art and Theatre Arts at Stony Brook University, and is currently the Associate Director of the Humanities Institute. His research is on creativity and cognition, with a special emphasis on the phenomenology of acting. This research is an outgrowth of his interest in subjectivity, on which he has published widely, including *Hearing Voices: Modern Drama and the Problem of Subjectivity.*

Bence Nanay is a Ph.D. student at the University of California, Berkeley. He started to do research with Richard Wollheim on the cognitive structure of character engagement and identification and published on these and other topics in aesthetics in *Journal of Aesthetics and Art Criticism* and in the *British Journal of Aesthetics.* His areas of specializations also include philosophy of mind and of biology.

Tobin Nellhaus is the Librarian for Drama, Film, and Theater Studies at Yale University. He has published on theater history and historiography, performance theory, critical realism, social theory, community-based performance, and humanities in the digital environment.

Martin Puchner is Associate Professor of English and comparative literature at Columbia University and author of *Stage Fright: Modernism, Anti-Theatricality and Drama,* as well as of *Poetry of the Revolution: Marx, Manifestos, and the Avant-Gardes.* He has written introductions and notes to *Six Plays by Henrik Ibsen, The Communist Manifesto and other Writings,* as well as to Lionel Abel's *Tragedy and Metatheatre.* He is coeditor of the forthcoming *Against Theatre: Creative Destructions on the Modernist Stage* and the *Norton Anthology of Drama.* He is also the editor of *Modern Drama: Critical Concepts* (forthcoming), and serves as the Associate Editor of *Theatre Survey.*

Michael L. Quinn was, at the time of his death in 1995, Professor of Drama at the University of Washington, Seattle, and the editor of *Theatre Survey.* He is the author of *Theater Semiotics: Prague School Theater Theory* and numerous articles on theater, drama, and performance.

Alice Rayner is Associate Professor in the Drama Department at Stanford University. She teaches courses in dramatic and performance theory, dramatic literature, and performance history. Her published work on the phenomenology of theater includes *To Act, To Do, To Perform: Drama and the Phenomenology of Action* and *Comic Persuasion: Moral Structure in British Comedy from Shakespeare to Stoppard.* Her essays on technology and culture have been included in *Discourse* as well as Michal Kobialka's *Of Borders and Thresholds* and Una Chaudhuri and Elinor Fuchs' *Landscape and Theatre.* She has written for *Theatre Journal* on Harold Pinter, on Suzan-Lori Parks (with Harry Elam), and most recently on a theory of practical work in theater. Other work includes essays on the phenomenon of the audience, on British playwright Caryl Churchill, and on *Hamlet.* Her most recent book is *Ghosts: Death's Double and the Phenomena of Theatre.*

David Z. Saltz is Associate Professor and Head of the Department of Theatre and Film Studies and Theory at the University of Georgia. He has published over twenty articles about the philosophy of theater, performance and digital technology, and modern drama in scholarly journals, books, and encyclopedias including the *Journal of Aesthetics and Art Criticism, Performance Research, Theatre Research International,* the *Oxford Encyclopedia of Aesthetics,* the *Blackwell Companion to Digital Humanities,* and the *Oxford Encyclopedia of Theatre and Performance.* He is coeditor of *Theatre Journal* and is the principal investigator of the innovative Virtual Vaudeville Project, funded by the National Science Foundation.

Mike Sell is Associate Professor of English at Indiana University of Pennsylvania. He wrote *Avant-Garde Performance and the Limits of Criticism: Approaching the Living Theatre, Happenings/Fluxus, and the Black Arts Movement.* He has written numerous articles on the Black Arts Movement and other movements of "Blackness." He is currently writing *The Avant-Garde: Race, Religion, Drugs, War,* the first multidisciplinary history of the tendency.

Julia A. Walker is Associate Professor of English and the Unit for Criticism and Interpretive Theory at the University of Illinois at Urbana–Champaign. She is the author of *Expressionism and Modernism on the American Stage: Bodies, Voices, Words.* She is currently working on a new book manuscript entitled *Modernity and Performance.*

Index